FOUNDATIONS OF

CLINICAL
MENTAL HEALTH
COUNSELING

Professional and Clinical Issues

FOUNDATIONS OF
CLINICAL MENTAL
HEALTH COUNSELING

Professional and Clinical Issues

EDWARD NEUKRUG

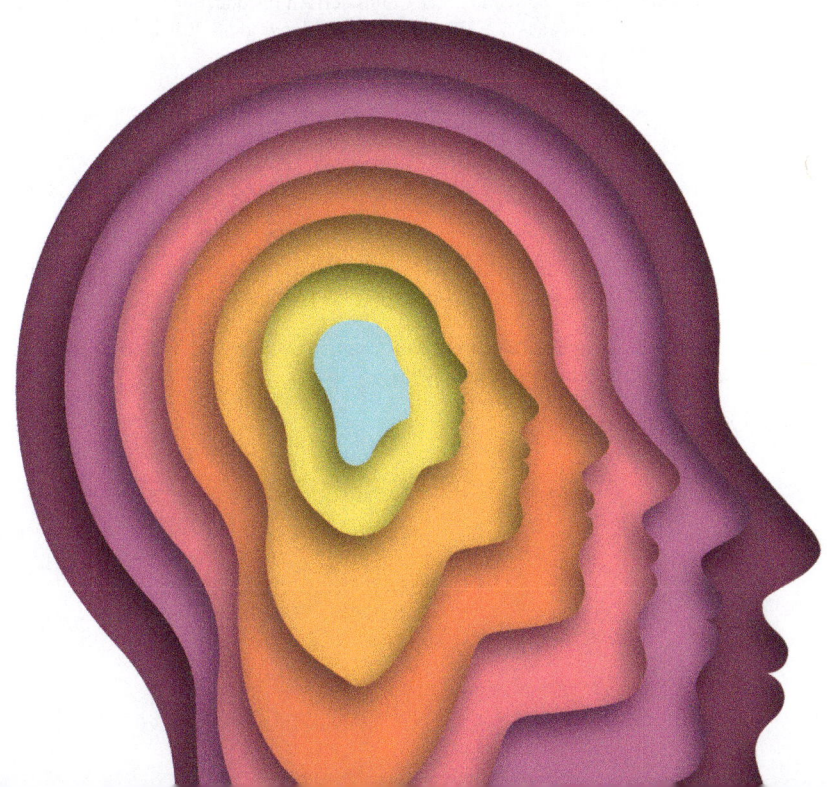

Bassim Hamadeh, CEO and Publisher
Amy Smith, Senior Project Editor
Jeanine Rees, Production Editor
Emely Villavicencio, Senior Graphic Designer
Kylie Bartolome, Licensing Coordinator
Natalie Piccotti, Director of Marketing
Kassie Graves, Senior Vice President, Editorial
Jamie Giganti, Director of Academic Publishing

Printed in the United States of America.

3970 Sorrento Valley Blvd., Ste. 500, San Diego, CA 92121

BRIEF CONTENTS

DETAILED CONTENTS

PREFACE

Hi there, and welcome to *Foundations of Clinical Mental Health Counseling*. This book surveys critical professional and clinical issues that every clinical mental health counselor (CMHC) should be knowledgeable about. The book is loosely divided in in two sections, with the first seven chapters focusing mostly on professional issues and the last five on clinical issues. I think you'll find the writing is down to earth and comprehensive. Hopefully, when you are finished, you will obtain a deep understanding of clinical mental health counseling and the work of the CMHC. The following offers a brief overview of each chapter.

Chapter 1, Defining Clinical Mental Health Counseling: Roles, Functions, and Characteristics of CMHCs and Related Professionals, begins by identifying work roles of the CMHC, usual credentials held, and professional memberships they tend to have. It then highlights the Council for the Accreditation of Counseling and Related Educational Programs (CACREP), which accredits clinical mental health counseling programs. Next, we examine important knowledge and skills of CMHCs, as noted by CACREP, and we list 15 critical roles and functions of CMHCs. We also briefly describe the nature of the work of counselors in other counseling specialty areas as well as related mental health professions. The chapter concludes with a discussion of evidence-based practice (EBP), common factors that influence positive outcomes for counseling relationships, and nine characteristics of the effective CMHC.

The second chapter, History and Current Trends in Clinical Mental Health Counseling, examines the history of, and current issues in, clinical mental health counseling. It starts by examining the precursors to modern-day counseling and then provides an overview of the vocational guidance movement at the turn of the 20th century, which was the basis for the development of the counseling field. It next examines the exponential growth of clinical mental health counseling from the 1960s through 1990. The chapter concludes with an examination of how clinical mental health counseling became part of the modern-day mental health landscape and then examines several current critical issues.

Chapter 3, Professional Associations in Clinical Mental Health Counseling and Related Professions, offers an overview of professional associations and begins by identifying benefits of these associations. It then provides an in-depth look at the American Mental Health Counselors Association (AMHCA) and the American Counseling Association (ACA) as well as several associations that are affiliated, or work closely, with these two organizations. It concludes with a brief overview of professional associations in related mental health fields.

Chapter 4, Clinical Mental Health Counselors' Work Settings, examines 14 common settings where CMHCs tend to work and the professional associations that tend to be associated with those settings. We provide short vignettes of people working in those settings throughout the chapter.

Chapter 5, Credentialing of CMHCs and Related Mental Health Professionals, offers a brief history of credentialing and distinguishes registration from certification from licensure. Next, we review a wide range of credentials for CMHCs, other counselors, and related mental health professionals. Finally, we examine three critical issues for licensed clinical mental health counselors: licensure portability, telemental health counseling, and parity with other professionals.

"Ethics" is the title of Chapter 6. Here, we examine the differences between values, ethics, morality, and the law and learn about the development of ethical codes in the helping professions. We spend a fair amount of time looking at the AMHCA and ACA ethics codes, identify how to determine which ethics code to use when a member of more than one association, examine ethical "hot spots," review ethical decision-making models, and explore CMHCs' perceptions of ethical behavior. We learn procedures for reporting ethical violations and identify several legal issues related to ethical violations, including civil and criminal liability, the role of ethics codes in lawsuits, the importance of malpractice insurance, and the use of best practices to avoid ethical violations.

Chapter 7, Culturally Competent Counseling, explores this ever-important topic. Here, we provide a rationale for culturally competent counseling with a special focus on diversity in the United States. We review nine reasons many diverse clients are distrustful of CMHCs. We then offer basic definitions of culturally competent counseling and highlight a number of terms related to an understanding of differentness, oppression, and social awareness. The chapter then reviews the four domains of the *Multicultural and Social Justice Counseling Competencies* (MSJCC) and identifies 12 factors that contribute to effective cross-cultural counseling and how these factors can be applied using the RESPECTFUL model of counseling. We note that culturally competent counseling and social justice have been called the "fourth" and "fifth" forces of helping.

Chapter 8, Abnormal (Atypical) Behavior, Diagnosis, and Psychopharmacology is the first chapter to focus on clinical issues and begins by explaining the intimate connection between these three areas. Within this chapter, we explore five models that explain abnormal behavior in different ways, offer an overview of the revised fifth edition of the *Diagnostic and Statistical Manual of Mental Disorders* (*DSM-5-TR*), and discuss advantages and disadvantages of a diagnosis. We then identify five categories of psychotropic medications and conclude with several important ethical, professional, and legal issues related to the content in the chapter.

Learning the importance of case conceptualization is the focus of Chapter 9, Case Conceptualization. Here, we examine the difference between theory-specific and non-theory-specific case conceptualization and then focus on the biopsychosocial model of case conceptualization. We note how this model can be used without a theory, but later in the chapter, we show how you can add a theoretical lens to the model. We also note how case conceptualization is important in developing a diagnosis and in treatment planning. We follow a case example throughout the chapter to illustrate these concepts.

Chapter 10, Case Management, focuses on a broad range of case management activities, including informed consent and professional disclosure statements, assessment for treatment planning, developing client goals, monitoring psychotropic medications, writing notes and reports, confidentiality of records, ensuring security of records, documenting clients contact hours, collaboration with other professionals, termination and making referrals, conducting follow-ups, and practicing time management.

In Chapter 11, Consultation and Supervision, focuses on two important aspects of clinical mental health counseling: consultation and supervision. We note that consultation examines how CMHCs can offer advice, knowledge, and direction to those who work with, or impact clients, in a time-limited manner, whereas supervision tends to be an ongoing relationship that focuses solely on client issues. We also discuss how consultation and supervision impact both the people with whom the consultant or supervisor is working as well as the larger system in which these people are involved (e.g., family, friends, co-workers). The chapter examines consultation and supervision separately, first focusing on definitions of the consultant and consultee and then reviewing the history of consultation as well as the types and stages of consultation. Then, it examines the supervision process, first defining the supervisor and supervisee and then examining models of supervisions. The chapter concludes with a discussion about several ethical and legal issues related to consultation and supervision.

The final chapter of the text, Chapter 12, Developing and Evaluating Mental Health Programs, examines program development and evaluation. We begin by looking at six steps in the development and evaluation of mental health programs, including identifying the target population, operationalizing the problem, identifying goals and objectives, designing specific strategies to reach goals and objectives, developing procedures to evaluate strategies used, and analyzing data from evaluation techniques. We elucidate these steps by offering an example of the development and evaluation of a program to manage emotions (emotional dysregulation). The chapter concludes with a discussion about how to prepare written evaluations, how to give an oral report, and concluded with ethical and legal issues related to program development and evaluation.

I certainly hope you learn and enjoy the book. Please know that I value your feedback, and I can be reached at eneukrug@odu.edu. Enjoy …

ACKNOWLEDGMENTS

I would like to thank Richie Kubilus, Jeanel Franklin, and Erin Woods for their important contributions to three of the chapters in the book. In addition, Mr. Kubilus and Ms. Franklin also helped with editing, ancillaries, and more. In addition, I am very thankful for a number of individuals who were willing to write vignettes concerning their experience in a wide range of counseling jobs. This included Drs. Tiffany Brannon, Kat Brown, Letitia Browne-James, Liliana Burciaga, Philip Daniels, Donette Deigh, Tony Dice, Jeanel Franklin, Cory Gerwe, Reggie Holt, Lauren Robins, Amber Samuels, Brittany Suggs, as well as Ms. Victoria Sepulveda and Mr. Matthew Michals-Voigt. A very special thanks to all the people from Cognella who assisted me, including Amy Smith, Senior Project Editor; Jeanine Rees, Production Editor; Emely Villavicencio; Senior Graphic Designer; Tiffany Mok, Senior Content Marketing Specialist; Jessica Rosa, Editorial Associate; and Christian Berk, Copy Editor. A special shout out to Kassie Graves, Senior Vice President, Editorial of Cognella who keeps me writing.

ABOUT THE AUTHOR

Dr. Edward Neukrug is the Batten Endowed Chair of Counseling in the Darden College of Education and Professional Studies at Old Dominion University in Norfolk, VA. He is also Executive Director of the International Institute for the Advancement of Counseling Theory (IIACT). He has been a teacher, therapist, and researcher for over 40 years. "Ed" has received numerous awards and accolades over the years, including twice being the recipient of the prestigious President's Award from the National Organization of Human Services, being named a Fellow of the American Counseling Association (ACA), and being conferred the Publications Award of ACA.

Dr. Neukrug has worked as a counselor at a crisis center, an outpatient therapist at a mental health center, an associate school psychologist, a school counselor, and as a private practice psychologist and licensed professional counselor. He has held a variety of positions in professional associations in counseling and human services and has published dozens of articles, book chapters, and related publications. Dr. Neukrug has also developed several helping and counseling videos, an interactive and animated website entitled Great Therapists of the Twentieth Century, a survey to assess one's theoretical orientation toward counseling, oral stories by well-known people of some of the famous therapists of the 20th century, and more. Most of these materials can be found on his IIACT website www.odu.edu/IIACT.

FIGURE 0.1 Dr. Edward Neukrug

Dr. Neukrug is well known for the multiple editions of his 13 books, which include: (1) The Dictionary of Counseling and Human Services, (2) Skills and Techniques for Human Service Professionals (2nd ed.), (3) Counseling Theory and Practice (3rd. ed.), (4) The World of the Counselor (6th. ed.), (5) Experiencing the World of the Counselor: A Workbook for Counselor Educators and Students (4th ed.), (4) Theory, Practice and Trends in Human Services: An Introduction to An Emerging Profession (6th ed.), (7) Essentials of Testing and Assessment for Counselors, Social Workers, and Psychologists (3rd ed., enhanced version), (8) A Brief Orientation to Counseling: Professional Identity, History, and Standards (3th ed.), (9) Skills and Tools for Today's Counselors and Psychotherapists, (10) Counseling and Helping Skills: Critical Techniques for Becoming a Counselor, (11) The SAGE Encyclopedia of Theory in Counseling and Psychotherapy, (12) Contemporary Theories of Counseling, and (13) Foundations of Clinical Mental Health Counseling: Professional and Clinical Issues. Dr. Neukrug has two children, Hannah and Emma.

Visit Dr. Neukrug's website at: www.counselingbooksetc.com to see all his books and videos. His ODU website is: https://sites.wp.odu.edu/eneukrug/.

CHAPTER 1

DEFINING CLINICAL MENTAL HEALTH COUNSELING

Roles, Functions, and Characteristics of CMHCs and Related Professionals

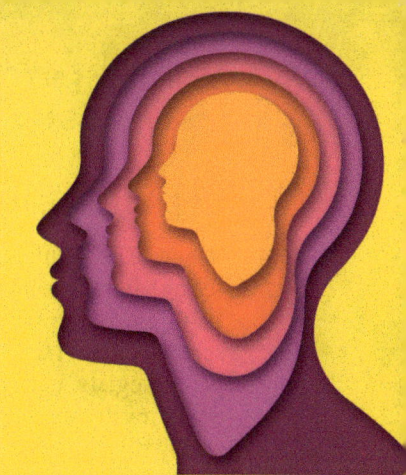

Learning Goals

- Understand the attributes that contribute to the definition of clinical mental health counseling.

- Identify and briefly discuss the two major professional associations—the American Mental Health Counselors Association (AMHCA) and the American Counseling Association (ACA)—to which many clinical mental health counselors (CMHCs) belong.

- Identify the Council for the Accreditation of Counseling and Related Educational Programs (CACREP), the accrediting body of CMHC programs, and discuss its advantages and disadvantages.

- Review the knowledge and skills needed by CMHCs, as defined by CACREP.

- Explore 15 critical roles and functions of CMHCs.

- Examine different types of counselors with which the CMHC may work, including addiction counselors; couples, marriage, and family counselors; pastoral counselors; rehabilitation counselors; school counselors; and student affairs and college counselors.

- Examine the different types of related mental health professionals with which the CMHC may work, including counseling and clinical psychologists; creative and expressive therapists; human service professionals; psychiatric mental health nurses; psychiatrists; psychoanalysts; psychotherapists; school psychologists, and social workers.

- Learn about evidence-based practice (EBP), common factors that positively influence counseling outcomes, and the nine characteristics of the effective CMHC: empathy, acceptance, genuineness, embracing a wellness perspective, cultural competence, the "it" factor, belief in one's theory, competence, and cognitive complexity.

INTRODUCTION

When I (Ed Neukrug) obtained my master's degree in student personnel counseling (i.e., college counseling), having a degree in clinical mental health counseling was not nearly as prevalent as it is today. At that time, obtaining a counseling degree would allow one to apply for a variety of jobs within almost any specialty area. However, it wasn't easy getting a job, as most helpers at that time were social workers and psychologists. I knew that if I got my foot in the door, I would have to explain what my degree was and prove my competence.

My first job as a crisis counselor was at a street-front, walk-in clinic called the "Rap House." Although our funding provided for the treatment of those with substance abuse issues, we often saw clients with other mental health problems. We also had a crisis hotline for people experiencing a mental health emergency, including suicidal and, occasionally, homicidal individuals. As a new counselor, I learned so much from this tremendous experience.

My next job was as an outpatient therapist at a mental health center, where I suspect I might have been the first employee with a degree in counseling. This position entailed a very large caseload, and I would often counsel individuals, couples, and families. I was supervised by, and consulted with, an in-house psychiatrist on diagnosis and medications. Like the Rap House, this agency also had a crisis line, for which every 9 days, I would stay overnight to answer emergency calls. To this day, I still haven't forgotten the sound of that very loud phone waking me up in the middle of the night.

After obtaining my doctorate in counseling, I started as a counselor educator, became a licensed psychologist, and owned a small private practice. Why a licensed psychologist and not a licensed professional counselor (LPC),[1] you ask? At that time, very few states offered licensure to counselors as LPCs. Fortunately, I lived in a state that allowed me to become a licensed psychologist, which was the only means through which I could obtain third-party payments. This was key to getting paid, so I could start my own small, private practice. However, when I moved to Virginia several years later, the opposite was true. I was a counselor educator at Old Dominion University and wanted to also do some private practice. However, the psychology licensing board would not license me as a psychologist—but I was allowed to obtain my LPC. Today, it is pretty much impossible to become a licensed psychologist with a degree in counseling. However, the field of counseling has progressed so that every state in the country now licenses LPCs, allowing them to work in any number of agencies or have a private practice.

Over the years, I've had many other "side jobs." I was a part-time school counselor and, for a while, a part-time school psychologist. Other times, I administered testing and assessment for various organizations. Regardless of where I may have worked, my heart and my identity were always as a clinical mental health counselor (CMHC). The outlook for CMHCs today is great! If this is the path you want to take, you'll likely have very few, if any, roadblocks.

This chapter begins by defining clinical mental health counseling. Then, we examine the knowledge and skills required to fulfill the roles and functions of the CMHC. From there, we offer brief descriptions of several related mental health professionals. Finally, we look at the nine characteristics of an effective helper.

WHAT IS CLINICAL MENTAL HEALTH COUNSELING?

Clinical mental health counseling (CMHC) is a master's level specialty area as identified by the Council for Accreditation of Counseling and Related Educational Programs (CACREP, 2016). CMHCs are found in a variety of mental health settings and work with a wide variety of clients (O*NET Online, 2023a).

---

1. In this book, I generally use the term "LPC" to denote a licensed CMHC. However, other terms are used interchangeably and vary based on the state in which one lives (e.g., LMHC and LCMHC).

Today, CMHCs conduct individual, group, couples, and family counseling and assist individuals with developmental adjustment issues as well as those who are struggling with mental health problems and disorders. Some of these mental health issues and disorders may include depression, anxiety, self-esteem issues, relationship and family problems, trauma, addictive disorders, career concerns, stress management, life transitions (e.g., retirement, job loss, or family status changes), psychotic disorders, and many others.

Those with a degree in clinical mental health counseling can become a licensed professional counselor (LPC)—sometimes called a licensed mental health counselor (LMHC), licensed clinical mental health counselor (LCMHC), or a similar variant of these names (American Counseling Association [ACA], 2023). Requirements to become an LPC vary state by state; however, they are often similar and generally include a master's degree in counseling, 2 years of post-master's supervised work experience, and passing a licensure exam. This allows the LPC to obtain third-party payments (e.g., payments from health insurance companies). It should be noted that in many states, one can obtain a degree in a related specialty area (e.g., rehabilitation, addictions, and school counseling) and still become an LPC if the counselor meets their state's coursework and field placement requirements. CMHCs can also become national certified counselors (NCCs) and certified clinical mental health counselors (CCMHCs) through the National Board for Certified Counselors (NBCC, 2023a). These credentials signify one's attainment of an important body of knowledge, and depending on the state you live in, the exams given to attain these credentials are used as the licensing exam for the LPC (see NBCC, 2023b, for the exam required in your state). We discuss the intricacies of credentialing in greater detail in Chapter 4.

The national professional organization for CMHCs is the American Mental Health Counselors Association (AMHCA). AMHCA used to be a division of ACA but disaffiliated in 2019 (Goodman, 2019). The mission of AMHCA is "to enhance the profession of clinical mental health counseling by setting the standard for collaboration, advocacy, research, ethical practice, and education, training, and professional development" (AMHCA, 2023a, Our Mission section), and its vision is "to position CMHCs to meet the health care needs of those we serve while advancing the profession" (AMHCA, 2023a, Our Vision section). AMHCA conducts many activities, including advocating for licensed counselors, providing workshops and conferences, offering malpractice insurance, providing a code of ethics, providing job links, helping clients find counselors, and publishing a newsletter and the *Journal of Mental Health Counseling*. AMHCA defines clinical mental health counseling and CMHCs as

> a distinct profession with national standards for education, training, and clinical practice. CMHCs are highly skilled professionals who provide flexible, consumer-oriented therapy. They combine traditional psychotherapy with a practical, problem-solving approach that creates a dynamic and efficient path for change and problem resolution. (AMHCA, 2023a, What Is a CMHC? section)

In addition to joining AMHCA, many CMHCs continue to join one or more of the divisions of ACA. ACA remains a vital association for CMHCs, due to its advocacy work, 19 specialty divisions, and one division affiliate. AMHCA, and ACA and its divisions, are discussed in greater detail in Chapter 3: Professional Associations.

The main accrediting body for clinical mental health counseling programs is CACREP, which accredits about 375 clinical mental health counseling programs across the country (CACREP, 2023a). Although programs do not have to become CACREP accredited, there are many advantages to doing so, including the following (CACREP, 2023b; Person et al., 2020; Urofsky et al., 2013):

- students having more developed professional identities
- counselors being less likely to be sanctioned for ethical violations
- programs attracting high-performing students and better-qualified faculty
- students experiencing a greater sense of competency in their clinical work

- programs offering longer field placements and more practical, hands-on experience
- programs producing students who are more knowledgeable about core counseling issues
- students having more job opportunities (e.g., some agencies only hire graduates from CACREP-accredited programs)
- students having an easier time becoming eligible to take credential exams (e.g., students in CACREP-accredited programs can take the National Counselor Exam [NCE] to become an NCC prior to graduation, whereas others must wait to complete postgraduate experience)

A competing accrediting body to CACREP is the Masters in Psychology and Counseling Accreditation Council (MPCAC, 2023a). MPCAC (2023b) accredits both psychology and counseling programs that "educate students in the science-based practice of counseling and psychological services" (para. 1). Thus far, MPCAC has accredited close to 60 programs; requires 48 semester hours, as opposed to CACREP's 60; and has competency in 11 broad areas, many of which are similar to CACREP. Students should be cautioned that completing an MPCAC-accredited program could make it difficult to obtain licensure in their state. However, the accreditation has a solid basis in counseling, and those who do go through an MPCAC-accredited program are well trained.

KNOWLEDGE AND SKILLS NEEDED BY CMHCs

The actual knowledge and skills needed by most CMHCs are delineated by CACREP, which requires that all master's level counseling specialty areas (i.e., addiction, career; clinical mental health; college and student affairs; marriage, couple, and family, rehabilitation counseling, and school) share core content knowledge in the following eight core curriculum areas: (a) professional counseling orientation and ethical practice, (b) social and cultural diversity, (c) human growth and development, (d) career development, (e) counseling and helping relationships, (f) group counseling and group work, (g) assessment and testing, and (h) research and program evaluation.

In addition to the core areas, each specialty area has unique content that needs to be incorporated into the specialty curriculum (CACREP, 2023c). Table 1.1 lists foundational knowledge, contextual dimensions, and practice issues that CACREP deems necessary for each CMHC to learn about as they complete their master's degree.

TABLE 1.1 Knowledge and Skills Needed for Clinical Mental Health Counseling

Foundations

- History and development of clinical mental health counseling
- Theories and models related to clinical mental health counseling
- Principles, models, and documentation formats of biopsychosocial case conceptualization and treatment planning
- Neurobiological and medical foundation and etiology of addiction and co-occurring disorders
- Psychological tests and assessments specific to clinical mental health counseling

Contextual Dimensions

- Roles and settings of CMHCS
- Etiology, nomenclature, treatment, referral, and prevention of mental and emotional disorders
- Mental health service delivery modalities within the continuum of care, such as inpatient, outpatient, partial treatment and aftercare, and mental health counseling services networks

- Diagnostic process, including differential diagnosis and the use of current diagnostic classification systems, including the *Diagnostic and Statistical Manual of Mental Disorders (DSM)* and the *International Classification of Diseases (ICD)*
- Potential for substance use disorders to mimic and/or co-occur with a variety of neurological, medical, and psychological disorders
- Impact of crisis and trauma on individuals with mental health diagnoses
- Impact of biological and neurological mechanisms on mental health
- Classifications, indications, and contraindications of commonly prescribed psychopharmacological medications for appropriate medical referral and consultation
- Legislation and government policy relevant to clinical mental health counseling
- Cultural factors relevant to clinical mental health counseling
- Professional organizations, preparation standards, and credentials relevant to the practice of clinical mental health counseling
- Legal and ethical considerations specific to clinical mental health counseling
- Record keeping, third-party reimbursement, and other practice and management issues in clinical mental health counseling

Practice

- Intake interview, mental status evaluation, biopsychosocial history, mental health history, and psychological assessment for treatment planning and caseload management
- Techniques and interventions for prevention and treatment of a broad range of mental health issues
- Strategies for interfacing with the legal system regarding court-referred clients
- Strategies for interfacing with integrated behavioral health care professionals
- Strategies for advocating for persons with mental health issues

Table 1.1: "Section 5C: Clinical Mental Health Counseling," 2016 CACREP Standards. Copyright © 2016 by Council for Accreditation of Counseling & Related Educational Programs.

In addition to the course content, all CACREP-accredited master's programs require a 100-hour practicum and 600-hour internship. In some states, licensing boards accept internship hours (e.g., 600 hours) toward the total number of post-master's supervisory hours needed to obtain licensure. CACREP requires 60 semester hours, or 90 quarter hours, for all their master's-level programs.

ROLES AND FUNCTIONS OF CMHCs

CMHCs and related counselors, such as addiction counselors and rehabilitation counselors, share several roles and functions critical to their job. Some job settings stress certain roles and functions more than others, but at some point in one's career, most—if not all—of these job functions are needed by these counselors (AMHCA, 2023b; O*NET, 2023a; U.S. Bureau of Labor Statistics, 2022). The following is a brief overview of some of the most important roles and functions:

- **assessment and diagnosis:** Conduct interviews with clients and make diagnoses to provide accurate treatment goals.
- **case management:** Participate in a broad range of activities that help run a practice or agency, such as completing paperwork, conducting evaluations, conducting follow-ups, completing billing, practicing time management, and assisting in marketing.
- **counseling and therapy:** Provide counseling and therapy individually, in groups, or with couples and families.

- **consultant:** Provide consultation for parents, colleagues, and professionals who work or interact with clients.
- **cultural competence:** Provide counseling and consultation for individuals from diverse backgrounds and continually update one's own attitudes and beliefs, knowledge, and skills about diverse groups.
- **crisis, disaster, and trauma work:** Have knowledge and expertise to work with those who have experienced a crisis, been exposed to a disaster, and/or have been traumatized.
- **maintaining records:** Know laws and ethical codes to ensure one is keeping client information accurately, confidentially, and securely.
- **testing:** Administer testing to clients to develop an accurate diagnosis, create a focused treatment plan, and provide information to important stakeholders (e.g., schools, courts, or lawyers), while increasing client insight.
- **psychoeducational activities:** Provide formal educational and informational activities for clients and the public to increase the understanding of mental health issues.
- **provide primary, secondary, and tertiary services:** Participate in numerous counseling activities, ranging from education and preventive services, working with non-severe mental health problems, and working to control severe mental health concerns.
- **social justice advocate:** Champion and defend clients' causes and rights, while organizing client and community support to provide needed services.
- **ethical and legal issues:** Practice within the parameters of one's ethical guidelines and respond appropriately to legal issues.
- **evaluation:** Assess client outcomes to ensure that the counselor's work is aimed towards ameliorating client problems.
- **supervisee/supervisor:** Participate in supervision to enhance skills and provide supervision to others that improves their skills.
- **implementation of counseling, education, and treatment plans based on specialized skills:** Participate in continuing education to gain knowledge regarding one's specialization.

COUNSELING AND RELATED HELPING PROFESSIONALS

As a CMHC, you will be working closely with several other professionals who have a similar knowledge base. It is important to know who those individuals are, how they are trained, and the credentials they are likely to have. We first highlight counselors, including couples, marriage, and family counselors; student affairs and college counselors; school counselors; rehabilitation counselors; addiction counselors; and pastoral counselors. Then, we focus on social workers, school psychologists, counseling and clinical psychologists; psychiatric mental health nurses; psychiatrists; psychoanalysts; creative and expressive therapists; human service professionals; and psychotherapists.

Counseling Professionals

This part of the chapter focuses on some of the many different types of counselors (see Figure 1.1). Although they are not discussed here, other counseling specialties include career counselors, gerontological counselors, genetic counselors, and more.

Addiction Counselors

Addiction counselors study a wide range of addictions, such as substance abuse (drugs and alcohol), eating disorders, gambling addiction, sexual addiction, and others (O*NET Online, 2023b). They are familiar with diagnosis and treatment planning, and they understand the importance of psychopharmacology in

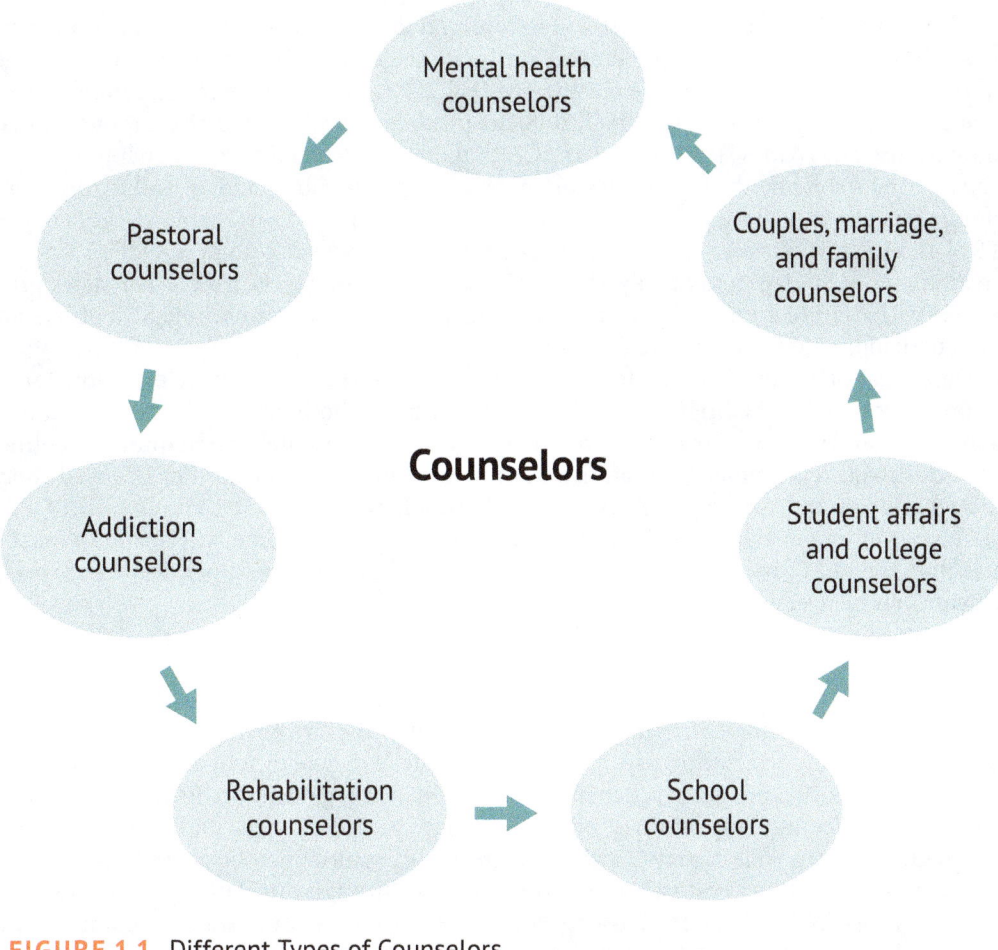

FIGURE 1.1 Different Types of Counselors

working with this population. They work in a variety of outpatient agency settings, inpatient rehabilitation centers, and private practices. As of 2019, 31 states have established state licensure statutes for substance use disorder (SUD) counselors, facilitating insurance billing eligibility for private and public insurance plans and opening avenues to practice independently (Ivan et al., 2019). The other 19 states, and the District of Columbia, offer some form of certification for SUD counselors. (See Addiction-counselors.com [2023] for up to date state requirements.)

CACREP provides accreditation standards for 60-credit addiction counseling programs. In addition to AMHCA, addiction counselors often belong to the International Association of Addictions and Offender Counselors (IAAOC), an ACA division. Many addiction counselors can become certified through their state, and NBCC offers a national certification as a master addiction counselor (MAC), which is currently under review. Depending on the state, individuals who go through a CACREP-accredited addiction counseling program may be able to obtain their LPC, although additional coursework, supervision, and/or other requirements may be required.

Couple, Marriage, and Family Counselors

Marriage, couple, and family counselors are specifically trained to work with couples and families and can be found in a vast array of agency settings, including private practice. While they have traditional coursework in the helping professions, these counselors tend to also have specialty coursework in systems dynamics, couples counseling, family therapy, family life stages, and human sexuality. The American Association of Marriage and Family Therapists (AAMFT, 2002–2023) and the International Association of Marriage and Family Counselors (IAMFC, 2018) are prominent professional associations for marriage and family counselors. IAMFC is a division of ACA that offers independent membership.

Although all 50 states and the District of Columbia have licensure for marriage and family therapists, the requirements can vary dramatically (Association of Marital and Family Therapy Regulatory Boards [AMFTRB], n.d.). While some states follow the curriculum guidelines set forth by AAMFT's Commission on Accreditation of Marriage and Family Therapy Education (COAMFTE, n.d.), other states prefer the 60-credit CACREP (2016) guidelines for marriage, couple, and family counseling. Still others have set their own curriculum guidelines for credentialing.

Most states that offer credentialing for marriage, couple, and family counselors allow for related helping professionals (e.g., CMHCs, social workers, and psychologists) to likewise obtain licensure as marriage and family counselors, provided they follow the state's curriculum guidelines and meet any additional requirements. In addition, in most states, LPCs and other licensed therapists can conduct couples and marriage counseling. Individuals who go through a 60-credit CACREP-accredited program in marriage, couple, and family counseling can become NCCs, and in most states, they can obtain their LPC. In certain circumstances, additional coursework, supervision, and specialized requirements may be needed.

Pastoral Counselors

While pastoral counselors sometimes have a counseling degree, they frequently have a degree in a related social service field (e.g., social work, psychology) or a master's degree in religion or divinity. Pastoral counselors often work in a private practice or within a religious organization. Provided that they have education in pastoral counseling, ministry, or theology, have passed an exam, and have additional experience, individuals from a wide variety of clinical degrees (e.g., counseling, social work, and psychology) can become national certified pastoral counselors (NCPCs) through the National Board for Certified Pastoral Counselors (NBCPC, 2023). Pastoral counselors, religious counselors, or counselors with a spiritual orientation might join the Association for Spiritual, Ethical, and Religious Values in Counseling (ASERVIC, 2023), an ACA division; the American Clinical Pastoral Education (ACPE, 2020); or both. Depending on their degree, pastoral counselors may be able to become NCCs and, in some states, LPCs, although additional coursework, supervision, or other requirements may be required. CACREP does not provide accreditation in pastoral counseling.

Rehabilitation Counselors

Rehabilitation counselors offer a wide range of services to people with physical, emotional, and developmental disabilities. "Rehab" counselors work in state vocational rehabilitation agencies, unemployment offices, and private rehabilitation agencies. Starting in 2023, rehabilitation counseling and clinical rehabilitation counseling programs are required, by CACREP, to offer 60 semester credits (Koker, 2018).

CACREP provides accreditation standards for 60-credit rehabilitation counseling programs. Many rehabilitation counselors join the American Rehabilitation Counseling Association, a division of ACA (ARCA, n.d.) or the National Rehabilitation Counseling Association (NRCA, n.d.). Rehabilitation counselors often choose to become certified rehabilitation counselors (CRCs) through a certification process offered by the Commission on Rehabilitation Counselor Certification (CRCC). Those with a degree in rehabilitation counseling can become NCCs and may be able to be licensed addictions counselors or LPCs in their state by meeting additional course, supervision, and/or other requirements (Peterson, 2020).

School Counselors

A school counselor has a master's degree in counseling and has taken coursework to become specialized in school counseling. Some states credential school counselors at the elementary, middle, and/or secondary levels, while other states prefer credentialing that covers kindergarten through 12th grade (K–12). Most school counseling programs are CACREP accredited, which currently requires 60 semester credit hours. The professional association for school counselors is the American School Counselor Association (ASCA, 2023). Previously a division of ACA, in 2018, ASCA disaffiliated from ACA, becoming an independent entity; however, the organizations continue to strive toward common goals. In recent years, the ASCA national model has been used as a training model for school counselors to apply within their schools and districts. Over the past few decades, there has been a large push to replace the term "guidance counselor" with "school counselor," as the latter term is seen as deemphasizing the guidance activities of the school counselor (Zyromski et al., 2019).

CACREP provides accreditation standards for 60-credit school counseling programs. Amongst other credentials, school counselors can become ASCA-certified school counselors *or* national certified school counselors (NCSCs). Individuals who go through a CACREP-accredited school counseling program can also become NCCs. In most states, school counselors can obtain their LPC, but they may be required to take additional coursework, supervision, or meet other expectations.

Student Affairs and College Counselors

College and student affairs counselors (postsecondary counseling) work in a variety of settings in higher education, including college counseling centers, career centers, residence life, student advising services, multicultural student services, and other campus settings where counseling-related activities occur. If attending a CACREP-accredit program, these counselors have taken 60 semester credits, including specialty coursework in college student development and student affairs practices. Two prominent professional associations of counselors in higher education settings are the American College Counseling Association (ACCA, n.d.; an ACA division) and the College Student Educators International (2004–2023; formerly, the American College Personnel Association and has kept the acronym ACPA). ACCA tends to focus on administration of student services, and ACPA tends to focus on counseling issues in college settings. Today, membership in ACCA is independent of ACA. Individuals who go through a 60-credit CACREP-accredited college counseling and student affairs programs can become NCCs. In most states, college and student affairs counselors can obtain their LPC but may need to take additional coursework, have supervision, or meet other requirements.

Related Mental Health Professionals

This section of the chapter examines related mental health workers (see Figure 1.2).

Counseling and Clinical Psychologists

Psychologists practice in a wide range of settings, including agencies, private practices, health maintenance organizations (HMOs), universities, business and industry, prisons, and schools. Although counselors will generally have the most contact with counseling psychologists, clinical psychologists, and school psychologists, there are many other types of psychologists, including cognitive and perceptual, community, developmental, educational, engineering, environmental, experimental, industrial/organizational, neuro, quantitative, social, and sports (American Psychological Association, 2023a). The professional association for psychologists is the American Psychological Association (2023b).

FIGURE 1.2 Related Mental Health Professionals

Relative to the practice of psychotherapy, all states offer licensure in counseling psychology, clinical psychology, or both, and many states allow individuals with a practitioner doctorate in psychology (PsyD) to become licensed as clinical or counseling psychologists. Clinical psychologists have historically worked with individuals with severe emotional disorders, whereas counseling psychologists have mostly worked with relatively healthy populations. However, the differences between counseling and clinical psychologists have become increasingly blurred in recent times. To obtain a license as a counseling or clinical psychologist, one must graduate from an American Psychological Association accredited doctoral program in clinical or counseling psychology and complete additional requirements identified by state licensing boards.

Psychologists have recently sought the right to prescribe medication for emotional disorders, and five states, the territory of Guam, and some branches of the federal government are now allowing psychologists to have limited prescription privileges. The professional association for clinical psychologists is Division 12 of the American Psychological Association, and the professional association for counseling psychologists is Division 17 of the American Psychological Association, which somewhat aligns with the mission and goals of ACA and AMHCA.

Creative and Expressive Therapists

Creative and expressive therapists include art, play, dance/movement, equine, poetry, and music therapists, along with others, who use creative tools to work with individuals experiencing significant trauma or emotional problems (Deaver, 2015). Through expressive therapies, individuals gain a deeper understanding of themselves, work through some of their issues, and decrease their symptoms. Expressive therapists work with individuals of all ages and do individual, group, and family counseling. They work in many settings and are often hired specifically for their ability to reach individuals through a medium other than language.

Many expressive therapists obtain degrees in counseling or social work and later pick up additional coursework in expressive therapy. However, there are specific programs that offer curricula in creative and expressive therapies, such as those approved by the American Art Therapy Association (AATA, 2022). Other related associations include the Association for Creativity in Counseling (ACC), a division of ACA; the American Dance Therapy Association (ADTA); the American Music Therapy Association (AMTA); and the Association for Play Therapy (APT). Although certifications exist for some kinds of creative and expressive therapies (see the Art Therapy Credentials Board, 2021), states generally do not license creative and expressive therapists. However, some creative and expressive therapists can become licensed if their degree is in a field credentialed by the state (e.g., counseling or social work). In other cases, the state licensing board may allow the individual to take additional courses and experiences (e.g., internships), so they have obtained the equivalency of existing state licenses requirements and apply for licensure in that field (AATA, 2022).

Human Service Professionals

Individuals who serve as human service professionals have generally obtained an associate's or bachelor's degree in human services. Some of these programs are accredited by the Council for Standards in Human Service Education (CSHSE), which sets specific curriculum guidelines for the development of human service programs. Individuals who hold these degrees are often found in entry-level support and counseling jobs and serve an important role in assisting counselors and other mental health professionals. The professional organization for human services is the National Organization of Human Services (NOHS, n.d.). The Center for Credentialing and Education (CCE, 2023) offers the human services–board certified practitioner (HS–BCP) credential for "human services practitioners seeking to advance their careers by acquiring independent verification of their practical knowledge and educational background" (para. 1). Some states now offer a credential as a qualified mental health professional (QMHP), and human services professionals can often become certified in addictions counseling. However, since they have an associate's or bachelor's degree, they cannot obtain licensure as a counselor or other mental health professional.

Psychiatric Mental Health Nurses

Primarily trained as medical professionals, psychiatric–mental health nurses (PMHNs) are also skilled in the delivery of mental health services (APNA, 2023). The professional association of PMHNs is the American Psychiatric Nurses Association (APNA). Most PMHNs work in hospital settings, while a few work in community agencies, private practice, or educational settings. Psychiatric–mental health nursing is practiced at two levels. The registered nurse–PMHN does basic mental health work related to nursing diagnosis and nursing care. The advanced practiced registered nurse (APRN) has a master's degree in psychiatric–mental health nursing and assesses, diagnoses, and treats individuals with mental health problems. Currently having prescriptive privileges in all 50 states (Stokowski, 2018), APRNs hold a unique position in the mental health profession.

Psychiatrists

A psychiatrist is a licensed physician who generally has completed a residency in psychiatry. This means that after graduating from medical school, they have gone on to complete extensive field placement training in a mental health setting. In addition, most psychiatrists have passed an exam to become board certified in psychiatry. Being a physician, the psychiatrist has expertise in diagnosing organic disorders, identifying and treating psychopathology, and prescribing medications for psychiatric conditions. Although, as just noted, some states, Guam, and branches of the federal government have granted psychologists prescription privileges for psychotropic medications (American Psychiatric Association, 2023; Robiner et al., 2019), psychiatrists take the lead in this important treatment approach and, in some cases, psychiatric nurses, nurse practitioners, and physician's assistants may as well.

Although psychiatrists spend extensive periods of time with patients during their schooling, they often have minimal skills and training in counseling and psychotherapy compared to counselors, social workers, and psychologists. However, some obtain advanced training on their own, and all serve an important role in integrative health practices with counselors and other mental health professionals. Psychiatrists are employed in mental health agencies, hospitals, private practice settings, and health maintenance organizations. The professional association for psychiatrists is the American Psychiatric Association (2023).

Psychoanalysts

Psychoanalysts are professionals who have received training in psychoanalysis from any of several recognized psychoanalytical institutes. In the past, the American Psychoanalytic Association (APsaA, 2009–2023) would only endorse psychiatrists for training at psychoanalytical institutes (Turkington, 1985); however, they now allow other mental health professionals to undergo training. Because most states do not license psychoanalysts, clients who see a psychoanalyst should make sure the analyst was trained at an institute sanctioned by APsaA and that they are a licensed psychiatrist, psychologist, social worker, counselor, or related mental health professional.

Psychotherapists

Psychotherapists are not associated with a specific mental health field or practice, and as such, most states do not offer legislation that would create a license for psychotherapists. Thus, in many states, individuals who have no mental health training can call themselves "psychotherapists." However, state legislatures generally limit the scope of psychotherapeutic practice to those individuals who are licensed mental health professionals (e.g., LPCs, LCSWs, or psychologists). In other words, anyone can generally claim to be a psychotherapist, but only licensed practitioners can practice psychotherapy.

School Psychologists

School psychologists have a master's or doctoral degree in school psychology and are licensed by state boards of education. Their work involves helping children succeed academically by working with children, families, teachers, school counselors, school administrators, community partners, and others (National Association of School Psychologists [NASP], 2021). A large portion of their work involves testing and assessment as well as helping students address their social and emotional health. Although most school psychologists work in schools, they are sometimes found in private practice, agencies, and hospital settings. The professional associations for school psychologists include the National Association of School Psychologists (NASP) and Division 16 of the American Psychological Association.

Social Workers

The term social worker generally applies to those who have an undergraduate or a master's degree in social work (i.e., MSW). While social workers were historically found working with the those who were marginalized, today's social workers provide counseling and psychotherapy for all types of clients in a wide variety of settings. These include child welfare services, government-supported social service agencies, family service agencies, private practices, and hospitals. In many ways, training as an MSW parallels training as a counselor, although past differences between these fields lead social work and counseling programs to emphasize different areas of the helping relationship. With additional training and supervision, social workers can become nationally certified by the Academy of Certified Social Workers (ACSW). Moreover, most states have specific requirements for becoming a licensed clinical social worker (LCSW). The professional association for social workers is the National Association of Social Workers (NASW).

CHARACTERISTICS OF THE EFFECTIVE CMHC

What makes the CMHC most effective when working with clients? First, client factors, such as readiness for change, psychological resources, and social supports, may affect how well a client does in counseling (Norcross & Wampold, 2019). In addition, it has become evident that counseling and psychotherapy work best when the counselor (a) knows the best available research-supported treatments; (b) uses their clinical expertise to understand the client's situation and chooses the most effective treatments for it; and (c) considers the client's personal preferences, values, and cultural background for such treatment. Called evidence-based practice (EBP; American Psychological Association, 2021), this approach to working with clients has become an important focus in training programs and work settings.

In addition to client factors and EBP, common factors underlying all therapeutic approaches have been shown to be related to positive client outcomes (Cuijpers et al., 2019; Norcross & Wampold, 2019). For instance, the abilities to build a working alliance as well as deliver a theoretical approach have been shown to be critical factors in positive client outcomes (Hilsenroth, 2014; Norcross & Lambert, 2018; Wampold, 2015, 2019; Wampold & Imel, 2015).

The ability to build a working alliance has been alluded to by almost every counselor and therapist, from Freud to the modern-day, new-age counselor (Neukrug, 2023). Based on the research (and, perhaps, some of my own educated guesses), this working alliance may be composed of the following six components: empathy, acceptance, genuineness, embracing a wellness perspective, cultural competence, and something I call the "it" factor.

Being able to deliver a theoretical approach includes knowing your approach well enough to build client expectations that it will work for the client's presenting problem (regardless of the approach) and being facile at implementing specific techniques from your approach to facilitate client change. I suggest that three characteristics important to delivering and being facile at your approach include: belief in one's theory, competence, and cognitive complexity. Let's take a deeper look at these three attributes along with the six components of a working alliance in the following sections (see Figure 1.3).

Empathy

Understanding our clients, or being empathic,

> … means that the therapist senses accurately the feelings and personal meanings that the client is experiencing and communicates this acceptant understanding to the client. When functioning best, the therapist is so much inside the private world of the other that he or she can clarify not only the meanings of which the client is aware but even those just below the level of awareness. Listening, of this very special, active kind, is one of the most potent forces of change that I know. (Rogers, 1989, p. 136)

FIGURE 1.3   Characteristics of the Effective Counselor

More than any component, empathy has been empirically shown to be related to positive client outcomes and is probably the most important ingredient to building a successful working alliance (Elliot et al., 2018; Norcross & Lambert, 2018). Whether one can truly understand the inner world of another has been discussed for centuries and was spoken of by such philosophers as Plato and Aristotle (Gompertz, 1960). However, Carl Rogers (1957) is given credit for bringing this concept to life in the 20th century. With respect to the counseling relationship, understanding through empathy is seen as a skill that can build rapport, elicit information, and help the client feel accepted (Egan, 2019; Neukrug, 2013, 2017, 2019, 2021).

Acceptance

Acceptance, sometimes called positive regard, is another component related to building a strong working alliance (Laska et al., 2014). Acceptance is an attitude that suggests that regardless of what the client says, they will feel accepted. Just about every counseling approach stresses the importance of acceptance (see Neukrug & Hays, 2023). For instance, person-centered counseling suggests that one core condition of helping clients open up about their experience is unconditional positive regard, or the ability to accept clients with "no strings attached." Behavior and solution-focused therapists suggest issues cannot be discussed, nor can goals be developed, if clients do not feel accepted. Reality therapy suggests that the suspension of judgment (i.e., acceptance) is one of the critical "tonics," or relationship-building skills, and psychoanalysis emphasizes the importance of analytic neutrality and empathy in building a relationship. Finally, cognitive-behavioral therapists note that relationship-building skills are critical to helping clients feel like they can learn about and apply the skills for change.

Genuineness

Genuineness refers to the counselor's ability to be authentic, open, and in touch with their feelings and thoughts within the parameters of the helping relationship (Rogers, 1957). Being real within the relationship has been shown to be related to positive outcomes in counseling (Nienhuis et al., 2018; Norcross & Lambert, 2018; Norcross et al., 2019). Thus, one may *not* have all aspects of their life "together," but within the counseling relationship, the counselor is real and seen by the client as being in a state of congruence (feelings, thoughts, and behaviors are in sync). Genuineness may also be related to emotional intelligence, which is the ability to monitor one's emotions; counselors and counseling students seem to possess this quality more than others (Gutierrez & Mullen, 2016; Martin et al., 2004). Rogers (1957) popularized the term "genuineness" (or congruence) and noted that it was a core condition in the counseling relationship, along with empathy and unconditional positive regard.

Research by Gelso et al. (2018) suggests that regardless of one's theoretical orientation, there exists an ongoing "real relationship," in which the client will see the counselor realistically, at least to some degree. This real relationship has at its core the ability of the client to recognize the genuine (or nongenuine) self of the counselor.

Embracing a Wellness Perspective

> The difference in professional quality of life between counselor with high and low Wellness levels [suggests that] greater Wellness translates to dramatically improved professional quality of life. (Lawson & Myers, 2011, p. 170)

Counselor stress, burnout, compassion fatigue, vicarious traumatization, and unfinished psychological issues can all hinder the CMHC's ability to have a working alliance (Beierel et al., 2021; Tschuschke et al., 2022). Such concerns can prevent a counselor from being empathic, lower their ability to show acceptance, lead to incongruence, and increase countertransference, or "the unconscious transferring of thoughts, feelings, and attitudes onto the client by the therapist" (Neukrug, 2023, p. 43).

To be effective, counseling students and counselors, in general, need to attend to their own wellness by embracing a wellness perspective. One method of assessing your level of wellness is through an examination of how well you are living out your values in five important areas (see Experiential Exercise 1.1).

Although many avenues to wellness exist, one that must be considered for all counselors is attending counseling themselves. Undergoing counseling can help counselors (a) attend to their own personal issues, (b) decrease the likelihood of countertransference, (c) examine all aspects of themselves to increase overall wellness, and (d) understand what it's like to sit in the client's seat. On a positive note, it appears counselors understand the importance of being in counseling, as 90.3% of counselors polled reported having attended counseling (Kalkbrenner & Neukrug, 2019; Kalkbrenner et al., 2019). So have you attended counseling? If not, have you found other ways to work on being healthy and well?

EXPERIENTIAL EXERCISE 1.1 Bull's-Eye Values Exercise

Relative to each of the following five domains, write a short statement regarding the type of person you would like to be and how you might develop yourself as you live out your life:

- work/education (career, education, and place of employment)
- relationships (partner, children, friends, coworkers, and relatives)
- personal growth (counseling, spirituality, religion, and creativity)
- physical health (exercise, diet, mind–body exercises, and addressing disease)
- leisure (avocations, recreation, relaxation, and play)

On the following bull's-eye, place an X In each of the five areas to reflect where you are today, with the bull's eye representing you fully living out your values and the outer circle representing extreme incongruence between how you are living and the values you want to embrace. Then, reflect on the short statement you wrote and how it relates to any discrepancies you find in your bull's-eye.

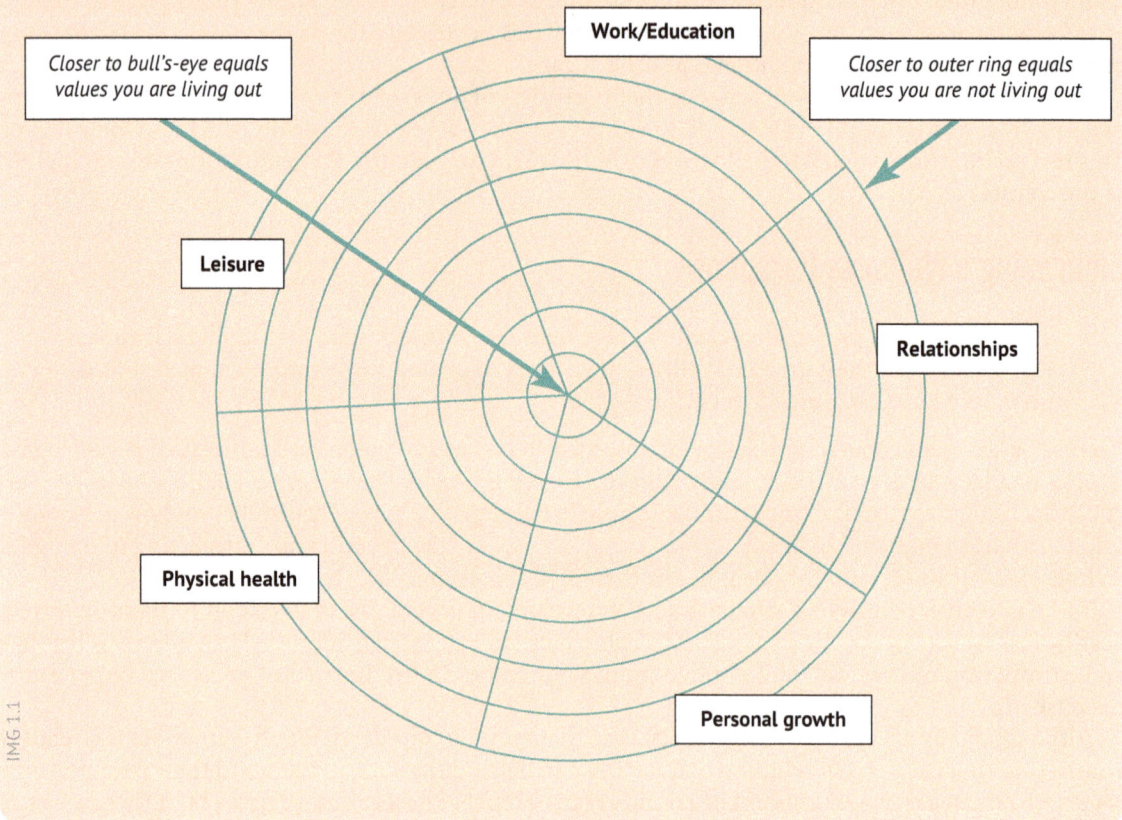

IMG 1.1

Cultural Competence

If you were distrustful of counselors, confused about the counseling process, or felt worlds apart from your helper, would you want to begin or continue in counseling? Assuredly not! Unfortunately, this is the situation for many diverse clients. In fact, it is now assumed that when clients from nondominant groups work with helpers from racial, ethnic, or cultural groups other than their own, there is a possibility that the client will frequently be talked down to, be misunderstood, be misdiagnosed, find counseling and therapy less helpful than their majority counterparts, attend counseling and therapy at lower rates than majority clients, and terminate counseling more quickly than majority clients (Escobar, 2012; Lo et al., 2013; National Alliance on Mental Illness, 2021; U.S. Department of Health and Human Services, 2014). Regrettably, it has become abundantly clear that many counselors have not learned how to effectively build a bridge—that is, form a working alliance with clients who are different from them.

Clearly, the effective counselor needs to be culturally competent if they are going to connect with clients (McAuliffe, 2020). One model that can help bridge the gap between the counselor and client's worlds is the RESPECTFUL model, which highlights 10 factors that should explored when working with clients:

- **R:** religious/spiritual identity
- **E:** economic class background
- **S:** sexual identity
- **P:** level of psychological development
- **E:** ethnic/racial identity
- **C:** chronological/developmental challenges
- **T:** various forms of trauma and other threats to one's sense of well-being
- **F:** family background and history
- **U:** unique physical characteristics
- **L:** location of residence and language differences (Lewis et al., 2011, p. 54)

The RESPECTFUL model offers one mechanism through which you can better understand the intersection of your client and your own various identities (see Experiential Exercise 1.2).

EXPERIENTIAL EXERCISE 1.2 **Understanding the Intersection of Your Identities**

Using the RESPECTFUL model, write a paragraph that describes each of the 10 characteristics as applied to you. Then, practice with a friend or peer to see if you can gather this important information from them.

The "It" Factor

I worked at a suicide crisis center where one of the counselors had an uncanny ability to make jokes on the phone that would result in suicidal clients laughing. If I had made those same jokes, it likely would have had the opposite effect! "So, is there a bridge nearby?" I would hear him say. This counselor had "it"—a way with words, a special vocal intonation, and a way of being that would get the client laughing—the *suicidal* client. Moreover, he knew he had "it" and he would use "it." I recognized that I didn't—well, I didn't have his "it"—so I knew better than to try to employ someone else's gift to make my clients laugh in the same manner. And, might I add, you should not try that technique! My "it" factor was simply listening and being empathic.

I believe all great counselors have their own "it" factor, although more often than not, great theorists want *us* to use *their* "it" factor. As such, Carl Rogers, who was great at showing empathy, unconditional positive regard, and genuineness, suggested we all use these core conditions. Albert Ellis, who was a master at showing how irrational one can be, suggested we all show our clients their irrational thinking. Michael White, who believed social injustices fueled mental illness, wanted all counselors to look at how individuals are oppressed by language. And of course, Sigmund Freud, who believed in the unconscious, told us to show analytic neutrality to allow the unconscious to be projected onto the therapist. I find that Salvadore Minuchin, the well-known family counselor, best described the "it" factor when he stated the following:

> The therapist's methods of creating a therapeutic system and positioning himself as its leader are known as joining operations. These are the underpinnings of therapy. Unless the therapist can join the family and establish a therapeutic system, restructuring cannot occur, and any attempt to achieve the therapeutic goals will fail. (Minuchin, 1974, p. 123)

So, what is your "it" factor? What do you have that is special and will enable you to bond? Is it the way you show empathy, the way you make people laugh, a tone, a look, or a way of being? Do you have "it"? See Experiential Exercise 1.3.

EXPERIENTIAL EXERCISE 1.3 **What Is Your "It"?**

Write down the unique personality characteristics that allow you to build a bond with others. Then, the instructor can make a master list on the board. After reviewing the list, discuss whether the characteristics are inherent or may be learned. Is it possible for a counselor to acquire new ways of bonding with clients as the counselor develops?

Compatibility With and Belief in a Theory

There are many theories to choose from when I do counseling, but most don't fit me. For one reason or another, I am simply not compatible with them. Maybe it's because they place too much emphasis on genetics, spirituality, or early child rearing, or maybe they're a little too directive or too nondirective. But for whatever reason, they just don't sit well with me, so I choose not to use them. Thankfully, however, there are enough theories out there with which I am compatible. I naturally align with them, so those are the ones I use. Wampold (2019) says that helpers "are attracted to therapies that they find comfortable, interesting, and attractive. Comfort most likely derives from the similarity of the worldview of the theory and the therapist's attitudes and values" (p. 54). Wampold and others go on to say that if you are drawn to a theory, and if you believe the theory works, then and only then are you likely to see positive counseling outcomes (Wampold, 2019; Wampold & Budge, 2012; Wampold & Imel, 2015). So what theories are you drawn to at this point in your counseling education? If you aren't sure yet, you'll have an opportunity to explore a variety of theories in your program. Hopefully, over time, you will feel an increased sense of compatibility with and belief in a theory.

Competence

Not surprisingly, counselor expertise and mastery (competence) has been shown to be a crucial element for client success in counseling (Hill et al., 2017; Shaw, 2020; Wampold, 2010, 2019). Competent counselors have a thirst for knowledge, and they continually want to improve and expand their expertise. Such counselors express this in many ways—through their study habits, their desire to join professional associations, their participation in mentoring and supervision, their reading of professional journals, their belief that education is a lifelong process, and by always broadening and deepening their unique approach to counseling. Competence also means counselors are not only concerned about their "relationships" with their clients but are also willing to look at the evidence of what works and apply appropriate treatment strategies to client problems (Hill et al., 2017). Finally, because these counselors feel confident about what they're doing, they can build expectations with their clients that what they do will help them get better. And in part, these expectations help clients get better (Wampold & Budge, 2012).

Competence is so important that Section I.C.1 of the *AMHCA Code of Ethics* (AMHCA, 2020) lists 16 items that delineate competent ethical behavior for a CMHC. The legal system reinforces these ethical guidelines because "competence is thus the touchstone by which the law will judge" (Kaslow et al., 2007; p. 488). Finally, clients pick up on incompetence. They can see it, smell it, and feel it. As you can imagine, incompetent counselors are sued more frequently and have clients who are less likely to improve.

Cognitive Complexity

The best helpers believe in their theory and are willing to question it. While this seems counterintuitive on the surface, it makes sense: you have a way of working that is efficacious, but you also have the humility to constantly examine whether your way *is* working in any given instance (Sommers-Flanagan, 2015). Counselors who have this capacity are often said to be cognitively complex. Not surprisingly, cognitive complexity has been shown to be related to empathy, open-mindedness, self-awareness, effectiveness with clients from diverse backgrounds, the ability to examine multiple perspectives, and being better at resolving ruptures in the counseling relationship (Castillo, 2018; McAuliffe & Eriksen, 2010). Such a counselor is willing to integrate new approaches into their usual way of practicing counseling and is a helper who doesn't believe their theory holds the lone "truth" (Wampold, 2019). So ask yourself the following: Do you have this quality? Are you able to self-reflect, question truth, take on multiple perspectives, and evaluate situations in complex ways? Counselor training programs are environments that seek to expand this type of thinking. Hopefully, in your program, you'll be exposed to such opportunities.

CONCLUSION

Now that we've looked at all nine characteristics, ask yourself this: Are you empathic, accepting, genuine, wellness oriented, and culturally competent? Do you know your "it" factor? Do you believe in your theoretical approach and are your compatibility with it? Are you competent and cognitively complex? Finally, as we start on our journey to help others, let's not forget to help ourselves—clearly, helping ourselves will significantly improve how we help others!

SUMMARY

This chapter sought to give you a basic overview of who the CMHC is, what the CMHC does, and some fundamental information about related mental health professionals. The chapter started with definitions of clinical mental health counseling and CMHCs. We noted that those with a degree in clinical mental health counseling can become licensed professional counselors (LPC's), which is sometimes called a licensed mental health counselor, a licensed CMHC (LCMHC), or some other variant. We also pointed out that all CMHCs can become a national certified counselor (NCC) as well as a certified CMHC (CCMHC) through the National Board for Certified Counselors (NBCC). We further noted that becoming licensed is the key to obtaining third-party payments. We then went on to note that the professional association for CMHCs is the American Mental Health Counselors Association (AMHCA), although many will also join the American Counseling Association (ACA) and one or more of its 19 divisions and 1 affiliate division.

The chapter next highlighted the advantages of accreditation of counseling programs and identified CACREP as the major accreditation body for CMHCs, accrediting over 375 programs nationally. A limited number of programs are also accredited by the Masters in Psychology and Counseling Accreditation Council (MPCAC). MPCAC has accredited close to 60 psychology and counseling programs and requires 48 semester hours, as opposed to CACREP's 60 credits. It also requires competency in 11 broad areas, many of which are similar to CACREP. We cautioned that graduates of an MPCAC accredited program may have some disadvantages in obtaining state licensure as compared to graduates from a CACREP accredited program.

We went on to note that all counseling programs are expected to cover knowledge and skills in each of eight core curriculum areas. But we also noted that each specialty area has its own knowledge and skills, and we addressed several of them in clinical mental health counseling that focused on foundations, contextual dimensions, and practice. We noted that all CACREP-accredited master's programs require a 100-hour practicum and 600-hour internship. The chapter also identified 15 important roles and functions for CMHCs on the job.

Moving on in the chapter, we briefly described a variety of counselors in addition to CMHCs, including addiction counselors; couples, marriage, and family counselors; pastoral counselors; rehabilitation counselors; school counselors; and student affairs and college counselors. Then, we briefly described other mental health professionals, including counseling and clinical psychologists; creative and expressive therapists; human service professionals; psychiatric mental health nurses; psychiatrists; psychoanalysts; psychotherapists; school psychologists, and social workers.

The last part of the chapter examined characteristics of the effective CMHC. First, we noted that client factors, such as readiness for change, psychological resources, and social supports, are likely to affect how well a client does in counseling. We then discussed the importance of using evidence-based practices with your client; this requires that counselors (a) know the best available research-supported treatments; (b) use their clinical expertise to understand the client's situation and choosing the most effective treatments for it; and (c) consider the client's personal preferences, values, and cultural background for such treatment. Finally, we identified two critical common factors related to positive client outcomes: the ability to build a working alliance and the ability to deliver a theoretical approach. We also identified nine characteristics of the effective counselor related to these two factors. These included six factors related to the working alliance: empathy, acceptance, genuineness, embracing a wellness perspective, cultural competence, and the "it" factor; and three factors related to delivering your theoretical approach: belief in one's theory, competence, and cognitive complexity.

KEY WORDS AND TERMS

addiction counselor
AMHCA Code of Ethics
ASCA-certified school counselor
ASCA national model
board certified
certified clinical mental health counselor (CCMHC)
client factors
clinical mental health counseling
clinical mental health counselor (CMHC)

clinical psychologist
cognitive complexity
college and student affairs counselors
common factors
compatibility with and belief in a theory
competence
congruence
counseling psychologist
countertransference

creative and expressive therapist
culturally competent
delivering a theoretical approach
embracing a wellness perspective
emotional intelligence
empathy
evidence-based practice (EPB)
genuineness
guidance counselor
human service professionals

human services–board certified practitioner (HS–BCP)
Journal of Mental Health Counseling
knowledge and skills
licensed clinical mental health counselor (LCMHC)
licensed mental health counselor (LMHC)
licensed professional counselor (LPC)
marriage, couple, and family counselors

master addiction counselor (MAC)
national certified counselor (NCC)
national certified school counselors (NCSCs)
national counselor exam (NCE)
pastoral counselor
psychiatric–mental health nurses
psychiatrist
psychoanalyst
psychologist

psychotherapist
PsyD
qualified mental health professional (QMHP)
rehabilitation counselors
RESPECTFUL model
roles and functions
school counselor
school psychologist
social worker
third-party payments
unconditional positive regard
working alliance

KEY NAMES

Ellis, Albert
Freud, Sigmund

Rogers, Carl
White, Michael

Minuchin, Salvador

PROFESSIONAL ASSOCIATIONS AND ORGANIZATIONS

Academy of Certified Social Workers (ACSW)
American Art Therapy Association (AATA)
American Association of Marriage and Family Therapy (AAMFT)
American Clinical Pastoral Education (ACPE)
American College Counseling Association (ACCA)
American Counseling Association (ACA)
American Dance Therapy Association (ADTA)
American Mental Health Counselors Association (AMHCA)
American Music Therapy Association (AMTA)
American Psychiatric Association (APA)
American Psychiatric Nurses Association (APNA)
American Psychoanalytic Association (APsaA)
American Psychological Association (APA)
American School Counselor Association (ASCA)
Art Therapy Credentials Board (ATCB)
Association for Creativity in Counseling (ACC)
Association for Play Therapy (APT)
Association for Spiritual, Ethical, and Religious Values in Counseling (ASERVIC)
Association of Marital and Family Therapy Regulatory Boards (AMFTRB)
Center for Credentialing and Education (CCE)
College Student Educators International (ACPA)
Commission on Accreditation of Marriage and Family Therapy Education (COAMFTE)
Council for Accreditation of Counseling and Related Educational Programs (CACREP)
Council for Standards in Human Service Education (CSHSE)
Division 12 of the American Psychological Association
Division 16 of the American Psychological Association
Division 17 of the American Psychological Association

International Association of Addictions and Offender Counselors (IAAOC)
International Association of Marriage and Family Counselors (IAMFC)
Masters in Psychology and Counseling Accreditation Council (MPCAC)
National Association of School Psychologists (NASP)
National Board for Certified Counselors (NBCC)
National Board for Certified Pastoral Counselors (NBCPC)
National Organization of Human Services (NOHS)
National Rehabilitation Counseling Association (NRCA)

CREDITS

CHAPTER 2

HISTORY AND CURRENT TRENDS IN CLINICAL MENTAL HEALTH COUNSELING

Learning Goals

- Learn about the varying philosophies and mental health professionals that were the precursors to modern-day counseling.
- Examine the emergence of the counseling profession and how its foundation was developed on the shoulders of vocational guidance during the first half of the 20th century.
- Understand how the 1960s through 1980s was a time of major growth and the establishment of clinical mental health counseling.
- Explore how clinical mental health counseling and licensure for CMHCs became a critical part of the mental health landscape over the past 30 years.
- Review how several current issues impact today's CMHCs, including professional associations; credentialing; licensure portability; telemental health counseling; interprofessional collaboration; salaries; ethical and legal issues, such as HIPAA, access to counseling records, and privileged communication; confinement against one's will; and cross-cultural and social justice issues.

INTRODUCTION

Can you imagine a woman being hanged as a witch because she was mentally ill, or being placed in a straitjacket and thrown into a filthy, rat-infested cell for the remainder of her life? Or can you envision a man being placed in a bathtub filled with iron filings to cure him of mental illness or bled to rid him of demons and spirits that caused him to think in demonic ways? What about having a piece of your brain scraped out to change the way you feel? Or being placed in a box that would receive "energy" and rid you of emotional and physical problems? These examples are a part of the history of our profession. (Neukrug, 2022, p. 29)

Although the history of clinical mental health counseling is only about 75 years old, its foundation goes back hundreds of years. This chapter discusses the precursors of clinical mental health counseling, examines the emergence of the counseling profession, reviews the growth and establishment of mental health counseling, and discusses how *licensed professional counselors* (LPCs)[1] are now a critical part of the mental health landscape. As noted in the opening quote, some of the history is not pretty, but it all represents the unfolding stories that eventually led to what we now call *clinical mental health counseling*.

The chapter concludes with a section that reviews current issues in clinical mental health counseling, including professional associations; credentialing; licensure portability; telemental health counseling; interprofessional collaboration; salaries; ethical and legal issues, such as HIPAA, confidentiality, privileged communication, and confinement against one's will; and cross-cultural and social justice issues.

FIGURE 2.1 A Golem. Golems were ancient inanimate objects, usually made from clay, which people believed could be brought to life to help them.

HISTORY

Precursors to Modern-Day Counseling

The first counselors were leaders of the community who attempted to provide inspiration for others through their teachings. They were religious leaders such as Moses (1200 B.C.), Mohammed (600 B.C.), and Buddha (500 B.C.). They were also philosophers like Lao-Tzu (600 B.C.), Confucius (500 B.C.), Socrates (450 B.C.), Plato (400 B.C.), and Aristotle (350, B. C.). (Kottler & Shepard, 2015, p. 30)

Since the dawn of existence, people have attempted to understand the human condition. Myths, magic, belief in spirits, ritualism, and sacred art have been used by people as means of gaining introspection and to understand the world around us (Ellwood & McGraw, 2014; see Figure 2.1). Forty thousand years ago—and still today—shamans, or individuals who have special status due to their mystical powers, have been viewed as caretakers of the soul and are thought to have knowledge of the future.

---

1. Throughout the book, I will generally use the term "LPC" to denote a licensed CMHC. However, other terms are used interchangeably and vary based on the state in which one lives (e.g., LMHC or LCMHC).

One of the first written treatises of a psychological nature can be traced back to an Egyptian papyrus of ca. 3000 B.C.E. that shows a primitive attempt to understand some basic functions of the brain (Breasted, 1930). Almost 1,000 years later, also in ancient Egypt, a wise man, who was obviously psychologically minded, wrote the following:

> If thou searchest the character of a friend, ask no questions, (but) approach him and deal with him when he is alone. … Disclose his heart in conversation. If that which he has seen come forth from him, (or) he do aught that makes thee ashamed for him, … do not answer. (Breasted, 1934, p. 132)

Following the advent of monotheistic religions, there have been abundant examples of humankind's attempt to understand and assist those struggling with psychological problems (Belgium, 1992). For instance, the Buddhist concept of duhkha speaks to the importance of developing insight into the nature of one's disappointment, pain, and suffering, which is inherent in life, and discovering how to overcome it (Epstein, 2013). Likewise, the Old and New Testaments offer many reflections on the healing powers of talk:

> The words of the reckless pierce like swords, but the tongue of the wise brings healing. (New International Version, 2022; Prov. 12:18)

Over the years, philosophers and theologians have reflected on the nature of the person, the soul, and the human condition. For instance, the Greek philosopher Hippocrates (460–377 B.C.E.) presented reflections on the human condition that challenged many of his contemporary's beliefs that emotional ills were the result of possession by evil spirits. In fact, some treatments for emotional problems that Hippocrates suggested would be considered modern by today's standards. For instance, for melancholia he suggested sobriety, a regular and tranquil life, and exercise short fatigue. However, he also suggested bleeding, if necessary, and for hysteria, he recommended getting married—an idea that would certainly spark the ire of many in today's world! Other Greek philosophers, like Socrates (470–399 B.C.E.) and Plato (437–347 B.C.E.), also reflected on the human condition. But perhaps most importantly for the history of the helping professions, there was Aristotle (384–322 B.C.E.), who reflected on the relationship between psychological processes and physiology and is often identified as the founder of psychology. Although, over the centuries, psychological ideas occurred throughout the world, current psychology is mostly based on modern-day Western thought, beginning in the 1400s.

The invention of the printing press in 1436 led to the spread of new ideas, scholarship, and philosophy throughout Europe and was partially responsible for the Renaissance in Europe between the 14th and 17th centuries. This modern era, as it is commonly called, led to individuals like the French philosopher René Descartes (1596–1650) to suggest that truth and knowledge come from deductive reasoning and the Western notion that the mind and the body are separate, often called mind–body dualism. Other Western philosophers, like John Locke (1632–1704) and James Mill (1773–1836), promoted the idea that the mind is a blank slate upon which ideas become imprinted. Such new knowledge set the stage for modern psychologists to study human experience. Individuals like these supplied the ingredients for the eventual development of the professions of psychology, psychiatry, social work, and counseling. Although psychological thinking occurred well before the 18th century, the treatment of the mentally ill left much to be desired during these times (see Box 2.1).

Despite the fact that the treatment of the mentally ill was horrific during the 1700s, the 1800s brought with it new ways of understanding and working with individuals and a shift in how mental illness was perceived. From believing individuals were possessed by demons and spirits, or their behaviors were solely a function of organic problems, people like the French physician Philippe Pinel (1745–1826) began to take a scientific perspective on mental illness and sought humane treatments for the mentally ill (Charland, 2018; Weissmann, 2008; see Figure 2.2).

BOX 2.1 The 1800s and the Establishment of Modern-Day Helping Professions

The Beginnings of the Modern Mental Hospital

In 1773, the Publick Hospital for Persons of Insane and Disordered Minds admitted its first patient in Williamsburg, Virginia. The hospital, which had 24 cells, took a rather bleak approach to working with the mentally ill. Although many of the employees of these first hospitals had their hearts in the right place, their diagnostic and treatment procedures would be considered subpar or inhumane today. For instance, some of the leading reasons patients were admitted included masturbation, "womb disease," religious excitement, intemperance, and domestic trouble—hardly reasons for admission to a mental institution. The treatment procedures included administering heavy doses of drugs, bleeding or blistering individuals, immersing individuals in freezing water for long periods of time, and confining people to straitjackets or manacles. Bleeding and blistering were thought to remove harmful fluids from the individual's system (Zwelling, 1990).

In the United States, Benjamin Rush (1743–1813), a physician and dedicated social reformer considered to be the founder of American psychiatry (Baxter, 1994), appealed for humane treatment of the poor and mentally ill. Similarly, during mid-1800s, Dorothea Dix (1802–1887) advocated for encouragement and respect, removal from stressors, and vocational training as treatments of choice for the mentally ill (Baxter, 1994). This increased focus on the treatment of the mentally ill eventually led to the founding of the Association of Medical Superintendents of American Institutions for the Insane in 1844, often seen as the forerunner of the American Psychiatric Association (APA). With advocates like Pinel, Rush, and Dix, treatment of the mentally ill improved but would still be considered horrible by today's standards.

FIGURE 2.2   Phillipe Pinel Releasing "Lunatics" From Their Chains

During the mid-1850s, people like Jean Martin Charcot (1825–1893), who studied hypnosis, and his student, Pierre Janet (1859–1947), who was intrigued by the subconscious, suggested there was a relationship between one's psychological history and current functioning (Solomon, 1918). These individuals influenced Sigmund Freud (1856–1939), the creator of the first comprehensive approach to psychotherapy, to believe mental illness could be understood through a psychological lens (see Figure 2.3).

It was also during this century that Charles Darwin's scientific analysis of the origins of species was the impetus for some of the first experimental psychologists. For instance, it was during this time that Wilhem Wundt (1832–1920) conducted experiments within the laboratory setting that examined the nature of spatial perceptions and human consciousness. Often identified as the modern-day founder of psychology, his methods subsequently led to the development of psychological tests, modern-day research methods, and early classification methods aimed at differences among people. As a result of these new "psychological" methods of understanding the person, the American Psychological Association (APA) was formed in 1892 (APA, 2023).

During the late 1800s, while psychologists were studying scientific methods and psychiatrists were increasingly seeing problems through a psychological lens, the first social workers were more interested in providing hands-on support to those most disenfranchised in society. For instance, those involved with the Charity Organization Societies (COS) would visit the poor, aid in educating children, give economic advice, and assist in alleviating the conditions of poverty (Popple et al., 2019). The COSs are seen as the beginnings of social casework, the process through which a client's needs are examined and a treatment plan is designed. Similarly, idealistic young staff from the *settlement movement* lived with the poor to offer help and guidance. In 1989, one of the best-known settlement houses, Hull House, was established by Nobel Peace Prize winner and social justice activist Jane Addams (1860–1935) in Chicago (Addams, 1910/2017; see Figure 2.4). These early, humane attempts to help people with their community-focused interventions are often seen as the precursors of the social work profession and the establishment of the National Association of Social Workers (NASW).

Although psychologists, psychiatrists, and social workers all had different perspectives on how to help individuals, each had their unique contribution to the early development of the major helping professions and set in motion the beginnings of the counseling profession (see Table 2.1 for an overview of the precursors).

FIGURE 2.3 "It's All in Your Head"

FIGURE 2.4 Social Reformer and Nobel Prize Winner Jane Addams

TABLE 2.1 Precursors to Modern-Day Counseling

Historical Person/Organization	Definition
Shamans (ca. 40,000 B.C.E.)	Mystical powers and caretakers of the soul
Monotheistic religions (6,000 B.C.E.–present)	Attempts to understand the human condition (e.g., Buddhist concept of *duhka*)
Egyptian papyrus of 3000 B.C.E.	A primitive attempt to understand basic brain functions
Hippocrates (460–377 B.C.E.)	Reflected on the human condition and had "modern-day" cures for melancholia
Socrates (470–399) and Plato (437–347)	Reflected upon the essence of human nature
Aristotle (384–322)	Reflected upon the relationship between psychological processes and physiology and is often identified as the founder of psychology
The Renaissance, printing press and "modern era" (1400–1700)	Birthed new ideas, scholarship, and philosophy
Descartes (1596–1650)	Believed truth and knowledge came from deductive reasoning and the mind is separate from the body
John Locke (1632–1704) and James Mill (1773–1836)	Promoted the idea that the mind is a blank slate upon which ideas become generated
"Modern" mental hospitals (ca. 1800s)	Mental hospitals with more humane treatments were founded.
Philippe Pinel (1745–1826)	Provided a scientific perspective on mental illness and advocated for the humane treatment of the mentally ill
Benjamin Rush (1743–1813)	A physician, social reformer, and founder of American psychiatry
Dorothea Dix (1802–1887)	Advocated encouragement and respect, removal from stressors, and vocational training for the mentally ill
Jean Martin Charcot (1825–1893)	Studied hypnosis for treatment of mental illness
Pierre Janet (1859–1947)	Studied the subconscious and looked at relationship between one's psychological history and current functioning
Sigmund Freud (1856–1939)	The creator of the first comprehensive theory of psychotherapy; viewed mental illness through a psychological lens
Association of Medical Superintendents of American Institutions for the Insane (1844)	The forerunner of the American Psychiatric Association (APA)
Wilhelm Wundt (1832–1920)	Examined the nature of spatial perceptions and human consciousness, which led to development of psychological tests, modern-day research methods, and early classification methods of understanding people; the modern-day founder of psychology
American Psychological Association (1892)	American Psychological Association was founded
Charity Organization Societies (ca. late 1800s)	Visited the poor, helped educate children, gave advice to those in need, alleviated poverty; the beginning of social casework

Jane Addams (1860–1935)	Social activist who stablished one of the first settlement houses (Hull House). Winner of the Nobel Peace Prize
Settlement houses (ca. late 1800s)	Used community interventions to help the poor, and many of their contributions were the precursors to the development of the NASW

1900 Through the 1950s: The Emergence of the Counseling Profession

The beginning of the counseling profession can be traced back to the vocational guidance movement during the early part of the 20th century, led by Frank Parsons (1854–1908; see Figure 2.5). Seen as the originator of vocational guidance in the United States, Parsons is often cited as the founder of the counseling profession (Briddick, 2009; Herr, 2013; McDaniels & Watts, 1994). Parsons was influenced by early psychologists' and psychiatrists' reflections on the nature of people and the reform movements of the time, such as the work of Jane Addams. As a result, he eventually established the Vocational Bureau, which assisted individuals in "choosing an occupation, preparing themselves for it, finding an opening in it, and building a career of efficiency and success" (Parsons, 1908, p. 3).

Parsons and other early vocational counselors used true reasoning in helping clients make sound vocational choices, which was a process of understanding oneself, knowing the requirements of different lines of work, and using a reasoning process to analyze the fit between oneself and the requirements of a job. This early counseling approach was a precursor to counselors encouraging clients to use their analytical skills to understand themselves (Herr, 2013; Jones, 1994). Vocational counseling would soon be incorporated into the schools and vocational guidance counselors, who were often half-time teachers, would eventually become full-time guidance counselors, now called school counselors (Neukrug, 2022).

With these skills at hand, and on the heels of doughboys (i.e., soldiers) returning from WWI needing vocational rehabilitation, in 1918, the Smith-Sears Soldier's Rehabilitation Act was passed, which offered much-needed vocational rehabilitation to soldiers disabled in the war (Chan et al., 2004; Peterson, 2020). In 1920, the Smith-Fess Act established state and federal vocational rehabilitation programs, which expanded services to individuals who had physical disabilities unrelated to the war. The vocational counselor, later to be known as the rehabilitation counselor, was a natural fit to work in these programs.

The vocational counseling movement was the foundation for a broader view of counseling when E. G. Williamson (1900–1979) developed the first comprehensive theory of counseling (as distinguished from Freud's theory of psychoanalysis) during the 1930s. Known as the Minnesota point of view (for the University of Minnesota, where Williamson was faculty in the psychology department), or trait-and-factor theory, Williamson's approach grew out of the ideas of Frank Parsons but was modified as a general approach to counseling. The approach involved five steps:

1. **analysis:** examining the problem and obtaining available records and testing for the client

2. **synthesis:** summarizing and organizing the information to understand the problem

FIGURE 2.5 Frank Parsons

FIGURE 2.6 Carl Rogers

3.   **diagnosis:** interpreting the problem

4.   **counseling:** aiding the individual in finding solutions

5.   **follow-up:** ensuring proper support after counseling had ended (Williamson & Darley, 1937)

With the rise of Nazism during the 1930s and 1940s, many existential–humanistic philosophers, psychiatrists, and psychologists fled Europe for the United States and dramatically influenced the field of psychotherapy and education in their new country. Meanwhile, during the 1930s, the federal government earmarked small amounts of money for mental health treatment, especially for research in mental health. Slowly, a new mindset to mental health treatment gained prominence—one that had an increasingly existential–humanistic perspective, as opposed to the then prevalent psychodynamic approach of Freud and others (du Plock & Tantum, 2019; Hoffman et al., 2019).

One of those influenced by the existential–humanists was Carl Rogers (1902–1987; see Figure 2.6). Called the most influential psychologists and psychotherapists of the 20th century (Simon, 2007), Rogers revolutionized counseling with his client-centered approach. His nondirective manner of working with individuals was shorter-term, more humane, more honest, and more viable for most clients compared to the psychodynamic approaches to counseling. The early 1940s saw the publication of Carl Rogers's book *Counseling and Psychotherapy*, which eventually had a major impact on the counseling profession (Rogers, 1942). Rogers and others in the newly established field of humanistic counseling and education were a major impetus for counseling to move from a vocational guidance and rehabilitation orientation to one with a much broader base (Hoffman et al., 2019). Rogers's approach was ripe for the times, as it reflected the increased focus on personal freedom and autonomy of the post–World War II years (Aubrey, 1977).

As a result of World War II, mental health providers and rehabilitation counselors became critical to the treatment of thousands of GIs coming home from the war (Hershenson et al., 2003); this was the primary reason the National Mental Health Act was passed in 1946, which gave states funding for research, training, prevention, diagnosis, and treatment related to mental health disorders. In 1949, the National Institute of Mental Health (NIMH) was created by Congress, which increased research and training in the mental health field and became the impetus for the 1955 Mental Health Study Act. This act also established the Joint Commission on Mental Illness and Health, which made several far-reaching recommendations that increased funding and services for mental health and mental illness. Meanwhile, with the passage of the 1954 Vocational Rehabilitation Act, Amendments, money was allocated for the expansion of services for the intellectually and psychiatrically disabled, for individuals who had become newly disabled, and for the development of master's level rehabilitation counseling programs (Chan et al., 2004).

Roger's client-centered, humanistic approach grew even more popular with the publication of his second book in 1951, *Client-Centered Therapy: Its Current Practice, Implications, and Theory*. In addition, affected by the push to depathologize individuals, this decade saw the promulgation of developmental theories in the areas of career counseling (e.g., Super, 1953), child development (e.g., Piaget, 1954), and lifespan development (e.g., Erikson, 1950). These theories stressed the notion that individuals would face natural and predictable tasks as they passed through the inevitable developmental stages of life and that knowledge of these developmental tasks could greatly aid counselors in their work with clients. A developmental and humanistic focus was much briefer than the psychodynamic theories of Freud, and others, that had been the primary approach to counseling and therapy. This approach was also a good fit for school counselors, college counselors, and the first CMHCs.

By 1952, the American Personnel and Guidance Association (APGA) was formed from a merger of four counseling-related associations, and it was not long before several divisions representing the growing diversity of counselors in the field emerged, including the American School Counselor Association (ASCA), the Association for Counselor Education and Supervision (ACES), the National Career Development Association (NCDA), the American Rehabilitation Counseling Association (ARCA), and the Counseling Association for Humanistic Education and Development (C-AHEAD). Although mental health counselors had similar training to these other counselors and could be found in some settings, they did not yet have the numbers to become an association.

The 1957 launch of the first satellite into space, the Russian satellite Sputnik, sent a chill through many Americans and spurred Congress to pass the National Defense Education Act (NDEA) in 1958, which allocated funds for training institutes that would quickly graduate secondary school counselors (Hanna, 2019). These counselors, it was hoped, would identify students gifted in math and science who could be future scientists. The obvious result of this legislation was the significant increase in secondary school counselors in the late 1950s and 1960s. The bill was extended to include the training of elementary school counselors in 1964.

Besides the dramatic increase in school counselors, the 1950s also saw the first full-time college counselors and the beginning of college counseling centers. With the GI Bill funding college expenses for World War II veterans, there was increased enrollment in colleges and an increased need for college counselors to address the needs of these soldiers as well as other students (Kraft, 2011). Other college student services offices that employed counselors expanded rapidly during this time (e.g., career centers). In addition, this decade saw counselors increasingly staffing vocational rehabilitation centers, working to address both the physical and psychological needs of individuals, especially those who had been seriously injured during World War II.

In tandem with the expansion of different kinds of counselors, the 1950s was a decade of growth for CMHCs. This increasing social acceptance toward counseling coincided with the development of new medications to treat a wide variety of mental health disorders, new laws expanding services for those with mental disorders, and the realization that many mental hospitals engaged in archaic practices and served merely as holding grounds. Consequently, these factors culminated in the release of large numbers of people from psychiatric hospitals, many of whom subsequently found needed services at local community agencies (Rochefort, 1984). These agencies needed to be staffed, and CMHCs were ready and willing. The 1950s was a time of rapid growth, but the most exciting era of counseling was still yet to come: the 1960s (see Table 2.2 for an overview of the progression of counseling in the 1900s through the 1950s).

TABLE 2.2 The 1900s–1950s: The Emergence of the Counseling Profession

Historical Event	Definition
Early 1900s: The vocational guidance movement	The precursor to counseling
Early 1900s: Frank Parsons	The "founder" of vocational guidance and counseling, who established the Vocational Bureau and the process of "true reasoning"
Early 1900s: Vocational counselors in schools	Eventually became "guidance counselors," now called "school counselors"

(Continued)

TABLE 2.2 (*Continued*)

Historical Event	Definition
1918: Smith-Sears Soldier's Rehabilitation Act	Vocational rehabilitation for soldiers disabled from war
1920: Smith-Fess Act	Established vocational rehabilitation programs and expanded vocational rehabilitation for individuals not impacted by war. Vocational counselors later became known as rehabilitation counselors.
1930s: E. G. Williamson	Developed the first comprehensive theory of counseling, known as Minnesota point of view or trait-and-factor theory
1930s: Existential–humanistic perspective	New mental health treatment arose that differed from the psychodynamic approach
1940s–1950s: Carl Rogers	His "client-centered approach" is introduced and begins to gain popularity. This approach is still widely used today.
1946: National Mental Health Act	Gave states funding for research, training, prevention, diagnosis, and treatment related to mental health disorders
1949: National Institute of Mental Health (NIMH)	Formed to focus research and training on mental health issues and was the impetus for the Mental Health Study Act in 1955 and the establishment of the Joint Commission on Mental Illness and Health
1954: Vocational Rehabilitation Act, Amendments	Allocated for the expansion of services for the intellectually and psychiatrically disabled and development of master's level rehabilitation programs
1955: Mental Health Study Act	Established the Joint Commission on Mental Illness and Health, which made far-reaching recommendations on increased funding and services for mental health and mental illness
1950s: An increase in counselors leads to formation of the APGA and divisions	School counselors, college counselors, rehabilitation, and mental health counselors increasingly needed to assist K–12 students, college students, and the mental health needs of the public
1952: APGA founded	APGA founded and several divisions formed
1954: Vocational Rehabilitation Act	Money allocated for expansion of services for individuals with intellectual and psychiatric disabilities along with the establishment of master's programs in rehabilitation counseling
1957 and 1958: Sputnik and NDEA	Sputnik results in the passage of the National Defense Education Act, which results in an increased need for school counselors

The 1960s–1980s: The Growth and Establishment of Clinical Mental Health Counseling

In addition to Carl Rogers's client-centered approach, which continued to gain popularity in the late 1950s and 1960s, several new and revolutionary approaches to counseling began to take shape during these decades. These included the cognitive approaches developed by Albert Ellis and Aaron Beck; the behavioral approaches of Albert Bandura, Joseph Wolpe, and John Krumboltz; the reality therapy approach of William Glasser; the Gestalt therapy approach of Fritz Perls; the communication approach of transactional analysis; and the existential approaches of Victor Frankl, Rollo May, and others (see Neukrug 2015; Neukrug & Hays, 2023). These theories were at least partially developed due to the increased need for mental health counseling, a greater acceptance of counseling, and people's preference for the shorter and more optimistic approach offered by these therapies compared to traditional psychodynamic approaches. Can you imagine being a young mental health professional during this time? The sheer number of new thought-provoking theories and approaches to working with clients would have been incredibly stimulating!

The need for mental health professionals expanded as a direct result of the passage of many legislative actions related to President Lyndon B. Johnson's Great Society initiatives during the early 1960s (Kaplan & Cuciti, 1986). One such law, the Community Mental Health Centers Act of 1963, funded the nationwide establishment of mental health centers to provide five essential services: (a) consultation and education for community and professional organizations, (b) inpatient facilities, (c) outpatient clinics, (d) emergency response, and (e) partial hospitalization (Erickson, 2021). These centers made it possible for individuals with diagnoses from adjustment disorders to schizophrenia to receive services. This act, and many others passed during this decade, greatly expanded the job pool for mental health counselors, school counselors, and rehabilitation counselors (Lambie & Williamson, 2004; Neukrug, 2023).

During the 1970s, several events increased the need for mental health counselors. For instance, the 1975 Supreme Court decision *O'Connor v. Donaldson* led to a massive reduction of individuals in state mental hospitals—from about 600,000 to under 200,000—by concluding individuals could not be held against their will if they were not in danger of harming themselves or others (Erickson, 2021; Rochefort, 1984; see Box 2.2).

BOX 2.2 *O'Connor v. Donaldson*

Kenneth Donaldson, who had been committed to a state mental hospital in Florida and confined against his will for 15 years, sued the hospital superintendent, Dr. J. B. O'Connor, and his staff for intentionally and maliciously depriving him of his constitutional right to liberty. Donaldson, who had been hospitalized against his will for "paranoid schizophrenia," said he was not mentally ill, and even if he was, the hospital had not provided him adequate treatment.

Over the 15 years of confinement, Donaldson, who was not in danger of harming himself or others, had frequently asked for his release, and had relatives who stated they would attend to him if he was released. Despite this, the hospital refused to release him, stating he was still mentally ill. The Supreme Court unanimously upheld lower court decisions stating the hospital could not hold him against his will if he was not in danger of harming himself or others (Behnke, 1999).

This decision, along with the increased use and discovery of new psychotropic medications, led to the release of hundreds of thousands of individuals across the country who had been confined to mental hospitals against their will and were not a danger to themselves or others.

With the release of individuals from these hospitals came an increased need for community mental health counselors and mental health services. Thus, in 1975, Congress expanded the original Community

Mental Health Centers Act from 5 to 12 services that mental health centers were required to provide, including the following:

1. short-term inpatient services
2. outpatient services
3. partial hospitalization (day treatment)
4. emergency services
5. consultation and education
6. special services for children
7. special services for the elderly
8. preinstitutional court screening
9. follow-up care for mental hospitals
10. transitional care from mental hospitals
11. alcoholism services
12. drug abuse services (GovTrack.us., n.d.)

The 1970s also saw the passage of legislation for individuals with disabilities, resulting in an increased demand for rehabilitation counselors and school counselors (U.S. Department of Education, 2017, 2020). For instance, the Rehabilitation Act of 1973 ensured vocational rehabilitation and counseling services were provided for employable adults who had severe physical or mental disabilities that interfered with their ability to obtain and maintain a job. The Education for All Handicapped Children Act of 1975 (PL94–142) guaranteed the right to an education, within the *least restrictive environment*, for all children identified as having a disability that interfered with learning. PL94–142 resulted in school counselors increasingly becoming an integral part of the team that would determine the disposition of students with disabilities. These two laws, which have been expanded over the years, are critical for CMHCs to understand when working with adults and children.

During this decade, a major shift in the training of counseling students took place. The influence of the humanistic movement had fully taken hold by the 1970s, and several individuals began to develop what became known as microcounseling skills training (Carkhuff, 1969; Egan, 1975; Ivey & Gluckstein, 1974). The teaching of these microcounseling skills was based on many of the skills deemed critical by Carl Rogers and other humanistic psychologists. These packaged ways of training counselors showed that basic counseling skills, such as attending behaviors, listening, and empathic understanding, could be learned in a relatively short amount of time and that the practice of such skills would have a positive impact on counseling outcomes (Ivey et al., 2018; Neukrug, 1980). It was also during this decade that the blossoming of publications in cross-cultural counseling began. Seminal works by Derald Sue, Paul Pedersen, William Cross, Donald Atkinson, and others began to make their way into counselor education curricula.

The 1970s was also the decade of increased professionalization in the field. For instance, during the early 1970s, the Association of Counselor Educators and Supervisors (ACES) provided drafts of standards for the accreditation of master's-level counseling programs. National credentialing became a reality when certification was offered for the first time by the Council on Rehabilitation Education (CORE) in 1973 and the National Academy for Certified Mental Health Counselors (NACMHC) in 1979 (Sweeney, 1991). This decade further saw President Jimmy Carter expand mental health services; Virginia become the first state to license mental health counselors in 1976; and the formation of a number of new divisions of APGA, including the American Mental Health Counseling Association (AMHCA) in 1978 (Colangelo, 2009; Weikel, 1985/2010). Increasingly, counselors could be found in community mental health centers, a wide range of agencies, and private practices (Smith & Robinson, 1995).

In 1981, the Council for Accreditation of Counseling and Related Programs (CACREP) was established, implementing the draft standards for accreditation of counseling programs that had been in development since the early 1970s (CACREP, 2023a). Today, CACREP accredits a wide variety of master's programs, including those in clinical mental health counseling. In 1983, APGA changed its name to the American Association of Counseling and Development (AACD), reflecting the organization's focus on modern-day helping. Within this decade, AACD continued to expand, adding an additional four divisions. In addition to accreditation, in 1982, the National Board for Certified Counselors (NBCC) was developed, offering a generic credential for all counselors—the national certified counselor (NCC)—as well as several specialty certifications, including the certified clinical mental health counselor (CCMHC) and national certified school counselor (NCSC; NBCC, 2023a, 2023b). Today, many states require passage of the NCC and/or the CCMHC exam as part of the licensure requirements to become an LPC.

The 1980s also saw dramatic changes in the delivery of mental health services due to the rise of managed care, such as health maintenance organizations (HMOs) and preferred provider organizations (PPOs), which became the primary health insurance providers (Kongstvedt, 2020; Schneiderman, 2018). Previously, clients who had medical insurance were generally free to choose the type of counseling services they desired and licensed professional they wished to see. However, HMOs and PPOs carefully monitored and limited which providers a client could see and the length of time the client could see the provider (see Table 2.3 for an overview of the 1960s through the 1980s).

TABLE 2.3 The 1960s–1980s: The Growth and Establishment of Clinical Mental Health Counseling

Historical Event	Definition
1960s: An increase in therapeutic modalities	Rogers's approach gains in popularity, and several new therapies founded, including cognitive approaches (Ellis and Beck), reality therapy (Glasser), Gestalt therapy (Perls), transactional analysis, and existential approaches (Frankl and May).
1960s: President Johnson's Great Society	Led to many mental health initiatives and programs
1963: Community Mental Health Centers Act	Provided seed money for short-term inpatient care, outpatient care, partial hospitalization, emergency services, and consultation and education services
1970s: Microcounseling skills training	The spread and influence of the humanistic way of learning skills
1970s: The spread of publications on multicultural counseling	Several seminal works published that set the stage for the inclusion of culturally competent counseling in counseling programs
1970s: ACES provides draft accreditation standards	Draft standards for master's level counseling programs
1973: CORE	CORE develops a national credential for rehab counselors.
1973: Rehabilitation Act of 1973	Ensured vocational rehabilitation services for those with physical and mental disabilities and is important for mental health counselors to be educated about

(Continued)

TABLE 2.3 *(Continued)*

Historical Event	Definition
1975: Education for all Handicapped Children Act	Ensured the right to an education, within the least restrictive environment, for children with a disability and is important for mental health counselors to know about
1975: *O'Connor v. Donaldson*	A Supreme Court decision that led to the release of hundreds of thousands of state mental hospital patients held against their will but not dangerous to themselves or others
1975: Expansion of Community Mental Health Centers Act	Services increased from 5 to 12.
1976: AMHCA formed	AMHCA became a division of APGA.
1976: Virginia licensing	Virginia became the first state in the country to license counselors.
1977: AMHCA established	AMHCA established as division of ACA
1979: Credentialing for mental health counselors	The National Academy for Certified Mental Health Counselors provided its first credential.
1980s: HMOs	HMOs limited services for the types of choices one has for counseling.
1981: CACREP Standards	The first accreditation standards dispersed, including accreditation standards for mental health counselors.
1982: NBCC established	Nonprofit organization that provides the National Counselor Certification for all counselors and specialty certifications, including certification as a CMHC. Today, states use these exams as part of the requirements to become an LPC.
1983: APGA becomes AACD	APGA changes its name to AACD.
HMOs and PPOs become popular	HMOs and PPOs limit who

The 1990s-Today: LPCs Become a Critical Part of the Mental Health Landscape

One of the most impactful changes in the field of counseling during the 1980s and 1990s was the increase in focus on multicultural counseling (Claiborn, 1991). This new emphasis was partly due to the CACREP requirement for multicultural counseling to be infused into the curricula of all accredited graduate programs; the ever-increasing volumes of work being published in the field of multicultural counseling; and the 1991 adoption by the Association of Multicultural Counseling and Development (AMCD; a division of ACA) of the Multicultural Counseling Competencies (MCC), which counseling training programs were encouraged to follow (Arredondo et al., 1996; Evans & Larrabee, 2002). After adding advocacy competencies in 2003 and later realizing the close relationship between multicultural counseling and advocacy, in 2015, the two competencies were updated and combined as the Multicultural and Social Justice Counseling Competencies (MSJCC; Ratts et al., 2016).

The 1990s also saw AACD become the American Counseling Association (ACA); membership soar past 55,000; and several new divisions founded, with AMHCA and ASCA representing the two largest divisions. At that point, ACA had 17 divisions and one affiliate division, representing the differing specialty areas in counseling, with close to 500 counselor training programs in the United States (Hollis & Dodson, 2000).

In 1996, the hold HMOs and PPOs had on the delivery of mental health services waned with the passage of the Mental Health Parity Act of 1996, which prevented annual or lifetime limits on mental health benefits by insurance companies. This was extended by the Mental Health Parity and Addiction Equity Act of 2008 and the Affordable Care Act of 2010, otherwise known as Obamacare (U.S. Department of Health and Human Services, 2021). These acts mandated mental health and substance use disorder services to be provided by insurance companies at the same level as physical illnesses and quickly increased the need for mental health providers, including LPCs.

Parallel with the mandate of mental health services, an increasing number of states passed licensure laws. Finally, in 2009, California became the last state to pass a mental health counselor licensure law (Shallcross, 2009). With licensure being the first important step toward counselors becoming independent providers and obtaining third-party reimbursement, this was no small feat. Today, LPCs can become providers for the vast array of managed care and health insurance companies, such as TRICARE, the largest health care organization for U.S. military families, and Medicare, which serves 43 million older Americans (ACA, 2015, 2023a; Walsh & Dasenbrook, 2010, 2016). It is through the advocacy work of AMHCA, ACA, NBCC, and other counseling associations that LPCs have quickly established themselves alongside other mental health professionals. Are you a member of one or more of these associations?

Today, all states provide some form of credentialing for addictions counselors, many of whom have degrees in clinical mental health counseling (University of Cincinnati Online, 2023), and in most states, addictions counselors, rehabilitation counselors, school counselors, and related professional counselors can become LPCs with some additional coursework and/or field experience. The expansion of clinical mental health counseling has been remarkable, and today, there are about 375 accredited clinical mental health counseling programs and LPCs in every state in the country, the District of Columbia, and Puerto Rico (ACA, 2023b; CACREP, 2023b). One result of this expansion was AMHCA disaffiliating with ACA in 2019 and becoming an independent association, similar to what ASCA had done in 2018. Although both AMHCA and ASCA are now independent associations, they continue to collaborate with ACA.

On October 17, 2020, President Trump signed Senate Bill 785, which mandated a federal government occupational classification for mental health counselors. The bill has resulted in increased hiring, training, and advancement of mental health counselors in federal agencies, such as VA hospitals (Bergman, 2020), and has been critical to the hiring of thousands of mental health counselors in federal jobs throughout the country.

Clinical mental health counseling has come a long way since its origins at the beginning of the 1900s. Today, mental health counselors can be found in a wide array of settings, and they work closely with mental health colleagues in related fields, such as human service professionals, social workers, psychologists, and psychiatrists (see Table 2.4 for an overview of the history of mental health counseling from 1990).

TABLE 2.4 The 1990s–Present: LPCs Become a Critical Part of the Mental Health Landscape

Historical Event	Definition
1991: MCCs developed	AMCD developed Multicultural Counseling Competencies (MCCs).
1996: Mental Health Parity Act	Limited the power of HMOs and PPOs by prohibiting annual or lifetime limits on mental health benefits
2008: Mental Health Parity and Addiction Equity Act	Mandated mental health and substance use disorder services to be provided by insurance companies at the same level as physical illnesses
2009: California Licensure Law	California became the last state to pass a mental health counselor licensure law, meaning counselors could now become independent providers and obtain third-party reimbursement in all states

(Continued)

TABLE 2.4   *(Continued)*

Historical Event	Definition
2010: Affordable Care Act	Reinforced and expanded the Mental Health Parity and Equity Addictions Act
2015: MSJCCs adopted	Multicultural and Social Justice Counseling Competencies developed
2017: CACREP-accredited rehabilitation counseling programs	CACREP took over accreditation of rehabilitation counseling programs from CORE.
2018–2019: ASCA and AMHCA disaffiliated from the ACA	ASCA, then AMHCA, decided they were large and unique enough to disaffiliate from ACA.
2020: Senate Bill 785	Senate Bill 785 mandated a federal government occupational classification for mental health counselors, which resulted in increased hiring, training, and advancement of mental health counselors in federal agencies, such as the VA.
2022: CMHCs were plentiful	In 2022, there were 375 CACREP-accredited clinical mental health programs and LPCs in every state of the country, D.C., and Puerto Rico.
2023: Mental Health Access Improvement Act	Mental health counselors became providers for Medicare, which covers 43 million older Americans.

CURRENT ISSUES FOR MENTAL HEALTH COUNSELORS

The final section of the chapter reviews pressing issues in clinical mental health counseling, including professional associations; credentialing; licensure portability; telemental health counseling; interprofessional collaboration; salaries; ethical and legal issues, such as HIPAA, access to counseling records, privileged communication, and confinement against one's will; and cross-cultural and social justice issues.

Professional Associations

Because mental health counseling covers a wide spectrum of counselors who work in many different types of settings, there is no "perfect" professional association to meet the needs of its entire constituency. However, the association that comes closest is AMHCA. The mission of AMHCA is "to enhance the profession of clinical mental health counseling by setting the standard for collaboration, advocacy, research, ethical practice, and education, training, and professional development" (AMHCA, 2023, Our Mission section), and its vision is "to position CMHCs to meet the health care needs of those we serve while advancing the profession" (AMHCA, 2023, Our Vision section). A few of the many activities AMHCA conducts are advocating for licensed counselors, providing workshops and conferences, offering malpractice insurance, providing a code of ethics, providing job links, helping clients find counselors, and publishing a newsletter and the *Journal of Mental Health Counseling*.

In many states, counselors with related degrees can become LPCs (sometimes called licensed CMHCs [LCMHCs] or some other variant of the name; ACA, 2022b). Thus, we often find LPCs who identify as CMHCs but initially started out as school counselors, addiction counselors, rehabilitation counselors, or other types of professional counselors. These professionals may also be members of ACA, ASCA, International Association of Addiction and Offender Counselors (IAAOC, a division of ACA), American

Rehabilitation Counseling Association (ARCA; a division of ACA), or the National Rehabilitation Counseling Association (NRCA). CMHCs with other interests may belong to one or more of the additional divisions of ACA noted in Chapter 1.

Credentialing

Counselors from many specialty areas are often interested in becoming a national certified counselor (NCC) through NBCC. This generic certification attests to the attainment of specific knowledge and skills deemed important as a counselor and is used as the test for licensure in several states throughout the country. In addition, a CMHC may also want to become a certified clinical mental health counselor (CCMHC) through NBCC. Passage of this test is also used by some states for counselor licensure—the gold standard for most mental health counselors (e.g., LPC, LMHC, and LCMHC). With the added benefits one gets from being licensed, it is not surprising that clinical mental health programs are flourishing (CACREP, 2023b). It is also not surprising that some rehabilitation counselors, addiction counselors, school counselors, or other professional counselors may also want to pursue this route, and as long as they have the prerequisite coursework and supervision, this is usually not difficult in most states.

In addition to becoming an LPC, CMHCs sometimes pick up other credentials, such as becoming a certified alcohol and drug counselor (CADC) or earning one of the three credentials offered by the National Certification Commission for Addiction Professionals (NCC AP): national certified addiction counselor, level 1; national certified addiction counselor, level II; and master addiction counselor (MAC; NCCAP, 2023). NBCC also offers the MAC certification, although this is currently on hold and being reviewed by NBCC.

Licensure Portability

Licensure portability is "the ability of a professional counselor licensed at the independent practice level to transfer their license to another state or U.S. jurisdiction when the counselor changes residence to that state or jurisdiction" (ACA, 2023c, What Is Licensure Portability? section). It became a critical issue for LPCs when all 50 states developed separate licensing laws, resulting in varied rules and regulations for attaining an LPC. Thus, when one counselor would move to another state or attempt to conduct telemental health counseling between states, becoming licensed in the other state or practicing across state lines was often a very difficult, or impossible, process. To remedy this, a number of associations have developed the Counseling Compact, and it is hoped that, within a few years, many more states will join this compact, allowing for interstate licensing (Counseling Compact, 2022, 2023). Chapter 4: Clinical Mental Health Counselors' Work Settings discusses this in a bit more detail.

Telemental Health Counseling

Suddenly, we were all online. Classes were all being taught online, and counseling went online. We saw our doctors online and ordered our food online. Our lives had changed dramatically. The age of telemental health counseling and other services was here. And it all started with a pandemic. Even though the pandemic has come and largely passed, there is little doubt that telemental health counseling will stay—probably not at the rates it was occurring during the pandemic but assuredly at higher rates than it was occurring prior to the pandemic (see Figure 2.7).

With telemental health counseling here to stay, counselors need to understand how to set up a telemental health platform, best practices for telemental health counseling, and the legal and ethical implications of

FIGURE 2.7 Telemental Health Counseling

telemental health counseling along with how it impacts the counseling relationship (Gilberston, 2020). Some specific questions counselors need to ponder include the following:

- "How will the privacy of the client be protected?"
- "Is the delivery of counseling as effective as in-person counseling?"
- "What kinds of ethical considerations do we need to consider with these new delivery systems?"
- "Will our traditional theories of counseling work well with these new delivery modes?" (Dilkes-Frayne et al., 2019; Liu et al., 2018).

Interprofessional Collaboration

Mental health counselors are increasingly being integrated into interprofessional settings, such as hospitals, medical practices, prisons, and various other agencies in which mental health professionals work and collaborate (Ghassemi, 2017; Franklin, 2022). Such interprofessional collaboration requires knowledge of each professional's specialty areas, roles and functions, and identity—knowledge often not taught about in graduate programs in counseling. As interprofessional collaboration amongst professionals continues to grow, it becomes increasingly important for all professionals to understand the duties, roles, functions, and separate identifies of one another and how to come together to offer effective management of the consumers and clients they serve.

Salaries

According to O*NET OnLine, the median wage of mental health counselors was $48,520 in 2023; however, this varied dramatically depending on the state in which one lived. In addition, these jobs have a bright outlook, meaning their projected growth is much faster than average. Finally, those who have an established private practice can easily make $100,000 a year or more.

Ethical and Legal Issues

In Chapter 6, we take an in-depth look at some of the important ethical and legal issues for CMHCs. Here, we highlight a few critical issues impacting the CMHC.

HIPAA

The passage of the Health Insurance Portability and Accountability Act (HIPAA) ensured the privacy of client records and adherence to rules concerning the sharing of such information (U.S. Department of Health and Human Services, 2017; Zuckerman, 2016). Covering all medical and counseling records, this important law underscores crucial elements of the helping relationship that all counselors need to know when doing practice.

Access to Counseling Records

The Freedom of Information Act of 1974 allows individuals access to any records maintained by a federal agency that contain personal information about the individual, and every state has followed along with similar laws for state agencies (National Security Archive, 1995–2017). Similarly, the Family Education Rights and Privacy Act (FERPA) guarantees parents the right to access their minor children's educational records (U.S. Department of Education, 2021). In addition, although ethical guidelines usually support a child's right to confidential counseling, it has generally been assumed that parents have the legal right to view their children's records (Attorney C. Borstein, personal communication, January 14, 2023). Similarly, with the exception of process notes (notes to jog your memory), clients generally have a legal right to view their counseling records, (ACA, 2014, Section B.6.e; Wheeler & Bertram, 2019).

Privileged Communication

Privileged communication is a conversation conducted with someone that state or federal law identifies as a person with whom conversations may be privileged. This means the person who hears the conversation has a legal right and responsibility to not reveal information about the conversation without the client's consent (Remley & Herlihy, 2020; Wheeler & Bertram, 2019). This includes such individuals as attorneys, medical doctors, licensed therapists, clergy, and spouses. Privileged communication varies from state to state, and every licensed professional should check on the extent of privileged communication they have within their state.

Confinement Against One's Will

Since the *O'Connor v. Donaldson* decision (1975), every state in the country has prohibited long-term confinement of clients against their will unless there is a clear indication that they are a danger to self or others (Behnke, 1999). Even in these cases, a court hearing to show cause is generally necessary. This law has had a dramatic effect on how CMHCs work with clients and the kinds of decisions they make concerning those clients who may not be quite ill enough to be committed but are also not well enough to adequately care for themselves. At times, clients such as these are cause for great concern for CMHCs.

Cross-Cultural and Social Justice Issues

There is little question that having an understanding of an individual's cultural, racial, ethnic, gender, sexual, and other identities is crucial for a successful counseling relationship. Counselors must have cultural competence and cultural humility if they are to connect and be successful with their clients. This important topic will be discussed more fully in Chapter 7, especially in light of the Multicultural and Social Justice Counseling Competencies (MSJCC) mentioned earlier (Ratts et al., 2016). Briefly, the competencies cover four domains: (a) counselor self-awareness, (b) client worldview, (c) the counseling relationship, and (d) counseling and advocacy interventions. Each of the first three domains are defined by attitudes and beliefs, knowledge, skills, and action. The last domain (counseling and advocacy) focuses on social justice work related to the following areas: intrapersonal, interpersonal, institutional, community, public policy, and international and global affairs (see Figure 2.8).

SUMMARY

This chapter examined the history that led to the development of, and current issues affecting, clinical mental health counseling. Starting with precursors to modern day counseling, we noted that attempts to understand the human condition go back thousands of years to early shamans and Greek philosophers. We pointed out that during the Renaissance (the 14th–17th centuries), new ways of understanding the person were promulgated, such as truth and knowledge coming from deductive reasoning, mind–body dualism, and the notion that the mind is a blank slate upon which ideas are imprinted.

The 1800s ushered in a more scientific perspective on mental illness and increasing advocacy for the humane treatment of the mentally ill and impoverished. Others began to look at how one's current functioning is impacted by the subconscious and explored mental illness through a psychological lens. This century also saw the first experimental psychologists, and their procedures eventually led to the development of psychological tests, research methods, and classifications of differences among people. These individuals were the first psychologists, psychiatrists, and social workers. For specific events and major players during the precursors to counseling, see Table 2.1.

The 1900s through 1950s brought about the emergence of the counseling profession, led by Frank Parsons, and the development of the Vocational Bureau. His ideas about true reasoning led to the first vocational counselors and part-time vocational guidance counselors in the schools, which would later become full-time guidance counselors, now called school counselors. In the early part of the 20th century, laws that supported vocational rehabilitation for returning soldiers from WWI were passed, resulting in the need for the first rehabilitation counselors. The vocational counseling movement eventually led to the first comprehensive theory of counseling, called the Minnesota point of view or trait-and-factor theory.

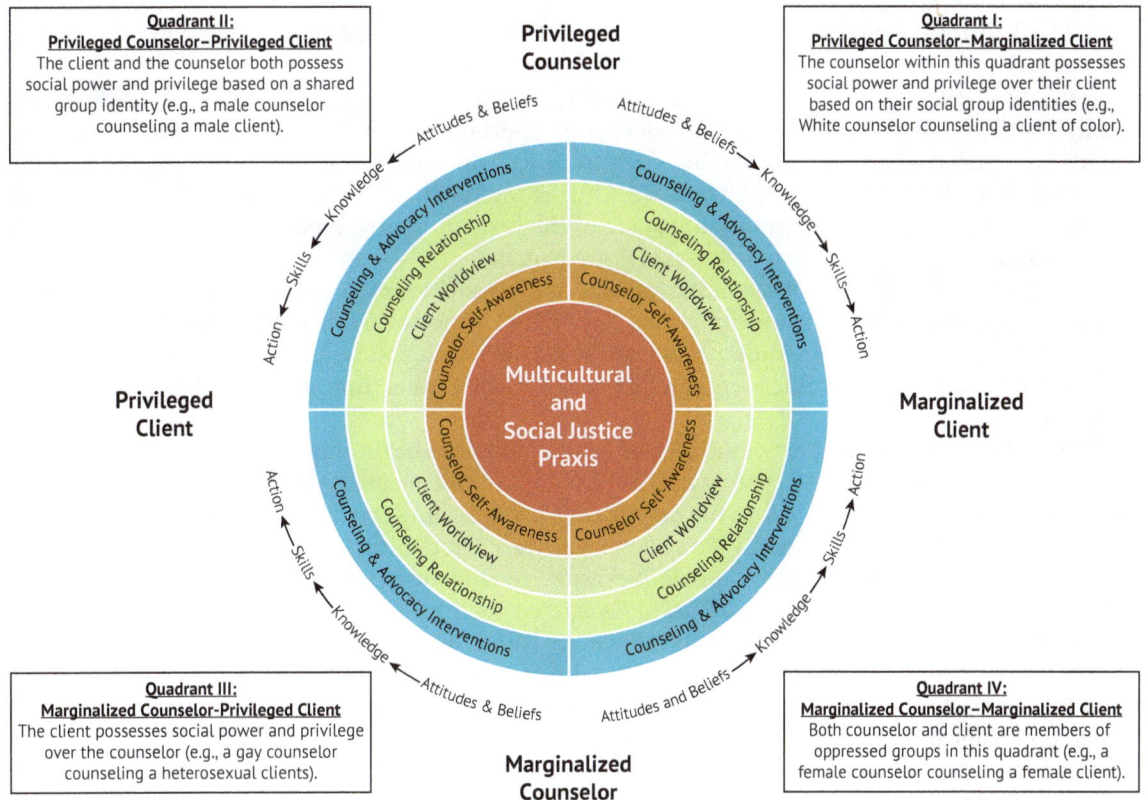

Quadrant II:
Privileged Counselor–Privileged Client
The client and the counselor both possess social power and privilege based on a shared group identity (e.g., a male counselor counseling a male client).

Quadrant I:
Privileged Counselor–Marginalized Client
The counselor within this quadrant possesses social power and privilege over their client based on their social group identities (e.g., White counselor counseling a client of color).

Quadrant III:
Marginalized Counselor–Privileged Client
The client possesses social power and privilege over the counselor (e.g., a gay counselor counseling a heterosexual clients).

Quadrant IV:
Marginalized Counselor–Marginalized Client
Both counselor and client are members of oppressed groups in this quadrant (e.g., a female counselor counseling a female client).

FIGURE 2.8 Multicultural and Social Justice Praxis

The fleeing of many existential–humanistic-oriented philosophers, psychologists, and psychiatrists from Nazism in Europe to the United States during the 1930s and 1940s impacted counseling and education. Slowly, a new mindset to mental health treatment arose—one that had an increasingly existential–humanistic flavor, as opposed to the then prevalent psychodynamic approach of Freud and others. One of these individuals, Carl Rogers, with his humanistic, client-centered approach to counseling, particularly impacted the way counseling was practiced.

After the second World War, several acts were passed that increased research on, and funding for, mental health and rehabilitation counseling. Around this same time, a push to depathologize individuals and promote developmental theories in career counseling, child development, and lifespan development were formed. This developmental and humanistic focus would greatly impact the beginning of clinical mental health counseling and counseling in general. It was also around this time that APGA was founded, although AMHCA was not yet a division. With the launching of Sputnik and the returning of GIs from WWII, there was great increase in school, college, and rehabilitation counselors. At the same time, CMHCs were beginning to become more prevalent and were increasingly found in agency settings. For specific events and names of major players from the 1900s to the 1950s, see Table 2.2.

The 1960s was an exciting time for counseling and therapy, as new cognitive, behavioral, Gestalt, transactional analysis, and existential approaches were developed. This was also around the same time that President Johnson's Great Society initiatives funded the expansion of mental health centers and other agencies. Meanwhile, the *O'Connor v. Donaldson* Supreme Court decision led to a massive reduction of individuals in state mental hospitals. As a result of all these factors, there was a great need for additional mental health professionals, including CMHCs, to work in the new developing agencies that serviced all these new clients.

The 1970s saw laws passed that provided counseling and services for individuals with disabilities and children with learning disabilities, most of which are important for CMHCs to understand. This decade was also the period when microcounseling skills training, which offered standardized ways of learning basic counseling skills quickly, was introduced. During the 1970s, draft standards for the accreditation of master's-level counseling programs and some of the first counseling credentials were created, with Virginia becoming the first state to offer an LPC credential.

During the 1980s, CACREP accreditation standards were adopted, APGA became AACD, and several counselor certifications were developed by NBCC. It was also during this decade that HMOs and PPOs began to carefully monitor and limit which clients a counselor could see and the length of time of counseling. For specific events and names of major players from the 1960s through 1980s, see Table 2.3.

CMHCs became a critical part of the mental health landscape beginning in the 1990s—and into the present day. It was then that AACD became ACA, divisions of and membership in ACA greatly expanded, the hold that HMOs and PPOs had on the delivery of mental health services waned, licensure expanded, and legislative initiatives increasingly gave counselors the right to practice. In 2009, California became the last state to pass a mental health counselor licensure law, and today, with advocacy by AMHCA, ACA, NBCC, and other counseling organizations, LPCs can receive third-party payments as independent providers for most insurance companies, such as TRICARE and Medicare.

Today, all states provide some form of credentialing for addictions counselors, many of whom have their degrees in clinical mental health counseling. In most states, addiction, rehabilitation, school, and related professional counselors can become LPCs with some additional coursework or field experience. Finally, Senate Bill 785 was passed in 2020, which mandates an occupational classification for mental health counselors and has resulted in increased hiring, training, and advancement of mental health counselors in federal agencies, such as the VA. For specific events and names of major players from the 1990s to the present, see Table 2.4.

The last section of the chapter reviewed pressing issues in clinical mental health counseling, including professional associations; credentialing; licensure portability; telemental health counseling; interprofessional collaboration; salaries; ethical and legal issues, such as HIPAA, access to counseling records, privileged communication, and confinement against one's will; and cross-cultural and social justice issues.

KEY WORDS AND TERMS

Affordable Care Act of 2010
behavioral approaches
blank slate
certified alcohol and drug counselor (CADC)
certified CMHC (CCMHC)
Charity Organization Societies (COS)
client-centered approach
clinical mental health counseling (CMHC)
cognitive approaches
college counselors
Community Mental Health Centers Act of 1963

confidentiality of records
confinement against one's will
cross-cultural counseling
developmental and humanistic focus
duhkha
Education for All Handicapped Children Act of 1975 (PL94–142)
existential approaches
existential–humanistic perspective
Family Education Rights and Privacy Act (FERPA)
Freedom of Information Act of 1974

Gestalt therapy approach
Great Society
guidance counselors
Health Insurance Portability and Accountability Act (HIPAA)
health maintenance organization (HMO)
Hull House
independent providers
interprofessional collaboration
Interstate Compact for Counselor Licensure
Joint Commission on Mental Illness and Health

Journal of Mental Health Counseling
licensed CMHC (LCMHC)
licensed professional counselor (LPC)
licensure portability
managed care
master addiction counselor
Mental Health Access Improvement Act
Mental Health Parity Act of 1996
Mental Health Parity and Addiction Equity Act of 2008
Mental Health Study Act
microcounseling skills training
mind–body dualism
Minnesota point of view
modern era

Multicultural and Social Justice Counseling Competencies (MSJCC)
Multicultural Counseling Competencies (MCC)
national certified addiction counselor (NCAC)
national certified counselor (NCC)
National Defense Education Act (NDEA)
National Institute of Mental Health (NIMH)
National Mental Health Act
O'Connor v. Donaldson
Obamacare
preferred provider organization (PPO)
printing press
privileged communication
psychodynamic approach
reality therapy approach

Rehabilitation Act of 1973
rehabilitation counselor
school counselors
Senate Bill 785
settlement houses
shamans
Smith-Fess Act
Smith-Sears Soldier's Rehabilitation Act
social casework
Sputnik
telemental health counseling
third-party reimbursement
trait-and-factor theory
transactional analysis
true reasoning
Vocational Bureau
vocational guidance movement
Vocational Rehabilitation Act of 1954 Amendments
vocational school counselor

PROFESSIONAL ASSOCIATIONS AND ORGANIZATIONS

American Counseling Association (ACA)
American Association of Counseling and Development (AACD)
American Mental Health Counseling Association (AMHCA)
American Personnel and Guidance Association (APGA)
American Psychiatric Association (APA)
American Psychological Association (APA)
American Rehabilitation Counseling Association (ARCA)
American School Counselor Association (ASCA)
Association of Counselor Educators and Supervisors (ACES)
Association of Multicultural Counseling and Development (AMCD)
Council for Accreditation of Counseling and Related Programs (CACREP)
Council on Rehabilitation Education (CORE)
Counseling Association for Humanistic Education and Development (C-AHEAD)
International Association of Addiction and Offender Counselors (IAAOC)
National Academy for Certified Mental Health Counselors (NACMHC)
National Association of Social Workers (NASW)
National Board for Certified Counselors (NBCC)
National Career Development Association (NCDA)
National Certification Commission for Addiction Professionals
National Rehabilitation Counseling Association (NRCA)

KEY NAMES

Addams, Jane
Aristotle
Atkinson, Atkinson
Bandura, Albert
Beck, Aaron
Charcot, Jean Martin
Cross, William
Darwin, Charles
Descartes, René
Dix, Dorthea
Ellis, Albert

Frankl, Viktor
Freud, Sigmund
Glasser, William
Hippocrates
Janet, Pierre
Johnson, Lyndon B.
Krumboltz, John
Locke, John
May, Rollo
Mill, James
Parsons, Frank

Pedersen, Paul
Perls, Fritz
Pinel, Phillipe
Plato
Rogers, Carl
Rush, Benjamin
Socrates
Sue, Derald
Williamson, E. G.
Wolpe, Joseph
Wundt, Wilhelm

CREDITS

PROFESSIONAL ASSOCIATIONS IN CLINICAL MENTAL HEALTH COUNSELING AND RELATED PROFESSIONS

Learning Goals

- Review the benefits of professional associations.
- Obtain an overview of the American Mental Health Counselors Association, including its ethics code, standards of care, credentials offered by AMHCA, membership categories, liability insurance, legislative initiatives, and more.
- Obtain an overview of the American Counseling Associations, including its divisions, membership benefits, branches, and organizations affiliated with and work close with the association, including the following:
  - American Counseling Association Foundation (ACAF)
  - Council for Accreditation of Counseling and Related Educational Programs (CACREP)
  - National Board for Certified Counselors (NBCC)
  - Center for Credentialing and Education (CCE)
  - American Association of State Counseling Boards (AASCB)
  - Healthcare Providers Service Organization (HPSO)
  - Chi Sigma Iota (CSI)

- Obtain an overview of related mental health professional organizations, including the following:
  - American Art Therapy Association (AATA)
  - American Association of Marriage and Family Therapists (AAMFT)
  - American Psychological Association (APA), the American Psychiatric Association (APA)
  - American Psychiatric Nurses Association (APNA)
  - National Association of School Psychologists (NASP)
  - National Association of Social Workers (NASW)
  - American Association of Pastoral Counselors (AAPC)
  - National Organization of Human Services (NOHS)

INTRODUCTION

Earlier in my career, I was very involved with several professional associations. My participation allowed me to network with other people, be mentored by experts, assist in the development of my specialty areas (e.g., the development of ethics codes), provide a vehicle to develop my leadership skills, and, of course, gain the benefits that professional associations provided. Perhaps most importantly, being part of a professional association provides one with a sense of professional identity and a place to call home. Although I am not as involved with the associations today, I still rely on them for their ethics codes; a sense of affiliation and to learn up-to-date knowledge through Listservs, workshops, and conferences; to read their journals and newsletters; to keep me up on cutting edge issues; for their advocacy work, and more. Professional associations provide me with a sense of identity and protect the identity of our profession.

Professional associations support the philosophical beliefs of and provide mechanisms to support their members (e.g., counselors), while protecting those who benefit from the work of their members (e.g., clients). They tend to have a large array of functions and are generally managed by an executive director who receives a salary, while paid assistants and volunteer members foster the mission and vision of the association. Although many believe professional associations are a relatively recent phenomenon, in fact, in the United States there were close to 1,000 psychologically oriented professional associations, societies, or organizations around the turn of the 20th century (Pickren & Fowler, 2003). The objectives and benefits of professional associations today vary but have evolved from those of early associations.

Today, there are professional organizations for just about any specialty area in the helping professions. The most prominent professional organization for CMHCs is the American Mental Health Counselors Association (AMHCA),

IMAGE 3.1

although many also join the American Counseling Association (ACA). This chapter describes some of the benefits of professional associations; provides details about two important counseling professional associations, AMHCA and ACA; and offers short descriptions of several professional associations within related mental health professions.

BENEFITS OF PROFESSIONAL ASSOCIATIONS

Each professional association in the helping professions has a unique outlook on how it aims to benefit its members. However, there are many benefits of professional associations that tend to be universal among these associations, including the following (AMHCA, 2023a; Huber et al., 2019):

- Job banks
- Networking
- Free webinars
- Membership directories
- Codes of ethics and standards for practice
- Opportunities for mentoring and networking
- Information on cutting-edge issues in the field
- Free, and for money, continuing education credits
- Education and advocacy about cutting-edge issues
- Free consultation on ethical and professional issues
- Lobbyists that advocate for the interests of the membership
- Collaboration communities for networking and discussions
- Newsletters and journals to discuss topics of interest to the membership
- National and regional conferences to discuss training and clinical issues
- Access to malpractice insurance, sometimes for free or at a discounted price

Perhaps most importantly, professional associations advocate for legislative initiatives. For instance, due to advocacy by AMHCA, ACA, NBCC, and other professional associations, LPCs can now receive third-party insurance payments for the 43 million individuals who are on Medicare (ACA, 2023a; AMHCA, 2023b). AMHCA and other associations hire lobbyists and spend money to advocate for new legislation that positively impacts clients and counselors and to make changes to older legislation that hindered the work of CMHCS. So, where do they get the money for their advocacy work? From your dues. If you are not a member of AMHCA or some other professional association, you are reaping the benefits from them but are not supporting them financially (see Experiential Exercise 3.1)!

EXPERIENTIAL EXERCISE 3.1 Determining Association Benefits

If you were the executive director of an association, what kinds of benefits would you want the association to give to its membership. In doing this, rank the items covered previously and add any of your own. Then, get into small groups, and see if there is some consensus based on your rankings.

PROFESSIONAL ASSOCIATIONS

The bulk of this chapter focuses on the two associations CMHCs tend to join: AMHCA and ACA. We include ACA divisions and affiliated groups that many counselors are involved with, and also provide, a brief overview of professional associations in related mental health professions.

American Mental Health Counselor Association and American Counseling Association

Whereas AMHCA has a specific focus on clinical mental health counseling, ACA, with its 19 divisions and affiliated groups, has a diverse focus which many CMHCs might find important. Let's look at each of these associations.

American Mental Health Counselors Association (AMHCA)

Founded in 1976 and established as APGA's 13th division in 1978 (now ACA), AMHCA was created for the expressed purpose of being a home base for counselors providing services in mental health agencies and other community-based settings (Weikel, 2010). This contrasted with APGA's primary membership at the time, which largely included school-based and vocational counselors (AMCHA, 2010; Colangelo, 2011). In 2019, AMHCA split from ACA and is now the largest clinical mental health counseling association in the world, with its current vision being "to position CMHCs to meet the health care needs of those we serve while advancing the profession" (AMHCA, 2023c, para 1). Its mission is to advance "collaboration, advocacy, research, ethical practice and education, training, and professional development" (AMHCA, 2023c, para. 2).

Currently, AMHCA has four affiliated groups: the Midwestern, North Atlantic, Southern, and Western regions (AMHCA, 2023d). Within these regions, there are 40 state divisions and the District of Columbia (some states do not have a division). AMHCA holds an annual conference; has an ethics code and provides ethics consultation; has two quarterly publications, the *Journal of Mental Health Counseling* and *The Advocate Magazine*; provides a Standard of Care document; provides certification in a number of areas; offers several membership categories; arranges free liability insurance for its students; advocates for legislative initiatives; offfers a variety of awards; provides a blog for every member; and provides a wide range of other services for CMHCs and related counselors. Let's take a closer look at some of these areas.

Ethics Code

The most updated version of the AMHCA Code of Ethics was written in 2020 and focuses on six sections: (a) commitment to clients, (b) commitment to other professionals, (c) commitment to students, supervisees, and employee relationships, (d) commitment to the profession, (e) commitment to the public, and (f) resolution of ethical problems (AMHCA, 2023e). This code will be examined more intensely in Chapter 6, which focuses on ethical issues for CMHCs.

In addition to the ethics code, AMHCA offers a list of most frequently asked questions related to ethical dilemmas, which you can review. AMHCA members can also seek guidance with ethical decision-making by submitting a concern to the AMHCA Ethics Committee, although the advice given is not legal advice.

Standards of Care

AMHCA publishes the AMHCA Standards for the Practice of Clinical Mental Health Counseling booklet that describes the minimal qualifications an LPC needs to be proficient in the field. This document defines such things as the scope of practice, educational standards, faculty and supervisor standards, credentialing, legal and ethical issues, and a number of additional areas that are particularly important in the training of LPCs (see Table 3.1). You are encouraged to download the standards and review them (see AMHCA, 2021).

TABLE 3.1 Outline of the Standards of Care

I. Introduction
    A. Scope of Practice
    B. Standards of Practice and Research

II. Educational and Pre-Degree Clinical Training Standards
    A. Program
    B. Curriculum
    C. Specialized Clinical Mental Health Counseling Training
    D. Pre-Degree Clinical Mental Health Counseling Field Work Guidelines

III. Faculty and Supervisor Standards
    A. Faculty Standards
    B. Supervisor Standards

IV. Clinical Practice Standards
    A. Post-Degree/Pre-Licensure
    B. Peer Review and Supervision
    C. Continuing Education
    D. Legal and Ethical Issues

V. Recommend AMHCA Training
    A. Biological Bases of Behavior
    B. Specialized Clinical Assessment
    C. Trauma-Informed Care
    D. Substance Use Disorders and Co-Occurring Disorders
    E. Technology Supported Counseling and Communications (TSCC)
    F. Integrated Behavioral Health Care Counseling
    G. Child and Adolescent Standards and Competencies
    H. Aging and Older Adults Standards and Competencies
    I. Forensic Evaluation Standards and Competencies
    J. Gender Identity Counseling Standards and Competencies

Table 3.1: Selection from "AMHCA Standards for the Practice of Clinical Mental Health Counseling," AMHCA Standards for the Practice of Clinical Mental Health Counseling, p. iii. Copyright © 2021 by American Mental Health Counselors Association (AMHCA).

AMHCA Credentials

In addition to becoming a licensed professional counselor (LPC) in their state, or becoming nationally certified by NBCC and other groups, a number of AMHCA credentials exist for students and advanced practitioners.[1] These include certifications for students, CMHCs under supervision, and CMHCs who are independently licensed as well as advanced certifications for CMHCs who specialize in any of the nine areas and those applying as a diplomate or fellow (see Table 3.2). These and other credentials for CMHCs are discussed further in Chapter 4.

---

1   As a reminder, I will generally use the term "LPC" to denote a licensed CMHC. However, other terms are used interchangeably and vary based on the state in which one lives (e.g., LMHC or LCMHC).

TABLE 3.2 AMHCA Certifications

Basic Certifications	I.	AMHCA Clinical Mental Health Counseling Student Certification
	II.	AMHCA CMHC Under Supervision Certification
	III.	AMHCA CMHC, Independently Licensed Certification
Advanced Certifications	I.	Clinical Mental Health Counseling Specialist
		A. Specialist in Child and Adolescent Counseling
		B. Specialist in Couples or Family Counseling
		C. Specialist in Developmental and Learning Disabilities Counseling
		D. Specialist in Geriatric Counseling
		E. Specialist in Integrated Behavioral Health Care Counseling
		F. Specialist in Military Counseling
		G. Specialist in Substance Use and Co-Occurring Disorders
		H. Specialist in Trauma Counseling
		I. Specialist in Forensic Evaluation
	II.	Diplomate in Advanced Clinical Mental Health Counseling Practice
	III.	Fellow in Clinical Mental Health Counseling Education and Research
	IV.	Fellow in Multiculturalism and Social Justice

Note. From "Credentialing Certifications" by American Mental Health Counselors Association, 2023e. Retrieved from https://www.amhca.org/members/career/credential/apply.

AMHCA Membership Categories

Several AMHCA membership categories exist, including clinical, regular, student, professional associate, and retired. In addition, if joining as an AMHCA member, one can join their state chapter for a reduced fee. See Table 3.3 for brief descriptions and the cost of these membership categories as of the writing of this book.

TABLE 3.3 AMHCA Membership Types

Membership Type	Cost	Description
Clinical	$183	This type of member must hold a master's or doctoral degree in counseling or a related field covering the basic principles of mental health counseling from a regionally accredited institution. The primary work is direct delivery of counseling services. Must hold state licensure or certification if available or be a certified CMHC if licensure/certification is not available. This is a voting member.
Regular	$183	This type of member must hold a master's or doctoral degree in counseling or a related field covering the basic principles of mental health counseling from a regionally accredited institution. This is a voting membership type.
Joint Dues Member	$147 + Membership Fee for Some States	This membership type is offered to clinical and regular members. It provides savings on AMHCA membership and state chapter membership when joining at the same time.

Emerging Professional	$84	This type of member must have completed a master's or doctoral degree and currently be in their first or second year of practice. Emerging professionals are eligible for an annual membership for up to 2 years in this membership category. Proof of recent graduation date may be required. This is a non-voting membership type.
Student	$84	This type of member must be enrolled at least half-time in a graduate program in counseling or a related discipline. Members are only eligible for this category for 3 years. Paid membership comes with free liability insurance. This is a non-voting membership type.
Associate	$79	Members of this type must have primary work responsibilities in human resources/personnel or be a supporter of the professional work of AMHCA. This is a non-voting membership type.
Retired	$79	This type of member must hold a master's or doctoral degree in counseling or a related field covering the basic principles of mental health counseling from a regionally accredited institution. This is a voting membership type.

Note. From "About: Memberships" by American Mental Health Counselors Association, 2023f. Retrieved from https://www.amhca.org/joinamhca.

Liability Insurance

A particularly important membership benefit in AMHCA is liability insurance through CPH and Associates (AMHCA, 2023g). Students who are members of AMHCA can obtain free liability insurance that covers up to $1,000,000 per claim and up to $3,000,000 for multiple claims in a year. Although colleges and universities generally have umbrella policies that cover students for their field experiences (e.g., practicum and internship), increasingly, programs are asking student to buy additional insurance; insurance through CPH and Associates is one good option.

Relative to students, the AMHCA policy "is designed to provide registered AMHCA students with professional liability, while performing therapeutic services (e.g., practicum) related to their counseling curriculum" (AMHCA, 2023g, What Coverage Does the Policy Provide? section). In addition to insuring students, CPH and Associates will insure LPCs and related mental health professionals for a cost.

Legislative Initiatives

AMHCA advocates for many legislative initiatives that benefit their members and clients (AMHCA, 2023h). Three recent pressing legislative initiatives have included advocacy for the recent passage of the Mental Health Access Improvement Act, which allows LPCs to receive third-party payments from the 43 million Americans who have Medicare; developing the Counseling Compact, which would allow counselors from one state to easily obtain a license in other sta"es; and expansion of medical and behavioral health care, so all individuals have access to these mental health services.

Conclusion

You can see that AMHCA offers many membership benefits to its members, with those discussed in the preceding sections being some of the most salient. Consider joining AMHCA as a student member, so you can reap some of these benefits, support the advocacy efforts of AMHCA, and become involved in this vibrant association.

American Counseling Association (ACA) and Its Divisions

The beginnings of ACA can be traced back to the 1913 founding of the National Vocational Guidance Association (NVGA), which was a vision of Frank Parsons, considered the founder of vocational guidance and sometimes of the counseling profession (Briddick, 2009a; Herr, 2013; McDaniels & Watts, 1994). After undergoing many name and structural changes over the years, today's ACA is the world's largest counseling association. This 57,000-member, not-for-profit association, serves the needs of all types of counselors to "promote the professional development of counselors, advocate for the profession, and ensure ethical, culturally-inclusive practices that protect those using counseling services" (ACA, 2023b, para. 2).

Divisions of ACA

Along with joining AMHCA, CMHCs may want to belong to ACA and/or one or more of ACA's divisions (some divisions can be joined without joining ACA). ACA currently sponsors 19 divisions and one affiliate division, all of which maintain newsletters and journals and provide a wide variety of professional development activities. ACA's divisions, along with the year they were officially founded and the journal(s) they publish, can be found in Table 3.4.

TABLE 3.4 Divisions of ACA and Their Associated Journals

Divisions	Associated Journal(s)
AADA: Association for Adult Development and Aging (1986)	*Adultspan*
AARC: Association for Assessment and Research in Counseling (1965)	*Measurement and Evaluation in Counseling and Development, Counseling Outcome Research and Evaluation*
ACAC: Association for Child and Adolescent Counseling (2013)	*Journal of Child and Adolescent Counseling*
ACC: Association for Creativity in Counseling (2004)	*Journal of Creativity in Mental Health*
ACCA: American College Counseling Association (1991)	*Journal of College Counseling*
ACES: Association for Counselor Education and Supervision (1952)	*Counselor Education and Supervision*
AHC: Association for Humanistic Counseling (1952)	*Journal of Humanistic Counseling*
AMCD: Association for Multicultural Counseling and Development (1972)	*Journal of Multicultural Counseling and Development*
ARCA: American Rehabilitation Counseling Association (1958)	*Rehabilitation Counseling Bulletin*
ASERVIC: Association for Spiritual, Ethical, & Religious Values in Counseling (1974)	*Counseling and Values*
ASGW: Association for Specialists in Group Work (1973)	*Journal for Specialists in Group Work*
CSJ: Counselors for Social Justice (2002)	*Journal for Social Action in Counseling and Psychology*

IARTC: International Association for Resilience and Trauma Counseling (2022)	*Journal for Social Action in Counseling and Psychology*
IAAOC: International Association of Addictions and Offender Counselors (1974)	*Journal of Addictions and Offender Counseling*
IAMFC: International Association of Marriage and Family Counselors (1989)	*The Family Digest, The Family Journal*
MGCA: Military and Government Counseling Association (1984)	*Journal of Military and Government Counseling*
NCDA: National Career Development Association (1986)	*Career Development Quarterly*
NECA: National Employment Counseling Association (1966)	*Journal of Employment Counseling*
SAIGE: Society for Sexual, Affectional, Intersex, and Gender Expansive Identifies (1997)	*Journal of LGBT Issues in Counseling*
ACSSW: Association of Counseling Sexology and Sexual Wellness (2021; Division Affiliate)	*Journal of Counseling Sexology and Sexual Wellness*

Note. The dates represent the year each ACA division was founded. Organizations may have an earlier establishment date.

Branches and Regions of ACA

In addition to its 19 divisions and one affiliate division, ACA has 55 chartered branches that include the 50 states, the District of Columbia, Puerto Rico, the Virgin Islands, the Philippines, and Europe. In addition, four regional associations support counselors throughout the United States, including the North Atlantic region, Western region, Midwestern region, and Southern region.

Associations That Are Affiliated or Work Closely With ACA

ACA works with several affiliates and organizations that contribute to the betterment of the counseling profession in unique ways. The following are brief descriptions of ACA affiliates and organizations:

- **American Counseling Association Foundation (ACAF):** ACAF offers support and recognition for a wide range of projects, including scholarships for graduate students, recognition of outstanding professionals, publishing materials for counselors that also advance the profession, resources for partnering with others, and support for counselors and others in need.
- **Council for Accreditation of Counseling and Related Educational Programs (CACREP):** CACREP is an independent organization that develops standards and provides accreditation processes for counseling programs.
- **National Board for Certified Counselors (NBCC):** NBCC provides national certification as a national certified counselor (NCC); certified clinical mental health counselor (CCMHC), national certified school counselor (NCSC), and master addiction counselor (MAC), although the MAC certification is currently under review.

- **Center for Credentialing and Education (CCE):** Created in 1995 as an affiliate of NBCC, CCE offers several credentials, including those as an approved clinical supervisor (ACS), board certified coach (BCC), board certified–telemental health provider (BC–TMH), distance credentialed counselor (DCC), global career development facilitator (GCDF), and human services–board certified practitioner (HS–BCP).
- **American Association of State Counseling Boards (AASCB):** AASCB fosters excellence in the counseling profession by facilitating an exchange of ideas and information among various member organizations, including ACA, on credentialing issues related to counselors. One large effort AASCB has focused upon in recent years is licensure portability from state to state (see www.aascb.org).
- **Healthcare Providers Service Organization (HPSO):** The ACA insurance trust has partnered with Healthcare Providers Service Organization (HPSO) to offer free liability insurance for students and professional liability insurance, at a cost, for others.
- **Chi Sigma Iota (CSI):** CSI is an honor society that promotes and recognizes scholarly activities, leadership, professionalism, and excellence in the profession of counseling.

Note that AMHCA also works closely with some of the aforementioned affiliates and organizations, particularly CACREP, NBCC, AASCB, and CCE.

Membership Benefits of ACA

Membership in ACA provides a number of unique opportunities and benefits, including

- a counselor directory;
- graduate student scholarships;
- professional liability insurance;
- computer-assisted job search services;
- networking and mentoring opportunities;
- links to ACA Listservs and 23 interest networks;
- consultation on ethical issues and ethical dilemmas;
- legislative updates and policy settings for counselors;
- assistance in lobbying efforts at the local, state, and national levels;
- links to ACA divisions and other relevant professional associations;
- counseling resources, including the ACA Code of Ethics, books, videos, audio files, electronic news, and journals;
- subscriptions to ACAs *Journal of Counseling and Development* (JCD), the monthly magazine *Counseling Today*, and other professional journals based on division membership; and
- professional development programs, such as conferences, online courses, free webinars and podcasts, continuing education workshops, and a variety of discount and specialty programs (e.g., rental cars, auto insurance, hotels, and discounts on books).

Related Professional Organizations

Today, behavioral health systems are often interdisciplinary, and it is common to work with several related professionals. Knowing a bit about them is important when working in close proximity to our "cousins" in the mental health professions. Thus, we briefly highlight several related professional associations, including the American Art Therapy Association (AATA), American Association of Marriage and Family Therapists (AAMFT), American Psychiatric Association (APA), American Psychiatric Nurses Association (APNA), American Psychological Association (APA), National Association of School Psychologists (NASP), National

Association of Social Workers (NASW), National Board for Certified Pastoral Counselors (NBCPC),and National Organization of Human Services

American Art Therapy Association (AATA)

Founded in 1969, AATA is open to any individual interested in art therapy (AATA, 2022). AATA is dedicated to "advanc[ing] art therapy as a regulated mental health profession and build[ing] a community that supports art therapists throughout their careers" (AATA, 2022, Our Mission section). Its vision is a "world where everyone has access to professional art therapy for improved mental health and well-being" ("Our Vision" section). The association establishes criteria for the training of art therapists, supporting licensing for art therapists, maintaining job banks, providing an ethics code, sponsoring conferences, providing an art therapist locator, and supporting research. Members receive two journals: *Art Therapy: Journal of the American Art Therapy Association* and *Arts & Health: An International Journal for Research, Policy and Practice.* Members of this association are sometimes licensed as LPCs or LCSWs if they complete additional requirements. Most states do not have licensure for art therapists.

American Association of Marriage and Family Therapists (AAMFT)

If you have a counseling degree, you may be interested in joining IAMFC, a division of ACA. However, AAMFT is another important association in the field of marriage and family counseling. Founded in 1942 as the American Association of Marriage and Family Counselors, AAMFT was established by family therapy and communication theorists. Today, AAMFT (2002–2023) "facilitates research, theory development and education ... [and develops] standards for graduate education and training, clinical supervision, professional ethics and the clinical practice of marriage and family therapy" (About the AAMFT, para. 1). AAMFT publishes the *Family Therapy Magazine* and *Journal of Marital and Family Therapy*, sponsors a yearly conference, provides an ethics code, provides access to couples and family therapists, and offers professional activities related to family counseling and family development. Members of this association are often licensed marriage and family counselors.

American Psychiatric Association (APA)

Founded in 1844 as the Association of Medical Superintendents of American Institutions for the Insane, today the American Psychiatric Association (which, like the American Psychological Association, uses the initialism "APA") has over 37,000 members (American Psychiatric Association, 2023a). Its mission is "to promote universal and equitable access to the highest quality care for all people affected by mental disorders, including substance use disorders; promote psychiatric education and research; advance and represent the profession of psychiatry; and serve the professional needs of its membership" (American Psychiatric Association, 2023b, Mission section). The American Psychiatric Association provides a wide range of services for psychiatrists, residents, and medical students, including the publishing of journals in the field of psychiatry, providing an annual conference, providing resources for the public, and being responsible for the development and publication of the *Diagnostic and Statistical Manual, Fifth Edition, Text Revision (DSM-5-TR)*. Members of the American Psychiatric Association are often licensed physicians and board-certified psychiatrists.

American Psychiatric Nurses Association (APNA)

Founded in 1986 with 600 members, APNA has over 13,500 members today. APNA (2023) is "committed to the practice of psychiatric-mental health (PMH) nursing and wellness promotion, through identification of mental health issues, prevention of mental health problems, and the care and treatment of persons with psychiatric disorders" (para. 2). The association also provides advocacy for psychiatric nurses to improve the quality of their mental health care delivery. APNA offers several continuing education and professional development activities, a variety of counseling and nursing-related resources, continuing education learning, an annual conference, and publishes the *Journal of the American Psychiatric Nurses Association*. Members of this associations are often credentialed nurses and have prescription privileges. Prescription privileges make psychiatric mental health nurses an important member of the interdisciplinary team that may work with CMHCs.

American Psychological Association (APA)

Founded in 1892 by G. Stanley Hall, the American Psychological Association started with 31 members and now maintains a membership of 133,000. The main purpose of this association is to "promote the advancement, communication, and application of psychological science and knowledge to benefit society and improve lives" (American Psychological Association, 2023, Our Work section). The association has 54 divisions in various specialty areas, publishes about 90 psychological journals, provides ethics codes, and offers a vast array of activities and resources for psychologists. The Counseling Psychology Division (Division 17) of the American Psychological Association shares many of the same goals and purposes of some divisions of ACA. Members of the American Psychological Association, particularly Divisions 12 (Clinical Psychology) and 17, are often licensed counseling psychologists or licensed clinical psychologists.

National Association of School Psychologists

The core purpose of the National Association of School Psychologists (NASP) is to empower school psychologists to "promote the learning, behavior, and mental health of all children and youth" at school, home, and throughout life (NASP, 2021). School psychologists have a master's or doctoral degree in school psychology and are credentialed by state boards of education. Their work involves helping children succeed academically, and to accomplish this goal, they work with children, families, teachers, school counselors, school administrators, and community partners. A large portion of their work involves testing and assessment and helping students address their social and emotional health. Although most school psychologists work in schools, you can sometimes find them in private practice, agencies, and hospital settings. In addition to NASP, some school psychologists join Division 16 of APA.

National Association of Social Workers (NASW)

The NASW was founded in 1955 as a merger of seven membership associations in the field of social work. Servicing both undergraduate- and graduate-level social workers, NASW has nearly 120,000 members. NASW (2023) seeks "to enhance the professional growth and development of its members, to create and maintain professional standards, and to advance sound social policies" ("Our Mission and Purpose" section). The association publishes five journals and other professional publications, has an ethics code, provides conferences at state and national levels, provides malpractice insurance, conducts advocacy for important issues, offers continuing education credits, and much more. NASW has 55 chapters from all 50 states, the District of Columbia, Puerto Rico, the Virgin Islands, Guam, and an international chapter. Master's-level members of NASW are often licensed clinical social workers (LCSWs).

National Board for Certified Pastoral Counselors

The National Board for Certified Pastoral Counselors (NBCPC, 2023) certifies individuals as national certified pastoral counselors (NCPCs). People from a wide variety of clinical degrees (e.g., counseling, social work, and psychology) can obtain their NCPC if they have education in pastoral counseling, ministry, or theology; have passed an exam; and have additional experience. Pastoral counselors, religious counselors, or counselors with a spiritual orientation might join the Association for Spiritual, Ethical, and Religious Values in Counseling (ASERVIC), a division of ACA; the American Clinical Pastoral Education (ACPE); or both. Depending on their degree, pastoral counselors may be able to become NCCs and, in some states, LPCs, if they meet additional requirements.

National Organization of Human Services (NOHS)

Founded in 1975, the mission of NOHS (n.d.) is "to support all Human Service Professionals in our primary purpose to assist individuals and communities to function as effectively as possible in all major domains of living" ("Our Mission" section). NOHS is mostly geared toward undergraduate students in human services or related fields, faculty in human services or related programs, and human service practitioners. Human service professionals are often assistants to licensed therapists, although many also work as equals in a practice (e.g., a human service professional who has a credential as an addictions counselor). NOHS provides webinars, continuing education credits, a biyearly conference, an ethics code, the magazine *Human Services Today*, and the *Journal of Human Services*. Members of NOHS can become HS–BCPs (see Experiential Exercise 3.2).

EXPERIENTIAL EXERCISE 3.2 Developing Your Professional Association

Now that we examined some of the most prevalent professional associations in the mental health field, let's develop a fictitious professional association. Use the following prompts to develop an association of your liking. You can do this on your own or in small groups:

- What is the name of your association?
- Develop an organizational chart that shows who runs the organization, who is employed by the organization, and who might be a volunteer for the organization.
- What kind of mental health practitioners do you attract to your organizations?
- Define your mission and vision statements.
- Are there certain professionals you would not allow as members (e.g., minimum of an undergraduate degree).
- What kind of credentials do your members tend to have?
- What legislative initiatives would you lobby for?
- Discuss what kind of workshops and conferences you might have?
- Will your association have a newsletter, magazine, and/or journal? What are their foci? What are their names?
- Is there an ethical code?
- Is their consultation regarding thorny ethical issues?
- List additional benefits of your association.
- What kind of membership categories do you have?
- What is the cost to join the different membership categories?

SUMMARY

This chapter examined professional associations in clinical mental health counseling and related mental health professions. First, we examined some of the many benefits of professional associations, listing 15 common ones and noting that in clinical mental health counseling, one of the most important benefits is lobbying for critical legislative initiatives, which is partially enabled by the funds provided from membership dues.

After examining benefits, we looked at two associations to which many CMHCs belong: AMHCA and ACA. We noted that AMHCA was founded in 1976, became APGA's (now ACA's) 13th division in 1978, and was one of the first ACA divisions that focused on mental health agencies and other community-based settings. Disaffiliating from ACA in 2019, AMHCA is now the largest clinical mental health counseling association in the world. We highlighted AMHCA's vision and mission statements and discussed the affiliated groups of AMHCA and some of the many benefits AMHCA offers. Some of the notable benefits include having an ethics code and providing ethics consultation; publishing two quarterly publications, the *Journal of Mental Health Counseling* and *The Advocate Magazine*; providing a Standard of Care document; providing certification in a number of areas, offering several membership categories, arranging liability insurance for practitioners and for free for its students; advocating and lobbying for legislative initiatives; supporting state and regional chapters; providing a variety of awards; offering a blog for every member; and providing a wide range of other services for CMHCs and related counselors.

Next, we highlighted ACA and its 19 divisions. We noted the emergence of ACA could be traced back to Frank Parsons and the founding of the National Vocational Guidance association. We pointed out that ACA is now the largest counseling association in the world. We then highlighted several affiliated associations and associations that work closely with ACA, including ACAF, CACREP, NBCC, CCE, AASCB, HPSO, and CSI. We also discussed a number of benefits of ACA, such as its publishing the *Journal of Counseling and Development* and its magazine, *Counseling Today*; offering national and regional conferences; providing a wide range of counseling resources; sponsoring 19 divisions and one affiliate division; supporting state chapters; lobbying for important legislative issues; providing an ethics code and consultation on ethical issues; offering legislative updates; providing listservs; offering networking and mentoring opportunities; providing job search services; offering liability insurance for free for students and at a cost for others; providing scholarships; and developing a counselor directory.

The last part of the chapter examined 10 well-known associations of related professional mental health organizations, including the American Art Therapy Association (AATA), American Association of Marriage and Family Therapists (AAMFT), American Psychiatric Association (APA), American Psychiatric Nurses Association (APNA), American Psychological Association (APA), National Association of School Psychologists (NASP), National Association of Social Workers (NASW), National Board for Certified Pastoral Counselors (NBCPC), and National Organization of Human Services. We highlighted the mission or vision statements of these associations as well as some of the main thrusts of the organizations. We also noted the kinds of credentials individuals who tend to join these organizations have.

Finally, the chapter asked you to consider what you would include if you were to develop a professional organization. You were prompted to determine the organizational structure, vision and mission statements, and other important factors you think would be needed to create a professional association.

KEY WORDS AND TERMS

19 divisions (ACA)
55 chartered branches (ACA)
ACA Code of Ethics
AMHCA Code of Ethics
AMHCA credentials
AMHCA membership categories
AMHCA Standards for the
  Practice of Clinical Mental
  Health Counseling
approved clinical supervisor
  (ACS)
art therapists
benefits of professional
  associations
board-certified coach (BCC)
board-certified psychiatrists
board-certified–telemental health
  provider (BC–TMH)
certifications
certified CMHC (CCMHC)
Counseling Today
counseling compact
credentialed psychiatric nurse

practitioner
credentialed school counselor
credentialed school psychologist
Diagnostic and Statistical Manual,
  Fifth Edition, Text Revision
  (DSM-5-TR)
distance credentialed counselor
  (DCC)
expansion of medical and
  behavioral health care
four regional associations (ACA)
global career development
  facilitator (GCDF)
human services–board certified
  professional
human service professionals
Journal of Counseling and
  Development
legislative initiatives
liability insurance
licensed clinical psychologist
licensed clinical social worker
licensed counseling psychologist

licensed marriage and family
  counselors
licensed physician
licensure portability
licensed professional counselor
master addiction counselor
membership benefits of ACA
Mental Health Access
  Improvement Act
national certified counselor
  (NCC)
national certified pastoral
  counselor (NCPC)
national certified school
  counselor (NCSC)
psychiatric mental health nurses
psychiatrist
psychologist
school psychologist
social worker
third-party insurance payment

KEY NAMES

Hall, G. Stanley
Parsons, Frank

PROFESSIONAL ASSOCIATIONS AND ORGANIZATIONS

American Art Therapy Association (AATA)
American Association of Marriage and Family Therapists (AAMFT)
American Association of Pastoral Counselors (AAPC)
American Association of State Counseling Boards (AASCB)
American Clinical Pastoral Education (ACPE)
American Counseling Association (ACA)
American Counseling Association Foundation (ACAF)
American Mental Health Counselors Association (AMHCA)
American Psychiatric Association (APA)
American Psychiatric Nurses Association (APNA)
American Psychological Association (APA)
Association for Spiritual, Ethical, and Religious Values in Counseling (ASERVIC)
Association of Medical Superintendents of American Institutions for the Insane
Chi Sigma Iota
Center for Credentialing and Education (CCE)

Council for Accreditation of Counseling and Related Educational Programs (CACREP)
Counseling Psychology Division (Division 17)
Division 12 of APA
Division 16 of APA
Division 17 of APA
Health Providers Service Organization (HPSO)
Healthcare Providers Service Organization (HPSO)
National Association of School Psychologists (NASP)
National Association of Social Workers (NASW)
National Board for Certified Counselors (NBCC)
National Board for Certified Pastoral Counselors (NBCPC)
National Organization of Human Services (NOHS)
National Vocational Guidance Association (NVGA)

CREDIT

CHAPTER 4

CLINICAL MENTAL HEALTH COUNSELORS' WORK SETTINGS

Ed Neukrug and Richie Kubilus

Learning Goals

- Learn about several work settings where you might find CMHCs, including
    - community mental health centers;
    - correctional facilities and related work settings;
    - couples, marriage, and family counseling centers;
    - gerontological settings;
    - HMOs, PPOs, EAPs;
    - integrated behavioral health care settings;
    - military and government;
    - pastoral, religious, and spiritual;
    - private practice settings;
    - rehabilitation agencies;
    - residential treatment centers;
    - substance abuse settings;
    - youth service agencies; and
    - other settings.
- Identify some of the different professional organizations with which CMHCs tend to affiliate based upon their chosen setting.

INTRODUCTION

I (Ed Neukrug) have worked as a crisis counselor, an outpatient therapist, a substance abuse counselor, a consultant, doing testing in the schools, as a counselor at a pastoral agency, and a counselor in private practice. And in all in of these settings, I was a CMHC. The places one can work as a CMHC are many, and you will have several settings to choose from once you obtain your degree.

This chapter offers a relatively brief overview of settings in which a CMHC may work as well as personal vignettes that highlight the experiences of those who currently work at these settings. By the end of this chapter, you may be surprised to find that you identify with a setting you had not previously considered. Regardless of the setting you ultimately choose, having a full knowledge of the many different agencies and what services they provide will benefit both you and your future clients. Let's take a brief look at these different settings, but first, complete Reflection Exercise 4.1.

> ## EXPERIENTIAL EXERCISE 4.1
> ### Brainstorming
>
> Spend the next 2 minutes brainstorming all the settings you know employ CMHCs. Now, with a partner, compare your lists. Were there any settings identified by your partner you had not considered or that surprised you?

WORK SETTINGS

As already noted, counselors can be found in many work settings, which gives CMHCs many possibilities for employment. Here we will take brief look at some of these settings including career and employment agencies; community mental health centers; correctional facilities and related work settings; couples, marriage, and family counseling centers; gerontological settings; HMOs, PPOs, EAPs; integrated behavioral health care settings; military and government; pastoral, religious, and spiritual settings; private practice settings; rehabilitation agencies; residential treatment centers; substance abuse settings; youth service agencies; and other settings.

Career and Employment Agencies

One's occupational choices significantly influence a person's way of life, including one's income, identity, meaning in life, educational attainment, hobbies, interests, friends, lifestyle, place of residence, personality characteristics, mental health, and more (Niles & Harris-Bowlsbey, 2021). Thus, it is not unusual to find CMHCs working in a variety of locations that offer career and employment counseling, including college career counseling centers, career management settings in business and industry, state employment offices, vocational rehabilitation offices, and private practices that focus on career transitions, and more.

Importantly, finding a job that matches one's personality orientation toward the world of work has been consistently shown to be related to job satisfaction, and career and employment counselors can assist clients in ensuring this fit (Hoff, 2020; Hodges, 2019; U.S. Bureau of Labor Statistics, 2022). Usually, this involves an assessment of a client's interests and aptitudes concerning their career development process. In fact, CMHCs, and counselors in general, are well trained in career counseling—more highly trained than any other mental health professional (see CACREP, 2016). Thus, CMHCs stand above others in their ability to offer career and employment counseling. In addition, such counseling can be quite lucrative! (See Vignette 4.1.)

VIGNETTE 4.1 Amber (MSEd, CCC, NCC, MBTI certified, LGPC)—A Career Counselor

Prior to my role as a career counselor at our university career center, I earned a BA in psychology and an MS in clinical mental health counseling. It was not until my internship in the final year of my master's program, however, that I gained an interest in career work, which was sparked by providing career counseling to undergraduate university students. Through this experience, I was exposed to the intersection of the personal and the professional, as I observed the frequently bidirectional relationship between these two areas in clients' presentations.

As a current doctoral candidate in counseling, I take a lifespan approach to career counseling and use an intersectional framework to guide me in helping the individuals I work with achieve short- and long-term career and life goals. As a certified career counselor (CCC), national certified counselor (NCC), Myers-Briggs Type Indicator (MBTI) certified practitioner, and licensed graduate professional counselor (LGPC), it is my goal to honor the diversity of experience and identity each client brings to the career counseling process.

In my current career practitioner role, I work primarily with graduate students across many areas of their career development. Specifically, I provide career counseling to master's and doctoral students to help them process career decisions, increase their preparation for internships and jobs, and identify and respond to challenges impacting employment opportunities. I also create and facilitate in-person and virtual career development workshops on career topics (e.g., career decision-making, salary negotiation, and interviewing preparation) and provide education about career-related documents (e.g., résumés, cover letters, and CVs). One of my favorite aspects of this job is building relationships with students and alumni through career counseling and being able to support and empower them in achieving their professional and life goals.

Community Mental Health Centers

Envisioned by President Kennedy and signed into law in 1963, the Community Mental Health Centers Act sought to establish 1,500 mental health centers around the country to be funded by the federal government and overseen by the National Institute of Health (Erickson, 2021). The Act aimed to provide new treatment centers for those who had previously been housed in unsafe, and sometimes inhumane, state institutions and public hospitals as well as provide services to individuals within their local community.

Although the act did help to establish many mental health centers, funding proved to be more of a challenge than originally anticipated, and the goal of 1,500 fully funded centers was never reached. Nonetheless, community mental health centers are still found today and receive subsidies through a patchwork of local, state, and federal sources as well as payment for affordable services by clients whose income is above a certain threshold. The clients served by community mental health agencies are often diverse, come from varying socioeconomic backgrounds, and present with a wide variety of issues. To provide quality service in community mental health centers, a counselor's cultural competence is exceedingly essential.

VIGNETTE 4.2   **Liliana (EdD, LCPC, CCTP)—A Community Mental Health Counselor**

I knew I had a calling to be a counselor since I was very young. Having grown up in a minoritized community, the need for mental health services amongst its members was very clear to me. I have spent a large portion of my clinical career working in community mental health because I have a knack for working with the people who need counseling the most.

I am a licensed clinical professional counselor in Illinois, and I hold both a master's degree in counseling psychology and a doctoral degree in counselor education and supervision. Working in community-based mental health centers allows counselors to provide holistic treatment by considering particular community strengths, resources, and needs. The majority of my clients have been impacted by societal systems and have experienced trauma. Being a community mental health counselor has helped me gain a different lens on how communities and societies impact a person and contribute to their mental health and resilience.

As a community mental health counselor, I primarily focus on intake assessments, individual and group counseling, crisis response, and serve as a behavioral health consultant for other medical providers. Since the clients I work with have a high prevalence of trauma, this is a specialty area for me. I am always seeking new knowledge and keep up to date on the most recent trauma research and treatment. Currently, I am also a counselor educator, which allows me to integrate my clinical experience in community mental health into all of my teaching and mentoring.

CMHCs who work at mental health centers can find jobs in any of a number of areas, including outpatient counseling, short-term inpatient services, day treatment for those with serious mental health problems, medication checks, emergency services, and more. Since they often work with individuals with a moderate to severe amount of impairment, it is essential that they have knowledge of evidenced-based treatment (EBP) and the *Diagnostic and Statistical Manual, Fifth Edition, Text Revision (DSM-5-TR)* as well as familiarity with psychopharmacology. Today, community mental health centers offer several potential employment opportunities (see Vignette 4.2).

Correctional Facilities and Related Work Settings

Today, the American criminal justice system holds approximately 2.3 million Americans in jails or prisons, with another 4.1 million on probation or parole (Maruschak & Minton, 2020). Since 1980, the U.S. prison population has grown by 500% (the Sentencing Project, 2022), and many of the people in custody are undereducated, come from dysfunctional families, have been abused, struggle with substance abuse, are mentally ill, and/or have been traumatized. After being released from prison, substance use disorders, poverty, and mental illness, often become worse and result in a 25% rearrest rate within the same year (Sawyer & Wagner, 2020). As such, the need for mental health services and counseling within the correctional system is paramount.

It is not surprising that counselors find themselves performing multiple functions when working with those who are, or have been, incarcerated. Some of these functions include mental health evaluations

VIGNETTE 4.3 **Kathleen (PhD, LPC-R)—Correctional Facility Counselor**

Growing up the only daughter in an Irish home, I was accustomed to helping care for others from a young age. Thus, for me, the transition to professional helper was natural. I possess both an MSEd in clinical mental health counseling and a PhD in counselor education and supervision. I have worked in many different settings, but working in the correctional setting afforded me the ability to combine my passion for social justice with mental health counseling.

Many incarcerated individuals, whether due to lack of access or stigma, have never had the opportunity to work with a counselor within the community setting, so I have a unique opportunity within the prison walls. I can provide services to those battling addictions, struggling with trauma, and grappling with anxiety and depression. I provide brief, solution-focused sessions as well as CBT group counseling. I respond to crisis situations and work closely with the facility psychiatrist for continuity of care. I also have the privilege of providing mental health in-service training to those employed at the facility.

This setting was not one I learned much about during my education, so joining the International Association of Addictions and Offender Counselors (IAAOC) provided me with access to those working within my setting and field. As an adjunct assistant professor, I now utilize many real-world examples from the correctional setting within my lectures and in-class activities. I am grateful for the opportunity to bring this special, often marginalized population into focus.

and assessment, social and emotional therapy, addiction counseling, vocational counseling and training, crisis intervention, consultations with other service providers, and assisting with day-to-day adjustment problems. CMHCs in these settings also prepare reports (e.g., sentencing, probation, and corrections violations), testify in court, maintain contact with family members, and make referrals to outside agencies prior to the incarcerated individual being released from prison (Hodges, 2019; Salisbury & Voorhis, 2022; see Vignette 4.3).

Couples, Marriage, and Family Counseling Agencies

Today, about 40% of marriages end in divorce, which is a lower rate than 10 years ago, when it reached a high of nearly 50% (U.S. Census Bureau, 2021). In addition, many couples struggle in their marriage, and this pain often reverberates through the family (Armstrong, 2022). Clearly, the need for couples, marriage, and family counseling is great. If you are interested in working in this area, many counseling agencies offer both individual, as well as, couples, marriage, and family counseling; however, there are some agencies that focus specifically on couples, marriage, and family work.

The social work profession has historically placed a strong emphasis on family issues and community advocacy, leading to the establishment of many family service agencies by social workers (Ritter et al., 2020). However, as counselors have increasingly included couples and family counseling in their repertoire

VIGNETTE 4.4 Letitia (PhD, LMHC, NCC, BCTHP, QCS)—A Couples and Family Counselor

I was born and raised in St. Thomas, U.S. Virgin Islands, and I knew from the age of 10 that I wanted to be a counselor, so I could help people deal with the intra- and interpersonal issues that adversely impacted their lives. Thus, in college I majored in psychology and subsequently obtained my master's in mental health counseling, becoming a licensed mental health counselor.

As a licensed mental health counselor, I have worked in various clinical settings, including community mental health centers, a department of juvenile justice's maximum-security facility, acute inpatient hospitals, and residential facilities. Currently, I own a virtual group practice in Orlando, Florida, where we serve families, couples, youth, children, and adults dealing with various mental health issues. One of the most crucial things I learned while working in these settings is the importance and influence that systems have on people's lives and communities, particularly the family system. Thus, as a counselor, I have found that whether I am doing individual, group, couples, or family work, I need to examine how the system impacts the client. I also ensure that I examine cross-cultural issues, as they are always impacted by the systemic issues within society. Finally, I believe using a trauma-informed approach helps uncover problems that resonate through the family and are often hidden and not talked about.

With my credentials and experience, I can supervise others who are seeking licensure as a counselor or marriage and family therapist. I find this to be one of the most interesting parts of my job, as I help others learn and grow as helpers. In addition, I am also a full-time professor and coordinator of the marriage and family therapy program at the school where I work.

of skills, they are now as likely as others to be hired by such agencies (Hodges, 2019). Often, these agencies receive partial funding through government grants, charities (e.g., United Way), or religious organizations. These agencies also receive payments directly from clients on a fee-for-service basis or via clients' insurance companies. Although many of these agencies have a religious affiliation, religion usually does not play a major role in the acceptance of clients for counseling.

To work with couples and families, specialized training is required, some of which is offered in the clinical mental health counseling specialty area that CACREP (2016) supports; however, those who obtain a degree in marriage, couples, and family counseling, which is an additional CACREP-accredited specialty area, have even more specialized training in this area (Barker & Chang, 2020; Johnson, 2019; Turner & West, 2018).

In most states, those who obtain their degree in couples, marriage, and family counseling can become credentialed as a licensed marriage and family therapist (LMFT, or some variation thereof). In addition, they can often be licensed as LPCs. Finally, since LPCs are generally CMHCs who are licensed, they too have the skills to do marriage and couples counseling (see Vignette 4.4).

Gerontological Settings

As the population of individuals over 60 years of age continues to rise (U.S. Census Bureau, 2020), so does the need for mental health services specific to this stage of life (Hodges, 2019). While older persons have traditionally been less amenable to counseling, this trend may end if counselors can create an environment that is conducive to, and empowering of, older individuals (Chapman, 2018; Fullen, 2018). Today, counseling for older persons is often provided through day treatment programs at community mental health centers, retirement communities, senior centers, religious organizations, social service agencies, and long-term care facilities, such as nursing homes (Ritter et al., 2020).

When working with older persons, prevention and treatment become important, and counselors often spend time assisting older persons with developmental challenges, the psychological impact of loneliness, physical illnesses, situational crises, loss and bereavement, and palliative and hospice care (Gladding & Newsome, 2018; Hodges, 2019). Counselors often must assist older persons with the psychological and physiological changes that accompany aging as well as the negative stereotypes placed upon them by society (see Vignette 4.5).

CMHCs working with this subset of the population offer individual, family, and group counseling as an effective means of treatment (Wallace & Sterns, 2022). Due to the emotional nature of client and family interactions with the counselor who works with older persons, CMHCs must navigate several skills and be prepared to deal with countertransference, the loss of a client, boundary issues, and overdependence.

VIGNETTE 4.5   Philip (PhD, LMHC, NCC, BC–TMH)—Gerontological Counselor

IMG 4.5

"Gerocounseling" is a field that is arguably underappreciated or avoided due to a lack of resources, training, or personal discomfort and fear of mortality. During high school, I chose to volunteer at a local hospice. Part of my experience was sitting with and holding the hands of individuals during their final days. Later in life, as I was working on my master's in counseling and marriage and family therapy, I became a caregiver to my grandparents who had neurocognitive disorders. What began as a personal desire to help my family turned into a professional passion to help other older adults and caregivers.

When I started my PhD in counseling and counselor education, I specialized in gerontology, beginning a journey of curiosity and practice. Through my research, I recognized a gap between play therapy and older adults, specifically individuals with neurocognitive disorders and their caregivers. After being trained in Theraplay level one, I was introduced to a clinician who applies Theraplay-informed interventions within their assisted-care home. After completing my dissertation, I started the process of translating a play therapy that could be implemented with older adults.

Currently, I work as a clinical assistant professor, counselor educator, consultant, licensed mental health counselor, and private practice owner. Part of my work is with individuals and families who are either older age (e.g., empty nesters, retired, or widowed) or caring for someone of older age. Another area of my service is helping people become more informed, allowing them to empower themselves, their families, and their decisions regarding death and dying (e.g., advance directives, health care surrogate, and end-of-life celebrations).

VIGNETTE 4.6   **Reginald (PhD, LPC, NCC, MAC, AADC, ICAADC)—Counselor at a Managed Behavioral Healthcare Organization**

My professional counseling career began at a medical center that offered mental health and addiction treatment services. Here, I conducted individual, group, and family therapy sessions for clients. Later, I was tasked with contacting managed behavioral healthcare organizations (MBHOs) to obtain authorizations for continued stay. This eventually led to the position of utilization review manager. My primary duties included participating in multidisciplinary treatment team meetings, conducting telephonic concurrent reviews with care managers employed by various MBHOs, and coordinating discharge and aftercare planning.

One day, a colleague encouraged me to apply for triage care manager at a top Fortune 500 health insurance and managed care company. Here, I gathered biopsychosocial assessment and treatment plan data to determine if the requested level of care was clinically appropriate when compared against the established level of care guidelines. I was later promoted to *team lead,* then clinical program manager, where I supervised a diverse team of behavioral health master's-degree-level clinicians. This group was responsible for applying medical necessity criteria to certify level of care placement for insured customers as well as conducting care coordination services for members diagnosed with serious mental illnesses (SMIs) and co-occurring behavioral health and medical conditions. Subsequent positions included senior behavioral network manager, accountable for developing a qualified network of credentialed providers, and facility contract manager, where I administered contracts and negotiated fee schedules for commercial and public-sector programs.

Managed care organizations play an essential role in delivering healthcare that is accessible, efficient, and effective for their members. I am proud of my combined experience of being a direct-care provider and a managed care team member—both roles significantly enhanced my practical knowledge of the many components that form the overall behavioral healthcare delivery system. Resultingly, I am a more informed and well-versed counselor educator!

HMOs, PPOs, and EAPs

Today, health maintenance organizations (HMOs) and preferred provider organizations (PPOs) actively refer to licensed counselors (Andrews, 2005–2023; Ritter et al., 2020; Schweiger et al., 2012). Whereas HMOs are health insurance companies that refer to health care specialists, including licensed counselors, within their network, PPOs generally allow referrals to providers who are in and out of network (U.S. Centers for Medicare and Medicaid Services, n.d.). Both HMOs and PPOs offer reduced fees, but with HMOs, the referral usually needs to go through one's primary care provider (PCP), which is often one's family practitioner. In addition, HMOs and PPOs sometimes offer in-house coaching or psychoeducation as part of their services. Finally, due to the overseeing of clinicians' work that is generally handled by HMOs and PPOs, some hire CMHCs to review the casework of other clinicians.

VIGNETTE 4.7 **Jeanel (PhD, LPC, NCC)—An Integrated Behavioral Health Care Setting**

IMG 4.7

My interest in integrated behavioral health care (IBH) began during the last year of my master's program, when I secured a practicum and internship position at an outpatient ambulatory care clinic. As a counseling intern, I provided individual counseling services to underinsured and uninsured adults. I also had opportunities to collaborate and consult with other health care professionals. I had never pictured myself working in a medical setting as a mental health counselor, but I soon developed a passion for interprofessional collaboration. I enjoyed learning about how these other professions addressed clients' health concerns as well as teaching others about mental health. By the end of my master's program, the mind–body connection had become clearer to me and informed how I conceptualized individual cases.

Since completing my master's program, I have worked in several interprofessional settings, all of which required me to understand the limits of my role as counselor and communicate the purpose of that role to other professionals I worked alongside. At times, I felt misunderstood by the professionals who were not in the mental health field, but I took pride in being able to clarify what my profession is and is not.

I believe my experiences in IBH have made me a stronger counselor, as I have had to clarify what it is that I do and also adapt my counseling style and session structure to meet the needs of my clients and the organization I work for. These experiences changed how I viewed myself as a counselor and expanded my conceptualization of what counseling could be.

In addition to HMOs and PPOs, employee assistant programs (EAPs) are programs that are already paid for by the employer and often focus on wellness and the prevention of mental health problems. EAPs sometimes offer coaching, counseling, psychoeducation, and other related services (e.g., relaxation, stress reduction, substance abuse awareness and recovery, and assistance with financial and legal problems). CMHCs in these settings also help to assess employee problems and increase employee satisfaction within the company. In addition, EAP counselors often provide referrals to a wide range of community services, such as mental health centers, substance abuse agencies, 12-step programs, lawyers, and private practice clinicians.

As an LPC, being a referral source for HMOs or PPOs can be particularly lucrative. In addition, working for HMOs, PPOs, or EAPs as a coach, counselor, psychoeducational provider, or coordinator of other activities is an increasingly important growth area for CMHCs (see Vignette 4.6).

Integrated Behavioral Health Care Settings

In recent years, there have been increasing numbers of CMHCs working in integrated behavioral health (IBH) care settings (Franklin, 2022). The blending of disciplines has created a unique work environment for mental health counselors, as they adapt their training, roles, and skills to function alongside non-mental health providers. Within IBH settings, CMHCs tend to do a mixture of counseling, consulting, and educative roles and usually provide short-term services based on the need of the setting. For instance, a CMHC might be hired by a physician's office to do short-term counseling with patients who have adjustment, anxiety, and depression disorders. Or, if working in a correctional facility, CMHCs would likely have a multitude of roles, such as being a counselor, being consultants to others who work in the setting, and being responsible for a wide variety of non-traditional counseling roles. Depending on the setting, if longer-term counseling is needed, these clients can be referred to outside services. IBH care settings are new and exciting areas to work in and have quickly become a large growth area for CMHCs (see Vignette, 4.7).

Military and Government

The military and government are unique work settings that offer a wide range of counseling opportunities. The general goals of counselors who work for the military or government are "to encourage and deliver meaningful guidance, counseling, and educational programs to all members of the Armed Services, their family members, and civilian employees of Local, State and Federal Governmental Agencies" (Military and Government Counseling Association [MGCA], n.d., para. 1). This is extremely important work, as some research has shown that over 30,000 active-duty military and veterans involved in post-9/11 wars have died of suicide and that such high rates are partly the result of "high exposure to trauma—mental, physical, moral, and sexual—stress and burnout, the influence of the military's hegemonic masculine culture, continued access to guns, and the difficulty of reintegrating into civilian life" (Suitt, 2021, p. 3).

Many significant changes have come about recently due to an increased awareness and focus on mental health concerns of military members and their families (Military OneSource, 2020). For instance, TRI-CARE, the major health insurer for those in the miliary, has approved counselors to obtain reimbursement, and LPCs have now been incorporated into the Veteran's Administration (VA) system (Bergman, 2020; National Board for Certified Counselors, 2023). CMHCs working with military or government personnel often find themselves functioning in several different roles at one time. For instance, they may provide educational programs related to advancement, help service members and government employees transition to civilian careers, provide prevention and psychoeducational programs (e.g., substance abuse), and conduct individual, group, and family counseling for military or government employees and their dependents. These counselors often work for a military family service center, an outpatient department of a military hospital or clinic, or serve as an in-house government employee, somewhat similarly to an EAP counselor. Taken altogether, career opportunities to work with this population are likely to continue to increase in the future (see Vignette 4.8).

Pastoral, Religious, and Spiritual Counseling Agencies

Many counselors who obtain a degree in mental health counseling are interested in work settings that have a religious or spiritual orientation or integrate religious or spiritual concerns into the counseling relationship (Cashwell, 2013; Schiffman, 2022; Shaler, 2019). In fact, religious and spiritual issues are becoming an increasingly important aspect of counseling. However, for many counselor trainees and seasoned professionals, this aspect of counseling feels uncomfortable, due to a lack of training (Hull et al., 2016; Shaler, 2019).

Some who do pastoral counseling are ministers who may have had some coursework in counseling and/or have pursued a master's degree in counseling. Others who have a strong religious orientation will obtain a degree in counseling and then seek employment in a setting that fosters their particular point of view (e.g., Christian counseling agencies). These individuals tend to integrate the basic precepts of their religious viewpoints with what they've learned in graduate school while maintaining basic counseling ethics. Obviously, at times, this makes for some interesting ethical and moral dilemmas, such as the

VIGNETTE 4.8 Donnette (PhD, LCPC, NCC)—Military and Government Settings

The field of mental health has always intrigued me! Originally, I considered majoring in psychology, but I soon realized my path was leading more toward becoming a counselor educator and licensed clinician. Soon after obtaining my undergraduate degree, I became a manager at a nonprofit organization that provided services to individuals with intellectual and developmental disabilities. Through that position, I found an interest in vocational rehabilitation. However, at that time, rehabilitation counseling was not yet accredited by CACREP; however, because my program was accredited by the Council on Rehabilitative Education (CORE), and by taking extra courses, I found I could still be eligible for licensure in my state.

As I completed my graduate studies, I interned at the Department of Affairs, which opened up a career of providing services to the military population. With no full-time positions open at my site, I decided to consider applying to doctoral programs. I knew I wanted to continue working with the military population, so I was fortunate to obtain a position as an education counselor with the Army National Guard. I also worked in a private practice to obtain the rest of my hours, finally becoming a board-certified, licensed clinical professional counselor.

After a few years, I was hired as an employee assistance program manager on an Army installation, providing prevention services to Department of Defense (DOD) civilians, service members and their family members. This setting is so unique because I have simultaneous opportunities to be an educator, counselor, and marketing professional. Through counseling and counselor education organizations (e.g., ACA, the Association of Counselor Education and Supervision [ACES], the Military and Government Counseling Association [MCGA], and the National Council of Rehabilitation Education [NCRE]), I continue my professional development and learn ways through which I can provide additional resources to these populations.

pro-life Christian counselor whose counselor education training has taught them to respect the clients' rights to make decisions for themselves, including those clients who might want to have an abortion. Besides pastoral and religious counselors, an increasing number of counselors have integrated a spiritual viewpoint into their counseling orientation (Shaw et al., 2012). These counselors tend be driven less by religious convictions and more by the belief that spiritual issues are primary to understanding a client's way of constructing meaning in their lives. CMHCs with a spiritual orientation can be found in all kinds of agency and mental health settings (see Vignette 4.9).

Private Practice

For a CMHC who embarks upon the journey of owning a private practice, there are significant pros and cons that should be factored into one's decision. For instance, owning a practice has several advantages, including the fact that the counselor is independent, has choices of where and when they want to work,

VIGNETTE 4.9 **Brittany (PhD, MPH, LPC-S)—Pastoral Counselor**

My interest in counseling began in 2013 during my final year of graduate public health studies. While matriculating through the program, I tirelessly sought a means to bridge the gap between global health, spirituality, and service to humankind. Consequential to this professional quest was an inner stirring to know the deeper things of God; a zealous curiosity ("yearning") to discover my purpose; and an enduring fervor for equity, justice, and defense of the oppressed (New International Version, Isaiah 1:17). At the crossroads of vocation ("calling") and career directions, a dual program in community mental health and pastoral counseling emerged as the integrative pathway among five distinct ambitions: pastoral guidance, community engagement, servant leadership, advocacy, and the promotion of holistic health care.

As a licensed professional counselor (LPC), counseling supervisor, and public health professional, I serve with a local faith-based, community mental health practice. Our practice setting provides myriad interprofessional counseling, wellness, consulting, and training services to individuals, couples, families, groups, churches, and agencies across demographics. In addition to these services, I coordinate our practice's practicum and internship orientations, facilitate staff telebehavioral health training meetings, and assist with the administrative components of our pastoral counseling services. Unique to the setting is our partnership with pastors and churches in championing mental health destigmatization and the cultivation of competent mental health responsiveness. In conjunction with these partnerships, we maintain the pastoral counseling program as a low-cost initiative to mitigate barriers to affordable and accessible mental health care.

The role of an LPC entails the ethical responsibility of engaging in ongoing counselor development through continuing education programs, webinars, and conferences. Connectedness with the ACA, American Association of Christian Counselors (AACC), American Clinical Pastoral Education Psychotherapy Commission (ACPEPC), Association for Multicultural Counseling and Development (AMCD), and Chi Sigma Iota (CSI) keeps me informed and in tune with the profession's advancement. This path of purpose continues to lead to rewarding growth, development, and holistic care for others in mind, body, and spirit.

has some autonomy over the cost of services, and can decide the type of work and theoretical approach with which they align (Hodges, 2019). On the other hand, with ownership comes many fiscal, administrative, ethical, and legal concerns. In addition, networking and establishing a clientele does not happen overnight (see Reflection Exercise 4.1).

Private practitioners need to give clients a professional disclosure statement, have clients provide informed consent, deal with billing and insurance company issues, address privacy issues and confidentiality concerns related to the Health Insurance Portability and Accountability Act (HIPAA) and other laws, maintain proper records, and have a transfer plan (called a professional will), in case the counselor becomes incapacitated (Brennan, 2013). With all these responsibilities, many counselors and mental health

VIGNETTE 4.10 **Victoria (PhD, LPC, CSAC, NCC)—An LPC in Private Practice**

IMG 4.10

I completed my master's degree in community counseling, now clinical mental health counseling, over 20 years ago and first worked in an agency providing prevention and reunification services to families involved with Child Protective Services (CPS) and foster care. I loved connecting with clients and helping families in their healing processes. I completed my doctoral degree in counselor education and supervision and started my career as a full-time faculty member, yet I felt something was missing in my work life.

After a few years of finding my professional footing, I discovered the balance I needed. Today, I am a single mother of two daughters, a licensed professional counselor, and a counselor educator, and I now have a small private practice where I see clients from all walks of life.

When I think about the wooden home where I have my practice, I think of the antique red oak timber beams that held up this space for over 170 years. I think of the people who have seen and touched it, and I wonder what the wood and adjoining walls have heard over the years. I have gratitude for the clients who have shared their stories, and if the wooden beams could talk, they may say they have heard it all.

The wood and I serve as a shock absorber for persons in crisis and foster an environment of safety, openness, and strength within a quiet space. The wood and I have heard so much within these walls, and I am honored and grateful to have clients trust me as they share their stories.

practitioners join existing practices that already have a process for dealing with most of these issues. Here, the independent practitioner will obtain a percentage of what they take in when seeing clients.

To network and expand their revenue-earning ability, private practitioners often do engage in activities in addition to counseling (Dasenbrook, 2023; Hodges, 2019). A few of the many possible activities include coaching, community organizing, marital and divorce mediation, parent education, consultation and training in business and industry, stress management and biofeedback, educationally oriented seminars and workshops, supervision, evaluations for adoption and custody, assessments, and professional writing.

Now that every state has licensure for counselors (ACA, 2023), there has been a sustained rise in the number of counselors who are in private practice. Today, many private practice counselors can be found conducting individual, group, couples, and family counseling for clients with "normal" life problems (primary and secondary prevention). However, private practice counselors are increasingly found working with those who have more intense impairments (tertiary prevention), and additional training in psychopathology, psychopharmacology, and assessment is sometimes needed to work with this population. With mandates from the Affordable Care Act for insurance companies to provide counseling and substance abuse services, it is likely that private practice will provide an additional venue of employment for many counselors who are drawn to this type of setting (ACA, 2012; see Vignette 4.10 and then Experiential Exercise 4.2).

REFLECTION EXERCISE 4.1 Starting Your Private Practice

A while back, after completing their degree, two of my students decided to start a private practice. Their parents helped get them set up. The only problem was they had no clients! They sat for many days, waiting for clients to show—and for the most part, they didn't. Obtaining clients is not easy and often occurs through word of mouth, paying for expensive ads, getting yourself known by presenting workshops, and more. If you are interested in starting a private practice, having some business sense and knowing the ins and outs of what it takes to start a private practice are essential.

EXPERIENTIAL EXERCISE 4.2 The Cost of a Private Practice

Make a list of items you would need to start up a private practice that includes five LPCs. Estimate the cost of purchasing items, rent, malpractice insurance, utilities, salaries, furniture, computers, and so on. Compare your list with others in class. What is the consensus of how much it would cost to start such a practice?

Rehabilitation Agencies

In the United States today, 26% of adults have a disability related to walking or using stairs; difficulty with select physical tasks like lifting, grasping, reaching, and pulling; difficulty with instrumental activities of daily living, such as taking medication, bathing, going to bed, preparing meals, and doing housework; mental disabilities, such as a learning disability, Alzheimer's or dementia, an intellectual disability, a developmental disability, or another mental disability; a seeing, hearing, or speaking disability; and problems with activities of daily living, such as dressing, bathing, eating, and toileting (Centers for Disease Control and Prevention [CDC], 2022, 2023). With such large numbers of individuals with disabilities, clearly, rehabilitation counseling is an essential component of a wellness program for these individuals.

Not surprisingly, the aim of rehabilitation counselors is to assist clients with physical, mental, developmental, or emotional disabilities and help them achieve personal, social, psychological or vocational aspirations. This may involve an assessment of client needs, the development and implementation of rehabilitation programs, and coordination of activities and services with other providers that promote an individual's ability to live more independently.

Individuals with disabilities are often counseled by those trained in clinical mental health or rehabilitation counseling at one or more of the following settings: state departments of vocational rehabilitation, community-based rehabilitation programs, schools, VA hospitals, independent living facilities, or private rehabilitation agencies (Hodges, 2019; Hartley & Tarvydas, 2023). Whereas state vocational rehabilitation agencies and VA hospitals obtain state and/or federal funding, private agencies predominantly rely upon insurance reimbursement, workers' compensation, and other client-related methods of payment. Recently, CACREP added rehabilitation counseling to its list of specialty areas that it accredits (CACREP, 2016). If you are interested in assisting clients with fostering independence and gaining essential life skills, working in a rehabilitation counseling setting might be the right place for you (see Vignette 4.11).

VIGNETTE 4.11 Matthew (MS, QRC, CRC)—A Rehabilitation Counselor

IMG 4.11

Growing up in central Minnesota, my first foray into the world of counseling and psychology was with an Advanced Placement (AP) psychology class I took in high school. From there, I attended North Dakota State University, earning a bachelor's in psychology. While working toward this degree, I was a psychiatric technician at the local psychiatric hospital. Some years later, I earned my master's in rehabilitation counseling from St. Cloud State University. After my master's program, I eventually became a qualified rehabilitation consultant (QRC), helping people return to the workforce after they have suffered a work-related injury.

As a QRC and certified rehabilitation counselor (CRC), I enjoy working with so many different types of people. I counsel people whose lives have been turned upside down by an unfortunate accident or illness, causing a sudden and drastic change to their means of earning a living. Some of my clients are unable to return to their previous vocations, often for lengthy periods of time. This, of course, presents myriad challenges for the individual client, as some even have difficulty completing what many might view as a relatively easy task (e.g., completing a job application form). Services such as job application feedback, job-seeking skills training, mock interviews, vocational testing, vocational counseling, and résumé development are offered to my clients. My clients often express feeling overwhelmed with trying to focus on getting better while also juggling the number of parties involved in their rehabilitation. As such, I provide medical management services to my clients to assist in the coordination of their medical care and treatment and the ascertainment of what sort of work restrictions their injury may present. Finally, I help my clients deal with the grief process regarding the social, cultural, and physical changes with which they are dealing.

Residential Treatment Centers

Residential treatment centers, which tend to have a rehabilitative focus, provide a live-in setting for the duration of treatment and offer counseling services (APA Dictionary of Psychology, 2023; Hodges, 2019; O*NET Occupational Information Network, 2015). These centers service many clients, including those who are, or have been, incarcerated; the developmentally delayed; substance abusers; delinquent youths; individuals with eating disorders; those with physical disabilities; those with mental illness, and more. Services provided in such settings vary, but they often include individual and group counseling; family counseling; vocational counseling; addiction counseling; medication management; client advocacy; and consultation with, and referral to, other professionals when the individual is ready to reenter the community (Blau et al., 2014; Hodges, 2018; O*NET Occupational Information Network, 2015).

Due to the wide range of clients who may be served in residential treatment centers, as with vocational rehabilitation settings, a team approach, involving a multidisciplinary team of professionals, and group treatment planning is often used. CMHCs who desire to work at a residential treatment center may find this to be a great prospect for employment (see Vignette 4.12).

> **VIGNETTE 4.12** **Lauren (PhD, LPC-R)—A Counselor at a Residential Treatment Center for Domestic Violence and Sex Trafficking Survivors**
>
> I have always been passionate about advocating for and helping those who are marginalized. From my undergraduate research on women in STEM majors to my current scholarship on the impact of social injustice and mental health inequity within the African American community, I have been driven to help those in need. This eventually led to my job as a residential program counselor for domestic violence and sex trafficking survivors.
>
>
>
> This comprehensive residential program provides individual and group counseling, psychiatric evaluation, substance abuse counseling, advocacy initiatives, recreational opportunities, financial planning, and career counseling for our clients. More recently, I became clinical director of the facility, and I am excited about the possibility of establishing increased interprofessional collaboration among those who work in different components of the program. I am hopeful that such collaboration and consultation can increase the success of all our clients.
>
> Although my basic counseling skills have been critical with my work with marginalized clients, I have found that counseling domestic violence and sex trafficking survivors has challenged me to cultivate advanced skills to best meet my clients' needs. While always valuing and utilizing the core conditions of unconditional positive regard and empathy, I find that using advanced skills in conjunction with these critical skills can lead to increased positive outcomes. Although my eventual goal is to become a counselor–educator, I believe my experiences in the field have allowed me to become a well-rounded and competent counselor and have given me knowledge and skills I can share in the classroom.
>
> *Lauren Robins, The World of the Counselor: An Introduction to the Counseling Profession, ed. Edward Neukrug, p. 566. Copyright © 2022 by Cognella, Inc. Reprinted with permission.*

Substance Abuse Settings

Approximately 25% of adults struggling with substance abuse also have a severe mental health problem (National Institute on Drug Abuse, 2020), and in general, substance abuse has run rampant in the United States (Substance Abuse and Mental Health Services Administration [SAMHSA], 2020). In fact, between July of 2021 and July of 2022, the CDC (2022) reports that 107,735 people died of a drug overdose. Clearly, substance abuse not only affects the users but also has a great impact on family members and society (Fisher & Harrison, 2020; Lissy, 2021).

As you might expect, the widespread abuse of substances provides an array of work settings for CMHCs, including hospital detoxification (detox) units, halfway houses, residential treatment centers, and drug and alcohol treatment centers (SAMHSA, n.d.). Recognizing the increased need for services, in 2009, CACREP developed the specialty area of addiction counseling, which allows more specialized and specific training and credentialing for CMHCs working in these settings (Hagerdorn et al., 2012). CMHCs working in substance abuse settings provide patient screening and intake, treatment planning, individual and group counseling, case management, crisis intervention, and consultations with interdisciplinary teams (see Vignette 4.13).

VIGNETTE 4.13 Tony (PhD, CSAC)—A Substance Abuse Counselor

IMG 4.13

I am 50-year-old husband and loving father of five. I am also a highly motivated addiction treatment counselor and program coordinator for an intensive outpatient treatment program that caters to veterans, law enforcement, firefighters, and other first responders who struggle with drug and alcohol problems. My past professional and personal experiences have shaped a deep-seated passion for the field of substance abuse counseling. The road that has led me to this point in my career has been long and enriching.

Several critical events along my journey have been especially instrumental in molding me into the counselor I am today. My father passed when I was young, and I spent my teenage years serving my family, of which I am the oldest of eight siblings. Through this experience, I developed my passion for helping others. This led to my pursuit of service-oriented occupations in my 20s, first as a paramedic and then as a firefighter. Wanting to expand my service, I became a U.S. Navy SEAL and honorably served my country. After returning from overseas, I encountered challenges reintegrating into society. I found myself turning to substance abuse to cope with posttraumatic stress.

As valuable as my professional experiences have been in shaping me, they come in a distant second to my journey of personal growth and self-discovery through PTSD and substance abuse. In fact, I now consider these challenges attributes. I have tasted the wrath of hopelessness and self-loathing and have walked the hard road of recovery. I once burned all my bridges and turned my back on everything I had once held dear. When I finally reached out for help, it was the hand of an addictions therapist that reached back. I am a product of a system that worked—a system to which I was subsequently drawn professionally. I could praise the numerous counselors that have been a part of my journey, but instead, I choose to honor them by becoming the best addictions counselor I can be!

Youth Services Agencies

With the increase in youth violence in the schools, the impact of adverse childhood experiences (ACEs), and the recognition of youth mental health needs, the importance of providing counseling services to youth has become clear (McWhirter et al., 2016; Nelson & Wines, 2021). Employment opportunities in such programs include CMHCs who work with foster children, delinquent youth at residential treatment centers, children at mental health centers and child and family services agencies, juvenile offenders at state correctional systems, child protective services, and more.

Clients who utilize youth service agencies require assistance in a variety of areas, such as family preservation, parent education, support for domestic violence and/or abusive situations, pregnancy support services, adoption support services, and countless others. CMHCs who work in such service agencies have a full range of responsibilities, including conducting intake interviews, providing case management, offering consultation and psychoeducation, making referrals to other agencies, and providing counseling for individuals, groups, and families (Henderson & Thompson, 2015). In addition to working in agencies, youth counselors are often found in private practice (see Vignette 4.14).

VIGNETTE 4.14   Tiffany (PhD)—A Youth Services Counselor

Upon completing my bachelor's degree at Eastern Kentucky University, majoring in psychology and juvenile justice, I realized I wanted to work with kids who were struggling with mental health diagnoses. I attended Lindsey Wilson College's CACREP program and earned my master of education in counseling. Today, I am a doctoral candidate at the University of the Cumberlands.

Working with youth has always been a passion of mine. While earning my bachelor's degree, I was a substitute teacher and worked for an after-school program. That experience led me to work with the school system as a teacher's assistant and behavior interventionist. My clinical background started during my graduate internship, at which I taught parenting classes and facilitated an intensive outpatient program's (IOP) substance abuse groups.

After moving to Virginia, I became a therapist at a lockdown mental health facility for youth between the ages 5 of 21. I enjoyed working with youth who exhibited high-risk behaviors. Youth in these services exhibited suicidal thoughts, ideations, or attempts; homicidal thoughts or attempts; sexually aggressive behaviors; and mental instability, often resulting in out-of-control behavior toward self or others. Youths were either court ordered for treatment or participated voluntarily.

Mental health and behavioral stability are vital with this population. These youths require intensive services at times, including, but not limited to, psychiatric monitoring and treatment services. As a therapist in a youth mental health facility, my role was to assist the family with weekly family therapy sessions and teach my clients healthy coping skills, communication skills, conflict resolution, and ways to address their triggers.

Other Settings

In addition to the settings already listed, counselors can be found at many other community agencies, including crisis centers, psychiatric hospitals, hospices, group homes, women's shelters, LGBTQIA centers, and departments of social services, to name just a few (see Brown, 2022; Hodges, 2019). A degree in clinical mental health counseling is versatile and provides the counselor with a wide range of opportunities for employment. In fact, one might find the counselor in any setting where helping others is crucial. If you are considering a job in counseling, review the agencies listed, but keep your options open (see Vignette 4.15 and then Table 4.1).

In addition to joining AMHCA and/or ACA, Table 4.1 lists divisions of ACA to which CMHCs might join based on the setting in which they work. In addition, other divisions of ACA as well as some of the other most popular professional associations are listed at the end of this table. Finally, there are many other professional organizations in the mental health field that you may want to join that are not on this list.

VIGNETTE 4:15 **Cory (PhD, LPC, NCC, CCTP)—Director of Counseling at an LGBTQ+ Center**

IMG 4.15

My favorite aspect of my job is feeling like I am part of something bigger than myself. My personal experiences as a member of the LGBTQ+ community moved me to pursue my counseling license, earn a PhD in counselor education, and become the director of counseling at a local LGBTQ+ nonprofit. More to the point, the adversity I faced during my coming out experience inspired me to help others navigate their identity. During that time, I was fortunate enough to be helped by a licensed counselor; this motivated my desire to create that safe and affirming space for others.

My setting is unique because we are a nonprofit that focuses on LGBTQ+ and HIV+ communities. Along with limited resources come specific challenges experienced by the community, such as isolation and rejection, above-average rates of suicidal ideation, and internalization of societal norms. Addressing these issues requires me to be exceptional in working with LGBTQ+ identity and crisis management.

As the director, I am responsible for recruiting and hiring staff, contractors, and interns; providing LGBTQ+ affirming workshops to the community; and managing budgets and records—all while having a medium-sized caseload. I also established—and continue to oversee—the Intimate Partner Violence Program. Clients who participate in this program have access to a crisis case manager who works with LGBTQ+ folks experiencing intimate partner violence. I am also currently involved with the state chapters of ACA and ACES, which assist me with networking, leadership support, and hiring staff. Additionally, I adjunct and teach graduate-level counseling courses and am a member of SAIGE, which keeps me anchored to the profession.

TABLE 4.1 Professional Organizations

Career and Employment Agencies (AMHCA and ACA)

National Rehabilitation Counseling Association (NRCA)

National Career Development Association (NCDA)

National Employment Counseling Association (NECA)

Community Mental Health Centers (AMHCA and ACA)

Correctional Facilities (AMHCA and ACA)

International Association of Addictions and Offender Counselors (IAAOC)

Couples, Marriage, and Family Counseling Centers (AMHCA and ACA)

International Association of Marriage and Family Counselors (IAMFC)

Family & Youth Service Agencies (AMHCA and ACA)

International Association of Marriage and Family Counselors (IAMFC)

American School Counselors Association (ASCA)

(Continued)

TABLE 4.1 Professional Organizations (*Continued*)

Gerontological Settings (AMHCA and ACA)

Association for Adult Development and Aging (AADA)

HMOs, PPOs, and EAPs (AMHCA and ACA)

Military and Government (AMHCA and ACA)

Military and Government Counseling Association (MGCA)

Integrated Behavioral Health Care Settings (AMHCA and ACA)

Pastoral, Religious, and Spiritual Counseling Agencies (AMHCA and ACA)

Association for Spiritual, Ethical, and Religious Values in Counseling (ASERVIC)

Private Practice Settings (AMHCA and ACA)

Rehabilitation Agencies (AMHCA and ACA)

American Rehabilitation Counseling Association (ARCA)

National Career Development Association (NCDA)

National Employment Counseling Association (NECA)

Residential Treatment Centers (AMHCA and ACA)

American Rehabilitation Counseling Association (ARCA)

International Association of Addictions and Offender Counselors (IAAOC)

National Rehabilitation Counseling Association (NRCA)

Substance Abuse Settings (AMHCA and ACA)

International Association of Addictions and Offender Counselors (IAAOC)

Youth Service Agencies (AMHCA and ACA)

American School Counselors Association (ASCA)

Association for Child and Adolescent Counseling (ACAC)

Additional Divisions of ACA You Might Want to Join

Association for Assessment and Research in Counseling (AARC)

Association for Counselor Education and Supervision (ACES)

Association of Counseling Sexology and Sexual Wellness (ACSSW)

American College Counseling Association (ACCA)

Association for Creativity in Counseling (ACC)

Association for Humanistic Counseling (AHC)

Association for Multicultural Counseling and Development (AMCD)

Association for Specialists in Group Work (ASGW)

Counselors for Social Justice (CSJ)

International Association for Resilience and Trauma Counseling (IARTC)

Society for Sexual, Affectional, Intersex, and Gender Expansive Identities (SAIGE)

(*Continued*)

TABLE 4.1 Professional Organizations (*Continued*)

<u>Other Popular Professional Associations</u>

American Art Therapy Association (AATA)

American Association of Marriage and Family Therapists (AAMFT)

American Clinical Pastoral Education Psychotherapy Commission (ACPEPC)

American Psychoanalytic Association (APA)

American Psychological Association (APA)

Division 17 of the American Psychological Association (Counseling Psychology)

National Rehabilitation Counseling Association (NCRA)

SUMMARY

This chapter examined a number of potential employment settings for CMHCs. Moving through the settings alphabetically, we first examined career and employment agencies, noting the importance of good career choices in one's life and that good career counseling is related to eventual job satisfaction. Career counseling can take place at agencies or in private practice.

Next, we highlighted the Community Mental Health Centers Act of 1963, which sought to develop 1,500 mental health centers and provided funds for outpatient counseling, short-term inpatient services, day treatment for those with serious mental health problems, medication checks, emergency services, and more. Today, community mental health centers continue to offer services for a wide variety of clients and are a type of agency at which many CMHCs find employment.

With 2.3 million Americans in jails and prisons and 4.1 million on probation or parole, it is not surprising that, as discussed in the chapter, we often find CMHCs in corrections facilities and related work settings (e.g., parole officers). In addition to counseling, these CMHCs offer a wide variety of services for their clients.

With high rates of divorce and many couples and families struggling with emotional pain, marriage, couples, and family counseling agencies are another place we often find CMHCs. Often, these agencies have a religious affiliation, although religion does not usually play a major role in counseling. CMHCs have training in couples, marriage, and family counseling, although those who have gone through a CACREP-accredited marriage, couples, and family counseling program have additional expertise in this area. These individuals can become LMFTs and, usually, LPCs, while CMHCs who are LPCs can engage in couples, marriage, and family counseling.

With an aging population in the United States, gerontological settings are an additional workplace we can find CMHCs. These counselors often assist older persons with developmental challenges, the psychological impact of loneliness, physical illnesses, situational crises, loss and bereavement, and palliative and hospice care.

HMOs, PPOs, and EAPS have become other places CMHCs can find work. Whereas HMOs are health insurance companies that refer to health care specialists, including licensed counselors, within their network, PPOs generally allow referrals to providers who are in and out of network. Employee assistant programs (EAPs) are programs that are already paid for by the employer and are often focused on wellness and the prevention of mental health problems. Counselors in these settings often provide in-house coaching, wellness workshops, or psychoeducation as part of their services. In order to ensure quality services of clients, counselors who work at HMOs and PPOs sometimes complete reviews of other counselors which HMOs and PPOs are referring clients to.

Integrated behavioral health (IBH) care settings, we noted, create a unique work environment for mental health counselors, as they adapt their training, roles, and skills to function alongside non-mental health providers. Within IBH settings, CMHCs tend to do a mixture of counseling, consulting, and educative roles and usually provide short-term services based on the need of the setting.

The military and government offer other settings for CMHCs, with the main goal being "to encourage and deliver meaningful guidance, counseling, and educational programs to all members of the Armed Services, their family members, and civilian employees of Local, State and Federal Governmental Agencies" (MGCA, n.d., para. 1). In recent years, counseling has become particularly important for veterans who have been exposed to trauma. These days, LPCs are approved to receive payments from TRICARE and recently have been approved to work in VA hospitals.

Pastoral, religious, and spiritual counseling agencies are another place we find CMHCs. CMHCs who are religious are more likely to work in a setting that fosters their point of view while maintaining counseling ethics. Those who are more spiritual tend to work with clients by helping them understand how spirituality is related to meaning in their lives.

Knowing that many students who receive a degree in clinical mental health counseling want to eventually go into private practice, we highlighted the pros and cons of private practice and the difficulty in starting a practice. We also noted that today's private practitioners may be working on primary, secondary, and tertiary prevention and that after passage of the Affordable Care Act, insurance companies must provide counseling and substance abuse services, thus increasing the likelihood of CMHCs having a client base.

Rehabilitation agencies is another setting where you might find CMHCs working alongside of those trained as rehabilitation counselors. With 26% of American adults having a disability, CMHCs and rehabilitation counselors are much needed. Many of these individuals work at state departments of vocational rehabilitation, community-based rehabilitation programs, schools, VA hospitals, independent living facilities, and private rehabilitation agencies.

There are a wide variety of residential treatment centers that provide a live-in setting for the duration of treatment and offer counseling and rehabilitative services. They tend to service those who are, or have been, incarcerated; the developmentally delayed; substance abusers; delinquent youths; individuals with eating disorders; those with physical disabilities; those with mental illness, and more.

With substance abuse running rampant in the United States, it's not surprising that we find CMHCs at hospital detoxification (detox) units, halfway houses, residential treatment centers, and drug and alcohol treatment centers. In addition to CMHCs, we might find those who have obtained a CACREP-accredited degree in addiction counseling at these agencies.

At youth service agencies, we find CMHCs who work with foster children, delinquent youth at residential treatment centers, children at mental health centers and child and family services agencies, juvenile offenders at state correctional systems, and more. These counselors conduct intake interviews, provide case management, offer consultation and psychoeducation, make referrals to other agencies, and provide individual, group, and family counseling.

Finally, we noted that there are many other settings in which we might find CMHCs. With such a large variety of settings, the counselor today has options they have never had in the past which makes the profession more exciting and versatile.

KEY WORDS AND TERMS

adverse childhood experience (ACE)

Affordable Care Act

community mental health centers

Community Mental Health Centers Act

correctional facilities and related work settings

couples, marriage, and family counseling centers

Diagnostic and Statistical Manual, Fifth Edition, Text Revision (DSM-5-TR)

employee assistant programs (EAPs)

evidenced-based treatment (EBP)

gerontological settings

Health Insurance Portability and Accountability Act (HIPAA)

health maintenance organization (HMO)

integrated behavioral health care settings

military and government

other settings

pastoral, religious, and spiritual settings

preferred provider organization (PPO)

primary and secondary prevention

primary care provider (PCP)

private practice settings

psychopharmacology

rehabilitation agencies

residential treatment centers

substance abuse settings

tertiary prevention

youth service agencies

CREDITS

CHAPTER 5

CREDENTIALING OF CMHCS AND RELATED MENTAL HEALTH PROFESSIONS

Learning Goals

- Learn about the relatively brief history of counselor credentialing in the United States.
- Understand the purposes of credentialing and the differences between registration, certification, and licensure.
- Review the varying credentials all counselors can obtain as well as specific credentials for clinical mental health counselors (CMHCs), marriage and family counselors, pastoral counselors, rehabilitation counselors, school counselors, and substance abuse counselors.
- Review the credentials that can be earned by those with related helping professions, including counseling and clinical psychologists, human service professionals, psychiatric–mental health nurses, psychiatrists, school psychologists, social workers.
- Highlight four critical credentialing issues for licensed clinical mental health counselors: licensure portability, telemental health counseling, parity for licensed clinical mental health counselors, and privileged communication.

INTRODUCTION

It was the 1980s, and I lived in New Hampshire and was teaching at a small, private college. I wanted to have a small private practice on the side, but there was no licensing for clinical mental health counselors in New Hampshire. Therefore, I decided to see if I could become licensed as a psychologist in New Hampshire and the bordering state of Massachusetts, even though my doctorate was in counselor education. The psychology boards put me through the wringer. They wanted to see my dissertation to make sure it was of a "psychological nature," and I had to have every one of my course instructors sign a statement saying they were licensed psychologists. I had to fly out to Ohio, where I received my master's and doctoral degrees, to track down all my professors. Luckily, they all were psychologists because there was no such thing as a licensed professional counselor (LPC)[1] in most states. After passing a grueling national exam and having the necessary post-doctoral supervision hours, I became licensed in both New Hampshire and Massachusetts as a psychologist. I was now able to obtain third-party payments and practice independently.

About 7 years later, I took a job at Old Dominion University in Norfolk, Virginia. Wanting to continue with a small private practice, I went to the psychology licensing board of Virginia, confident they would license me as a psychologist, having already been licensed in two other states. However, with Virginia having been the first state to license counselors, the psychology board said, "You're a counselor. We only license psychologists." I thought, "Good, that is the license I should have anyway." So I eventually submitted my materials, took an oral exam, and became an LPC. I started to work at a small private practice in Virginia. However, at that time, there were many insurance companies that would not pay LPCs but would pay licensed psychologists.

Today, things have changed dramatically. Every state in the country has licensure for counselors, LPCs can receive third-party payments from most insurance companies, and one need not go through the rigmarole I went through. However, there are still impediments to licensure, like the fact that it is not easy to move from one state to another and maintain your license, as each state has unique requirements (i.e., lack of licensure portability).

This chapter provides a brief overview of the history of credentialing in counseling; examines the purpose of credentialing and the three types of credentials, registration, certification, and licensure; highlights the kinds of credentialing counselors can obtain; provides an overview of credentials in related mental health professions; and discusses a few issues related to credentialing, including licensure portability, telemental health counseling, parity for counselors in the sometimes competitive world of therapy, and privileged communication.

A BRIEF HISTORY OF CREDENTIALING IN COUNSELING

> It is the year 1224 in the city of Sicily, a young physician gathers his credentials to file for a medical license. He collects proof that he has studied for over eight years in physick, surgery, and logic. He proudly adds a letter from his master physician mentor, extolling his extraordinary skill in leech placement and uncanny facility in astrology. The young physician nervously heads off, credentials in hand, to be examined in public by a committee of master physicians. If he passes, the emperor himself will issue a medical license. If he fails, he will be jailed if he attempts to practice medicine again (Scoville & Newman, 2009, para. 1).

As you can see from the quote, credentialing in the allied health professions started at least as far back as the 13th century, when the Holy Roman Empire set requirements for the practice of medicine (Hosie, 1991). Interestingly, the process of obtaining a credential today is not dissimilar to the process in 1224 Sicily. First, you study for several years. Then, you demonstrate that a mentor (e.g., a supervisor) deems you ready, and, finally, you take a credentialing exam. Finally, if you fail the exam, and practice without a license, you could get jailed!

---

1. As a reminder, I will generally use the term "LPC" to denote a licensed CMHC. However, other terms are used interchangeably and vary based on the state in which one lives (e.g., LMHC or LCMHC).

Although the first credentialing of counselors can be traced to the certification of school counselors during the 1940s (Bradley, 1995), counselor credentialing in the form of certification and licensure did not take off until the 1970s. For instance, in 1974, rehabilitation counseling became one of the first counseling specialty areas to obtain certification for its members through the Commission on Rehabilitation Counselor Certification (CRCC, 2021; Livingston, 1979). As the world's largest rehabilitation counseling organization, 40,000 people have participated in CRCC's certification process, and 15,000 are currently credentialed rehabilitation counselors (CRCs).

Meanwhile, advocacy by professional counselors and associations to obtain licensure for counselors began slowly in the 1960s but picked up steam in 1976, when Virginia became the first state to pass a licensing law for counselors. Today, all 50 states, Puerto Rico, the District of Columbia, Guam, American Samoa, and the Northern Mariana Islands offer licensing, and the American Counseling Association (ACA) has identified thousands of LPCs in every state (see ACA, 2023a, 2022b). As the number of jobs for mental health counselors is expected to increase at a particularly fast rate, the number of LPCs is also likely to rise dramatically (Olfson, 2016; O*Net Online, 2022).

The National Board for Certified Counselors (NBCC), established in 1982, "provides national certifications that recognize individuals who have voluntarily met standards for general and specialty areas of counseling practice" (NBCC, 2023a, para. 1). Today, there are over 70,000 national certified counselors (NCCs), and NBCC offers three additional certifications: nationally certified school counselor (NCSC), nationally certified clinical mental health counselor (NCMHC), and master addiction counselor (MAC), although the MAC certification is currently under review and inactive (NBCC, 2023b).

Finally, in 1995 the Center for Credentialing and Education (CCE) was developed as an affiliate to NBCC (CCE, 2023a). Today, CCE credentials 25,000 practitioners globally in a variety of fields, including counseling. CCE offers credentials as an approved clinical supervisor (ACS), board-certified coach (BCC), board-certified–telemental health provider (BC–TMH), distance credential counselor (DCC), global career development facilitator (GCDF), and human services–board-certified practitioner (HS–BCP).

PURPOSE AND TYPES OF CREDENTIALING

Today, credentialing cuts across many professions and can be found in many forms. Credentialing offers many benefits to the profession, consumer, and counselor (Bloom, 1996; Corey et al., forthcoming). The following are a few of these benefits of credentialing:

- **increased professionalization**: Credentialing increases the status of the members of a profession.
- **the delimitation of one's professional identity**: Credentialing defines the content of a profession and the scope of practice of the professional.
- **attainment of parity for the professional**: Relative to such things as status, salary, insurance reimbursement, and more, credentialing provides a mechanism for a professional group (e.g., counselors) to obtain parity with other mental health professionals.
- **providing a process for reporting poor practice**: Credentialing offers a mechanism for consumers and professionals to report subpar practices of professionals, and if the complaint is found to be warranted, the professional will be sanctioned in any of a number of ways (e.g., a warning, a fine, the need for continuing education, loss of license, and if particularly egregious, taken to court to face criminal charges).
- **preventing others from practicing in a specific field**: Credentialing highlights those who are better trained and, with some credentials, offers a mechanism that prevents people who do not have a credential from practicing.

Although credentialing takes many forms, the three most common types include registration, certification, and licensure. Registration, the simplest form of credentialing, involves "the act or process of entering information about something in a book or system of public records" (*The Britannica Dictionary*, 2023). Relative to professional groups, registration is generally overseen by the state in which one lives and only involves the listing of the members of a particular professional group, which implies each registered individual has acquired minimal competence, such as a technical or college degree or an apprenticeship in their particular area of expertise. Generally, registration involves a modest fee, and today, states rarely provide registration for CMHCs or other mental health professionals, opting instead for the more rigid credentialing standards of certification or licensure.

Certification involves the formal recognition that individuals within a professional group have met certain predetermined standards of professionalism (ACA, 2023a, 2023c). Although more rigorous than registration, certification is less demanding than licensure. Generally, certification is seen as a protection of a title (Remley & Herlihy, 2020); that is, it attests to a person's attainment of a certain level of competence but does not define the scope and practice of a professional (what a person can do and where they can do it). A yearly fee is usually required to maintain certification.

Certification is often overseen by national boards, such as NBCC (2023a). Although national certification suggests a certain level of competence in a professional field has been achieved, unless a state legislates that the specific national certification will be used at the state level, such certification carries little or no legal clout. Many individuals nevertheless obtain certification because it indicates they have mastered a body of knowledge, which can be important for hiring and promotion and can draw clients to one's practice by helping them feel at ease with the counselor's knowledge base. Some certifications also exist on a state-by-state basis. For instance, in Virginia, there are several certifications for substance abuse or addictions counselors. State certifications usually do not carry with them the ability of the practitioner to obtain third-party payments (see Virginia Department of Health Professions, n.d.). Each counselor should check with their own states' credentialing boards to know the specific scope of practice of their state's certifications. Certification often requires ongoing continuing education, such as 20 hours of workshops in one's area of certification, every year or two, with ethics often being a piece of the continuing education requirement.

The most rigorous form of credentialing is licensure. Generally regulated by states, licensure denotes that the licensed individual has met rigorous standards and that individuals without licenses cannot practice in that particular professional arena (ACA, 2023a, 2023c). Whereas certification protects only the title, licensure generally defines the scope of practice, or what an individual can and cannot do. For instance, in Virginia, the counselor licensing law not only defines the requirements one must meet to become licensed but also defines what is meant by counseling, who can do it, the limits of confidentiality and privileged communication, legal regulations related to suspected violations of the law (e.g., child abuse), and other various restrictions and regulations (Virginia Board of Counseling, 2022).

In terms of day-to-day professional functioning, the most important aspect of counselor licensure is that state licensure almost always carries with it legislation that mandates third-party reimbursement privileges. Such legislation requires insurance companies to reimburse licensed individuals for counseling and psychotherapy. As with certification, licensure generally involves a yearly fee, and usually, continuing education credits are mandated. Like certification, a portion of those credits generally needs to be related to ethics training.

You will find idiosyncratic usages of the words certification and licensure depending on the state in which you live. Therefore, check your state regulations to be sure that you know how credentialing operates where you live (see Experiential Exercise 5.1).

EXPERIENTIAL EXERCISE 5.1 **Creating Your Own Credential**

Using the following prompts, create your own hypothetical certification or license:

1. In what specialty area would you want the person to be credentialed?

2. Would you create a certification or a license?

3. Who would oversee your credential (e.g., the state, a nonprofit organization, or a for-profit organization)?

4. What would you require for a person to become credentialed (e.g., an exam, a master's degree, internship, and/or supervision)?

5. How much would you charge for your credential, and would there be a yearly renewal fee?

6. Would you require continuing education for a person to maintain their credential?

7. Would you have your own ethics code?

8. What would happen if a person was accused of an ethical violation and the complainant came to your credentialing board for action?

CREDENTIALING FOR COUNSELORS

There are dozens of different credentials for counselors, and this section explores some of the most popular and, perhaps, most important credentials. Often, with additional course work, supervision, and an exam, a counselor can become credentialed in an area other than what their specialization area was during their master's program. The following is a review of credentials all counselors can obtain, followed by information pertaining to the credentialing of clinical mental health counselors, marriage and family counselors, pastoral counselors, rehabilitation counselors, school counselors, and substance abuse counselors.

All Counselors

All counselors who obtained a master's or doctorate degree from a regionally accredited educational institute can become a national certified counselor (NCC) through NBCC. In addition, as previously noted, counselors may consider obtaining the specialty certifications offered by CCE, including approved clinical supervisor (ACS), board certified coach (BCC), board certified–telemental health provider (BC–TMH), distance credential counselor (DCC), or global career development facilitator (GCDF). Finally, all counselors should consider obtaining specialty certifications in areas in which they have, or want to gain, expertise, that are offered in the states in which they live.

The aforementioned credentials are some of the most common credentials amongst counselors. However, some less common certifications include certifications as a Christian counselor, forensic counselor, pastoral counselor, co-occurring disorder specialist, and others (e.g., National Association of Forensic Counselors, n.d.). As you continue through your career, you will undoubtedly come upon many of these certifications—and others—that you may be interested in. Finally, in many states, counselors with degrees other than clinical mental health counseling can become LPCs if they take additional coursework and meet other specific state requirements (e.g., supervision hours or a licensing exam).

Clinical Mental Health Counselors

As discussed previously, those with a degree in clinical mental health counseling can become licensed professional counselors (LPCs), or an equivalent. Such a license is almost always given by a state's board of counseling, or some variant (e.g., the board of health regulations).

Attainment of an LPC often involves a minimum of 2 years of post-master's supervised work experience and passage of an exam. All states have adopted the national counselor exam and/or the national clinical mental health counselor exam, offered by NBCC, as their licensing exam(s). The LPC is one of only a few credentials that allows counselors to obtain third-party payments (e.g., payments from health insurance companies). LPCs can generally perform most forms of counseling (e.g., individual counseling, addiction counseling, couples and family counseling, and counseling for severe disorders) as long as they have knowledge in these areas. Counselors should check their state law to see what kinds of limitations, if any, are placed on LPCs. In many states, one can have a degree in a related specialty area (e.g., rehabilitation, addictions, or school counseling) and still become an LPC if they meet their state's coursework, field placement, and supervision requirements.

Increasingly, states are requiring those who seek licensure to have graduated from a university accredited by the Council for Accreditation of Counseling and Related Educational Programs (CACREP, 2016), or its equivalent. Such universities require 60 semester hours, or 90 quarter hours, of counseling courses that are focused on eight common-core content areas, other coursework specifically focused on the work of the clinical mental health counselor, and a 200-hour practicum and 600-hour internship (see Chapter 1). In addition to course content, a whole host of other program requirements are a hallmark of CACREP accreditation (e.g., program evaluation, faculty to student ratios of 10–1, professional development plans for struggling students, and much more).

Clinical mental health counselors can also become certified in most, if not all, of the national certifications noted earlier by NBCC and CCE. In addition, states often offer certifications in several areas in which there tends to be a state or national trend or need (e.g., substance abuse or physical abuse counseling). In some cases, states require certification in a specific area for employment in certain jobs, and certification demonstrates to potential clients and colleagues that one has obtained mastery in the area in which the counselor is certified.

Finally, the American Mental Health Counselors Association (AMHCA) has developed several beginning and advanced certifications to acknowledge expertise in the field. Highlighted in Chapter 3 and expanded upon here, they include the certifications listed in Table 5.1 (AMHCA, 2023a).

TABLE 5.1 AMHCA-Sponsored Certifications

Certification Type	Required Qualifications
Basic Certifications	
AMHCA clinical mental health counseling student certification	For students enrolled in a master's in counseling degree or higher, this certification identifies individuals as specializing in clinical mental health counseling and acknowledges their commitment to the field.
AMHCA clinical mental health counselor under supervision certification	This certification is for those who have completed their master's degree and are under supervision but not yet licensed. It demonstrates the individual has basic knowledge of the profession.
AMHCA clinical mental health counselor, independently licensed certification	If one is already licensed as an LPC, this certificate demonstrates the individual acknowledges the importance of applying learned concepts and is continuing to develop expertise through ongoing professional development.

Advanced Certifications	
Clinical mental health counseling specialist	These certifications imply the LPC has advanced training, knowledge, and expertise in any of the following nine areas: 1. specialist in child and adolescent counseling 2. specialist in couples or family counseling 3. specialist in developmental and learning disabilities counseling 4. specialist in geriatric counseling 5. specialist in integrated behavioral health care counseling 6. specialist in military counseling 7. specialist in substance use and co-occurring disorders 8. specialist in trauma counseling 9. specialist in forensic evaluation
Diplomate in advanced clinical mental health counseling practice	One who receives status as a diplomate has demonstrated advanced knowledge, leadership in professional organizations, awards and acknowledgements, and ongoing continuing education activities.
Fellow in clinical mental health counseling education and research	LPCs who have demonstrated advanced knowledge and conducted research in clinical mental health counseling are acknowledged by being bestowed the designation "fellow."
Fellow in multiculturalism and social justice	The "fellow" designation acknowledges deep understanding and application of multicultural and social justice advocacy, intervention services, supervision, and research in the areas of multiculturalism and social justice.

Marriage and Family Counselors

In 1987, the Association of Marital and Family Therapy Regulatory Boards (AMFTRB) was established by the American Association of Marriage and Family Therapists (AAMFT) to address licensure and certification issues. Today, all 50 states have licensing laws that cover the 50,000 licensed marriage and family therapists (LMFTs)—some of which have degrees from CACREP-accredited programs, while others have degrees from programs accredited by the Commission on the Accreditation of Marriage and Family Therapy Education (AAMFT, 2002–2023; AMFTRB, n.d.; COAMFTE, n.d.). Some states have separate boards of marriage and family counselors, while other states subsume marriage and family counseling under the counseling licensure board or other health boards. Finally, in most states, LPCs can practice couples and family therapy without obtaining a license as a marriage and family counselor.

Pastoral Counselors

The National Board for Certified Pastoral Counselors (NBCPC, 2023) offers a certification as a national certified pastoral counselor (NCPC) at three levels, with level 1 (NCPC 1) focused on those with a bachelor degree and level 2 (NCPC 2) and level 3 (NCPC 3) focused on master's and doctoral degrees in "counseling, pastoral counseling, divinity, ministry, social work (or equivalent)" (NBCPC, 2023, Certification Requirements, Education section).

Certification as a board-certified Christian counselor (BCCC) can be obtained from the American Association of Christian Counselors (AACC; 2023) and requires a master's degree in counseling or a related field, identity as a Christian caregiver, and 60 contact hours of education or training in how to incorporate biblical principles and counseling theory and skills.

Depending on their degree, pastoral counselors may be able to become NCCs and, in some states, LPCs, although additional coursework, supervision, and an exam is often required. If they have an LPC, or related license, pastoral counselors may work in private practice, while some pastoral counselors work within a religious organization.

Rehabilitation Counselor (CRCs)

As previously noted, in 1974, rehabilitation counseling became one of the first counseling specialty areas to obtain certification for its members through the Commission for Rehabilitation Counseling certification (CRCC, 2021; Livingston, 1979). Today, the commission credentials 15,000 certified rehabilitation counselors (CRCs) and certifies rehabilitation counselors as vocational evaluation specialists in leadership and in diversity and inclusive leadership. Those with a degree in rehabilitation counseling can often become LPCs in their state by meeting additional requirements (Peterson, 2020).

School Counselors

> Professional school counselors are required by law and/or regulation in every state, the District of Columbia, Guam, Puerto Rico, and the Virgin Islands to obtain a state-issued credential in order to be employed in public schools. In some states, this credential is called "certification" while in others it is termed "licensure" or "endorsement." (ACA, 2012, p. 2)

States sometimes credential school counselors at specific levels (e.g., elementary, middle, or secondary grades), while other states offer a credential that endorses counselors to practice K–12 (ACA, 2012; American School Counselor Association [ASCA], 2023a). Although state requirements to become a credentialed school counselor tend to be similar in nature, the name of a credential can vary and may be called a certification, license, or endorsement. Usually, the state board of education bestows the credential, and today, all school counselors in the 50 states, the District of Columbia, Guam, Puerto Rico, and the Virgin Islands are given one of these credentials. Despite their different names, in terms of scope of practice, these credentials imply a similar work focus. For the most part, school counselors cannot practice independently or receive third-party payments, regardless of the name of their credential. However, with additional course work and other requirements, in many states, school counselors can become LPCs if they wish.

In addition to credentialing by the state board of education, a school counselor can become a national certified school counselor (NCSC) by NBCC, an ASCA certified school counselor (ACSC) through ASCA, and/or certified through the National Board for Professional Teaching Standards (NBPTS; ASCA, 2023b; NBCC, 2023b; NBPTS, 2023).

Substance Abuse Counselors

As of 2019, 31 states offered licensure for substance abuse counselors and 20 states and the District of Columbia offered certification (U.S. Department of Health and Human Services, 2019). As you probably can guess, licensure allows the substance abuse counselor eligibility for third-party payments and generally requires a master's degree or higher in counseling or a related helping profession.

Many states have a variety of credentials for substance abuse counselors at different levels. For instance, in Virginia alone, one can become an associate addiction counselor (AAC), a certified alcohol and drug counselor (CADC), a certified advanced alcohol and drug counselor (CAADC), a certified substance abuse counselor assistant (CSAC-A), and a certified substance abuse counselor (CSAC; Center for Addiction Studies and Research, 2022a). Of these, only the CAADC requires a master's degree. Besides educational requirements, other requirements also apply (e.g., coursework, field experience, and super-vision). If you want to find the types of substance abuse credentials in your state, a good source is the Center for Addiction Studies and Research (2022b).

Meanwhile, the National Certification Commission for Addiction Professionals (NCCAP) offers three types of certifications (NAADAC, 2023a). The educational requirements for these certifications are a high school diploma, college degree, and master's degree to become a national certified addiction counselor, level I; national certified addiction counselor, level II; and master addiction counselor, respectively. To become credentialed, individuals must meet additional requirements, such as supervised work experience and passing an exam. Currently, 22 states use NAADAC's exam to certify substance abuse counselors (NAADAC, 2023b). In addition to NAADAC's master addiction counselor certification, NBCC also offers a master addiction counselor (MAC) certification, although it is currently under review (NBCC, 2023b).

Counselors with degrees in specialty areas other than addiction counseling can generally pick up the additional coursework and other requirements to become credentialed as a substance abuse counselor. In addition, counselors who have a master's degree in addiction counseling can often become an LPC, although they sometimes need to acquire additional requirements, depending on the state (e.g., specific coursework and supervision).

Summary of Credentials for Counselors

The many credentials discussed in this chapter only scratch the surface of the types of credentials coun-selors can obtain. Table 5.2 summarizes the major credentials we just examined.

TABLE 5.2 Credentialing of Counselors

Type of Professional	Type of Credential	Administered By
All Counselors	National certified counselor (NCC)	NBCC
	Approved clinical supervisor (ACS)	CCE
	Board certified coach (BCC)	CCE
	Board certified–telemental health provider (BC–TMH)	CCE
	Distance credential counselor (DCC)	CCE
	Global career development facilitator (GCDF)	CCE
Clinical Mental Health Counselors	Licensed professional counselor (LPC or similar variant)	Individual states
	Clinical mental health counseling student certification	AMHCA
	Clinical mental health counselor under supervision certification	AMHCA
	Clinical mental health counselor, independently licensed certification	AMHCA
	Specialist in child and adolescent counseling	AMHCA

(Continued)

TABLE 5.2 (*Continued*)

Type of Professional	Type of Credential	Administered By
	Specialist in couples or family counseling	AMHCA
	Specialist in developmental and learning disabilities counseling	AMHCA
	Specialist in geriatric counseling	AMHCA
	Specialist in integrated behavioral health care counseling	AMHCA
	Specialist in military counseling	AMHCA
	Specialist in substance use and co-occurring disorders	AMHCA
	Specialist in trauma counseling	AMHCA
	Specialist in forensic evaluation	AMHCA
	Diplomate in advanced clinical mental health counseling practice	AMHCA
	Fellow in clinical mental health counseling education and research	AMHCA
	Fellow in multiculturalism and social justice	AMHCA
Marriage and Family Counselors	Licensed marriage and family therapists (LMFT)	Individual States
	Certified marriage and family therapists	NCA
Pastoral Counselors	National certified pastoral counselor (NCPC) I, II, and III	NBCP
	Board certified Christian counselor (BCCC)	AACC
Rehabilitation Counselors	Certified rehabilitation counselors (CRC)	CRCC
School Counselors	Credentialed school counselors	State boards of education
	National certified school counselor (NCSC)	NBCC
	ASCA certified school counselor	ASCA
	Certification	NBPTS
Substance Abuse Counselors	License or certification	Individual states
	Certified alcohol and drug counselor (CADC)	Individual states
	Certified advanced alcohol and drug counselor (CAADC)	Individual states
	Certified substance abuse counselor assistant (CSAC-A)	Individual states
	Certified substance abuse counselor (CSAC)	Individual states
	National certified addiction counselor, level I and level II	NAADC
	Master addiction counselor	NAADC
	Master addiction counselor	NBCC

CREDENTIALS IN RELATED HELPING PROFESSIONS

Although written over 30 years ago, this quote is still relevant today:

> It is recognized that there is competition for clients among professionals providing mental health services and that there is also concern about the degree of preparation and expertise of a number of professions to deliver those services. (Garcia, 1990, p. 495)

Competition between credentialed mental health professionals is real, and whether a professional is credentialed makes a huge difference in one's ability to obtain clients. Let's look at some of the different credentials in the closely related professions of human service professionals, social workers, school psychologists, make this one first, prior to human service professionals. psychiatric–mental health nurses, and psychiatrists. Like credentialed counselors, these certifications and licenses represent some of the most popular and important credentials.

Counseling Psychologists and Clinical Psychologists

The first push for credentialing doctoral-level psychologists came during the 1950s (Cummings, 1990). Today, every state offers licensure for doctoral-level psychologists, generally in the areas of counseling psychology and clinical psychology. In addition, many states now offer hospital privileges for licensed counseling psychologists and licensed clinical psychologists. Such privileges afford psychologists the right to treat those who have been hospitalized with serious mental illness. Not surprisingly, psychologists have recently sought to gain the right to prescribe medication for emotional disorders, and five states, the territory of Guam, and some branches of the federal government are now allowing psychologists to have limited prescription privileges. As you might expect, this has been met with much opposition, particularly from the American Psychiatric Association (American Psychological Association, 2023; O'Connor, 2022; Robiner et al., 2019). In addition to licensure, the American Board of Professional Psychology (ABPP) offers 15 Board Certifications in the following psychology areas: behavioral and cognitive, clinical child and adolescent, clinical health, clinical neuropsychology, clinical, counseling, couple and family, forensics, geropsychology, group, organizational and business, police and public safety, rehabilitation, school, psychoanalysis, and serious mental illness (ABPP, 2023).

Human Service Professionals

Human service professionals have generally obtained an associate or bachelor's degree in human services, are often found in entry-level support and counseling jobs, and sometimes assist counselors and other mental health professionals. The Center for Credentialing and Education (CCE, 2023b) offers the Human Services–Board Certified Practitioner (HS–BCP) credential for "human services practitioners seeking to advance their careers by acquiring independent verification of their practical knowledge and educational background" (para. 1). At the state level, numerous other certifications can also be obtained for human service professionals, including certifications as substance abuse counselors, qualified mental health practitioners (QMHP), and more. Check your state for what certifications are available for human service professionals. Not having one of these state certifications can sometimes prevent a person from obtaining a job.

Psychiatric–Mental Health Nurses

There are two levels of psychiatric–mental health nurses: basic and advanced. Basic psychiatric–mental health (PMH) nurses generally do not have advanced degrees and can work with clients and families doing entry-level psychiatric nursing. In contrast, psychiatric–mental health advanced practice registered nurses (PMH–APRN) are generally registered nurses (RNs) with a master's or doctoral degree in psychiatric–mental health nursing and have passed a board certification exam sponsored by the American Nurses Credentialing Center (ANCC, n.d.). PMH–APRNs can offer a wide range of mental health services, prescribe medication, function as independent practitioners in their own medical practice, and receive third-party reimbursement in many states (American Psychiatric Nurses Association [APNA], 2023). Nurses can also become certified through ANCC in a number of specialty areas (e.g., gerontology, lifespan, healthcare, and many others).

Psychiatrists

Psychiatrists are physicians, and licensure as a physician is a state responsibility and generally not specialty specific; thus, licensed physicians are not licensed as pediatricians, psychiatrists, surgeons, and so forth. Therefore, a physician who obtains a license within a state can theoretically practice in any area of medicine. However, because the ability to be paid by insurance companies is sometimes related to being board certified, and because hospital accreditation standards generally require the hiring of board-certified physicians, almost all physicians today are board certified in a specialty area. Being board certified means that the physician has had additional experience in the specialty area and has taken and passed a rigorous exam in that area. Thus, most psychiatrists are not only licensed physicians within the state in which they practice but are also board certified psychiatrists (American Board of Psychiatry and Neurology [APBN], n.d.). Psychiatrists can also become certified in many areas of psychiatry and medicine.

School Psychologists

School psychologists have a master's or doctoral degree in school psychology, and since they mostly work in the schools, like school counselors, they are credentialed by state boards of education. Also, like school counselors, school psychologists may be certified, or licensed, depending on the state. In addition, being a licensed school psychologists does not mean school psychologists can work independently and receive third-part payments, although some school psychologists may be able to obtain licensure as a psychologist in their state and work in private practice. In addition, school psychologists can become national certified school psychologists (NSCPs) through the National Association of School Psychologists (NASP, 2021, 2022). Currently, there are 17,253 NSCPs.

Social Workers

On the national level, several credentials exist for the many types of master's-level social workers offered by the National Association of Social Workers (NASW, 2023). Experienced social workers can hold a credential as an "ACSW" from the Academy of Certified Social Workers. Those who have more clinical experience can become a qualified clinical social worker (QCSW), and advanced clinicians can become a diplomate in clinical social work (DCSW). In addition, advanced practice specialty credentials can be obtained in several areas (e.g., addictions), and many clinical social workers become licensed in their states as licensed clinical social workers (LCSWs; Association of Social Work Boards, 2023).

Summary of Credentials for Related Helping Professions

The many credentials discussed in this chapter only scratch the surface of the types of credentials that can be obtained by related mental health professionals. Table 5.3 summarizes the major credentials we just examined.

TABLE 5.3 Credentialing in Related Helping Professions

Type of Professional	Type of Credential	Administered By
Counseling and Clinical Psychologists	Licensed psychologist (LP)	Individual states
	15 board certifications in psychology areas	ABPP
Human Service Professionals	Human services–board certified practitioner (HS–BCP)	CCE
Psychiatric–Mental Health Advanced Practice Registered Nurse	Board certification	ANCC
	Many other certifications	ANCC
Psychiatrists	Licensed physician	Individual states
	Board certified psychiatrist	American Board of Psychiatry and Neurology
	Many other certifications	Other boards
School Psychologists	Credentialed school psychologist	State boards of education
	National certified school psychologist	NSCP
Social Workers	Licensed clinical social worker (LCSW)	Individual states
	Academy of Certified Social Workers (ACSW)	NASW
	Qualified clinical social worker (QCSW)	NASW
	Diplomate in clinical social work (DCSW)	NASW
	Advanced practice specialty credentials in many areas	NASW

CRITICAL ISSUES IN THE CREDENTIALING OF CLINICAL MENTAL HEALTH COUNSELING

Although there are many important issues that revolve around the credentialing of clinical mental health counselors, four that are of particular importance in recent years include licensure portability, telemental health counseling, parity for licensed clinical mental health counselors, and privileged communication. Let's look at these important issues.

Licensure Portability

Because requirements for licensure often vary considerably from state to state, if a counselor is licensed in a particular state, it is sometimes difficult for that person to become licensed in a different state or practice between states when conducting telemental health counseling. In recent years, The Counseling Compact Commission (2022, 2023), which is made up of states that have endorsed its legislative initiative and four counseling organizations, including ACA, NBCC, AMHCA, and the American Association of State

EXPERIENTIAL EXERCISE 5.2
What Credentials Would You Want to Obtain?

Based on the credentials you read about in the chapter, or others you may know about, write a paragraph discussing which credentials you would want to obtain and why they would be important to you. In class, discuss your responses.

Counseling Boards (AASCB), have endorsed the Counseling Compact, which would allow counselors to practice in other compact states. They note the following:

> The Counseling Compact is an interstate compact, or a contract among states, allowing professional counselors licensed and residing in a compact member state to practice in other compact member states without need for multiple licenses. (Counseling Compact, 2023, What is the Counseling Compact? section)

As of the writing of this book, there are 22 states that have enacted legislation, and 18 states that have pending legislation to become members of the Compact (see the "Compact Map" for updates: https://counselingcompact.org/map/). It is expected that in late 2023, applications to become a member of the Compact will open, and licensed professional counselors will be able to apply to practice in other states.

Telemental Health Counseling

The COVID-19 pandemic changed the world in many significant ways, including a dramatic shift toward telemental health counseling. Understanding that clients could no longer be seen in person, insurance companies readily agreed to allow licensed therapists to see clients via telemental health methods. However, several issues were immediately raised, including the following:

- Was telemental health as effective as in-person counseling?
- Could licensed therapists conduct sessions from one state, while the client was in another state?
- How could licensed therapists assure privacy, confidentiality, security, and compliance to the Health Insurance Portability and Accountability Act (HIPAA)?
- Were therapists adequately trained in the use of technology necessary for telemental health counseling?
- Were clients adequately trained in the use of technology, and did they have the technology to be a participant in telemental health counseling?
- How would a licensed therapist respond if there was an emergency with a client (e.g., the possible need for hospitalization or a client who was suicidal or homicidal)?

With these concerns in mind, counselors need to understand how to set up a telehealth platform, best practices for telehealth counseling, the legal and ethical implications of telehealth counseling, and how telehealth counseling impacts the counseling relationship (Gilberston, 2020). One way to help ensure that a counselor has expertise in telemental health counseling is to become a board certified–telemental health provider (BC–TMH; CCE, 2023a). With the monumental changes that have occurred due to the pandemic, no longer will counselors be able to say they "must" see their clients in the office.

Parity for Licensed Clinical Mental Health Counselors

Of social workers, psychologists, psychiatric mental health nurses, and psychiatrists, counselors were the last to obtain licensure in all 50 states. This resulted in them lagging behind other licensed mental health professionals in obtaining third-party payments from all potential sources. However, in recent years, licensed counselors have made a number of strides, which have put them in line with most other licensed therapists. For instance, they were finally included as providers for TRICARE, the large health care organization for U.S. military families; included as providers for Medicare, which insures 43 million older Americans; and allowed employment at VA hospitals (ACA, 2015, 2023d; Department of Veteran Affairs, 2018; NBCC, 2023c; Walsh & Dasenbrook, 2010, 2016). Counselors have come a long way and are now essentially aligned with other licensed therapists in their ability to obtain third-party reimbursement and their access to working in a variety of agencies and settings.

Privileged Communication

Privileged communication is the right of the client to expect that communication with the counselor is confidential, as defined by state or federal statute. Such privilege is generally given to licensed therapists, lawyers, priests and ministers, and spouses.

A 1996 Supreme Court ruling, *Jaffee v. Redmond*, involving the case records of a social worker, upheld the right for licensed professionals to maintain the confidentiality of their records. Describing the social worker as a "therapist" and "psychotherapist," the ruling suggested all licensed therapists who hold privileged communication have a right to withhold information about their clients (Remley et al., 1997). However, how the right to privilege is defined can vary state by state, and each licensed therapist should check on this important legal rule in their state. Further discussion on the right to privilege is included in Chapter 6: Ethics.

SUMMARY

This chapter examined credentialing of clinical mental health counseling and related professionals. We began the chapter by noting that credentialing in the helping professions started many centuries ago, although modern-day credentialing can be traced back to the certification of school counselors during the 1940s. We pointed out that certification of rehabilitation counselors was initiated in 1974 and that Virginia was the first state to license counselors in 1976. We also highlighted the fact that all 50 states now license clinical mental health counselors as LPCs, or a variant of that name. We noted that NBCC was founded in 1982 and today certifies counselors as nationally certified school counselors (NCSCs), nationally certified clinical mental health counselors (NCMHCs), and master addiction counselors (MACs), although the MAC certification is currently under review and inactive.

The chapter next examined some of the purposes and types of credentialing. We pointed out several benefits of credentialing, including increased professionalization, delimitation of one's professional identity, attainment of parity for the professional, offering a process for reporting bad practice, and preventing others from practicing in a specific field. We then gave definitions of three forms of credentialing: registration, certification, and licensure. We noted that registration is simply the registering of a group, certification protects a title, and licensure defines the scope and practice of what one can do. We noted that states generally regulate licensure and that certification can involve a state or nationally regulating body. We highlighted the importance of licensure in mandating third-party reimbursement privileges.

The next section of the chapter provided an overview of credentialing for different types of counselors, including all counselors, clinical mental health counselors, marriage and family counselors, pastoral counselors, rehabilitation counselors, school counselors, and substance abuse counselors. We then described credentialing in the related helping professions of counseling and clinical psychologists, human service professionals, psychiatric–mental health nurses, psychiatrists, school psychologists, social workers.

The chapter concluded by examining four critical issues in the credentialing of clinical mental health counseling: licensure portability, telemental health counseling, parity for clinical mental health counselors, and privileged communication. Relative to licensure portability, we discussed the recent development of the Counseling Compact Commission, which hopes to soon develop an interstate compact for licensed counselors. For telemental health counseling, we raised several issues that are important when practicing this form of counseling. We next noted that counselors have come a long way in achieving parity with other mental health professionals in that they have recently become providers for TRICARE and Medicare and are now employable at VA hospitals. Counselors, today, can get reimbursed from most insurance companies and funding organizations in a similar way as licensed social workers and licensed psychologists. Finally, when discussing privileged communication, we noted the right of a licensed therapist to keep client information confidential but warned that such privilege can vary by state law.

KEY WORDS AND TERMS

"ACSW"

ASCA Certified School Counselor (ACSC)

beginning and advanced certifications

benefits of credentialing

board-certification

board-certified Christian counselor (BCCC)

board-certified coach (BCC)

board-certified psychiatrists

board-certified–telemental health provider (BC–TMH)

certification

certified advanced alcohol and drug counselor (CAADC)

certified alcohol and drug counselor (CADC)

certified rehabilitation counselor (CRC)

certified substance abuse counselor (CSAC)

certified substance abuse counselor assistant (CSAC-A)

clinical mental health counseling student certification

clinical mental health counselor exam

clinical mental health counselor, independently licensed certification

clinical mental health counselor under supervision certification

counseling compact

credentialed rehabilitation counselors (CRCs)

credentialed school counselors

credentialed school psychologists

diplomate in advanced clinical mental health counseling practice

diplomate in clinical social work (DCSW)

distance credential counselor (DCC)

fellow in clinical mental health counseling education and research

fellow in multiculturalism and social justice

15 board certifications in psychology

global career development facilitator (GCDF)

human services–board-certified practitioner (HS–BCP)

Jaffee v. Redmond

licensed clinical psychologists

licensed clinical social worker

licensed counseling psychologists

licensed marriage and family therapists (LMFT)

licensed physician

licensure

licensure portability

licensed professional counselor

master addiction counselor (MAC)

Mental Health Access Improvement Act

national certified addiction counselor, level I and II

national certified counselor (NCC)

national certified pastoral counselor (NCPC)

national certified school counselor (NCSC)

national certified school psychologist (NSCP)

national clinical mental health counselor exam

national counselor exam

nationally certified clinical mental health counselor (NCMHC)

nationally certified school counselors (NCSC)

parity for licensed clinical mental health counselors

pastoral counselors

privileged communication

protection of a title

psychiatric mental health nurses

psychiatric-mental health advanced practice registered nurses

psychiatrist

qualified clinical social worker (QCSW)

registration

school psychologists

scope of practice

specialist in child and adolescent counseling

specialist in couples or family counseling

specialist in developmental and learning disabilities counseling

specialist in forensic evaluation

specialist in geriatric counseling

specialist in integrated behavioral health care counseling

specialist in military counseling

specialist in substance use and co-occurring disorders

specialist in trauma counseling

telemental health counseling

third-party payments

third-party reimbursement privileges

PROFESSIONAL ASSOCIATIONS AND ORGANIZATIONS

Academy of Certified Social Workers (ACSW)
Approved Clinical Supervisor (ACS)
American Association of Christian Counselors (AACC)
American Association of Marriage and Family Therapists (AAMFT)
American Association of State Counseling Boards (AASCB)
American Board of Professional Psychology (ABPP)
American Board of Psychiatry and Neurology (ABPN)
American Counseling Association (ACA)
American Mental Health Counselors Association (AMHCA)
American Nurses Credentialing Center (ANCC)
American Psychiatric Association (APA)
American Psychiatric Nurses Association (APNA)
American Psychological Association (APA)
American School Counselor Association (ASCA)
Association of Marital and Family Therapy Regulatory Boards (AMFTRB)
Center for Addiction Studies and Research (CASR)
Center for Credentialing and Education (CCE)
Commission for Rehabilitation Counseling Certification (CRCC)
Council for Accreditation of Counseling and Related Educational Programs (CACREP)
Counseling Compact Commission (CCC)
International Association of Marriage and Family Counselors (IAMFC)
National Association of School Psychologists (NASP)
National Association of Social Workers (NASW)
National Board for Certified Counselors (NBCC)
National Board for Certified Pastoral Counselors (NBCPC)
National Certification Commission for Addiction Professionals (NCCAP)

CHAPTER 6

ETHICS

Learning Goals

- Understand the differences between values, ethics, and morality as well as their relationship to the law.
- Learn about the development of, and need for, ethical codes in the mental health professions.
- Review highlights of the American Mental Health Counselors Association's (AMHCA) ethics code, the American Counseling Association's (ACA's) ethics code and note the ethics codes of other counseling related mental health professions.
- Identify how to determine which ethics code to use and when it might be best to use a combination of codes.
- Examine ethical "hot spots" and consider how a counselor might respond to them.
- Review and learn how to implement models of ethical decision-making, including problem-solving, moral, social constructionist, and developmental models.
- Explore and discuss CMHCs' perceptions of ethical behavior.
- Learn procedures for reporting ethical violations.
- Learn about legal issues related to ethical violations, particularly civil and criminal liability, the role of ethical codes in lawsuits, the importance of malpractice insurance, and the use of best practices to avoid ethical violations.

INTRODUCTION

When working at a mental health center, I had a suicidal client leave her session saying she was going to kill herself. I immediately told my supervisor, who said, "Get in my car." We chased her down, stopped her, and had her involuntarily committed. Another time, I was testing a high school student who I suspected had been molested. I asked her if she had been sexually assaulted, and she began to sob and told me she had been raped. Her parents and authorities were informed, and we successfully got her into counseling. Another time I was working with a colleague who was misrepresenting his credentials. I sat down with him, shared my thoughts, and told him if he did not rectify the situation, I would have to report him to the licensing board. I used to do problem pregnancy counseling when abortion was legal throughout the country. I wonder if my ethical responsibility toward client self-determination would, today, clash with the law if I was counseling a client who was wanting an abortion in a state where it was illegal. How would I handle that? How might you handle that?

If you have not yet faced difficult ethical dilemmas, at some point in your career, you will. These dilemmas can be complex, and finding the best response is often tricky. Thus, in this chapter we discuss values, morality, ethics, best practices, and the law, so you have a knowledge base to draw from when faced with difficult ethical dilemmas.

DEFINING VALUES, ETHICS, MORALITY, AND THEIR RELATIONSHIP TO THE LAW

Always do what is right. It will gratify half of mankind and astound the other.

—Mark Twain

Although not constantly faced with situations such as the ones just described, in our work as counselors, we are periodically confronted with complicated and delicate ethical dilemmas. In these moments, we need to respond in the best manner possible, and it helps if we know the differences between our values, morals, ethical responsibilities, and legal obligations.

Whereas one's values are those thoughts and behaviors that represent "the principles and priorities that are important to us" (Simon et al., 1995, p. 4), one's morals reflect the values from an individual's family, religious sect, culture, or nationality, which are handed down to us (Gert, 2020). In contrast, ethics generally describes the collectively agreed-upon preferred or expected behaviors of a professional group (Moyer & Crews, 2017; Remley & Herlihy, 2020). Therefore, our values, sense of morality, and professional ethics can all conflict with one another—which can get messy. For instance, one's values might suggest abortion should be a complicated decision by any person; one's moral beliefs might state that abortion is murder; and one's professional ethics might assert a client's right to self-determination, including the right to an abortion. Imagine a minister who has these values and moral beliefs who is also a counselor. This person could face several conflicting thoughts, beliefs, and feelings and may respond differently depending on which "hat" they are currently wearing. At times, trying to make sense of one's values, moral beliefs, and professional ethics can be quite an undertaking! And to make things even more confounding, sometimes the law contradicts with one's values, sense of morality, and even professional ethics. Or as Supreme Court Justice Potter Stewart is reported to have said, "There's a big difference between what we have the right to do and what is right." This is why when professional ethics are not in line with legal statute, ethics codes generally state that one should try to either change the law or make the code fit the law.

THE DEVELOPMENT OF AND NEED FOR ETHICAL CODES

The development of ethics codes in the helping professions is relatively new and began with the 1953 adoption, by the American Psychological Association, of its code of ethics, followed by the 1960 code of the National Association of Social Workers (NASW) and the 1961 ACA code. Because ethical standards often mirror changes in society, associations' guidelines have undergone several major revisions over the years (see ACA, 2014; AMHCA, 2020; American Psychological Association, 2017; NASW, 2021a, 2021b). Today, there are several purposes of ethics codes, which (Barksy, 2022; Corey et al., 2024; Remley & Herlihy, 2020):

- protecting consumers;
- furthering the professional standing of the organization;

- making a statement about the maturity and professional identity of a profession;
- offering a framework for the sometimes-difficult ethical decision-making process;
- guiding professionals toward behaviors that reflect underlying values desirable in the profession; and
- offering one measure of defense if the professional is sued for malpractice.

Although offering considerable assistance in a professional's ethical decision-making process, there are limitations to codes (Moyer & Crews, 2017; Robinson et al., 2020). For instance,

- codes do not always address "cutting-edge" issues;
- it is sometimes difficult to enforce ethical violations in the codes;
- codes do not address some issues and offer no clear way of responding to other issues;
- the public is often not involved in the code construction process, and public interests are not always considered; and
- there are sometimes conflicts within the same code, between different related codes, between the code and the law, between the code and licensing boards, and between the code and a counselor's value system.

Deciding what to include in a code can be difficult (Burkholder et al., 2020; Kaplan et al., 2017; Ponton & Duba, 2009). For instance, those who develop ethics codes will often reflect upon, and struggle with, which societal values to include in codes. And despite careful consideration of which values to include, the chosen values will not be reflective of all individuals. For instance, the idea of "self-determination," or the notion that we all should have the ability to decide for ourselves what is in our own best interest, is not a value held by all individuals in society, especially those who value the opinions of extended family or authority figures when making important decisions. Yet this is often listed in codes as a critical part of the ethical decision-making process. Similarly, people debate the universality of so-called universal truths. For example, the idea that "thou shalt not kill" seems universal, yet many would hold that killing is ethical if it is sponsored by the state, such as in war, capital punishment, or assisted suicide. Thus, deciding what principles to include in a code often involves a fair amount of debate among, and reflection by, members of professional associations, as they try to develop a code that fits most counselors and can seem reasonable to most clients. Despite wrestling with many different values, those who developed the ethical guidelines of the three major helping professions of counseling, psychology, and social work ended up producing remarkably similar codes.

CODES OF ETHICS

Although ethics codes in the helping professions are very similar, there are some differences. Here, we highlight paraphrased versions of the AMHCA and ACA codes, note codes of other select counseling associations, and list codes of related professional associations in the helping professions. This is followed by a short discussion of how to decide which ethics codes to use when making difficult ethical decisions.

AMHCA and ACA Ethics Codes

Most clinical mental health counselors adhere to the AMHCA Code of Ethics and/or the ACA Code of Ethics. Box 6.1 paraphrases the AMHCA (2020) code—greatly reducing it. Thus, it is critical that, at some point, you also review the code in its entirety, which can be found at the "News and Events" section of the AMHCA website (www.amhca.org). If your instructor, or you, would prefer examining the ACA (2014) code, or want to compare the two codes, a paraphrased version of the ACA code can be found in Appendix A and the full code can be found in the "Knowledge Center" of the ACA website (www.counseling.org; see Box 6.1 and then Exercise 6.1).

BOX 6.1 **Outline of the AMHCA Code of Ethics**

Preamble of the AMHCA Code of Ethics

CMHCs abide and are guided by the principles of the AMHCA code and use ethical decision-making processes. CMHCs follow state and federal laws and other regulations and try to resolve differences between those laws and the ethics code when they exist. When resolution is not possible, they may need to follow the law.

I. **Commitment to Clients**
   A. **Counselor–Client Relationship**
      1. **primary responsibility:** There is a primary responsibility of CMHCs to ensure (a) the autonomy and self-determination of clients, except in cases of harm to self or others, and to use a professional disclosure statement to guide their clients and (b) that clients understand the counselor's professional orientation, values of the counselor, the counseling process, how emergencies are dealt with, knowledge of counselor supervision, and business practices.
      2. **confidentiality:** Clients have a right to confidentiality and should know (a) the limits including exceptions due to the law; (b) that records will not be shared without client permission; (c) info will not be shared except under certain circumstances (the law, harm to self or others, legal rules); (d) info is only given out with a release of info form or from a court order; (e) anonymity of the client info is critical; (f) info received about clients from other agencies should not be forwarded without client permission; (g) the validity of data received; (h) when case reports are presented to others they should not reveal clients names; (i) to keep confidentiality of reports and records; (j) that tapes are only recorded with written permission; (k) clients own the right to confidentiality; (l) with family and groups, each member has the right to confidentiality; (m and n) all electronic information needs to be controlled to ensure confidentiality; (o) deceased clients may have the a right to confidentiality; and (p) third-party payers can obtain info about a client only after the client authorizes such usage.
      3. **dual/multiple relationships:** CMHCs should (a) avoid dual/multiple relationships especially when they impair counselor judgment; (b) seek consultation if they are going to have a dual/multiple relationship with a client; (c) take precautions (e.g., supervision, informed consent) when there is a dual/multiple relationship; and (d) not accept clients when they have an evaluative relationship with them.
      4. **exploitive relationships:** CMHCSs do not have (a) romantic or sexual relationships with clients or their family members; (b) romantic relationships with former clients, and if they do, the burden is on the CMHC to show harm has not transpired; and (c and d) avoid exploitive relationships based on factors like duration of counseling, time in counseling, termination issues, clients personal history and mental status, adverse issues that can impact the client, values of the counselor, and lack of cultural competence.

(continued)

5. **counseling environments:** Counseling should be accessible to all clients, including those with disabilities, and should always be amenable to confidentiality.

B. **Counseling Process**

1. **treatment plans:** With all clients, treatment plans should have some promise for success.

2. **informed consent:** Clients should (a) provide informed consent based on knowledge of counselor credentials, confidentiality limits, use of assessments, diagnoses, billing, reporting to others, and counselor's approach to therapy; (b) be able to have others provide informed consent when they cannot (e.g., children, those who are emotionally unable to, etc.); (c) know that consent is ongoing, and may need to be reassessed at times; and (d) know the limits and risks relative to online counseling services.

3. **multiple clients:** When counselors provide services to two or more persons, they should (a) clarify the relationship with each person; (b) reassess the relationships if objectivity is not achieved; (c) ensure that confidentiality applies to all; and (d and e) ensure that with group members compatible goals and precautions are taken to avoid harm to each group member.

4. **clients served by others:** CMHCs should avoid counseling relationships when a person is in a helping relationship with others, except when the client is informed and agrees. When clients (a) change helpers but have not terminated with the former helper, CMHCs should encourage the client to terminate the first relationship and (b) when working with multiple helpers, permission to work collaboratively should be obtained when appropriate.

5. **termination and referral:** Clients should be (a) given help for continued treatment when the counselor is on vacation or following termination, if needed; (b) terminated from counseling if it is no longer helpful or when the agency does not allow continued counseling; (c) terminated if the client does not pay fees or insurance denies treatment but should be given other referrals; (d) can be terminated if they do not want suggested referrals; (e) know that CMHCs will work collaboratively after making referrals; and (f) if needed, be given steps to develop a plan to avoid being harmed or suicidal during termination or referral.

6. **the use of technology supported counseling and communications (TSCC):** CMHCs realizes that (a) TSCC includes a wide range of categories (Telehealth, videos, internet, etc.); (b) all laws prevail when using TSCC and continuity of care should be ensured, as best as possible; (c) CMHCs are not required to offer services via TSCC, (d) should be sufficiently trained in TSCC; (e) they should be familiar with the laws in the state they are licensed and the state where the client presides; (f) they have client contact info in case there is an emergency; (g) if the state requires client communications via TSCC be included in the client record, the clients should be informed; (h) clients should be informed when text messages or emails are not encrypted; (i) unsecured chat rooms should be discouraged; (j) they should have separatee personal and professional profiles and clients should use professional confidential channels when contacting CMHCS; and (k) obtaining info about a client from internet searches is discouraged except when there is an issue of client safety, when necessary for forensic evaluations, or at the client's request.

(continued)

7. **clients' rights:** Clients should be treated with dignity and have the right to (a) quality services; (b) confidentiality and knowing it's limits; (c) the times of sessions, fee info, emergency procedures, third-party payment processes, termination and referral procedures, and advanced info about collection agencies; (d) purposes and goals of counseling; (e) knowledge, education, training, and practice limitations of the CMHC; (f) participation in treatment plan; (g) info about their treatment plan; (h) info and/or consultation about progress; (i) refuse treatment and advised about the consequences of refusing; (j) an emotional and physical safe space; and (k) knowledge of the termination process and the ability to terminate at any time.

8. **end-of-life care for terminally ill clients:** CMHCS ensure clients receive quality end-of-life care, are aware of their ability to work with such clients, consult with professional and legal entities regarding state laws, and have the option of respecting confidentiality regarding end-of-life plans after consulting with such entities.

C. **Counselor Responsibility and Integrity**

1. **competence:** CMHCs (a) know the limits of their expertise; (b) provide services based on their expertise; (c) maintain ongoing education; (d) represent their expertise and credentials accurately; (e) conduct teaching based on careful preparation and accuracy; (f) remain open to new procedures that show efficacy; (g) are culturally competent; (h) provide services only when they are mentally and physically healthy; (i) maintain high standards and professional conduct; (j) resolve ethical issues with colleagues directly and when informal resolution is not appropriate, seek out formal options (e.g., licensing boards); (k) empower clients; (l) maintain respect for clients at all times; (m) attempt to understand diverse cultural backgrounds and how their values and beliefs impact counseling; (n) engage in continuing education and current trends; (o) develop plans for termination of practice, death, or incapacitation by having a colleague assigned as a custodian; and (p) avoid language offensive to individuals.

2. **non-discrimination:** CMHCS do not condone or engage in any forms of discrimination or sexual harassment and educate themselves about their own biases.

3. **conflict of interest:** CMHCs avoid conflict of interests and consult with all parties when there may be one.

D. **Assessment and Diagnosis**

1. **selection and administration:** CMHCs choose assessment instruments that (a) are valid, reliable, and cross-culturally appropriate; (b) meet the client's needs; (c) are not outdated or obsolete; (d) are appropriate for the context in which they are working in (e.g., academic, professional training); (e) are explained to the client and the client is told who will receive the report; and (f) given in an appropriate environment.

2. **interpretation and reporting:** CMHCs respect the rights and dignity of clients involved in assessment and (a) base their results on multiple pieces of information; (g) consider cross-cultural issues when making decisions about the client; (c) ensure the validity of computerized assessment; (d, e, f) clearly explain results in reports in a nonjudgmental manner; (g) ensure confidentiality and security of reports; (h) ensure that staff respect confidentiality of reports; and (i) do not release reports without a release of information or when the court requests one and legal concerns are followed.

(continued)

3. **competence:** CMHCs (a) only use tests in which they are appropriately trained; (b) seek continuing education for assessment techniques; and (c) ensure that supervisees are adequately trained.

4. **forensic activity:** When conducting forensic assessment, CMHCs (a) have the appropriate knowledge; (b) offer findings without bias; (c) inform clients of the limits of confidentiality; (d) use instruments appropriate for evaluation; (e) provide testimony that is adequately supported by assessments; (f) provide their qualifications that support their ability to make conclusions during testimony; (g) usually do not do forensic evaluations for their clients or counsel individuals for which they are doing a forensic evaluations; and (h) do not advocate for the legal system, perpetrators, or victims of criminal activity.

E. **Recordkeeping, Fee Arrangements, and Bartering**

1. **recordkeeping:** CMHs (a) are careful to protect the confidentiality of client records; (b) establish a process for, transfer, storage, and disposal of client records; (c) inform clients when they exceed state requirements for maintaining records; and (d) keep ALL communications regarding treatment, including emails and texts.

2. **fee arrangements, bartering, and gifts:** CMHCS (a) know cultural norms relative to bartering and gifts; (b) usually refrain from accepting goods and services for counseling but may barter if there is no exploitation; (c) offer pro bono, volunteer, or reduced services when possible; and (d) consider the implication of accepting gifts.

F. **Other Roles**

1. **consultant:** MHCs (a) focus on the issues to be resolved, not on personal characteristics of the consultant; (b) secure an agreement that specifies the nature of the consultation; (c) ensure that they and the client can follow through on the consultation plan; (d) encourage growth, autonomy, and self-direction; (e) keep all information confidential; and (f) avoid conflicts of interests.

2. **advocate:** CMHCs advocate on the individual, institutional, professional, and societal level for clients and communities. They (a) avoid conflicts of interest, avoid inappropriate relationships, and are sensitive to cross-cultural issues; (b) may encourage clients to advocate for themselves; (c) are clear and accurate in their communication when speaking on behalf of a counseling organization; and (d) speak factually.

II. **Commitment to Other Professionals**

A. **relationship with colleagues:** CMHCs treat colleagues with respect, give credit for publications, do not accept or offer referral fees, and try to rectify unethical conduct informally but go to the appropriate board or ethics committee when they cannot.

B. **clinical consultation:** CMHCs may seek consultation from other mental health professionals and when acting as a consultant, provide critical and supportive feedback.

III. **Commitment to Students, Supervisees, and Employee Relationships**

A. **relationships with students, interns, and employees:** CMHCs respect supervisees, students, and employees and do not exploit them, counsel them, engage in sexual behavior with them, or harass them. In addition, they (a) ensure that they accurately represent their training, experience, and credentials; (b) have their students or supervisees notify their clients if they are in supervision; (c) ensure ethical behaviors by them; and (d) provide a written informed consent document for supervision.

(continued)

B. **commitment for clinical supervision**
    1. **confidentiality of clinical supervision:** Supervision helps ensure good treatment, provides gatekeeping, and is confidential. Supervisors do not disclose information except when (a) there is imminent danger; (b) it is mandated by law; (c) there is a written confidentiality waiver; (d) a release of records is permitted by law; and (e) when information has been deidentified for educational and training settings.

IV. **Commitment to the Profession**

A. **teaching:** CMHCS ensure that when teaching, their information is accurate, current, and educational.

B. **research and publications:** Researchers seek advice if their research deviates from the original plan with human participants. Researchers are (a) open and honest; (b) protect the participant from danger or harm, minimize distress; (c) tell participants they can withdraw at any point; (d) ensure participants that information obtained is confidential; (e) offer informed consent to institutions involved in the research; and (f) ensure those institutions involved in the research are given feedback and acknowledgement.

C. **service on public or private boards and other organizations:** When serving on government or organizational capacities, CMHCs adhere to the CMHC Code of Ethics.

V. **Commitment to the Public**

A. **public statements:** When making public statements, CMHCS accurately represent their background and credentials and ensure public statements will aid the public in making informed decisions.

B. **marketing:** CMHCS ensure accurate information is given when marketing their professional services.

VI. **Resolution of Ethical Problems**

The American Mental Health Counselors Association and its constituent boards and committees do not investigate ethical complaints. If a member has their license suspended or revoked by a state licensure board, the AMHCA board of directors can suspend or revoke their membership.

Adapted and reduced from "AMHCA Code of Ethics," pp. 1–17. Copyright © 2020 by American Mental Health Counselors Association (AMHCA). Adapted with permission.

EXPERIENTIAL EXERCISE 6.1 **Examining Ethics Codes**

Using the paraphrased or full versions of the AMHCA or ACA code, students can pick items that they think are important and the instructor can lead a discussion about that item in class.

In addition to AMHCA and ACA's ethics codes, there are ethics codes of several divisions and affiliated groups of ACA. Highlighting just a few of these, the American School Counselors Association (ASCA) and the International Association for Marriage and Family Counselors (IAMFC) both have their own codes (ASCA, 2022; IAMFC, 2017). Also, the Association for Specialists in Group Work has Guiding Principles for Group Work that supplements the ACA code and other codes (ASGW, 2021). In addition, the National Board for Certified Counselors (NBCC) and the Commission on Rehabilitation Counselor Certification (CRCC) both have separate codes for counselors (CRCC, 2023; NBCC, 2016).

Related Codes of Ethics

Besides ACA and its divisions and affiliates, there are ethics codes of several related mental health professions. For instance, there are ethical codes from the American Psychological Association (2017), NASW (2021a), American Association of Marriage and Family Therapists (AAMFT, 2015), American Psychiatric Association (2013), and National Organization of Human Services (NOHS, 2015). Although there is certainly much in common between the various ethical standards, differences do exist.

Which Code Should You Use?

If you were a member of AMHCA and ACA and were also a national certified counselor (bestowed by NBCC), which code should you use? Although similar, there are differences, and deciding which code, or codes, to use when faced with a difficult ethical dilemma could be a tedious process. Summarizing some of the opinions in the literature and experts on ethics, here are a few tips when deciding which code to adhere to (ACA, 2014; AMHCA, 2020; Barsky, 2019; 2021; B. Canfield & M. E. Wade, personal communications, September 10, 2020):

- Ensure your informed consent process includes a statement about which code(s) you use and adhere to that statement.
- Usually use the code of the professional association(s) to which you belong.
- When deciding which of multiple codes to use, do not use a code because it happens to agree with your point of view.
- If you are a member of multiple associations, decide if one code takes precedence because of your type of employment and affiliation (if you are a CMHC, use the AMHCA, not the NCC code).
- If multiple codes have equal standing and disagree with one another, generally use the one that has stricter guidelines.
- You probably need to adhere to a specific code if legal requirements require you to (e.g., some state licensing boards require adherence to certain codes).
- If there is a conflict between codes and the law, try to resolve the conflict, but if this is not possible, it may be okay to follow the law if you are working in the best interest of your client.
- Use an ethical decision-making model, and include the varying suggestions listed by the different codes in your decision-making process (see decision-making models later in this chapter).

ETHICAL "HOT SPOTS" FOR COUNSELORS

By examining complaints filed against counselors, inquiries made by helpers regarding ethical problem areas, and research that examines ethical concerns with which counselors most struggle, we can identify some areas where counselors are most likely to face difficult ethical decisions, or as I like to call them, ethical hot spots (Carlisle et al., 2022; Çerkez et al., 2018; Wilkinson et al., 2019). As you read the hot spots in Table 6.1, you may notice that some of the items could fit under more than one category.

TABLE 6.1 Ethical "Hot Spots" Grouped Into Logical Categories

Category	Ethical Hot Spot
Counseling Relationship/ Boundaries	Bartering for counseling services
	Encouraging clients to text a counselor
	Expressing strong feelings toward a client
	Giving clients one's personal phone number
	Pressuring a client to receive needed services
	Becoming sexually involved with a former client
	Hugging a client (e.g., to say hello, say goodbye, or console a client)
	Attending a client's wedding, graduation, or other formal ceremony
	Conducting counseling while walking through a park or another informal way
	Selling a product to your client related to the counseling relationship (e.g., a book)
Values and Culture	Publicly advocating for a cause
	Referring a client because of cultural differences
	Referring a prospective client because of religious differences
	Accepting clients only from specific cultural, ethnic, or gender groups
	Referring a client before the first session because of values differences
	Choosing not to counsel an LGBTQ+ client because of values differences
	Encouraging clients' autonomy and self-determination without regard for their cultural background
Confidentiality	Seeing a minor without parental consent
	Not reporting when you suspect spousal abuse
	Guaranteeing confidentiality for group members
	Guaranteeing confidentiality for couples and families
	Withholding information about a minor despite a parent's request
	Sharing confidential information with an administrative supervisor or a colleague who is not your clinical supervisor
	Warning a third party (e.g., spouse, significant other, sexual partner) of exposure to a communicable and life-threatening disease
	Breaking confidentiality because of foreseeable harm (formerly called "duty to warn"; see Reflection Exercise 6.1)
Legal and Professional Issues	Misrepresenting a credential to the public
	Breaking the law to protect your client's rights
	Allowing a mandated client to refuse counseling services
	Not allowing clients to view process notes about them (notes to jog one's memory)
	Refraining from making a diagnosis to protect a client from a third party (e.g., an employer)

(Continued)

TABLE 6.1   (*Continued*)

Category	Ethical Hot Spot
Professional Responsibility	Taking on medication compliance monitoring
	Using techniques that are not theory or research based
	Not being a member of a professional association in counseling
	Not providing pro bono services to clients who cannot afford services
	Failing to obtain necessary continuing education credits for a credential
	Allowing a client access to a counselor's personal social media (e.g., Facebook)
	Reporting a colleague's unethical conduct, without first consulting the colleague
	Not creating a specific informed consent document focused on distance counseling
	Not contacting another mental health professional with whom your client is actively working
Technology	Having a professional website that is not accessible for people with hearing and visual impairments
	Viewing a client's personal information online without informing your client (e.g., Twitter, Facebook, or blog; see Activity 6.1)

REFLECTION EXERCISE 6.1   The Tarasoff Case and Foreseeable Harm

In this case, a client named Prasenjit Poddar, who was being seen at the counseling center at the University of California at Berkeley, told his psychologist that because of his girlfriend's recent threats to break up with him and date other men, he intended to kill her (Paul, 1977). As a result, his psychologist informed his supervisor and the campus police of his client's threat, at which point the campus police detained the client. The supervisor reprimanded the psychologist for breaking confidentiality, and finding no reason to detain Poddar further, the campus police released him. Two months later, he killed his girlfriend, Tatiana Tarasoff. Tarasoff's parents sued the university, therapist, supervisor, and police and won their suit against all but the police. The decision, which was seen as a model for duty to warn (now called foreseeable harm), was interpreted by courts nationally to mean that a therapist must make all efforts to prevent danger to another or self.

EXPERIENTIAL EXERCISE 6.2   Ethical Hot Spots

After reflecting on the ethical hot spots in Table 6.1, discuss them in small groups and come up with four scenarios related to four hot spots and discuss how the issue might be dealt with. Then, present the salient points of your discussion to the class.

RESOLVING ETHICAL DILEMMAS: MODELS OF ETHICAL DECISION-MAKING

Given the practical limitations of ethical guidelines noted earlier, models of ethical decision-making have been devised to assist in the ethical decision-making process (Burkholder et al., 2020; Cottone & Claus, 2011; Welfel, 2016). This section of the chapter examines four types of models: problem-solving, moral, social constructionist, and developmental. These models are not mutually exclusive; that is, they can be used in conjunction with one another. Regardless of the model used, the cultural, religious, and worldview (CRW) identities of the counselor and client should be taken into account when the counselor is faced with a difficult ethical decision (Bray, 2019; Hendricks et al., 2015; Luke et al., 2013).

Problem-Solving Models

Problem-solving models provide the clinician with a step-by-step approach to making ethical decisions. A practical and hands-on approach, these models are particularly useful for the beginning clinician. One eight-step, practical model, developed by Corey et al. (2024), consists of

1. identifying the problem or dilemma,
2. identifying the potential issues involved,
3. reviewing the relevant ethical guidelines,
4. knowing the applicable laws and regulations,
5. obtaining consultation,
6. considering possible and probable courses of action,
7. enumerating the consequences of various decisions, and
8. deciding on the best course of action.

This and other similar models can greatly aid the clinician in the sometimes-thorny ethical decision-making process.

Moral Models (Principle and Virtue Ethics)

Whereas Corey's model emphasizes pragmatism, other models stress the role of moral principles in ethical decision-making and focus on principled ethics or virtue ethics (Hill, 2004). Karen Kitchener's principled ethics model is often described as foundational for developing ethical codes (Kitchener, 1984, 1986; Urofsky et al., 2008) and encourages counselors to embrace the attitudes of (a) autonomy, which has to do with protecting the independence, self-determination, and freedom of choice of clients; (b) nonmaleficence, which is focused on "doing no harm" when working with clients; (c) beneficence, which highlights promoting the good of society which can be fostered by focusing on the well-being of the client; (d) justice, which refers to providing equal and fair treatment to all clients; and (e) fidelity, which is related to maintaining trust in the counseling relationship (e.g., keeping conversations confidential) and being committed to the client within that relationship. A sixth moral principle, veracity, is attributed to Meara et al. (1996), which has to do with being truthful and genuine with the client within the context of the counseling relationship. The clinician who adheres to the moral model will use all these principles to guide their decision-making process.

Whereas principled ethics encourages counselors to focus on adhering to certain principles, virtue ethics suggests the character of the counselor is critical to ethical decision-making (Kleist & Bitter, 2013). For instance, Meara et al. (1996) suggest that virtuous helpers are prudent, or careful and tentative in their decision-making; maintain integrity; are respectful; and are benevolent. Others suggest that helpers should be self-aware, compassionate, understanding of cultural differences, motivated to do good, and have a vision concerning decisions that are made (Welfel, 2016). Obviously, such virtues should drive a counselor's actions.

Social Constructionist Perspective

A recent addition to ethical decision-making, the social constructionist perspective, sees knowledge (e.g., information in codes about how to make wise ethical decisions) as intersubjective, changeable, and open to interpretation (Cottone, 2011; Guterman & Rudes, 2008; Raskin & Debany, 2017). This perspective suggests realities are socially constructed, constituted through language, organized and maintained through narratives (stories), and assumes there are no essential truths (Freedman & Combs, 1996). Taking a postmodern perspective, they believe traditional ways of viewing ethical dilemmas can, at times, be problematic, often as the result of the language used and embedded in one's culture and in society. Such language, they suggest, is sometimes oppressive of others, particularly those from nondominant groups. They question what we often take for granted when making ethical decisions, such as having a client's diagnosis drive the decision-making process or having one's theoretical perspective push a counselor toward certain ways of acting. Instead, the social constructionist looks to have a dialogue with others to develop new ways of understanding situations. These others may include the client, others intimately involved with the client (partners, significant others, etc.), and the counselor's supervisor. And sometimes, they suggest all should sit and talk together about the solution.

Although fully aware of ethical guidelines, those who embrace a social constructionist perspective do not expect "answers" to come from a code, within themselves, or within other people. They view dialogue among people as critical to understanding the multifaceted stories that the client holds and view such dialogue as a mechanism to develop new stories. The social constructionist approaches clients with humility, as equals, with wonder, and as collaborators with whom solutions to ethical problems can be jointly worked out with them and others.

Developmental Models

Developmental models, created by individuals like *Lawrence Kohlberg* (1984), *William Perry* (1970), and *Robert Kegan* (1982, 1994), suggest counselors at "higher levels" of development have some qualities that make the ethical decision-making more nuanced and complex than counselors who are at lower levels of development. (Lloyd-Hazlett & Foster, 2017; Wagner & Hill, 2015). Although not developed to address ethical codes, these models have been applied to our understanding of how individuals respond to such codes. They assert counselors at lower levels of development want "the answer" to complex questions that might face them, such as those involved in difficult ethical decisions. These counselors often adhere to a rigid view of the truth and expect (or, at the very least, hope) that such formal documents as ethical codes hold the answer to complex ethical dilemmas. They are also likely to look at those in positions of authority and power (e.g., supervisors) as being able to quickly tell them the correct answer when faced with thorny ethical dilemmas. Such counselors can be said to be making meaning from what Perry calls a dualistic perspective, in that they view the world in terms of black-and-white thinking, concreteness, rigidity, oversimplification, stereotyping, self-protectiveness, and authoritarianism. In contrast, higher-level counselors, sometimes called individuals committed in relativism, are more complex thinkers, open to differing opinions, flexible, empathic, sensitive to the context of the ethical dilemma, and nondogmatic (Lambie et al., 2009; Lambie et al., 2010; Lloyd-Hazlett & Foster, 2017; McAuliffe & Eriksen, 2010). Although few adults (or counselors) reach the highest levels of development, these models suggest that, if afforded the right opportunities, most can.

You can see how individuals at lower levels would make ethical decisions in very different ways than individuals at higher levels, even when the ultimate decision is the same. Counselor education programs often offer opportunities to support and challenge students to move toward these higher levels of development (Landon & Schultz, 2017; Letourneau, 2016; Purgason et al., 2016).

Summarizing and Integrating the Models

After reviewing the different models in Table 6.2, read the ethical dilemma presented in Case Study 6.1. First, consider separately how the problem-solving, moral, and social constructionist models would approach the ethical dilemma faced in the vignette. Then, using the developmental model, consider how a person of higher development could integrate all the models in responding to the dilemma. When you complete the ethical dilemma, consider Reflection Exercise 6.2.

TABLE 6.2 Summary of Ethical Decision-Making Models

Moral Models	Theoretical Assumptions	Principles or Key Points	Role of the Counselor
Problem-Solving Model	Uses a step-by-step, practical, pragmatic, and hands-on approach.	*Eight steps*: identifying the problem or dilemma, identifying the potential issues involved, reviewing the relevant ethical guidelines, knowing the applicable laws and regulations, obtaining consultation, considering possible and probable courses of action, enumerating the consequences of various decisions, and deciding on the best course of action	Go through the steps one by one.
Principle Ethics	These six principles are foundational to ethical codes. Decisions are based on these principles and on what should be done.	*Six principles*: autonomy, nonmaleficence, beneficence, justice, fidelity, and veracity	Consider the six principles in making an ethical decision.
Virtue Ethics	The focus is on the character of the counselor, who strives to make ideal decisions based on these virtues.	*Four virtues*: prudence, integrity, respectfulness, and benevolence	The counselor needs to be self-aware, compassionate, culturally astute, consider doing good, have a vision, and embrace the four virtues in making an ethical decision.

(Continued)

TABLE 6.2 (*Continued*)

Moral Models	Theoretical Assumptions	Principles or Key Points	Role of the Counselor
Social Constructionist Model	Knowledge in codes is intersubjective, changeable, and open to interpretation. Realities are socially constructed, constituted through language, organized, and maintained through narrative (stories). There are no essential truths. Ethical dilemmas may be the result of inequities in society subtly supported through language.	Solutions to ethical dilemmas come out of a dialogue between a counselor, their clients, their supervisor, and others.	The counselor approaches the client with humility, as an equal, with wonder, and as a collaborator with whom solutions to ethical problems can be jointly worked out.
Developmental Model	Counselors at "lower" levels of development have less of some qualities effective in ethical decision-making than those who are at "higher" levels. All individuals can increase their levels of development.	*Dualistic counselors:* black-and-white thinking, concreteness, stereotyping, oversimplification, self-protectiveness, and authoritarianism *Relativistic counselors*: complex thinkers, open to differing opinions, flexible, empathic, sensitive to the context of the ethical dilemma, and nondogmatic	The counselor embodies qualities of the relativist, in an effort to work through ethical dilemmas.

CASE STUDY 6.1   **Using the Ethical Decision-Making Models**

Angela, an 84-year-old great-grandmother, has 4 children and 13 grandchildren and is dying of pancreatic cancer. Her disease is debilitating, and she is in quite a bit of pain. Therefore, as her counselor, you have agreed to see her periodically in her home. You know that she only has a few precious months to live. At one point, during a counseling session, she tells you her pain is getting the best of her and the morphine given to her barely takes the pain away. She is a proud woman and does not want her children or her grandchildren to see her suffer. She asks you whether you could expedite her death by giving her a dose of morphine she knows will kill her. Although you refuse, she tells you that if you don't help her out, she'll do it on her own. She tells you that she wants her children and grandchildren to remember her as a healthy strong woman, not sickly. You leave thinking she is likely going to kill herself. What should you do? Carefully consider the following questions:

1. Consider the four ethical decision-making models, and using the ethical code of AMHCA and/or ACA, come to a decision about what you should do.
2. Do your morals play a role in the decision you make?
3. What place do your values play in any decision you make?
4. What does the ethics code suggest you might do?
5. What place might the legal system play in your decision?

EXPLORING CMHCS' PERCEPTIONS OF ETHICAL BEHAVIOR

Even though ethical codes guide our behavior, perceptions of what is, or is not, ethical can vary greatly. For instance, when a sample of CMHCs were asked to rate whether 76 potential counselor situations were ethical, a great deal of disparity was found on a number of items, as shown in Table 6.3 (Carlisle et al., 2022; review Table 6.3, and then complete Experiential Exercise 6.3).

TABLE 6.3 Percentage of Counselors Rating Behaviors as Ethical

Behavior	Percent Ethical
1. Showing unconditional acceptance to my clients	98.5
2. Making a diagnosis based on the *DSM-5*	95.3
3. Providing services to an undocumented worker (sometimes referred to as having "illegal" status)	92.9
4. Using an interpreter when a client's primary language is different from yours	92.0
5. Using self-disclosure as a purposeful counseling technique	90.8
6. Counseling a terminally ill client who wishes to explore a hastened death	90.5
7. Verifying the identity of a distance client whom you cannot see, prior to beginning a counseling session	88.0
8. Providing counseling over the internet (i.e., distance counseling)	87.4
9. Referring a client because of interpersonal conflicts between you and your client	85.8
10. Keeping client records on your office computer	83.7
11. Consoling your client by touching him or her (e.g., placing your hand on his or her shoulder)	77.8
12. Allowing a mandated client to refuse counseling services	75.0
13. Not being a member of a professional association in counseling	74.4
14. Conducting a counseling session while walking with a client through a park	72.9
15. Hugging a client (e.g., to say hello or goodbye or to console a client)	72.8
16. Publicly advocating for a cause that is different from widely held views in your professional organization	68.0
17. Attending a client's wedding, graduation ceremony, or other formal ceremony	64.1
18. Sharing confidential client information with your administrative supervisor	64.0

(Continued)

TABLE 6.3 (*Continued*)

Behavior	Percent Ethical
19. Referring a client due to cultural differences	59.9
20. Telling your client you are angry at them	59.8
21. Warning a third party (e.g., a spouse, significant other, or sexual partner) of exposure to a communicable and life-threatening disease of one of your clients	58.2
22. Taking on medication compliance monitoring	57.0
23. Not allowing clients to view process notes about them (notes to jog one's memory)	56.9
24. Withholding information about a minor client despite a parent's request for information	56.9
25. Encouraging autonomy and self-determination regardless of the client's culture	54.7
26. Referring a prospective client due to religious differences between the counselor and the client	56.1
27. Guaranteeing confidentiality for couples and families	51.6
28. Encouraging clients to text you if they need you	51.0
29. Based on personal values, choosing not to counsel and, instead, referring an LGBTQ+ client to another counselor	50.4
30. Refraining from making a diagnosis to protect a client from a third party (e.g., an employer)	49.4
31. Reporting a colleague's unethical conduct without first consulting with the colleague	46.9
32. Referring a client before the first session because your personal values conflict with the presenting problem on the client's intake document	43.6
33. Not reporting when you suspect that your client is being abused by their spouse	45.9
34. Giving clients your personal phone number	44.4
35. Bartering (accepting goods or services) for counseling services	42.6
36. Breaking the law to protect your client's rights	42.2
37. Not providing pro bono or other free services to clients who cannot afford services (e.g., free counseling, lectures, disseminating counseling related information, or psychoeducational groups)	41.7
38. Having a professional website that is not accessible for people with hearing and visual impairments	41.6
39. Not contacting another mental health professional with whom your client is actively working	40.2
40. After completing all PhD coursework, using the acronym "ABD" (all but dissertation) with your name on business cards and other written forms of communication	40.0
41. Becoming sexually involved with a former client, at least 5 years after the counseling relationship ended	39.8
42. Using the same informed consent document when conducting face-to-face and distance counseling	37.3
43. Guaranteeing confidentiality for group members	36.9
44. Selling a product to your client that is related to the counseling relationship (e.g., a book)	35.6
45. Using techniques that are not theory or research based	32.8
46. Sharing confidential client information with a colleague who is not your supervisor	28.5
47. Charging for individual counseling while seeing all members of a family	28.1
48. Seeing a minor without parental consent	27.5

TABLE 6.3 (*Continued*)

Behavior	Percent Ethical
49. Pressuring a client to receive needed services	26.6
50. Based on knowledge and interests, accepting clients who are only from specific cultural, ethnic, or gender groups	25.6
51. Viewing your client's personal information online (e.g., Twitter, Facebook, blog, Google) without informing your client	25.4
52. Setting your fee higher for clients with insurance than for those without	24.4
53. Accepting a client when you haven't had training in their presenting problem	22.7
54. Counseling clients from a different culture with little or no cross-cultural training	21.7
55. Becoming sexually involved with a person your client knows well	19.4
56. Not having malpractice coverage (on your own or by your agency/setting)	18.0
57. Referring clients unhappy with their same sex attraction for sexual orientation change therapy (e.g., "reparative" or "conversion therapy")	17.9
58. Not allowing clients to view their counseling records (excluding process notes—notes used to jog your memory)	13.3
59. Trying to change your client's personally held beliefs or values	13.1
60. Engaging in multiple relationships with your clients (e.g., your client is also your child's teacher)	12.6
61. Revealing confidential information if a client is deceased	11.3
62. Not having a plan to transfer your clients should you become incapacitated	9.5
63. Accepting a gift from a client that's worth more than $25	9.0
64. Not confirming a medical diagnosis before warning a third party of a potentially hazardous exposure to a disease	8.4
65. Providing distance counseling across state lines without verifying one's legal professional status within the client's state of residence	7.2
66. Kissing a client as a friendly gesture (e.g., greeting)	6.9
67. Telling your client you are attracted to them	6.9
68. Trying to persuade your client to not have an abortion, even though they want to	5.4
69. "Friending" clients on your personal social networking sites (e.g., Facebook)	4.6
70. Failing to explain the risks and benefits of a new technique or developing theory that will be used with a client	4.3
71. Failing to provide access to emergency services information for distance clients	4.1
72. When conducting distance counseling, using software without confirming it meets HIPAA regulations	3.6
73. Not taking action when a severely depressed client suggests they have decided to commit suicide	3.1
74. Contacting another professional with whom the client is in a helping relationship without telling the client	3.0
75. Treating transgender individuals as pathological	2.7
76. Treating same sex attractions as pathological	2.3

Table 6.3: Kristy L. Carlisle, Dana H. Levitt, and Edward S. Neukrug, Selection from "Mental Health Counselors' Perceptions of Ethical Behaviors," Counseling and Values, vol. 67, no. 1, pp. 96–100. Copyright © 2022 by American Counseling Association. Reprinted with permission.

EXPERIENTIAL EXERCISE 6.3 **Discussing Controversial Ethical Behaviors**

After reviewing the counselor behaviors in Table 6.3, identify four or five you think are particularly controversial. Write down your thoughts about the behavior. If your instructor suggests, and with other students, discuss the items chosen. Are there any items that several students chose? If so, while referring to the AMHCA (2020) and/or ACA (2014) code, see if you are able to come to a consensus on how to work with that dilemma. The full version of the AMHCA Code of Ethics can be found in the News and Events section of https://www.amhca.org/home and the full version of the ACA Code of Ethics can be found by clicking the Knowledge Center at www.counseling.org.

REPORTING ETHICAL VIOLATIONS

The AMHCA (2020) code suggests that if a colleague is impaired, shows incompetence, or acts in an unethical manner, one should first attempt to rectify the situation informally with the that person. If this fails, they should report the situation to the licensing board and/or ethics committee of the professional association to which the colleague belongs. Like the AMHCA code, the ACA's ethical code (2014) first encourages complainants to try and resolve the issue informally by discussing the situation directly with the counselor who is suspected of violating the guideline (see Reflection Exercise 6.3). If no resolution is found, or if substantial harm is suspected, then counselors are asked to take "further action," which could include any or all of the following: "referral to state or national committees on professional ethics, voluntary national certification bodies, state licensing boards, or appropriate institutional authorities" (ACA, 2014, Standard I.2.b; see Reflection Exercise 6.3).

When a complaint is received, ethics committees first examine whether they have the jurisdiction to address the complaint. For instance, if a complaint comes to the ACA ethics committee concerning a licensed counselor and the counselor in question is not a member of ACA, then the ethics committee will likely refer the complainant to the ethics committee of the licensing board within the state the person is licensed.

Recent studies have indicated the most common disciplinary actions for ethical violations include fines (54%), mandatory continuing education (45%), and receiving a reprimand (28%). Indefinite suspension and probation fall just beneath these, both with a frequency of about 19% (Ahia & Boccone, 2017). However, studies have demonstrated a major discrepancy between whether states take disciplinary actions at all and what disciplinary measures are taken in response to specific ethical violations (Wilkinson et al., 2019).

REFLECTION EXERCISE 6.3
The Importance of an Informal Resolution of an Ethical Violation

A friend of mine reported a psychologist to the psychology licensing board for writing inferior assessment reports. However, she did not go directly to the psychologist. She, who was also a psychologist, ended up being reprimanded by the licensing board because she had not first gone to the professional she was accusing. The accusations against the professional were never addressed.

If you had a colleague who was acting unethically, would you be able to talk to them directly? Would it depend on the seriousness of the ethical violation? What would prevent you from talking to your colleague?

LEGAL ISSUES RELATED TO ETHICAL VIOLATIONS

Some legal issues related to ethics are important to know about when working as a CMHC. These include the concepts of civil liability and criminal liability, the role of ethical codes in lawsuits, the importance of malpractice insurance, and engaging in best practices to avoid lawsuits.

Civil and Criminal Liability

Because some complainants consider potential suspension or expulsion from a professional group too mild a punishment, they may opt to initiate a civil lawsuit or, if they suspect a possible criminal act, report it to the authorities in hopes of criminal prosecution of the counselor. Whereas "criminal liability is the responsibility under the law for a violation of federal or state criminal statute, civil liability is the responsibility one has as a result of having violated a legal duty to another" (personal communication, C. Borstein, Esq., January 25, 2023). This was widely recognized in the O. J. Simpson legal travails. Because the burden of proof in a criminal case is "beyond a reasonable doubt" but in a civil case is "by a preponderance of the evidence," it's not too surprising that Mr. Simpson was found guilty in a civil court but not guilty in a criminal court. To highlight these differences, imagine the scale of justice. In a criminal case, the scale needs to sharply drop to one side to establish the defendant's guilt beyond a reasonable doubt; in a civil suit, where the penalty is money rather than potential incarceration, the scale need tilt only slightly in the plaintiff's favor to obtain a verdict and a potential judgment.

In instances of alleged malpractice, complainants most often initiate civil suits against counselors, although counselors could also be charged with criminal violations in the criminal courts. For example, if a counselor is alleged to have had sex with a client in violation of a state statute, a prosecuting attorney (e.g., district attorney) could bring criminal charges against the counselor in criminal court while the client (the alleged victim) may pursue a civil court action against the counselor for monetary damages. Anyone can bring a civil lawsuit alleging virtually anything; however, outlandish cases are generally dismissed in a timely manner, and some states have even set up procedures to penalize an individual for arbitrary and capricious acts of malicious prosecution and abuse of process in filing unwarranted lawsuits.

The Role of Ethical Codes in Lawsuits

Generally, ethical guidelines are not legal documents, although some states pass statutes stating an ethical code is a legal document that helpers must follow (NASW, 2023). When not a legal document, whether a counselor is involved in a criminal or civil suit, a professional association's code of ethics can still be an important piece of evidence. For instance, a counselor would have a difficult time defending having had sex with a client because all ethics codes greatly frown or disallow such behavior. However, cases are often not clear-cut. For example, consider a case in which a counselor has sex with a former client. The former client feels abused and brings the case to a prosecutor, who determines that the AMHCA Code of Ethics clearly states that counselors "should not knowingly enter into a romantic or sexual relationship with a former client" (AMHCA, 2020, Section I.A.4.b) and decides to bring criminal charges against the counselor. However, during the trial, the counselor's attorney brings the the AMHCA code to court, which also states, "If a CMHC chooses to enter into such a [sexual] relationship, the burden to demonstrate that neither coercion nor harm to the client has transpired is on the CMHC and not the former client" (AMHCA, 2020, Section I.A.4.b), which clearly implies sexual relationships can be consensual in some circumstances. You can see that ethics codes can be complex, and even contradictory at times.

Malpractice Insurance

In today's litigious society, there is little doubt that counselors need to be particularly careful because even when they are faithfully following their ethical code and the law, they might still be sued. Remember, anyone can be sued by anybody! Certainly, this does not mean a counselor will lose a frivolous suit. However, if a counselor finds themselves in the dubious position of not having malpractice insurance and subsequently loses a civil suit, that counselor may be haunted by the monetary settlement for the rest of their life. There is little question that in today's world, malpractice insurance is a necessity. Although most schools and agencies purchase an umbrella malpractice insurance policy, it is still prudent to carry additional insurance protection. Also, if you work in a setting that has purchased a malpractice policy, review it carefully, study its monetary limits, and examine any possible exclusions to the policy (see ACA, 2023 and AMHCA, 2023). For instance, are you covered if you work after hours? What if your employer lets you run a workshop for your own personal profit at the agency on the weekend? Are you still covered?

Although colleges and universities almost always carry malpractice insurance for students doing practicum and internship, again, it is always best to check and see if the school does, indeed, have a policy as well as the monetary limits of such a policy. Both AMHCA and ACA provide free malpractice insurance for students (ACA, 2022; AMHCA, 2022), and the typical cost of $1,000,000 worth of malpractice insurance for a self-employed licensed professional tends to be a few hundred dollars, but can vary dramatically, depending on the state in which you live (see Healthcare Providers Service Organization, 2021).

Avoiding Lawsuits: Best Practices

As one can see from the discussion on ethics and the importance of malpractice insurance, making ethical decisions can be an arduous and potentially career-threatening process. It is, therefore, essential that clinicians are equipped with the clinical knowledge and tools necessary to make the best decisions when working with clients. Showing a court you have followed best practices in your profession can be critical in winning a lawsuit. Although ethical guidelines are generally not legal documents, following your professional association's code of ethics can be one important piece of evidence showing you have adhered to best practices. Corey and his colleagues (forthcoming) describe additional ways in which a clinician can ensure that they have been following best practices. Highlighting some of these ways, they note that clinicians should

- know relevant laws;
- maintain good records;
- keep your appointments;
- ensure security of records;
- stay professional with clients;
- document treatment progress;
- have a sound theoretical approach;
- preserve appropriate confidentiality;
- obtain informed consent from clients;
- maintain the confidentiality of records;
- report cases of abuse as required by law;
- treat only within your area of competence;
- avoid imposing your values or influence on clients;
- obtain written permission when working with minors;
- refer when it is in the best interest of your client to do so;
- be attentive to your clients' needs and treat them with respect;
- avoid engaging in sexual relationships with current or former clients;

- obtain permission from a client to consult with others, whenever possible;
- make sure that clients understand the information that you present to them;
- ensure that clients understand that they can terminate counseling at any point;
- know cultural and clinical issues related to bartering and accepting or giving gifts;
- monitor your reactions to clients, especially when countertransference is involved;
- assess clients and explain diagnoses and treatment plans and their risks and benefits;
- provide a professional disclosure statement and obtain informed consent regarding the course of treatment;
- keep appropriate boundaries and know the limitations of multiple relationships (e.g., counseling a person who is a neighbor); and
- know how to appropriately assess for clients who may pose a danger of harming self or others and what to do if you think a client poses a threat.

SUMMARY

This chapter began by distinguishing between values, ethics, and morality as well as the role that legal issues may play when making important ethical decisions. We then discussed the development of, and need for, ethical codes, noting there are several purposes of ethics codes as well as limitations to codes.

As the chapter continued, we highlighted the ethics codes of AMHCA and of ACA. The AMHCA code was summarized in the chapter, and a summary of the ACA code was posted in Appendix A. However, we encouraged you to read the full codes and provided the websites on which they can be found. We also noted there are several other codes from counseling organizations, including those of ASCA, IAMFC, NBCC, and CRCC as well as codes of related professional groups, including NASW, AAMFT, NOHS, the American Psychological Association, and the American Psychiatric Association. We then highlighted eight points to consider when one is affiliated with more than one code.

The chapter next examined over 40 ethical "hot spots" for counselors, noting that they generally fit into several categories, including counseling relationships and boundaries, values and culture, confidentiality (we looked at the Tarasoff case and foreseeable harm), legal and professional issues, professional responsibility, and technology.

We identified four models of ethical decision-making and examined them in some detail, including problem-solving, moral, social constructionist, and developmental models. We also noted that regardless of the model used, the cultural, religious, and worldview (CRW) identities of the counselor and client should be considered when making difficult ethical decisions. We offered Table 6.2 as a summary of the models.

The chapter next identified 76 potential ethical concerns of CMHCs and highlighted whether a sample of CMHCs viewed each situation as ethical or unethical. We suggested you examine those ethical concerns and reflect upon, and discuss, the most controversial ones in class. After reviewing the potential ethical concerns, we discussed the importance of trying to resolve unethical behavior of a colleague, informally, with that person, except when there is potential of substantial harm to another. If an attempt at an informal resolution does not work, it was suggested to report the person to the licensing board and/or the ethics committee of the counselor's professional organization.

We concluded the chapter by examining legal issues related to ethical violations, such as distinguishing between civil and criminal liability, the role of ethical codes in lawsuits, the importance of malpractice insurance, and a number of best practices counselors should adopt in the interest of working effectively and avoiding lawsuits.

KEY WORDS AND TERMS

ACA Code of Ethics
AMHCA Code of Ethics
autonomy
beneficence
benevolent
best practices
character of the counselor
civil liability
committed in relativism
criminal liability
cultural, religious, and worldview
  (CRW) identities
development of, and need for,
  ethical codes
developmental models
dualistic perspective
duty to warn
ethical hot spots

ethics
ethics codes of several
  divisions and affiliated
  groups of ACA
ethics codes of several related
  mental health professions
fidelity
foreseeable harm
Guiding Principles for Group
  Work
integrity
justice
legal issues related to ethical
  violations
limitations to codes
malpractice insurance
models of ethical decision-
  making

moral models
morals
nonmaleficence
postmodern
principled ethics
problem-solving models
prudent
respectful
several purposes of ethics
  codes
social constructionist
  perspective
Tarasoff case
values
veracity
virtue ethics
which code should you use?

KEY NAMES

Kegan, Robert
Kitchener, Karen
Kohlberg, Lawrence
Perry, William

PROFESSIONAL ASSOCIATIONS AND ORGANIZATIONS

Healthcare Providers Service Organization (HPSO)

CHAPTER 7

CULTURALLY COMPETENT COUNSELING

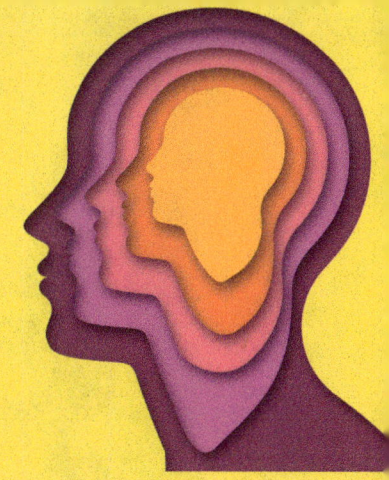

Learning Goals

- Learn about the importance of culturally competent counseling.
- Review nine reasons many diverse clients are wary and distrustful of counseling.
- Understand basic definitions of culturally competent counseling.
- Become knowledgeable of important words and terms related to an understanding of differentness, oppression, and social awareness.
- Review and obtain an understanding of the four domains of the Multicultural and Social Justice Counseling Competencies (MSJCC).
- Relative to the MSJCCs, understand how privilege and marginalization impact the counseling–client relationship.
- Review 12 factors that contribute to culturally competent counseling.
- Learn how to implement the 12 factors that contribute to culturally competent counseling by using the RESPECTFUL model of counseling.
- Highlight culturally competent counseling and social justice as the "fourth" and fifth" forces of helping.

INTRODUCTION

Every person is like all persons, like some persons, and like no other persons …

(Kluckohn & Murray, 1953, p. 335)

Growing up in New York City was a world unto itself: the diverse ethnic foods, the multicultural music, the people—oh, how I loved to watch the people. Walk down a Manhattan street, and you can watch an endless sea of people, a sea that seems to change color as it flows by you, a sea whose shape transforms constantly; and if you flow with it long enough, you can visit every part of the world. There is no question that New York gave me a multicultural perspective many people don't have. However, despite this exposure to a variety of cultures and ethnic groups, I never really got below the surface. I could taste the foods, I

IMAGE 7.1

could see the people, and I could listen to the music, but that experience was from a detached perspective. Even though I might see the brightly colored clothes of a Nigerian person, I still didn't know that person. Even though I could taste the sushi, I didn't understand the world of Japanese people. And even though I could listen to Latin music, I didn't really understand the people.

This chapter examines the demographics of the United States and argues for the necessity of counselors understanding, and being accepting of, many diverse individuals if they are to be effective. It then strengthens this argument by providing nine examples of why some diverse clients are wary and distrustful of counselors and counseling. Next, we offer definitions of culturally competent counseling and follow this up with a number of words and terms counselors should know. The chapter then moves on to a discussion of the Multicultural and Social Justice Counseling Competencies (MSJCC), which is a roadmap for how to be a culturally competent counselor. The chapter concludes by suggesting 12 factors that contribute to culturally competent counseling and how to apply them.

WHY CROSS-CULTURAL COUNSELING?

There is little doubt that we live in a pluralistic country and are thus called to offer counseling services to clients from many diverse backgrounds (see Table 7.1). In fact, the United States is becoming increasingly diverse, and by the year 2043, nondominant racial groups are expected to comprise the majority of the population. By 2060, America will look quite different than it does today (U.S. Census Bureau, 2020; see Table 7.1).

TABLE 7.1 Changes in Racial and Ethnic Composition of the United States Over Time

	Non-Hispanic White	Hispanics	African-American	Asian	American Indian	Native Hawaiian/ Other Pacific Islander	Two or More Races
2020	61.3%	17.8%	13.3%	5.7%	1.3%	.2%	2.6%
2060	44.3%	27.5%	15%	9.1%	1.4%	.3%	6.2%

These changing demographics are a function of several factors, such as higher birth rates within nondominant populations; most legal immigrants now being Asian, Black, and Latinx; and immigration rates being the highest in American history (U.S. Census Bureau, 2022; U.S. Department of Homeland Security, 2022). Like past immigrants, many immigrants today claim a strong affiliation to their cultural heritage. These factors have also led to changes in the religious composition of the United States (Public Religion Research Institute, 2021). Although still decidedly Christian (about 72%), the United States is less Christian than in the past, as Buddhists, Hindus, Jews, Muslims, other religions, and non-affiliated individuals, have become more widespread. In addition, about 6% of non-Christians are atheists or agonistics (see Table 7.2).

TABLE 7.2 Number and Percentage of Individuals from Select Racial, Ethnic, Religious, Sexual Orientation, and Gender Identity Groups in the United States

	Number (in Millions)	Percentage
Ethnicity/Race		
White	251,238,736	75.8%
Black/African American	45,077,134	13.6%
American Indian and Alaska Native	4,308,843	1.3%
Asian	20,218,420	6.1
Native Hawaiian and Other Pacific Islander	994,349	0.3
Two or More Races	9,612,032	2.9%
Hispanic/Latinx	62,643,959	18.9%
White/Not Hispanic	196,549,565	59.3%
Sexual Orientation and Gender Identity		
Lesbian/Gay	~4,200,000	1.0/1.5
Bisexual	~13,500,000	4.0%
Transgender	~2,400,000	.7%
LGBT	24,000,000	7.1%
Straight/Heterosexual	~290,550,000	86.3%
Religion		
Total Christian		44%
White Mainline Evangelical Protestants		14%
White Mainline (Nonevangelical) Protestants		16%
White Catholics		12%
Mormon		< 2%
Jehovah's Witness		< 2%
Orthodox Christian		< 1%
Hispanic Catholics		8%
Black Protestants		7%
Hispanic Protestants		4%
Protestants of Color		4%
Other Catholics of Color		2%
Jewish		1%
Muslim		1%
Hindu		1%
Buddhist		.5%
Unitarian Universalist		.2%
Other Religion		1%
Unaffiliated		23%
Atheist or Agnostic		6%
Total Affiliated With a Religion		72%

Note. Data on ethnicity/race is from the U.S. Census Bureau (2019), on sexual orientation and gender identity from Jones (2022), on religion from the Public Religion Research Institute (2021). Data on sexual orientation and gender identity may be low due to the social stigma of identifying as LGBTQ+.

In addition to increasing ethnic, cultural, and religious diversity, there has been greater acceptance of diversity in gender identity, gender role stereotypes, gender equality, and same-sex relationships (Ekstam, 2022; Pew Research Center, 2013; 2019; Notestine & Leeth, 2020; Parker et al., 2022; Szymanski & Carretta, 2019). Increased understanding and acceptance of differences seems more the norm today, although there are clearly many who are not happy with these changes.

Changes in local, state, and federal laws have precipitated a gradual move toward acceptance of diversity in our culture and have given many Americans a heightened sensitivity to, and awareness of, the many diverse groups that make up the United States. With changing laws and demographics, and because CMHCs should ethically and morally be able to effectively counsel all clients, it is crucial that CHMCs make sure their approach to helping works with a wide variety of clients. Unfortunately, this has not always been the case.

WHY SOME CLIENTS ARE WARY OF COUNSELING

Imagine being distrustful of counselors, confused about the counseling process, or feeling worlds apart from the counselor you were seeing. Would you want to begin, or continue in, a counseling relationship? Assuredly not. Unfortunately, this is the way it is for many clients from diverse backgrounds. In fact, when compared to Whites, culturally diverse clients are more likely to be spoken down to, find the counseling relationship less helpful, seek mental health services at lower rates, and terminate the counseling prematurely (Escobar, 2012; Lo et al., 2013; National Alliance on Mental Illness [NAMI], 2023; Smith & Tremble, 2016; U.S. Department of Health and Human Services, 2014). The reasons for diverse clients being distrustful of counseling are historical and complicated; however, the following are *nine reasons some clients are wary of counseling* (Hays & Erford, 2018; McAuliffe, 2020a, 2020b; Sue et al., 2019):

- **the melting pot myth:** For many years, mostly Whites saw the United States as a melting pot, believing individuals form different cultures would assimilate into "American" culture. Although some assimilation occurs with individuals from all cultures, the history of immigration in the United States has mostly seen new immigrants, from similar backgrounds, living in the same communities and maintaining their unique ethnic and cultural background. This cultural mosaic has brought beauty and differences to this country. If counselors assume clients should "melt into" the greater American culture, they are likely to make the clients feel as if they should be somebody other than who they are.

  example: A counselor encourages a client who lives with individuals from their own culture, in a poorer section of town, to move to a "safer [and Whiter] part of town." The client feels as if they are being "pushed" to do something they do not want to do and to leave those with whom they are most comfortable. It leaves them feeling conflicted about their counselor.

- **inability to adapt the counseling relationship:** Most counseling theories are developed from a Eurocentric, White, male perspective and emphasize individualism, expression of feelings, cause and effect, self-disclosure, and the importance of insight. Clients from some cultures, however, may not value these attributes and would feel uncomfortable with such an approach. Despite this, some counselors find it difficult, or never even consider, adapting their approach to the cultural perspective of the client.

  example: A Vietnamese client is encouraged to talk about their feelings regarding their family's immigration to the United States, even though their posture and tone of voice suggest they are not comfortable with this. Expression of feelings is not the norm in Vietnam, and the client feels embarrassed, put on the spot, and wronged when they try to refuse.

- **lack of understanding of social forces:** Counselors are well trained in examining how internal forces (e.g., thoughts, unconscious factors, or feelings) impact the kinds of choices made by clients. However, such a focus sometimes neglects how external forces, such as prejudice and discrimination, can impact a client.

  example: A female client who is being paid less at her job than her male counterparts, is distraught about the pay inequity. The counselor asks, "What are you saying to yourself to make you feel so badly." In this case, it might be better for the counselor to help the client advocate for an equitable pay raise.

- **ethnocentric worldview:** If a counselor assumes the client's worldview should be similar to their worldview, the counselor may have a negative reaction to a client who believes differently about certain subjects. The counselor may even believe the client's reactions are an indication of emotional instability or client misunderstanding. The counselor should, instead, respect client's worldview.

  example: A counselor inadvertently offends a Muslim client when she says to her, "Have a wonderful Christmas." The counselor shows nonverbal indignation when the client states they don't celebrate Christmas.

- **ignorance of one's own unconscious bias:** Research has shown that almost everyone has some amount of unconscious bias toward certain groups. However, when a counselor makes no attempt to monitor their bias, it can impact clients in negative ways.

  example: A counselor who believes he is accepting of all gender identities unconsciously believes being transgender is against the laws of nature. When working with a transgender female, the counselor is not aware that he grimaces when the client describes the transitioning process. The client drops out of counseling.

- **inability to understand cultural differences in the expression of symptomatology:** Expression of symptoms can vary dramatically as a function of the cultural background of the client. A counselor who assumes that certain symptoms are indicative of pathology may not realize the client is simply expressing a common symptom from the client's culture. This can clearly lead to misdiagnosis and mistreatment.

  example: A Puerto Rican born client living in New York City presents with somatic complaints and is immediately referred to his family practitioner, as the counselor believes there is a medical concern. Although ensuring the health of the client may be fine, the counselor didn't realize that somatization is a common way of showing grief in some Latinx cultures, and in this case, it was a response by the client to dearly missing their daughter, who is back in Puerto Rico.

- **unreliability of assessment and research instruments:** Over the years, assessment and research instruments have notoriously been culturally biased. Although they have improved, an astute counselor should ensure all instruments are effective with all populations before using them.

  example: A diverse client is given a cognitive ability test by a counselor to assess the client's ability at being a firefighter. Although the test predicts well for Whites, it predicts poorly for many diverse clients and should not be used in this instance. It would have been best if another form of assessment (e.g., a performance-based assessment that measures actual on-the-job performance) had been used.

- **institutional discrimination:** Because racism, heteronormativity, prejudice, and bias, are embedded in society, they often go unrecognized and become a natural but unhealthy part of organizations and institutions.

    example: A mental health agency consistently has African Americans males diagnosed as schizophrenic at higher rates than other clients. Actually, African Americans do not have higher rates of schizophrenia, but training programs and mental health centers have done a poor job understanding how to properly conduct a clinical interview with African American males, and they often get misdiagnosed.

- **individualistic perspectives:** Whereas Whites tend to view the world from an individualistic perspective (I can pick myself up from my bootstraps), some cultural groups have historically had a collectivistic perspective, where consulting parents, elders, or wise individuals in their culture is the norm. If counselors assume a client should be the deciding force in decision-making, they may turn off a client, or even upset the broader system, as they push the client to decide without consulting an important person within the client's circle.

    example: A client who is American Indian wants to consult with their elders before making an important decision regarding getting married. The counselor, however, suggests the client should make the decision on their own, as this would be a sign of maturity. The client feels confused, upset, and caught between two different cultural beliefs. Having the client consult with their elders would have been more natural and healthier in this case.

These nine examples highlight some of the reasons the counseling relationship has *not* been effective for many clients from diverse backgrounds. They demonstrate the need for counselors to be culturally competent and for greater sensitivity in counseling diverse clients. By attending to these issues, and similar ones, counselors can improve their understanding of diversity, be able to make better treatment plans, see a decrease in the dropout rate when counseling clients who are diverse, and see an increase in client satisfaction with the helping process.

DEFINING CULTURALLY COMPETENT COUNSELING

Is it possible to connect with and understand a client who is from a cultural, racial, ethnic, or other background different from you own? What critical skills are necessary for counselors to learn if they are to work effectively with clients from nondominant groups? These are some of the crucial questions that must be asked when defining culturally competent counseling. McAuliffe (2020c) suggests culturally competent counseling is "a consistent readiness to identify the cultural dimensions of clients' lives and a subsequent integration of culture into counseling work" (p. 5). Sue and Torino (2005) suggest culturally competent counseling "can be defined as both a helping role and process that uses modalities and defines goals consistent with the life experiences and cultural values of clients, utilizes universal and culture-specific helping strategies and roles, recognizes client identities to include individual, group, and universal dimensions, and balances the importance of individualism and collectivism [emphasis added] in the assessment diagnosis and treatment of client and client systems" (p. 6; see Figure 7.1).

In addition to the these two definitions, culturally competent counseling involves having knowledge of words and terms critical to understanding clients. Let's take a look at some of them.

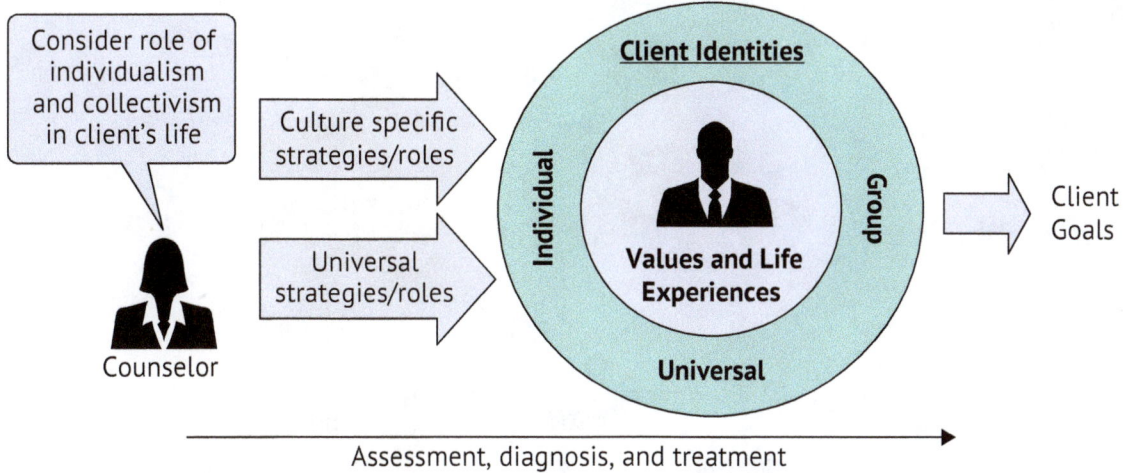

FIGURE 7.1 Defining Culturally Competent Counseling

WORDS AND TERMS TO KNOW

To understand differences and to communicate effectively with others, it is important to know definitions of commonly used words and terms related to cross-cultural counseling. Let's examine some of these terms including culture; ethnicity; intersectionality. microaggressions; minorities and nondominant groups; oppression; prejudice; privilege; race; religions and spirituality; sexual orientation and gender identity; social class (class); stereotypes, and racism; systemic inequality, and other words and terms.

Culture

Shared values, symbols, language, and ways of being in the world are some of the words associated with culture. One's culture is expressed through common values, habits, norms of behavior, symbols, artifacts, language, and customs (McAuliffe, 2020c; Sewell, 2009; Spillman, 2016).

Ethnicity

When a group of people shares a common ancestry, such as similar language, values, religion, foods, and artistic expressions, they are said to be of the same ethnic group (Jenkins, 2007; McAuliffe et al., 2020d). Ethnicity is based on long-term patterns of behavior that have some historical significance, not on genetics.

Intersectionality

Today, the counseling and psychology professions suggests intersectionality is when "membership in multiple marginalized identities results in unique circumstances that cannot be effectively captured through the examination of just one axis of identity" (Shin et al., 2017, p. 462). Using this focus, we can see how several social identity positions discussed in this chapter, such as race, social class, gender, sexual orientation, and others, overlap to create unique systems of discrimination and disadvantages for marginalized clients (Ali & Lee, 2019; see Figure 7.2). For instance, a Black woman experiences discrimination, racism, and sexism in a different way than a White woman, Asian woman, or Black man. Thus, learning

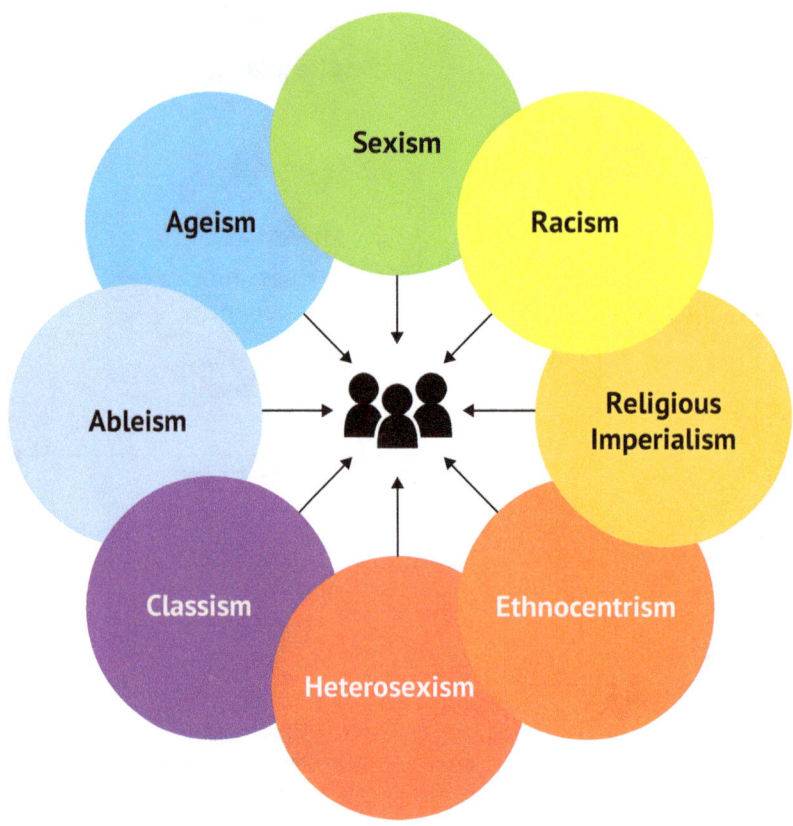

FIGURE 7.2 Examples of Intersectionality of Identities.

about the impact of each client's intersecting social identity positions can help counselors determine how to best work with, and advocate for, them in creative and meaningful ways.

Microaggressions

Microaggressions are subtle, sometimes unconscious, behaviors that denigrate others and are usually experienced through individual interactions directed toward individuals from diverse cultures (Groth-aus et al., 2020; Nadal, 2011; Sue et al., 2019). Examples include statements like, "You don't seem 'gay' [or 'Black,' or …]," and "My ancestors made it in this country; I don't see why your family can't," as well as providing poor or slow service at a restaurant or store and differential treatment by police or others in positions of power.

Minorities and Nondominant Groups

Historically, the word minority described any person or group of people who are singled out because of their cultural or physical characteristics and are systematically oppressed by those individuals who are in a position of power (Macionis, 2019). Using this definition, minorities could conceivably be the numerical majority of a population, as was the case for many years for Blacks in South Africa and as is the situation with women in the United States. In recent years, we have seen the counseling profession increasingly use the term nondominant group rather than, or in addition to, minority because the term nondominant group suggests there are social causes (the oppression by dominant groups) causing distress to other (nondominant) groups.

Oppression

Oppression is the systematic restriction from, and access to, opportunities and tends to be targeted toward individuals based on age, gender, sexuality, race, disability status, ethnicity, and religion (Grothaus et al., 2020). The systemic nature of oppression makes it difficult to "prove" because it is supported by existing policies and institutional practices.

Prejudice, Stereotypes, and Racism

Generally, all three of these words are related to preconceived ideas or attitudes people have toward others. Whereas prejudice has to do with judging a person or group based on preconceived notions (e.g., gays are no good; therefore, I hate John because he's gay), stereotyping is the rigidly held belief that most or all members of a group share certain characteristics, behaviors, or beliefs (e.g., Asians are intelligent people, or Native Americans are alcoholics; Jennings, 2015; Pickering, 2017). Racism is believing one racial group is superior to another (e.g., Whites are better than Blacks) and is based on social construction of race (Arthur, 2007).

Privilege

When a population is systemically granted power, access, and opportunities because of the social categories they are perceived to belong to, they have privilege. Those with privilege can influence others, control resources, and place themselves in situations where they are the powerbrokers in society (Johnson, 2006; Kishimoto, 2018; Tarver & Herring, 2019).

Race

According to Chou, "In the biological and social sciences, the consensus is clear: **race is a social construct**, not a biological attribute" (2017, Does "Race" Still Mean Something? section, para. 2). Race has traditionally reflected visible phenotypic characteristics, such as eye color, hair texture, skin color, body shape, and size, and has historically been thought to be based on genetic differences. However, this concept has been debunked, and race is now seen as a social construction based on ambiguous categorization of people's perceived characteristics (McAuliffe et al., 2020e). In fact, research on the human genome shows humans share much more genetically than was once thought, with genetic differences between two people only being 0.1% (Duello et al., 2021; National Human Genome Research Project, 2018.

Religion and Spirituality

Religion is an organized set of practices and beliefs that has moral underpinnings and helps define a group's way of understanding the world (Cipriani, 2016; Fox et al., 2020). In contrast, spirituality is seen as residing in a person and defines the person's understanding of self in relationship to others and to a self-defined higher power, or lack thereof. Because religion is concerned with values from an external referent group and spirituality has more to do with internal processes, important differences exist between how one would counsel a person struggling with religious concerns (e.g., value differences

> ## REFLECTION EXERCISE 7.1   What Race Are You Anyway?
>
> Although most people tend to think of themselves as one race or another, take a look at what happened in one study that examined the genetic heritage of a group of students at Pennsylvania State University:
>
>> About 90 students took complex genetic screening tests that compared their samples with those of four regional groups. Many of these students thought of themselves as "100 percent" White or Black or something else, but only a tiny fraction of them, as it turned out, actually fell into that category. Most learned instead that they shared genetic markers with people of different skin colors. (Debunking the concept of race, 2005, para. 2)
>
>> Reflect on your "race." Are you sure you are what you think you are? How might your assumptions about your race be right or wrong? How might your assumptions of your race have affected your understanding of yourself and others? How might your assumptions about your race be a social construction that is it is developed through conversations we have with others?

between self and a religious group) versus a person struggling with spiritual concerns (e.g., finding meaning in life).

Sexual Orientation and Gender Identity

Whereas sexual orientation is the sexual feelings, romantic attractions, longings, and attachments one has toward a person or others (Szymanski & Carretta, 2020), one's sex is defined by one's genitals and associated reproductive organs, gonads, chromosomes, and hormones. However, .7% of individuals are born with bodies that differ from what is considered standard male or female, such as external genitalia of one gender and internal genitalia of another and are identified as people who are intersex (Blackless, 2000; InterACT, 2021). Differing from one's sex, a person's gender identity is an individual's internal experience of self relative to maleness, femaleness, or some combination thereof (Szymanski & Carretta, 2020). One's gender expression, on the other hand, includes the ways in which a person outwardly presents themselves through visible characteristics, such as mannerisms and attire. Finally, one may have romantic attractions to men, women, both, or none (Szymanski & Carretta, 2020). However, romantic attractions may or may not be in sync with one's sexual feelings towards a person. As you can see, there is an infinite number of potential combinations, as highlighted in the genderbread person (see Figure 7.3).

These days, the initialism *LGBTQIA* is used to describe individuals who are lesbian, gay, bisexual, transgender, questioning, intersex, and/or asexual (Szymanski & Carretta, 2020). However, this leaves a host of other individuals who may identify as agender, pansexual, polygender, and more. In fact, partly to be more inclusive, the Association for Lesbian, Gay, Bisexual, and Transgender Issues in Counseling, a division of the American Counseling Association (ACA), is now called the Society for Sexual, Affectional, Intersex, and Gender Expansive Identities (SAIGE; see www.saigecounseling.org; see Reflection Exercise 7.2).

The Genderbread Person v4  by *it's pronounced* METROsexual.com

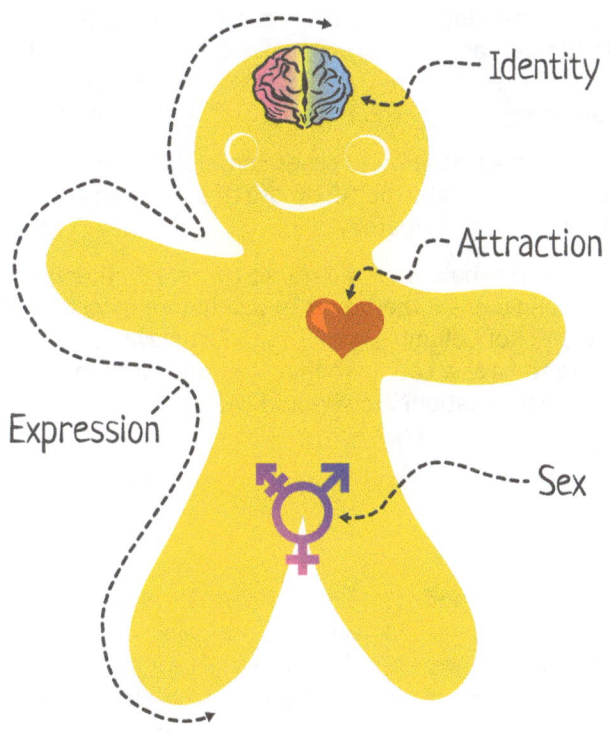

⊘ means a lack of what's on the right side

 **Gender Identity**
⊘ ⟶ Woman-ness
⊘ ⟶ Man-ness

Gender Expression
⊘ ⟶ Femininity
⊘ ⟶ Masculinity

Anatomical Sex
⊘ ⟶ Female-ness
⊘ ⟶ Male-ness

Identity ≠ Expression ≠ Sex
Gender ≠ Sexual Orientation

Sex Assigned At Birth
☐ Female ☐ Intersex ☐ Male

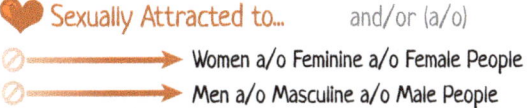 **Sexually Attracted to...**   and/or (a/o)
⊘ ⟶ Women a/o Feminine a/o Female People
⊘ ⟶ Men a/o Masculine a/o Male People

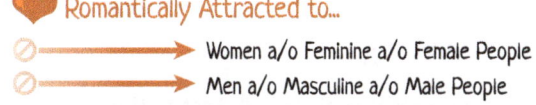 **Romantically Attracted to...**
⊘ ⟶ Women a/o Feminine a/o Female People
⊘ ⟶ Men a/o Masculine a/o Male People

Genderbread Person Version 4 created and uncopyrighted 2017 by Sam Killermann   For a bigger bite, read more at www.genderbread.org

FIGURE 7.3 The Genderbread Person

REFLECTION EXERCISE 7.2 **Sexual Orientation Change Efforts (Conversion and Reparative Therapy)**

In recent years, guidelines developed by AMHCA and ACA regarding sexual orientation change efforts, referred to in the past as conversion therapy or reparative therapy, state that all counselors refrain from using or referring to these therapies due to their lack of scientific efficacy and the harm they can cause to clients. For instance, ACA (2023) states the following:

> The American Counseling Association opposes conversion therapy because it does not work, can cause harm, and violates our Code of Ethics. It is an attempt to treat something that is not a mental illness. (para. 1)

When dealing with clients who wish a referral to conversion therapy, they ask counselors to discourage this practice and explain the potential deleterious effects of such treatment. Meanwhile, 20 states, the District of Columbia, and Puerto Rico have banned the practice (PBS News Hour, 2023). If you were to have a client who was seeking to change their sexual orientation, how might you handle that situation? How would the previous statement by ACA drive what you do?

Social Class (Class)

Social class, socioeconomic status, and class are often used interchangeably. Collectively, this construct is based on a person's education, income, and wealth and represents the perceived ranking of an individual within society and the amount of power an individual wields (Goodspeed-Grant et al., 2020; Macionis, 2019; Vitt, 2020). It also denotes access to, or restriction from, resources. For example, one who has lower income, little education, and no measurable wealth has lower class status and may experience barriers to needed resources to meet their basic needs.

Systemic Inequality

> Slavery was America's "original sin." It was not solved by the framers of the U.S. Constitution, nor was it resolved by the horrendous conflict that was of the American Civil War. It simply changed its odious form and continued the generational enslavement of an entire strata of American society. (Allen, 2020, para. 2)

Systemic inequality, sometimes called systemic or institutional racism, has to do with how society systemically oppresses and discriminates against certain nondominant groups (O'Dowd, 2020, para. 3). For instance, within the United States, those who are wealthy, White, heterosexual, able-bodied, and male tend to have more advantages and opportunities than others, despite existing laws, institutional policies, and practices designed to foster equity for various populations.

Other Words and Terms

The American Psychological Association (APA, 2021) has Inclusive Language Guidelines that define most words and terms of which you should be aware. You are encouraged to download them, for free, at https://www.apa.org/about/apa/equity-diversity-inclusion/language-guidelines.pdf.

THE MULTICULTURAL AND SOCIAL JUSTICE COUNSELING COMPETENCIES

> Both the multicultural and social justice counseling perspectives acknowledge the importance of diversity and recognize that oppression has a debilitating effect on mental health. Together, both perspectives promote the need to develop multiculturally and advocacy competent helping professionals. (Ratts, 2011, p. 24)

Until 2015, there were two distinct sets of competencies—multicultural and social justice. However, recognizing the intimate relationship between the two, they were merged into the Multicultural and Social Justice Counseling Competencies (MSJCC); (Ratts et al., 2015, 2016). Today, the competencies reflect the minimum standards needed by all counselors if they are to work effectively with diverse clients (Bray, 2019; Counselors for Social Justice, 2021).

There are four domains of the competencies: (a) counselor self-awareness, (b) client worldview, (c) counseling relationship, and (d) counseling and advocacy interventions. Each of the first three domains are defined by attitudes and beliefs, knowledge, skills, and action. The last domain focuses on social justice work related to the following areas: intrapersonal, interpersonal, institutional, community, public policy, and international and global affairs (see Figure 7.4).

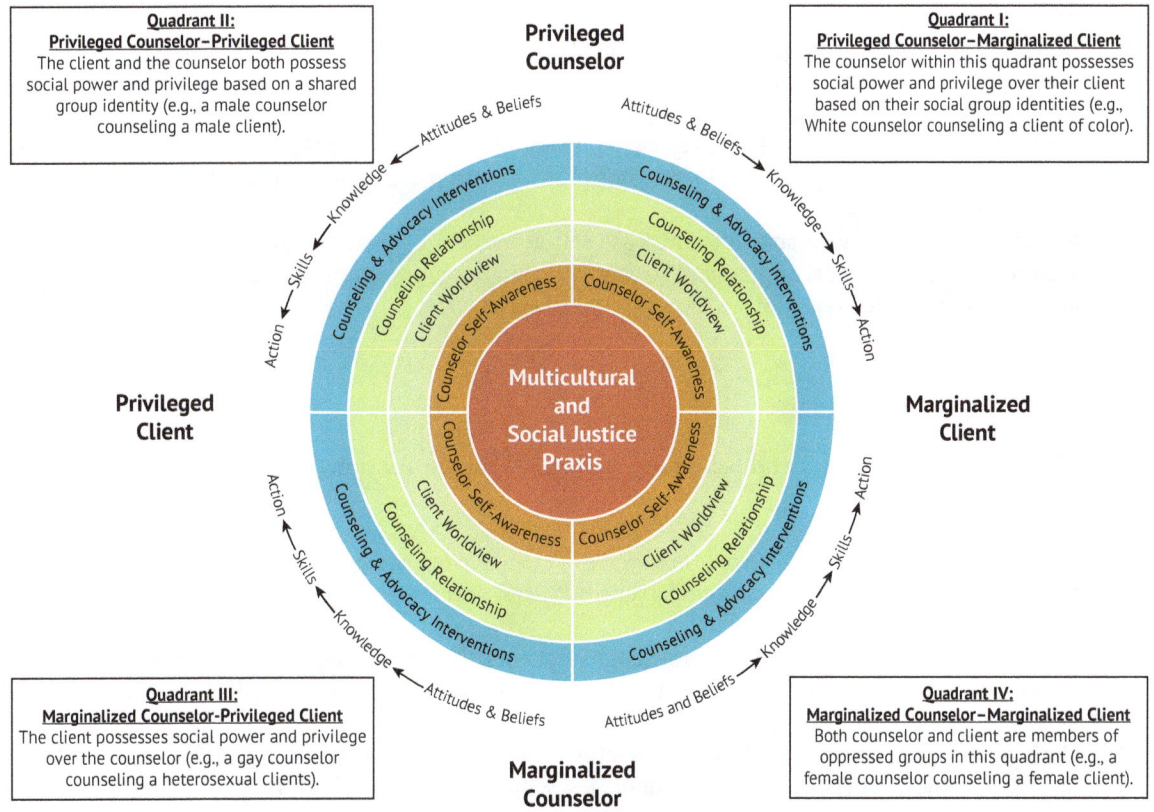

FIGURE 7.4 The Multicultural and Social Justice Competencies

There is a logical sequence to the MSJCCs, in that it begins with self-awareness (inner circle of Figure 7.4). Here, the counselor works on becoming increasingly aware of their own cultural values, beliefs, and biases. Next, there is natural movement toward understanding the client's worldview and how it is impacted by culture, oppression, power, discrimination, and privilege. Understanding self and other leads to a stronger counseling relationship that takes into account the nature of how the factors, just noted, impact the client and the counselor. Finally, when counselors are tuned into how "power, privilege, oppression and social group status shape the counseling relationship," they are better at understanding and suggesting personal interventions the client can embrace and social interventions the client or counselor can take (Ratts et al., 2016, p. 42). Here, we see how specific actions on the part of the client, or on the part of the counselor, can actively address social maladies and assist clients in living a more enriched life. Finally, by juxtaposing privileged or marginalized counselors with privileged or marginalized clients, we can examine how these four positions (the four quadrants) might also impact the counseling relationship. Let's take a close look at the four domains.

Domain I: Counselor Self-Awareness

The following are the attitudes and beliefs, knowledge, skills, and actions associated with the first domain—counselor self-awareness:

- **attitudes and beliefs:** Counselors "are aware of their social identities, social group statuses, power, privilege, oppression, strengths, limitations, assumptions, attitudes, values, beliefs, and biases."
- **knowledge:** Counselors "possess an understanding of their social identities, social group statuses, power, privilege, oppression, strengths, limitations, assumptions, attitudes, values, beliefs, and biases."
- **skills:** Counselors "possess skills that enrich their understanding of their social identities, social group statuses, power, privilege, oppression, limitations, assumptions, attitudes, values, beliefs, and biases."
- **action:** Counselors "take action to increase self-awareness of their social identities, social group statuses, power, privilege, oppression, strengths, limitations, assumptions, attitudes, values, beliefs, and biases." (Ratts et al., 2015; see Experiential Exercise 7.1)

Domain II: Client Worldview

The following are the attitudes and beliefs, knowledge, skills, and actions associated with the second domain—the client worldview:

- **attitudes and beliefs:** Counselors "are aware of clients' worldview, assumptions, attitudes, values, beliefs, biases, social identities, social group statuses, and experiences with power, privilege, and oppression."
- **knowledge:** Counselors "possess knowledge of clients' worldview, assumptions, attitudes, values, beliefs, biases, social identities, social group statuses, and experiences with power, privilege, and oppression."
- **skills:** Counselors "possess skills that enrich their understanding of clients' worldview, assumptions, attitudes, values, beliefs, biases, social identities, social group statuses, and experiences with power, privilege, and oppression."

Excerpts taken from Manivong J. Ratts, et al., The Multicultural and Social Justice Counseling Competencies. Copyright © 2015 by American Counseling Association. Reprinted with permission.

EXPERIENTIAL EXERCISE 7.1 The Counselor's Awareness About Privilege

Awareness of the kinds of privilege some have is important when working with clients, as it helps us understand that due to life circumstances, some clients have a much more difficult time than others. This exercise helps us examine the kinds of privilege we have had in our lives and can be done in one of two ways:

- **if done in a classroom:** Stand in a line about 10 feet away from the instructor while facing the instructor. The instructor will then read each of the statements found in Appendix B, and each student should simply follow the instructions (take a step back or forward for each statement). This will visually show you who has grown up with more privilege.
- **if done on your own:** Read the statements and place a plus sign next to each statement if you were to take a step forward and a minus sign next to each statement if you were to take a step back. Students can then count all their plusses and minuses and add them up (e.g., 7 plusses and 5 minuses equals 2 plusses overall). Then, the instructor can obtain the average score from the class and each student can compare their score to the average score.

After the exercise is completed, students can discuss the following questions:

- How advantageous is it to have privilege in our society?
- How disadvantageous is it to not have privilege in our society?
- If you grew up with privilege, what would your life be like if you hadn't had it?
- If you grew up with little privilege, what would your life be like if you did have it?
- How might your experience of privilege impact how you do counseling?

- **action:** Counselors "take action to increase self-awareness of clients' worldview, assumptions, attitudes, values, beliefs, biases, social identities, social group statuses, and experiences with power, privilege, and oppression" (Ratts et al., 2015; see Reflection Exercise 7.3).

REFLECTION EXERCISE 7.3 Counselor's Knowledge About Clients

Read the case description in Part 1, and then based on your knowledge of visually impaired, indigent Irish Americans, consider how you might have greeted this man if he had come to your office and what kind of treatment planning you might consider. Then, go on to Part 2, and read how knowledge of the visually impaired and of Irish Americans could have been helpful. Discuss your thoughts on this case in class.

Part 1
Case description: John McGowan, a 70-year-old visually impaired widower with a strong Irish heritage and culture, was brought to a clinician's office by his adult daughter after finding him disheveled, still in his pajamas, and crying over a bowl of uneaten cereal when she checked on him at noon. Between sobs, John could not convey to his daughter what had precipitated this latest incident.

(continued)

When making the appointment, the daughter told the receptionist that her father had experienced other "weepy" episodes since Thanksgiving (3 months ago), but previously she had always been able to coax him out of them by playing some lighthearted Irish music. Since Thanksgiving, her father had had difficulty sleeping and seemed to have lost interest in most things that had previously given him pleasure. She added that her mother, who also strongly identified as Irish, had died suddenly of a heart attack 15 months ago. Her father had always depended on his wife to "be his eyes" and to care for his daily needs. They had met while still in parochial high school and became engaged shortly after graduation. When John was 19, he suffered severe visual impairment from a car accident, which prevented him from completing a plumber's apprenticeship. During their subsequent 48-year marriage, his wife supported them both, and neighbors cared for their daughter during work hours. John spent his days reading Braille versions of poetry and fiction, with unrealized aspirations of being a writer. Since his wife died, he had learned to use a cane but resisted the idea of having a Seeing Eye dog. As a result, he was mostly confined to his small apartment, leaving only to have a drink on Saturday night at the local bar, to attend Sunday mass, and to visit his daughter's family. He had very limited financial resources because he was no longer covered by his deceased wife's pension; however, the daughter was so concerned that she agreed to pay "out of pocket" for her father's treatment (Hansen et al., 2000, p. 656).

Part 2

The following is a description of how a clinician might work with this client if they had knowledge of the visually impaired and of indigent Irish Americans:

Imagine that Dr. Smith has knowledge and experience in working with visually impaired, indigent Irish Americans. With this background, she may have decided to meet initially with John alone—out of respect for the characteristically strong Irish sense of privacy. She would use the "sighted guide technique" for greeting him in the waiting area, asking simply, "Would you like to take my arm?" On entering her office, the clinician would inquire if John wanted a description of the space, being sure to note the possible seating options and the location of windows and lighting (because some visually impaired individuals are adversely affected by glare and illumination). She might begin the interview with factual questions regarding his current living situation, the extent of his visual impairment, and his recent medical and psychological symptoms, only later broaching. the more emotion-laden topic of the death of his wife. Likely, she would consider multiple hypotheses regarding the etiology of his depression, including his unresolved grief over the death of his wife, his lack of adequate independent coping skills in her absence, the contribution of his Irish heritage to his reluctance to ask for help and to his fatalistic outlook, the isolation and depression common in visually impaired individuals, the possibility of an organically based onset, plus the real-world economic constraints impinging on his life. The culturally competent psychologist would search for a delicate balance between the need to verbalize facial or bodily gestures to compensate for John's lack of visual acuity and his traditional Irish culture's prohibition regarding overt emotional expressiveness. In keeping with the cultural mandate to avoid direct expressions of difference or conflict, the psychologist would be likely to use humor and storytelling to indirectly explore differences between herself and John (Hansen et al., 2000, pp. 656–657).

Domain III: Counseling Relationship

The following are the attitudes and beliefs, knowledge, skills, and actions associated with the third domain—the counseling relationship:

- **attitudes and beliefs:** Counselors "are aware of how client and counselor worldviews, assumptions, attitudes, values, beliefs, biases, social identities, social group statuses, and experiences with power, privilege, and oppression influence the counseling relationship."
- **knowledge:** Counselors "possess knowledge of how client and counselor worldviews, assumptions, attitudes, values, beliefs, biases, social identities, social group statuses, and experiences with power, privilege, and oppression influence the counseling relationship."
- **skills:** Counselors "possess skills to engage in discussions with clients about how client and counselor worldviews, assumptions, attitudes, values, beliefs, biases, social identities, social group statuses, power, privilege, and oppression influence the counseling relationship."
- **action:** Counselors "take action to increase their understanding of how client and counselor worldviews, assumptions, attitudes, values, beliefs, biases, social identities, social group statuses, and experiences with power, privilege, and oppression influence the counseling relationship" (Ratts et al., 2015; see Experiential Exercise 7.2).

EXPERIENTIAL EXERCISE 7.2 Talking About Cultural Differences in the Counseling Relationship

Sometimes, no one wants to acknowledge the elephant in the room. For instance, when a client is culturally different than the counselor, the counselor and the client often think about their differences but never discuss them. Sometimes this is fine, but in ongoing helping relationships, it is often important to acknowledge differences and talk about how the client's identity has impacted their life, including their relationship with the counselor. Do you possess the skills to "talk race" or other diversity issues with clients in a positive way?

Find a person, in or out of class, who in some way identifies as a member of a nondominant group. Using the following questions, or others, see if you and the person can talk openly and honestly by sharing your responses with each other to the following questions. In class, discuss the ease you had in doing this exercise:

1. Have you experienced any discrimination, prejudice, or bias in your life?
2. When you have faced discrimination, prejudice, or bias in your life, how did you react?
3. What kind of privilege do you think you were denied due to your class, gender, race, sexual orientation, cultural identity, or other differences?
4. What is it like to be [insert the nondominant group to which the interviewee belongs]?
5. How do you think cultural differences could influence a counseling relationship?
6. If I was your counselor, is there anything I could do to positively impact a counseling relationship with you?

Domain IV: Counseling and Advocacy Interventions

The following are the different types and examples of interventions associated with the fourth domain—counseling and advocacy interventions:

- **intrapersonal:** "The individual characteristics of a person such as knowledge, attitudes, behavior, self-concept, skills, and developmental history."
  - **intrapersonal interventions:** Counselors "address the intrapersonal processes that impact privileged and marginalized clients."
- **interpersonal:** "The interpersonal processes and/or groups that provide individuals with identity and support (e.g., family, friends, and peers)."
  - **interpersonal interventions:** Counselors "address the interpersonal processes that affect privileged and marginalized clients."
- **institutional:** "Represents the social institutions in society such as schools, churches, community organizations."
  - **institutional interventions:** Counselors "address inequities at the institutional level."
- **community:** "The community as a whole represents the spoken and unspoken norms, values, and regulations that are embedded in society. The norms, values, and regulations of a community may either be empowering or oppressive to human growth and development."
  - **community interventions:** Counselors "address community norms, values, and regulations that impede the development of individuals, groups, and communities."
- **public policy:** "Public policy reflects the local, state, and federal laws and policies that regulate or influence client human growth and development."
  - **public policy interventions:** Counselors "address public policy issues that impede on client development with, and on behalf of clients."
- **international and global affairs:** "International and global concerns reflect the events, affairs, and policies that influence psychological health and well-being."
  - **international and global affairs interventions:** Counselors "address international and global events, affairs and polices that impede on client development with, and on behalf of, clients" (Ratts et al., 2015; see Experiential Exercise 7.3).

Power and Privilege Within the Counseling Relationship

In the four quadrants highlighted in Figure 7.4, the nature of the counselor–client relationship is described as a function of whether the group identity of the counselor, and client, is marginalized or privileged. There is an assumption that "power, privilege, and oppression influence the counseling relationship to varying

---

EXPERIENTIAL EXERCISE 7.3   Advocating Locally and Globally

I'm confident that the vast majority of students entering the helping professions want to be of service to those who are marginalized and those struggling with life problems. Although the counseling relationship can assist a client in raising their self-esteem and in helping clients learn how to advocate for themselves, another way to help our clients is through institutional, community, public policy, and global advocacy interventions. In small groups, brainstorm ways your group could advocate for individuals. Make a list, and then share it with the class. If class members agree to participate, pick one or two of the items on the list and follow through with them.

degrees" (Ratts et al., 2016, p. 36), and an individual's affiliation with a group identity can play itself out within the counseling relatinship. A counselor who is from a social group identity of privilege may view and act differently toward a client who is from a marginalized social group identity compared to a client who is from a priviliged social group identity. Similarly, a client who is from a marginalized social group may experience a counselor who is from a social group of privilege differently from a counselor who is also from a marginalized social group. Thus, understanding your own background and considering how it impacts your counseling relationship is critical to succesful counseling outcomes.

12 FACTORS THAT CONTRIBUTE TO CULTURALLY COMPETENT COUNSELING

Now that we have defined culturally competent counseling, gave descriptions of some words and terms frequently used by culturally competent counselors, and highlighted the MSJCCs, let's see if we can come up with some common factors that contribute to culturally competent counseling (e.g., Hays & Erford, 2018; McAuliffe, 2020a; Ratts et al., 2015; 2016; Sue et al., 2022). The following are 12 factors that contribute to culturally competent counseling:

- Counselors have self-awareness of their own attitudes and beliefs, knowledge, and skills and are able to use this knowledge effectively in the helping relationship (Domain I of the MSJCC).
- Counselors demonstrate to their clients that they understand their clients' attitudes and beliefs, knowledge, and skills (Domain II of the MSJCC).
- Counselors understand the influence of differences between their clients and themselves in the counseling relationship and acknowledge them when appropriate (Domain III of the MSJCC).
- Counselors help clients learn how to advocate for themselves, and counselors advocate for their clients, when appropriate (Domain IV of the MSJCC).
- Counselors understand and try to adapt to how differences, or similarities, between counselor and client privilege and marginalization impacts the counseling relationship and discuss such differences when appropriate.
- Counselors understand the intersection of various client identities (sexual, cultural, gender, etc.) and consider their complexities when counseling clients.
- Counselors understand the nine reasons clients may be wary of the counseling relationship and do their best to not embody any of them.
- Counselors attempt to understand the client's individual, group, and universal aspects of self.
- Counselors consider whether the client comes from a collectivist or individualistic culture when helping the client set goals and make decisions.
- Counselors are curious, respectful, and humble with their clients.
- Counselors are real, genuine, and empathic with their clients.
- Counselors obtain additional knowledge and skills, including supervision, to enhance their ability to work with a variety of clients from diverse backgrounds.

USING THE RESPECTFUL MODEL TO APPLY THE 12 FACTORS

You may remember from Chapter 1 that we described the RESPECTFUL model as one mechanism of understanding clients. This model suggests that you inquire about the following 10 aspects of the person:

- **R**: religious/spiritual identity
- **E**: economic class background

- **S:** sexual identity
- **P:** level of psychological development
- **E:** ethnic/racial identity
- **C:** chronological/developmental challenges
- **T:** various forms of trauma and other threats to one's sense of well-being
- **F:** family background and history
- **U:** unique physical characteristics
- **L:** location of residence and language differences (Lewis et al., 2011, p. 54)

Using the RESPECTFUL model and applying the 12 factors that contribute to culturally competent counseling, see if you can successfully work with a person who is different from you (see Experiential Exercise 7.4).

THE FOURTH AND FIFTH FORCES

Within the past 25 years, the training in and practicing of multicultural counseling has flourished, CACREP began requiring training in social and cultural counseling, research on cultural competency has mushroomed, and books and articles on cross-cultural counseling have grown exponentially. There is little doubt that a multicultural counseling and social justice focus has become a critical component of what the counselor does. As multicultural counseling gained a foothold, it became evident that a close cousin of culturally competent counseling—social justice and advocacy work—was not far behind in importance (Ratts, 2009). So important have cultural competence and social justice become that many today identify them as the fourth and fifth forces of helping, after the psychodynamic, behavioral, and humanistic traditions of counseling.

EXPERIENTIAL EXERCISE 7.4   Becoming a Culturally Competent Counselor

For this exercise, select and complete either option 1, option 2, or both.

Option 1
Pair up with a student you would like to learn more about. It would be particularly powerful exercise if you could find someone from a culture with which you have little familiarity. Then, with this person, inquire about the items in the RESPECTUL model while applying the 12 factors that contribute to culturally competent counseling. When you are finished, ask the person how comfortable they felt with you. Better yet, have one or two other classmates watch you do the interview and solicit their feedback as well. What areas do you need to work on?

Option 2
Outside of class, find a person who identifies differently than you (e.g., gender, sex, racial group, or ethnicity). Try to pick someone you would have difficulty relating with. Then, using the RESPECTFUL model while applying the 12 factors that contribute to culturally competent counseling, interview that person about their life and problems they may be experiencing. When you are finished, ask the person how comfortable they felt with you. Better yet, have one or two other classmates watch you do the interview and solicit their feedback as well. What areas do you need to work on?

The counselor of today works differently than the counselor of 25 years ago. Today's counselor sees each counseling relationship as a cross-cultural experience, and this counselor applies wisdom from the MSJCC to help each client feel embraced, understood, supported, and has a sense that someone is in their corner advocating for them.

SUMMARY

This chapter started with an examination of the pluralistic nature of the United States and the fact that the country will continue to become more diverse in terms of religion, race, sexual orientation, culture, and more. It was noted that in recent years, there has been greater acceptance of diversity in the United States, although some are clearly not happy with that.

Despite greater acceptance of diversity, diverse clients have a number of reasons for being wary of counseling. Nine of those reasons were highlighted in this chapter, including counselors buying into melting pot myth, an inability to adapt the counseling relationship to the clients cultural background, a lack of understanding of social forces, an ethnocentric worldview, ignorance of unconscious bias, an inability to understand cultural differences in the expression of symptomatology, the use of unreliable assessment and research instruments, ignorance of institutional discrimination, and a focus on individualistic perspectives.

The chapter went on to give two definitions of culturally competent counseling, including McAuliffe's (2020c) statement that it is "a consistent readiness to identify the cultural dimensions of clients' lives and a subsequent integration of culture into counseling work" (p. 5), and Sue and Torino's (2005) belief that it "can be defined as both a helping role and process that uses modalities and defines goals consistent with the life experiences and cultural values of clients, utilizes universal and culture-specific helping strategies and roles, recognizes client identities to include individual, group, and universal dimensions, and balances the importance of individualism and collectivism in the assessment diagnosis and treatment of client and client systems" (p. 6).

We next went on to define several important words and terms related to cross-cultural counseling, including culture; ethnicity; intersectionality. microaggressions; minorities and nondominant groups; oppression; prejudice; privilege; race; religions and spirituality; sexual orientation and gender identity; social class (class); stereotypes, and racism; systemic inequality, and other words and terms. We also noted that the in 2021, the American Psychological Association published its *Inclusive Language Guidelines*, which defines most words and terms of which you should be aware.

The chapter spent a fair amount of time reviewing the Multicultural and Social Justice Counseling Competencies (MSJCC). We noted that there are four domains of the competencies: (a) counselor self-awareness, (b) client worldview, (c) counseling relationship, and (d) counseling and advocacy interventions. Each of the first three domains are defined by attitudes and beliefs, knowledge, skills, and action. The last domain focuses on social justice work, related to the following areas: intrapersonal, interpersonal, institutional, community, public policy, and international and global affairs. We also noted there is movement in each domain from self-awareness to understanding the client's worldview, to understanding self and other in the counseling relationship, to understanding how power, privilege, oppression and social group status shape the counseling relationship.We also noted that understanding how privilege, or marginalization, on the part of the counselor and client, impacts the relationsihp between the two.

The chapter next identified 12 factors that contribute to culturally competent counseling, and we used the RESPECTFUL model as one way to practice how these factors can be used in the counseling relationship. The chapter concluded with a note that cultural competent counseling and social justice work have become so important that some now call them the fourth and fifth forces of helping.

KEY WORDS AND TERMS

agender
asexual
bisexual
class
collectivistic perspective
conversion therapy
cultural mosaic
culture
Domain I: counselor self-awareness
Domain II: client worldview
Domain III: counseling relationship
Domain IV: counseling and advocacy interventions
ethnicity
fifth force
four domains of the competencies
fourth force
gay

gender expression
gender identity
genderbread person
Inclusive Language Guidelines
individualism and collectivism
institutional racism
intersectionality
intersex
lesbian
logical sequence to the MSJCCs
melting pot
microaggressions
minority
Multicultural and Social Justice Counseling Competencies (MSJCC)
nondominant group
oppression
pansexual
polygender

prejudice
privilege
questioning
race
racism
religion
reparative therapy
Respectful model
sex
sexual orientation
sexual orientation change efforts
social class
socioeconomic status (SES)
spirituality
stereotyping
systemic inequality
systemic racism
transgender
12 factors that contribute to culturally competent counseling

PROFESSIONAL ASSOCIATIONS AND ORGANIZATIONS

Society for Sexual, Affectional, Intersex, and Gender Expansive Identities (SAIGE)

CREDITS

CHAPTER 8

ABNORMAL (ATYPICAL) BEHAVIOR, DIAGNOSIS, AND PSYCHOPHARMACOLOGY

Ed Neukrug and Erin Woods

Learning Goals

- Understand the intimate connection between abnormal (atypical) development, diagnosis, and psychopharmacology.

- Review five models that explain abnormal (atypical) development in dramatically different ways: the genetic and biological model, the psychodynamic model, the learning model, the humanistic approach, and the postmodern and social constructionist approach.

- Introduce the history of diagnosis and provide a brief introduction to using the *Diagnostic and Statistical Manual, Fifth Edition, Text-Revision* (*DSM-5-TR*).

- Review advantages and disadvantages of diagnosis.

- Provide an overview of five major categories of psychotropic medications, including antipsychotics, mood-stabilizing drugs, antidepressants, antianxiety agents, and stimulants.

- Examine the ethical, professional, and legal issues regarding the impact of cultural background on symptom expression; when it may be efficacious to diagnose or refrain from diagnosing; when it might be beneficial, or harmful, to confine a person against their will; insurance fraud; and gatekeeping of impaired graduate students.

INTRODUCTION

My uncle was schizophrenic. How he got that way, I'm not sure. He ended up homeless on the streets of New York City, and his brothers and father would periodically try to help him as best as they could. He was hospitalized, lived in group homes, and placed on medication. Nothing seemed to help a great deal. Did he have a genetic predisposition to schizophrenia? Was there some sort of childhood trauma he experienced or were there environmental toxins that might have led him down this road? I don't know and will very likely never know. Could he be helped today with some of the newer therapies and anti-psychotic medications? I'm not sure. I do know that research on the causes of schizophrenia, treatment models that can help a person who experiences schizophrenia, and medication that can assist a person with schizophrenia continues today.

There have been times in my life that I've been seriously depressed and even had suicidal thoughts. Were these times natural responses to difficult situations? Would another person not have been depressed if in my shoes? Do I have a predisposition to depression when under stress? I'm not sure. I do know that during my darkest times, therapy and antidepressants have helped lift me out of my depression. I was not destined to remain depressed as my uncle seemed destined to remain schizophrenic.

This chapter explores abnormal (atypical) development, diagnosis, and psychopharmacology. There is a close relationship between these three areas, as our development is a factor in determining which of the 21% of us will end up with a mental disorder each year, the diagnosis of those individuals who have mental disorders, and what medications might be used to help in the treatment of mental disorders. Let's take a look at abnormal (atypical) development, diagnosis, and psychopharmacology.

WHY STUDY ABNORMAL DEVELOPMENT, DIAGNOSIS, AND MEDICATION?

With evidence that over one-fifth of Americans have a diagnosable mental disorder within any year (Substance Abuse and Mental Health Services Administration, 2020), regardless of where you are employed, you will be working with clients who (a) have serious emotional problems, (b) have been given or need a diagnosis for treatment purposes, and (c) are taking, or need, medication. Although controversy exists about defining abnormality, developing a diagnosis, and using psychotropic medications, all CMHCs today deal with these issues (Allsopp et al., 2019; Perkins et al., 2018; Stein et al., 2020). This has not always been the case.

Counselor–educators and counselors have historically had a disdain for diagnosing and labeling and have, at times, opposed

FIGURE 8.1 Vincent Van Gogh: *At Eternity's Gate*

the use of psychotropic medication (Bonino & Hanna, 2018; Gaete et al., 2017). In fact, learning about psychopathology and the development of mental disorders was frowned upon in counseling programs until the turn of the century (Eriksen & Kress, 2005, 2006, 2008). There were many reasons for this. First, the early history of the counseling profession was largely influenced by humanistic approaches to counseling, which downplayed the notion of abnormal development, the role of diagnosis, and the use of medication. This influence also led counselors to believe training in psychopathology and diagnosis would lead counselors to stigmatize individuals unduly. In addition, many counselors, and counselor educators, believed counselors should only work with "normal" individuals, using a preventive and wellness model, not what was called a deficit model, which was often the treatment of choice when working with those with severe mental disorders. However, in recent years, psychopathology, diagnosis, and psychopharmacology have become important parts of the work of CMHCs for several reasons, including the following:

- Diagnosis can sometimes be helpful in the development of treatment plans, and treatment plans may include the use of medication.
- CMHCs are increasingly working with severely disturbed clients, and they need to know how the diagnosis is related to treatment planning and choice of medication.
- Licensing boards and accrediting bodies require knowledge of psychopathology, diagnosis, and psychopharmacology.
- CMHCs need to know diagnostic procedures, evidence-based practices (EBPs), and the appropriate use of medication if they are to receive reimbursement from insurance companies and demonstrate the efficacy of their work.
- Greater acceptance of mental disorders, treatment planning, and the use of medication by the public have resulted in CMHCs needing to know at least as much about their clients' diagnoses as they know!
- To be ethical and stay competitive, CMHCs need to be on the cutting edge of changes in diagnoses, new models of working with clients with mental disorders, and new medications.
- A diagnostic system offers clinicians a common language with which to discuss client issues.

THE INTIMATE RELATIONSHIP BETWEEN ABNORMAL BEHAVIOR, DIAGNOSIS, AND MEDICATION

Using the following definition, it is likely that many of us have experienced some form of abnormal behavior, and as a species, we tend to want to understand and classify behaviors that are different from the norm:

> [Abnormal behavior is] behavior that is atypical or statistically uncommon within a particular culture or that is maladaptive or detrimental to an individual or to those around that individual. Such behavior is often regarded as evidence of a mental or emotional disturbance, ranging from minor adjustment problems to severe mental disorder. (American Psychological Association, 2022)

Classification systems, such as those found in the *Diagnostic and Statistical Manual, Fifth Edition, Text Revision (DSM-5-TR)*, help us understand a mental disorder, enable us to research which treatment options work best, and help us choose which medications should be used with various disorders.

Today, most clinicians believe that the development of mental disorders is the result of a complex interaction of genetic, biological, sociological, and psychological factors. We may and probably should argue about the term "abnormal," but no matter what you call it, many individuals exhibit atypical behaviors that are described in the *DSM-5-TR*. We may and probably should argue that diagnosis is stigmatizing, but we should keep in mind that people have been helped by appropriate diagnoses and subsequent treatment plans. And we probably should argue about the overuse of medication, but it is now clear that some people are helped, and even "miraculously" improved, by taking medication.

PERSONALITY DEVELOPMENT AND ABNORMAL BEHAVIOR

Several models of personality development offer us an understanding of abnormal or atypical behaviors that result in what we call a mental disorder. Here, we examine five such models: the genetic and biological model, psychodynamic model, learning model, humanistic approach, and postmodern and social constructionist approach.

Genetic and Biological Explanations of Development

Genetics, which is the science of hereditary characteristics, is a subset of biology, which is the science of life. Biology, therefore, includes genetic factors, but genetics does not include all biological factors. For instance, if we say biological factors can affect the development of intelligence in children, we are referring to such things as prenatal care, nutrition, exposure to toxins, hormonal changes, genetics, and so forth. However, when we assert genetics can affect the development of intelligence in children, we are focused on what specifically impacts the expression of the genes for intellectual ability, not other factors that can impact intelligence.

The nature-versus-nurture debate, as it relates to personality formation, has a long and turbulent history, which continues today. However, the schisms among genetic determinists, environmental advocates, and intrapsychic zealots are clearly much more muted than ever before. This is partially because the concept of heritability has changed, with genes no longer being seen as deterministically causing behavior. Today's views of genetics assume that in most cases there are complex environmental influences on the action of genes (Mukherjee, 2016; Patron et al., 2019). For instance, after an extensive review of the literature, Clark and Watson (2008) note that genetics, as well as an individual's experiences, both play an essential role in the expression of each individual's unique personality.

The linking of biology, including genetics, with environmental factors in the development of personality moves the counseling profession toward an approach that is truly holistic. Conduct a literature review today, and you'll find research suggests that most mental disorders have some genetic basis, but for any individual, a disorder is only expressed if several genes are turned on by environmental influences at specific times (Mukherjee, 2016):

> Once we perceive organisms—humans—as assemblages built from genes, environments, and gene-environment interactions, our view of humans is fundamentally changed. "No sane biologist believes that we are entirely the product of their genes." (p. 485)

Conclusion

From a genetic and biological basis, abnormal behavior is a function of the genetics we are born with and internal and external biological and environmental factors to which we are exposed. From this perspective, it makes intuitive sense to consider using biological and other interventions when working with clients, including such things as psychotherapy, stress reduction, exercise, eating well, sleeping well, ensuring we receive proper light, psychopharmacology, and so forth. All these factors, in some manner, affect one or more major biological system and can affect our mood positively or negatively.

Psychodynamic Understanding of Development

Psychodynamic therapies, sometimes called post-psychoanalytic approaches, can be loosely defined as approaches "that postulate that unconscious mental activity affects our conscious thoughts, feelings, and behavior" (Cabaniss et al., 2017, p. 4). A whole range of psychodynamic theories exist, which started with Sigmund Freud but go on to those who practice a neo-Freudian, object relations, attachment, ego psychology, intersubjective perspective, and any of a number of other post-psychoanalytic approaches (Bishop, 2015; Jacobs, 2017). Although these approaches vary dramatically as therapeutic practices, they have common elements regarding the development of the person, including the following:

- **drives:** Psychodynamic theorists believe part of our biological makeup consists of drives, often largely out of our consciousness that try to fulfil the needs they represent. Although Freud believed we were motivated by unconscious drives related to sex and aggression, other psychodynamic theorists believe our drives include a drive for perfection, wholeness, attachment to others, and more.
- **early childhood development:** The psychodynamic understanding of parenting styles suggests the manner in which our parents or guardians interact and model for us early in life impacts the development of our personality in conscious and unconscious ways. In addition, the earlier poor parenting, or trauma, takes place, the more difficult it is to unravel one's personality development as memory, and images, are much-less clear at early stages of development.
- **an unconscious:** Psychodynamic theorists suggest our unconscious directs large portions of behaviors in ways to get one's individual's needs met and is driven by our drives. Thus, some part of our waking life is controlled by our unconscious mind and can sometimes even fool our conscious mind.
- **a conscious mind:** Our conscious mind contains all of what we are aware of and is often said to largely house our ego, which is the part of our self that attempts to deal with the external world, meet our needs, and develop our sense of self.

Many psychodynamic approaches also speak about how defense mechanisms reduce anxiety that arises from unacceptable impulses we experience if our drives become overwhelming. Unconsciously, defenses such as repression, intellectualization, denial, rationalization, projection, and many others keep us from allowing our drives to become all encompassing.

Although largely shaped by early attachments, the newer psychodynamic approaches believe our personality styles change over our lifespan as we engage in ongoing interactions with others and our environment. Thus, abuse, oppressive cultural experiences, or positive relationships (e.g., therapy) can continue to impact our sense of self over our lifetimes.

Finally, because this approach believes there is a complex interaction of our drives, parenting style, ongoing interactions, and unconscious motivations a person can only gain knowledge of self through an in-depth relationship, usually over years, with a therapist who can help unpack all of these factors.

Conclusion

From a psychodynamic perspective, psychopathology is the result of a complex number of factors. It assumes the past is critical to current-day functioning; that significant others, particularly parents or guardians, are critical to the development of the person; that interaction with others over one's lifespan and external factors, such as cultural influences, can impact the individual's developing self; that unconscious factors and defense mechanisms need to be explored if change is to occur; that psychopathology is more likely to become embedded in one's personality the earlier in life one experiences poor parenting and/or trauma; and that it takes time to unravel all of these factors in therapy (Wilson, 2015).

Learning Theory and the Development of the Person

Learning theory suggests individuals learn behaviors through operant conditioning, classical conditioning, or modeling (social learning), and therefore, it places emphasis on how positive or negative reinforcement, models, and the pairing of an unconditioned stimulus with a conditioned stimulus affect our personality development (Bandura et al., 1963; Jozefowiez & Staddon, 2015; Maia & Jozefowiez, 2015; Skinner, 1971; Wolpe, 1969). Operant conditioning is generally considered the most common type of conditioning and occurs when behavior is reinforced, thus increasing the probability of that response occurring again, or punished, which decreases the probability of a response occurring. B. F. Skinner, and others, delineated many principles of operant conditioning, each of which is crucial to the shaping of behaviors and the development of personality. A small portion of these include the following:

- positive reinforcement: any stimulus that when presented following a response, increases the likelihood of that response
- negative reinforcement: any stimulus that when removed following a response, increases the likelihood of that response
- punishment: applying an aversive stimulus to decrease a specific behavior. Punishment is often an ineffective method of changing behavior, as it may lead to undesirable side effects (e.g., counter-aggression).
- schedules of reinforcement: the numerous ways in which a stimulus can be arranged to reinforce behavior—based on elapsed time and frequency of responses
- discrimination: the ability of a person to respond selectively to one stimulus but not respond to a similar stimulus
- generalization: the tendency for stimuli that are similar to a conditioned stimulus to take on the power of the conditioned stimulus
- extinction: the ceasing of a behavior because it is not reinforced
- spontaneous recovery: the tendency for responses to recur after a brief period after they have been extinguished

Skinner, and other learning theorists, developed first-wave cognitive behavioral approaches, which assert reinforcements often occur very subtly and in ways that we may not immediately recognize (Nye, 2000; Skinner, 1971; Wolpe, 1969). Therefore, things like changes in voice intonation, subtle glances, TV shows that appeal to us, or body language could subliminally affect our personality development. They note that by examining a situation closely, one could attain an understanding of the types of reinforcement contingencies that were instrumental in shaping an individual's behavior.

Over the years, learning theorists such as Albert Ellis (Ellis & Harper, 1997) and Aaron Beck (Beck, 2020) included a cognitive framework into their understanding of development, which suggests that in addition to behaviors being reinforced, so do the ways in which people think. Called second-wave cognitive behavioral approaches, they suggest one's maladaptive thoughts can be identified, replaced, or changed, and new adaptive thoughts and behaviors can become adopted and reinforced. Even more recently, third-wave cognitive behavioral approaches, such as dialectical behavioral therapy (DBT), developed by Marsha Linehan, and acceptance and commitment therapy (ACT), developed by Stephen Hayes, look at how self-acceptance, mindfulness, changing context, stepping outside of self to examine self, and identifying new values and healthy behaviors are critical in the change process and allow us to develop new ways of acting and thinking that can be reinforced (see Neukrug & Hays, 2023).

Because abnormal development is seen to be a result of a complex array of reinforcement contingencies, learning theorists believe change can occur at any point in the life cycle if new ways of being can be reinforced. Summarizing some of the major points of many of today's learning theorists, we find the following:

- Individuals are born capable of developing a multitude of personality characteristics.
- Reinforcement of behaviors and cognitions can occur in very subtle and complex ways.
- Abnormal development is largely the result of the kinds of behaviors and cognitions that have been reinforced.
- The manner in which behaviors and cognitions are reinforced is intimately related to one's context, or environment.
- By accepting one's current state and examining one's way of being in the world, one can identify important values and move toward adopting new cognitions and behaviors that move one toward new goals and values that are cherished.

Conclusion

From a learning perspective, psychopathology is the result of dysfunctional behaviors and faulty cognitions that are conditioned, sometimes in very subtle and complex ways. Because maladaptive behaviors and cognitions are believed to be largely learned, they can be changed, and new functional behaviors and cognitions can be adopted. Modern-day learning theorists have an optimistic and antideterministic view of the person and believe people need to accept themselves, become aware of values and behaviors they want to strive toward, change their context, and use reinforcement contingencies and other techniques to move toward new values and goals.

The Humanistic Understanding of Development

The following words, by Carl Rogers, encompass much of which humanists believe to be foundational in the development of the person:

> In my experience I have discovered man to have characteristics which seem inherent in his species, and the terms which have at different times seemed to me descriptive of these characteristics are such terms as positive, forward-moving, constructive, realistic, trustworthy. (Rogers, 1957, p. 200)

This approach asserts that people are born good, are naturally positive, are looking toward the future, and have the capacity to construct and reconstruct their reality (Crocker & Philippson, 2005; Moreira, 2012; Rogers, 1980). Steeped in phenomenology, humanism, and existentialism, this approach suggests each person's reality is unique, one's core is good, and at any point in existence, one can choose new ways of being in the world.

Relative to psychopathology, this approach suggests people become neurotic, or even psychotic, due to restraints and expectations, sometimes called conditions of worth, which are placed on them by other people (Rogers, 1951, 1957, 1959, 1980). They suggest children and adults sometimes act in ways to please others to obtain a sense of acceptance, even if this pleasing self is not our real self. In essence, the person has learned that by acting in an incongruent or nongenuine fashion, they will receive acceptance. This nongenuine way of living then becomes their way of relating to the world and prevents the person from becoming self-actualized—that is, becoming one's true self. This is when one's self-actualizing tendency is thwarted.

Humanists do not use the term "abnormal" and feel strongly that this term, and others like it, are stigmatizing and inaccurate. They believe all dysfunctional behaviors are the result of individuals having restraints and expectations placed on them, which eventually result in disengagement from self. The story of Ellen West epitomizes this kind of response to an untenable situation, with unfortunate results (see Box 8.1).

BOX 8.1 The Story of Ellen West

As described by Rogers (1961/1989), Ellen West was a client who underwent psychotherapy by a number of well-known, nonhumanistically-oriented therapists (a client Rogers knew about but never saw himself). Rogers noted that Ellen felt she had to follow her father's wishes (conditions of worth) and not marry the man she loved. Consequently, she disengaged herself from her feelings by overeating and becoming quite obese. A few years later, she again fell in love but instead married a distant cousin, due to pressure from her parents. Following this marriage, she became anorectic, taking 60 laxative pills a day, again as an apparent attempt to divorce herself from her feelings. She saw numerous doctors, who gave her differing diagnoses, treated her dispassionately, and generally denied her humanness. Eventually, disenchanted with her life, Ellen committed suicide.

   This story, Rogers noted, gives a poignant view of what it's like to lose touch with self—to be incongruent. As Ellen West felt she needed to gain the conditional love of her parents, she gave up the most valuable part of self—her "real" self. This led to a life filled with self-hate and a sense of being "out of touch." Eventually, she was viewed by therapists as mentally ill, which Rogers implied might have added to her feelings of estrangement and her eventual suicide. From Rogers perspective, the therapists treated Ellen West dispassionately, didn't believe her, and didn't trust her decision-making process. Although we may not always agree with out clients, it is important that we build a trusting relationship based on empathy, genuineness, and positive regard if we are going to have positive client outcomes.

Conclusion

The humanistic approach downplays, and in many cases challenges, the concept of abnormality. Instead, humanists see the use of the term "abnormal behavior" as an attempt to objectify and isolate people. If we call the individual "abnormal," we take away their humanness and treat the person as if there is something innately wrong with them. In contrast, humanists would say so-called abnormal behavior is a healthy response to an unhealthy situation. In other words, abnormal behavior is the individual's attempt to survive in a world that places conditions of worth on the person. What is abnormal, say the humanists, is the attempt to call something abnormal that is natural.

Postmodernisms and Social Constructionism's View of Development

Postmodernism has sometimes been defined as the questioning of modernism. Whereas modernists propose that truth can be discovered and that underlying structures (e.g., id, ego, and superego) are responsible for shaping one's understanding of the world, postmodernists, such as Michael White and David Epston, the developers of narrative therapy, suggest much of what has been handed to us as "truth" is only the modernist's particular "take" on reality (Rice, 2015). In fact, they suggest those who assume there are certain inherent mechanisms that lead toward a particular personality style have become entrenched in believing *that* particular truth. In contrast, social constructionism views knowledge and truth as constructed through conversations and social interaction (Gergen, 1985, 2015). Fitting comfortably alongside postmodernism, this philosophy suggests that the language used and the discourses we have with others are key factors in the development of reality. In other words, nothing is fixed. Freedman and Combs (1996) suggest four premises that summarize postmodernism and social constructionism: realities are socially constructed, realities are constituted through language, realities are organized and maintained through narrative, and there are no essential truths.

Because reality is constantly changing and a function of language and social interaction, it is assumed one can never fully know another; "all one can know is the verbal expressions of another's experiences" (Rudes & Guterman, 2007, p. 388). It is also assumed that interaction with oppressive systems can, and does, impact individuals in harmful ways and creates realities that become cruel and harsh for the individual.

Postmodernists and social constructionists question any counselor who states they know the client's inner world by understanding the functioning of some hypothesized inner structures (e.g., id, ego, and superego; incongruent versus congruent self; self-actualization, etc.). Hypothetically, what I say is the color blue may be someone else's red; what I say is depression may be experienced differently by another; and what I say is happiness also may be experienced differently by another (see Box 8.2).

BOX 8.2 Color Therapy

Imagine there was a counseling approach that stated color preference was an indication of mental health. The closer a person's favorite color was to red on the color spectrum, the healthier they were. Those who liked red most were very healthy, those who liked orange were pretty healthy, those who liked yellow were somewhat healthy, and so forth, down the spectrum to green, then blue, and then those who liked violet—who were really unhealthy. Now, imagine this approach became so popular it was accepted throughout the land, and most people "knew" color preference was related to mental health.

Now, imagine a client sees a "color counselor." Naturally, one of their first questions would be to ask the client what their favorite color is. They say, "Blue." Well, immediately, the counselor assumes the client is not mentally healthy. After all, blue is way down the list toward violet. So the counselor begins to treat them and tries to change their favorite color. They even have a systematic way of having the client work up the hierarchy toward red. If the client practices the system every day, they will eventually get closer to red, says the counselor. After a few months, the client has worked their way up to green, and the counselor says they think that the client might want to consider taking some medication, as medication will help them experience the red more often. And the counselor tells them that after a few years of experiencing more red, they can try to reduce their medication because maybe they can begin to like red on their own.

Frustrated they are not making progress quickly enough, the client decides to see a new counselor. The new counselor is clearly unconventional and does not even believe in color therapy. The counselor asks the client to tell them what their problem is. The client states, "Well, everyone says that liking blue is bad, and so I must be mentally ill. What do you think?" This counselor replies by saying, "How about we don't focus on the color right now. Instead, let me ask you this: What do you want your life to look like? Where do you want to take therapy? What do you want as your end goal? What would make you happier?"

(continued)

With counselor number one, there is an external reality based on preconceived notions about colors. And this reality has been bought into by many. In fact, a whole system of working with clients has been developed. And almost everyone "knows" and believes in this approach. The second counselor, however, does not have these preconceived ideas and, indeed, even questions the moral authority that asserts that this reality exists. This counselor does not believe there are any internal structures that mediate mental health based on color. This counselor is the post-modern, social constructionist counselor!

Conclusion

Postmodernists and social constructionists turn the concept of abnormality on its head. From their perspective, abnormal behavior is simply a social construction—a construct that has been developed by certain individuals within the helping professions who have tended to be in power (e.g., psychiatrists—and maybe even counselors) and have subtly, but forcefully, pushed their viewpoint onto the rest of the mental health field. They also believe that through dialogue and new knowledge, people can build new constructions of their sense of self. They believe the world would have been different if instead of the mental health professions focusing on symptoms, they had focused on how relationships and systems of oppression shape the world:

> One might wonder how the field of counseling could have been enhanced if, in the early 1950s when the *DSM* was first published, the American Counseling Association (then the American Personnel and Guidance association) had published a complementary diagnostic framework, perhaps a "Manual of Client Core Issues" (MCCI). This diagnostic guide would not have focused on symptoms of pathology but rather on psychosocial and relational formulations of client struggles that tend to be problematic. (Halstead, 2015, pp. 6–7)

Which Model to Use?

Today, most CMHCs can derive some "truth" from each of the models. The genetic and biological model offers us hope that, through science, behaviors can be modified and help a person feel better. The psychodynamic model reminds us of the importance of how early child-rearing practice can impact us consciously and unconsciously and should be attended to, while the learning perspective highlights the power that reinforcement of certain behaviors and cognitions have and the importance of accepting self while moving on toward new goals. The humanistic perspective tells us to remember the good in every person and to not objectify people and reduce them to something other than what they are—a person trying to struggle to find their sense of self. And the postmodern and social constructionist approach yells out to us: "Question everything!" Try theories out, adapt new approaches, but don't get too caught up in the "truth" of any one approach. This approach also reminds us about how oppressive forces can negatively impact the person. Perhaps, we can learn a bit from all of these ideas on the development of the person.

DIAGNOSIS AND MENTAL DISORDERS

Derived from the Greek words *dia* (apart) and *gnosis* (to learn), the term diagnosis refers to the process of making an assessment of an individual from an outside, or objective, viewpoint (Douglas Harper, 2019). Attempts have long been made to classify mental disorders. For example, in 1733, physician named George Cheyne referred to a group of "psychosomatic, nervous, and depressive symptoms" as "English malady" (Horowitz, 2021, p.11). Despite earlier attempts at diagnostic classification, it was not until 1952 that the American Psychiatric Association published the first comprehensive diagnosis system called the *Diagnostic and Statistical Manual (DSM-I)*; (American Psychiatric Association, 2022a; Horowitz, 2021). Although, this first modern-day effort at a diagnostic system was received with much criticism, it provided a foundation for future generations to build upon.

The *DSM* has been revised multiple times over the years. In 1994, *DSM-IV* was released, and in 2000, an additional text revision, known as *DSM-IV-TR*, became available with 365 diagnoses (American Psychiatric Association, 1994, 2000). The *DSM-5*, with over 500 diagnoses, was published in May of 2013, and its text revision (*DSM-5-TR*) was published in 2022. Today's *DSM-5-TR* offers 22 broad diagnostic categories and their subtypes (see Appendix C). The last category, "Other conditions that may be a focus of clinical assessment," includes Z codes, which are not considered mental disorders but could be clinically significant, such as such as abuse/neglect; relational problems; psychosocial, personal, and environmental concerns; educational/occupational problems; housing and economic problems; and problems related to the legal system.

In most of the 22 categories, the *DSM-5-TR* offers other specified and unspecified disorders that can be used when a provider believes an individual's impairment is clinically significant, but it does not meet the specific diagnostic criteria in that category. Depending on whether you include all possible combinations of diagnoses within diagnostic categories (e.g., subtypes and specifiers), there are somewhere between 150 to 550 possible diagnoses.

Within the *DSM-5-TR*, the sections that were most updated from *DSM-5* included Prevalence, Risk and Prognostic Factors, Culture-Related Diagnostic Issues, Sex- and Gender-Related Diagnostic Issues, Association With Suicidal Thoughts or Behavior, and Comorbidity (American Psychiatric Association, 2022a). A couple of notable changes included the addition of a new diagnosis, prolonged grief disorder, which was added to the Trauma- and Stressor-Related Disorders section and symptom codes related to current and past suicidality or non-suicidal self-harm. In addition, this update included a work group on 19 experts on cultural issues that made suggestions for change, including revisions in language usage through the book (American Psychiatric Association, 2022b). However, despite a long revision process, the *DSM* still has its critics (Ghaemi, 2018; Jackson, 2012; Kinderman et al., 2017; Kress et al., 2005; Miller, 2012; see Table 8.1).

TABLE 8.1 Advantages and Disadvantages of the *DSM*

Disadvantages	Advantages
Does not predict outcomes of counseling	Can help with case conceptualization
Does not examine etiology	Can lead to good treatment planning, including proper use of medication, with proper diagnosis
Can reinforce the counselor's tendency to use a medical model of treatment and objectify clients	Facilitates communication among professionals
Does not fully account for contextual and social factors	Fosters research on diagnostic categories
Can lead to labeling and stigmatization of the client	Helps the client understand their emotional problems
Can be dehumanizing to the client	Offers a model to test hypotheses concerning treatment outcomes
Fosters an objective view of the client and minimizes the counseling relationship	Provides a sense of what is "normal" for most people
Lack of sound scientific evidence supporting many diagnostic categories	Provides a forum for professionals to discuss nomenclature and treatment

Making and Reporting Diagnoses

Diagnosis is a complex, multi-step process, which may include ordering diagnoses; identifying subtypes, specifiers, and severity of diagnoses; using a provisional diagnosis; and listing medical conditions and psychosocial/environmental disorders.

Ordering Diagnoses

Individuals often have more than one diagnosis, with the first diagnosis being called the principal diagnosis (American Psychiatric Association, 2022a). This diagnosis is usually the most salient factor that resulted in the person seeking treatment. The secondary and tertiary diagnosis should be listed in order of need for clinical attention. All the diagnoses have a specific code, generally an F code. For instance, a recurrent major depressive episode has a code of "F33." In addition, subtypes, specifiers, and severity codes help distinguish diagnoses, and sometimes, a specific form of provisional diagnosis will be used.

Subtypes, Specifiers, and Severity

Subtypes for a diagnosis can be used to help communicate greater clarity. They can be identified in the *DSM-5-TR* by the instruction "Specify whether" and represent mutually exclusive groupings of symptoms (i.e., the clinician can only pick one). For example, attention-deficit/hyperactivity disorder (ADHD) has three subtypes to choose from: predominantly inattentive, predominantly hyperactive/impulsive, or a combined presentation. Specifiers, on the other hand, are not mutually exclusive, so more than one can be used. The clinician chooses which specifiers, if any, apply. The ADHD diagnosis offers only one specifier that is "in partial remission" (American Psychiatric Association, 2022a, p. 69). Some diagnoses offer an opportunity to rate the severity of the symptoms. For the ADHD diagnosis, there are three options regarding severity: mild, moderate, or severe. Severity can also be identified through dimensional diagnosis. For instance, autism spectrum disorder has "Table 2 Severity levels of autism spectrum disorder" (American Psychiatric Association, 2022a, p. 58), which classifies autism on three levels of severity: "requiring support," "requiring substantial support," and "requiring very substantial support." Similarly, schizophrenia has the user reference a "Clinician-Rated Dimensions of Psychosis Symptom Severity" chart (pp. 852–853) to rate symptoms on a 5-point Likert scale. Returning to our earlier example of a recurrent major depressive disorder, if it is a moderate case, then we would write the following: Major Depressive Disorder, Recurrent, Moderate, F33.1.

Provisional Diagnosis

When a clinician has a strong inclination a client will meet the criteria for a diagnosis but does not yet have enough information to make the diagnosis, they may use a provisional diagnosis. Once the criteria are confirmed, the provisional label can be removed. These situations often occur when a client is not able to give an adequate history or further collateral information is required. Although some of the following are not specifically cited in *DSM-5-TR*, they are often used:

- rule out: The client exhibits many of the symptoms but not enough to make a diagnosis at this time; it should be considered further (e.g., rule out major depressive disorder).
- traits: This person does not meet the necessary criteria; however, they present with many of the features of the diagnosis (e.g., borderline traits or cluster-B traits).
- by history: Previous records (another provider or hospital) indicated this diagnosis; however, records can be inaccurate or outdated (e.g., alcohol dependence by history).

- by self-report: The client claims this as a diagnosis, but it is currently unsubstantiated; these can be inaccurate (e.g., bipolar by self-report).

MEDICAL CONDITIONS AND PSYCHOSOCIAL/ENVIRONMENTAL DISORDERS

In addition to identifying mental disorders, the listing of medical conditions and psychosocial and environmental disorders are encouraged, if relevant. Major medical disorders can be listed, especially if they impact one's psychological state. Their codes can be found in the *International Classification of Diseases-10 (ICD-10)*, which is the diagnosis book used by medical professionals and also includes a list of *DSM-5-TR* diagnoses. Psychosocial and environmental conditions are listed as Z codes, which can be found in *DSM-5-TR*. Thus, if we were to list a secondary mental disorder diagnosis as well as a medical diagnosis (from *ICD-10*) and a psychosocial/environmental code (from *DSM-5-TR*) along with the major depressive disorder code, we would list a number of diagnoses that would look like this:

- Major depressive disorder, recurrent, moderate, F33.1
- Generalized anxiety disorder, F41.1
- Type 2 diabetes mellitus without complications, E11.9
- Problems in relationship with spouse or partner, Z63.0

You can see how diagnoses can help a clinician fully understand many of the issues going on in a person's life. In addition, a diagnosis can be critical to the determination of whether one is to recommend the use of psychotropic medication. Let's look at this sometimes-important adjunct to counseling.

PSYCHOPHARMACOLOGY

Whether medication should be used as an adjunct to counseling and how one broaches this possibly delicate topic with clients are increasingly important issues for CMHCs and other mental health professionals (Preston et al., 2021; Sinacola et al., 2019). If counselors are to make informed decisions about a referral for medication, they should know the pros and cons of their usage (see Table 8.2) and should have some basic knowledge about psychotropic medications (Preston et al., 2021). With a host of possible medications available (see Schatzberg & DeBattista, 2019), the following represents a brief overview of some commonly used psychotropic drugs. Although classification systems of psychotropic drugs vary, almost all systems describe medications in most or all of the following five groups: antipsychotics, mood-stabilizing drugs, antidepressants, antianxiety agents, and stimulants (National Institute of Mental Health, 2022; Preston et al., 2021; Videbeck, 2019). Let's look at each of these.

Antipsychotics

During the early 1950s, antipsychotic drugs were used extensively for the first time (Nasrallah & Tandon, 2017). This first wave of antipsychotic drugs changed the field of mental health dramatically, as individuals with severe psychotic symptoms were finally treated with some success, resulting in the release of tens of thousands of individuals from mental institutions.

Sometimes called neuroleptics, antipsychotic drugs are generally used for the treatment of schizophrenia as well as schizoaffective disorders and the manic phase of bipolar disorder (Videbeck, 2019). Less frequently, these drugs are used in the treatment of Alzheimer's disease, aggressive

TABLE 8.2 Advantages and Disadvantages of Psychotropic Medications

Advantages of Medication	Disadvantages of Medication
The efficacy of medication use is easily studied.	Only counseling can address the complexity of the human condition.
If they work, medications can help quickly.	Counseling can lead to autonomy; drugs can lead to dependence.
The quick response of medications can instill hope.	The quick effects of medications lessen the desire for clients to work on their problems.
The quick response of medication can lead to more effective work in therapy.	Most psychotropic medications have some side effects.
The quick response of medication can reduce the likelihood of a serious mental illness occurring again (e.g., schizophrenia).	The side effects of some psychotropic medications are serious and long-lasting.
Medication may help some people that psychotherapy won't help.	Research on the effects of some psychotropic medications is mixed and confusing.
Sometimes medications are more cost effective than psychotherapy.	Psychotropic medications do not solve life's problems; only the individual can do this.
Due to their biological basis, some mental disorders can only be treated by medication.	Individuals should not have to rely on something that is not naturally found in their bodies.

behavior, and anxiety, and insomnia. There are three broad classes of antipsychotic drugs that include the conventional antipsychotics, and atypical antipsychotics, sometimes called second-generation antipsychotics (Sherman & Field, 2017; Videbeck, 2019). Some of the classic antipsychotic and second-generation drugs used in these disorders are listed in Table 8.3.

TABLE 8.3 Antipsychotic Medications

Conventional Antipsychotics		Atypical or Second-Generation Antipsychotics	
Generic Name	Trade Name	Generic Name	Trade Name
Chlorpromazine	Prolixin	Aripiprazole	Abilify
Droperidol	Inapsine	Asenapine Maleate	Saphris
Fluphenazine	Thorazine	Clozapine	Clozaril
Haloperidol	Haldol	Iloperidone	Fanapt
Loxapine	Loxitane	Lurasidone	Latuda
Molindone	Moban	Olanzapine	Zyprexa
Perphenazine	Trilafon	Olanzapine/Fluoextine	Symbyax
Thioridazine	Mellaril	Paliperidone	Invega
Thiothixene	Navine	Quetiapine	Seroquel
Trifluoperazine	Stelazine	Risperidone	Risperdal
		Ziprasidone	Geodon

Antipsychotics can dramatically alter the course of an individual's life who is having an acute psychotic episode, as the quicker an individual can recover from a psychotic episode, the greater the likelihood of decreasing or eliminating the intensity of future psychotic episodes. Although antipsychotic medications can help an individual who has a long history of psychotic behavior live a more normal life, they are often not a cure. For these individuals, normal cognitive functioning is often not restored, and they are frequently left seeming somewhat stilted in their thinking and ability to respond.

Depending on the type and dosage of medication, several side effects may occur. For instance, some individuals may have one or more of the following side effects (Goldberg & Ernst, 2019; Procyshyn et al., 2019):

- **Anticholinergic side effects**, including dry mouth, blurred vision, constipation, urinary retention, decreased memory, and decreased libido, occur in some individuals.
- **Extrapyramidal side effects (EPS)**, including muscle spasms, Parkinson-type symptoms, and motor restlessness, occur in some individuals.
- **Tardive dyskinesia**, which includes involuntary movements of the tongue, lips, and facial muscles, can occur in some individuals who have taken high dosages of antipsychotic medications over a long period of time, although it has occasionally been seen when the medications are taken for short periods in lower doses.
- **Blood disorders**, which can lead to death if not treated, have been found with some of the newer antipsychotic medications.
- **Other side effects**, such as a fast heartbeat, rigidity, agitation, sedation, weight gain, and skin pigmentation, occur in some individuals.

Mood-Stabilizing Drugs

During the 1800s, an element called lithium was found to have positive effects in the treatment of several bodily afflictions (Kamali et al., 2017). In the early 1950s, lithium was rediscovered as an effective treatment for the manic phase of bipolar disorder (then called manic depression). Because it does not have the same dramatic effects during the depressive phase of the illness, antidepressants are often also prescribed. For individuals who take lithium, the level of drug must be assessed through a blood test, as too much lithium can cause severe side effects and too little will be ineffective in treatment. Like antipsychotics, lithium can produce a number of side effects, including gastrointestinal problems, excessive thirst, excessive urination, hand tremors, a metallic taste, fatigue, lethargy, and mild nausea; however, the side effects are generally viewed as less serious than those with the antipsychotic medications. Although lithium has been used in the treatment of other disorders, it is often an early treatment of choice for bipolar disorder.

Although lithium has shown some success with the treatment of bipolar disorder, in recent years, other mood stabilizing drugs have also been shown to be helpful for individuals in the manic phase, including anticonvulsant medications, such as Tegretol and Topamax, and benzodiazepines (antianxiety drugs), such as alprazolam and diazepam (a.k.a., Zanax and Valium; Kamali et al., 2017; McElroy & Keck, 2017).

Antidepressants

The use of amphetamines during the 1930s was one of the first attempts to treat depression psychopharmacologically (Pirodsky & Cohn, 1992). Known on the street as "speed," this medication did little except stimulate a person's central nervous system temporarily, which would led to a "crash" and more serious depression. In addition, consistent use of amphetamines can lead to paranoia and health problems.

The 1950s saw a dramatic shift in the treatment of depression with the identification of two classes of antidepressants, called monoamine oxidase inhibitors (MAOIs) and tricyclics (Krishnan, 2017; Nelson, 2017). Until the 1990s, these drugs were the medications of choice in the treatment of depression, with the tricyclics being used more frequently because they tended to have fewer side effects. However, the last 30 years have seen the widespread use of a new class of antidepressants called selective serotonin reuptake inhibitors (SSRIs; Videbeck, 2019). SSRIs have been called "miracle drugs" by some, due to their limited side effects and often-dramatic results. In fact, these drugs have been so effective that there is some evidence they can help make an individual who already feels relatively well, feel even better. For these reasons, drugs such as Prozac, Luvox, Paxil, Lexapro, Celexa, and Zoloft have very quickly become commonplace in American society. Although some early research suggested these drugs increase the risk for suicide, especially in children (Bridge et al., 2007), more recent research has disputed this (Courtet & Lopez-Castro, 2017; Henein et al., 2016; Stübner et al., 2018). However, out of an abundance of caution, warnings continue to be given to individuals taking these medications. In addition to the treatment of depression, SSRIs also show promise in treating other disorders, including obsessive–compulsive disorder (OCD), panic disorder, some forms of schizophrenia, eating disorders, alcoholism, obesity, and some sleep disorders. Besides SSRIs, several atypical antidepressants, which also improve brain cell communication, seem to be promising in the treatment of depression. Some of these include Wellbutrin, Mirtazapine, Nefazodone, Trazodone, Vilazodone (Viibryd), and Vortioxetine (Trintellix).

Antianxiety Medications

The use of modern-day antianxiety medications started with the development of Librium, which came on the market in 1960 and was soon followed by Valium. These medications, and other benzodiazepines, were better tolerated and less addictive than barbiturates (e.g., phenobarbitol), the previous treatment of choice (Sheehan, 2017). However, tolerance of and dependence on benzodiazepines can be developed, and there is a potential for overdose on these medications.

Today, benzodiazepines, such as Valium, Librium, Tranxene, Xanax, and others, are frequently used for generalized anxiety disorders, as they have a calming effect on the individual (Videbeck, 2019). In conjunction with psychotherapy, these medications can be an effective agent in treating such disorders. Benzodiazepines have also been shown to reduce stress, relieve insomnia, and manage alcohol withdrawal (Nishino et al., 2017). In addition, they have been used in conjunction with some antidepressants for the treatment of OCD and in treating social phobias and posttraumatic stress disorder (PTSD; Sheehan, 2017). Two other nonbenzodiazepines, Buspar and Gepirone, have been found to be effective for use in generalized anxiety disorders and can be an alternative to the more popular benzodiazepines. In addition, these drugs show some efficacy in the treatment of depression, especially for those who are exhibiting anxiety disorders (Robinson & Rickels, 2017).

Stimulants

Probably the first modern-day stimulant used to treat emotional disorders was cocaine, which was first discovered in the mid-1800s. However, due to its addictive qualities, cocaine has never become a treatment of choice. In 1887, amphetamines, which had many of the same stimulant qualities as cocaine but were less addictive, were synthesized (DeBattista, 2017; Fawcett & Busch, 1998). Over the years, amphetamines were used, mostly unsuccessfully, as diet aids, antidepressants, and to relieve the symptoms of sleepiness. However, during the 1950s, amphetamines were found to have a paradoxical effect in many children diagnosed with ADHD—they seemed to calm them down and help them focus. Today, the use of stimulants in the treatment of ADHD is widespread, with the three most common drugs being Ritalin, Cylert, and Dexedrine. In addition to treating ADHD, stimulants have been found to be successful in the treatment of narcolepsy and are somewhat successful in treating residual attention deficit disorder in adults.

Unfortunately, these drugs are often sold on the street as a stimulant to help people feel good but can have a wide range of serious side effects.

Psychopharmacology has come a long way since the 1950s, when the first modern-day psychotropic medications were introduced. Increasingly, the medications used for a wide array of disorders are more effective and have fewer side effects than in the past. As the mechanism for psychological disorders becomes increasingly understood, new and even more effective medications can be developed to target the underlying physiological mechanisms causing disorders.

ETHICAL, PROFESSIONAL, AND LEGAL ISSUES

This section highlights a few prominent ethical, professional, and legal issues relative to when cultural background impacts symptom expression, when it may be efficacious to diagnosis or refrain from diagnosis, insurance fraud, and gatekeeping of impaired graduate students.

Symptoms as a Function of Cultural Background

Differences in symptoms as a function of cultural background are common, and in recent years, the American Psychiatric Association (2013, 2022a) has asked clinicians to understand and acknowledge such differences. For example, Latin American culture broadly acknowledges that ataque de nervios (attack of nerves) is a common disorder related to difficult and burdensome life experiences, wherein a person may exhibit "intense emotional upset, including acute anxiety, anger, or grief; screaming and shouting uncontrollably; attacks of crying; trembling; heat in the chest rising into the head; and becoming verbally and physically aggressive. Dissociative experiences (e.g., depersonalization, derealization, amnesia), seizure-like or fainting episodes, and suicidal behavior are prominent in some *ataques* but absent in others" (American Psychiatric Association, 2022a, p. 874). A clinician who ignores the client's culture could easily misdiagnose a client who presents with symptoms like this and begin to treat the client with inappropriate strategies. To assist in understanding differences in symptomology, the *DSM-5-TR* offers definitions of some cross-cultural symptoms and identifies how cross-cultural issues impact a wide range of diagnoses. In addition, the *DSM-5-TR* offers a section entitled Cultural Formulation Interview (CFI), which helps clinicians understand the kinds of values, experiences, and influences that have come to shape the client's worldview and provides an outline for interviewing clients from diverse backgrounds appropriately (Desilva et al., 2018).

To Diagnosis or Not

Although the following study was conducted way back in 1973, the misdiagnosis of individuals continues today:

> A group of eight pseudopatients presented themselves to mental hospitals. One was a psychology graduate student, three were psychologists, one a pediatrician, one a psychiatrist, one a painter, and one a housewife. These subjects presented themselves to 12 mental hospitals in five states. The only symptoms they displayed in the admissions offices were saying that they felt their lives were empty and hollow and that they heard voices saying "empty, hollow, thud." The researchers chose these symptoms because they could not find one case of "existential psychosis" in the literature. Once admitted, the pseudopatients ceased showing any symptoms at all. Mental health professionals diagnosed all but one of these people as schizophrenic, and the length of hospitalizations ranged from 7 to 52 days. The professional staffs of the hospitals never detected the fraud, although many actual patients were suspicious and questioned the fake patients. (Swenson, 1997, p. 449)

Noting the potential misuse and abuse of diagnosis, the AMHCA (2020) and ACA (2014) codes of ethics address a number of important issues when making a diagnosis, noting the importance of taking special care when diagnosing, being culturally sensitive in making a diagnosis, recognizing the historical and social prejudices that have resulted in the misdiagnosis and pathologizing of marginalized clients, and considering refraining from making a diagnosis if it will harm the client or others (ACA, 2014, Section E).

Ivey and Ivey (1998) suggest that rather than assuming there is something inherently wrong with a person, we should view problems as a "logical response to developmental history" (p. 334) and natural responses to issues in the family, community, and broader culture. This approach does not suggest discontinuing the use of diagnosis; rather, it offers a humanistic and antideterministic alternative to understanding the person. For instance, for a person who is "paranoid," they suggest one views that person as an individual who is vigilant about looking out for injustice, and for a person who is "obsessive–compulsive," they suggest this person is good at "maintaining order and a system […] necessary for job success" (p. 338). Today, the controversy over what is abnormal and the use of diagnosis still exists, although it has calmed down a bit. When you are called to diagnose a client (and you will be), you may want to reflect on these issues and carefully consider how your diagnosis will be used.

Refraining from Diagnosis

Even if you think a diagnosis is accurate and will likely be helpful in many ways to a client, there may be times when you need to refrain from making a diagnosis. It is important to weigh the advantages and disadvantages of making the diagnosis and carefully consider whether the diagnosis would be beneficial or detrimental for the client. For instance, there may be cases when a diagnosis would cause a person to lose their job. In this case, one must weigh the legal and ethical implications of not diagnosing (e.g., there may be sound reasons for the job to want to know about a diagnosis) and the implications to the client if you did diagnose (e.g., job loss might result in poverty for some individuals). The ACA Code of Ethics supports this careful consideration:

> Counselors may refrain from making and/or reporting a diagnosis if they believe it would cause harm to the client or others. Counselors carefully consider both the positive and negative implications of a diagnosis. (ACA, 2014, Section E.5.D; see Reflection Exercise 8.1)

EXPERIENTIAL EXERCISE 8.1 Would You Refrain From Making a Diagnosis?

The following are three situations which could come up in your role as a CMHC. Consider each of them and discuss in small groups. Share your ideas in class:

1. Your client is in the military, and you know making a diagnosis of a major depressive disorder episode will likely impact their ability to move up in rank.

2. The setting in which your client works does not allow for any substance abuse, and your client has a substance abuse diagnosis due to his use of marijuana. Making the diagnosis could end up with the client losing their job.

3. Child Protective Services (CPS) has been called by the estranged spouse of a client you are seeing because the spouse is bitter and wants to gain custody of their children. You believe your client is an excellent parent, but you are pretty sure that if you diagnose them as having bipolar disorder, CPS will remove the children from the house. You believe they do have a bipolar disorder but also believe it is under control, and when it is not, the client has their parents take care of the children.

Insurance Fraud

Today, certain diagnoses are often not reimbursed by insurance companies. Although there may be a tendency by some to alter a client's diagnosis, so they obtain reimbursement, this act is unethical and could constitute insurance fraud. With this practice being cited as one of a number of common complaints made against licensed professional counselors (LPCs; Carlisle et al., 2022; Wilkinson et al., 2019), counselors must learn to inform clients of what will and will not likely be reimbursed, work with clients when faced with certain diagnoses that are not reimbursable (ACA, 2014, Section H.2.a), and be honest with insurance companies and other third parties:

> Counselors are accurate, honest, and objective in reporting their professional activities and judgments to appropriate third parties, including courts, health insurance companies, those who are the recipients of evaluation reports, and others. (ACA, 2014, Section C.6.b)

Impaired Graduate Students

At times, I have sat in a faculty meeting when a faculty member brought up the name of a student and suggested they be approached because it seemed apparent they had severe emotional problems. Sometimes I have agreed with the faculty member's assessment; other times I have not. For me, this issue is similar to the old debate concerning the use of the term "abnormal behavior." In terms of students, it first challenges me to define what a "severe emotional problem" is and then asks me to ponder whether I believe such students can be assisted to the point that they can be effective counselors (see Foster & McAdams, 2009; Letourneau, 2016). The ACA ethical code suggests the following:

> Counselor educators, through ongoing evaluation, are aware of and address the inability of some students to achieve counseling competencies. Counselor educators do the following:

1. assist students in securing remedial assistance when needed,

2. seek professional consultation and document their decision to dismiss or refer students for assistance, and

3. ensure that students have recourse in a timely manner to address decisions requiring them to seek assistance or to dismiss them and provide students with due process according to institutional policies and procedures. (ACA, 2014, Section F.9.b; see Reflection Exercise 8.2)

> **EXPERIENTIAL EXERCISE 8.2**
> **How to Approach an Impaired Graduate Student**
>
> If you were in charge of a CMHC program, what kind of gatekeeping would you have for "impaired" students. How would you define "impaired"? How would decisions be made regarding "impaired" students? What kind of decisions would be made? Discuss in class.

SUMMARY

This chapter introduced the concepts of abnormal behavior, diagnosis, and psychopharmacology, noting that the three are inextricably connected. Whereas it used to be unusual for counseling programs to examine these concepts, changes in the field have made it increasingly common and important.

We began the chapter by exploring how five models attempt to explain abnormal behavior. We first noted there is a strong connection between genetic, biological, and environmental factors in the development of personality. We concluded that it makes sense to consider using biological and other interventions when working with clients, including such things as psychotherapy, stress reduction, exercise, eating well, sleeping well, ensuring we receive proper light, psychopharmacology, and so forth.

The psychodynamic understanding of development examined how a number of attributes impact behavior, including drives, early childhood development, the unconscious mind, the conscious mind, interactions with others, defense mechanisms, and parenting styles. We noted it takes time to develop abnormal behaviors and time to unravel their complexity in therapy.

Looking at learning theorists, we found that first-wave cognitive–behaviorists view abnormal development as a function of operant conditioning, classical conditioning, and modeling, and we listed some important concepts related to operant conditioning. In recent times, most learning theorists have included a cognitive perspective that stated our cognitions are also reinforced and can lead to healthy functioning or irrational ways of thinking (second wave). We also noted that third-wave cognitive behaviorists believe that context, self-acceptance, and moving toward important values is critical to change.

The humanistic perspective suggests people are born good, naturally positive, look toward the future, and have the capacity to construct and reconstruct their reality. This philosophy is steeped in phenomenology, humanism, and existentialism and approaches each individual as unique. We pointed out that, often, people are impacted by conditions of worth, which result in them acting how they think others would want them to act, rather than being genuine or real. Humanists suggest that instead of viewing this reaction as pathology, one should view it as a natural reaction to a difficult situation.

Finally, postmodernists and social constructionists view reality as being socially constructed through language and organized and maintained through narratives and social interaction. Therefore, they believe abnormal behavior to be socially constructed such that there are no essential truths and that individuals can change through dialogue and social interaction with others.

If one believes there are deviant behaviors, then it is natural to want to classify them. This is what the complex process of diagnosis achieves. Thus, this chapter offered a brief history of *DSM* and then described the *DSM-5-TR*, the major diagnostic classification system for mental disorders. We explored some of the advantages and disadvantages of the *DSM*. We noted that the *DSM-5-TR* diagnostic categories are in sync with the 10th edition of the *ICD-10*.

We went on to note that diagnosis is often a critical conceptualization and communication tool, and we highlighted the aspects of making and reporting diagnoses. This included how to order diagnoses; identifying subtypes, specifiers, and severity of diagnoses; how to use a provisional diagnosis (e.g., rule out, traits, by history, and by self-report); and the importance of listing medical conditions and psychosocial/environmental disorders. Understanding this process can help clients receive the care that best fits their needs.

If an accurate diagnosis is made, then treatment planning becomes easier, and part of treatment may be the use of psychotropic medications. Thus, the chapter examined five classes of drugs often used in the treatment of a wide range of emotional disorders. They included the antipsychotics, mood-stabilizing drugs, antidepressants, antianxiety agents, and stimulants. A brief history of the use of various psychopharmacological agents was provided, along with descriptions of some of the major psychotropic medications currently in use and some of their side effects.

As the chapter continued, we highlighted a number of ethical, professional, and legal issues. We first discussed the fact that cultural background can impact symptom expression and noted that *DSM-5-TR* includes a cultural formula interview to help ensure diagnoses are accurate. We also noted that diagnoses can be stigmatizing, misused, and abused, especially for those who are marginalized. We then talked about the importance of framing diagnoses in positive ways. Knowing that diagnoses can sometimes be harmful to people, we highlighted the section from the ACA ethics code that supports the decision to not diagnose in certain situations. We also encouraged all CMHCs to report diagnoses accurately, as purposely listing an untrue diagnosis can constitute insurance fraud. Finally, we discussed how a counseling program conducts gatekeeping when it believes a student has severe emotional problems and may need support, remedial assistance, or be removed from a program. We noted three steps the ACA Code of Ethics suggests when dealing with this kind of gatekeeping situation.

KEY WORDS AND TERMS

abnormal (atypical) development

acceptance and commitment therapy (ACT)

amphetamines

antianxiety agents

antianxiety medications

anticholinergic side effects

anticonvulsant medications

antidepressants

antideterministic

antipsychotic drugs

antipsychotics

ataque de nervios

atypical antidepressants

atypical antipsychotics

barbiturates

benzodiazepines

biology

bipolar disorder

blood disorders

born good

by history

by self-report

classical conditioning

cocaine

cognitive framework

complex environmental influences on the action of genes

complex interaction of our drives, parenting style, ongoing interactions, and unconscious motivations

conditioned stimulus

conditions of worth

conscious mind

construct and reconstruct his or her reality

conventional antipsychotics

Cultural Formulation Iinterview (CFI)

defense mechanisms

deficit model

diagnosis

Diagnostic and Statistical Manual (DSM-I)

Diagnostic and Statistical Manual, Fifth Edition, Text Revision (DSM-5-TR)

dialectical behavioral therapy (DBT)

dimensional diagnosis

discrimination

drives

ego

evidenced-based practices (EBP)

existentialism

extinction

extrapyramidal side effects (EPS)

F codes

first-wave cognitive behavioral approaches

first wave of antipsychotic drugs

generalization

genetic and biological model

genetics

heritability

humanism

humanistic approach

incongruent

International Classification of Diseases-10 (ICD-10)

learning model

learning theory

lithium

looking toward the future

manic depression

medical conditions

modeling (social learning)

modernism

monoamine oxidase inhibitors (MAOIs)

mood-stabilizing drugs

narcolepsy

narrative therapy

naturally positive

nature versus nurture

negative reinforcement

neuroleptics

nonbenzodiazepines

nongenuine

ongoing interactions with others and with our environment

operant conditioning

other side effects

other specified disorders

ordering subtypes

paradoxical effect

phenomenology

pleasing self

positive reinforcement

postmodern and social constructionist approach

postmodernism

postmodernists

post-psychoanalytic approaches

preventive and wellness model

principal diagnosis

prolonged grief disorder

provisional diagnosis

psychodynamic model

psychodynamic therapies

psychopharmacology

psychosocial and environmental disorders

psychotropic drugs

punished

punishment

real self

realities are constituted through language

realities are organized and maintained through narrative

realities are socially constructed

reinforced

reinforcement contingencies

rule out

schedules of reinforcement

second-generation antipsychotics

second-wave cognitive behavioral approaches

selective serotonin reuptake inhibitors (SSRIs)

self-actualized

self-actualizing tendency

severity

social constructionism
specifiers
spontaneous recovery
stimulants
subtypes
tardive dyskinesia

there are no essential truths
third-wave cognitive behavioral
  approaches
traits
tricyclics
true self

unconditioned stimulus
unconscious
unspecified disorders
Z codes

KEY NAMES

Beck, Aaron
Ellis, Albert
Epston, David

Freud, Sigmund
Hayes, Stephen
Linehan, Marsha

Rogers, Carl
Skinner, B. F.
White, Michael

CREDIT

Fig. 8.1: Vincent Van Gogh, "At Eternity's Gate," 1890.

CHAPTER 9

CASE CONCEPTUALIZATION

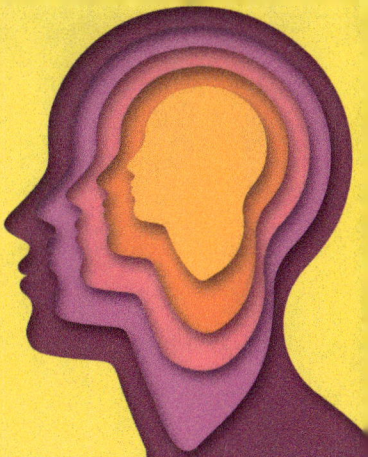

Learning Objectives

- Define case conceptualization.
- Understand the difference between theory-specific and non-theory specific case conceptualization.
- Describe the biological, psychological, and sociocultural domains of the biopsychosocial assessment model of case conceptualization and demonstrate how it is implemented.
- Describe the various aspects of assessment: informal techniques, ability testing, personality assessment, and the clinical interview. Show how they can be used to gather information for the biopsychosocial model.
- Show how themes and ideas about causation are generated from the assessment process of the biopsychosocial model.
- Demonstrate how the case conceptualization process can be used to help determine an accurate diagnosis.
- Define the treatment planning process and demonstrate how it is an outgrowth of the case conceptualization process.
- Briefly define four schools of counseling and psychotherapy and demonstrate how a theoretical lens can be applied to the case conceptualization process.

INTRODUCTION

When I first started out as a counselor, after a client walked into my office, I would introduce myself and then ask them something like, "How can I help you today." After this initial question, I would do a lot of listening and, perhaps, a small amount of inquiry. I spent little time gathering information or trying to formulate what was going on with the client. As I became more seasoned, I learned that because I hadn't developed a process for assessing what was going on with the client, I often missed important issues (e.g., abuse, trauma, addictions), as those problems would come up much later in the therapeutic relationship. It was at this point that I realized I needed to assess what was going on with the client—usually as soon as they came into the office. Thus, I started to implement an assessment phase of counseling. I realized that gathering information and then conceptualizing client problems could quickly help build the therapeutic relationship and assist me in reaching accurate goals more quickly. This case conceptualization

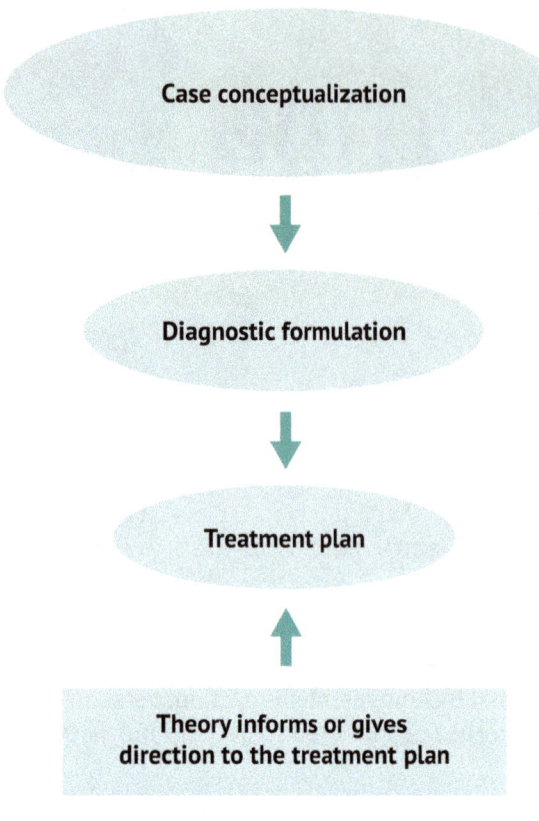

FIGURE 9.1 Case Conceptualization, Diagnosis, Treatment Planning, and Theory

process, which has to do with the methods we use to understand our clients, is the major focus of this chapter.

In this chapter, we define case conceptualization, examine how case conceptualization can be theory or nontheory specific, review the biopsychosocial assessment model of case conceptualization, offer an overview of the assessment process, show how to use the biopsychosocial model with a client, demonstrate how case conceptualization naturally leads to a diagnosis, discuss a four-step model of treatment planning that evolves out of the case conceptualization process, show how the case conceptualization process can be used through a theoretical lens, and give you an opportunity to apply case conceptualization, diagnostic formulation, and treatment planning to a client.

DEFINING CASE CONCEPTUALIZATION

Sometimes called case formulation, case conceptualization is the process that new and seasoned counselors use to collect information from a variety of sources, understand the client's situation, develop a diagnosis, and form treatment strategies that can lead to successful outcomes (Zubernis & Snyder, 2016). Sperry and Sperry (2020) define it in the following way:

Basically, case conceptualization is a method for understanding and explaining a client's concerns and for guiding the treatment process. It functions like a "bridge" to connect assessment and treatment with clinical outcomes. (p. 4)

In addition, as counselors mature, they increasingly integrate their theory into the case conceptualization process, and the treatment strategies they use reflect the theory they embrace (see Figure 9.1).

THEORY AND NON-THEORY-SPECIFIC CASE CONCEPTUALIZATION

Some models of case conceptualization suggest the counselor views the process through the lens of their favored theoretical perspective. For instance, Berman (2019) offers a case conceptualization process for no less than 10 different theoretical orientations (e.g., psychodynamic, behavioral, cognitive, emotion-focused, and constructivist). This approach to case conceptualization

initially involves the clinician deciding on a theoretical perspective and developing a hypothesis about the factors that cause and maintain the problems to then guide a personally meaningful intervention, test the hypothesis, and revise the intervention accordingly. (Bucci et al., 2016, p. 517)

However, others note that theory-specific case conceptualization models can be particularly trying for new counselors, who are still struggling to understand their own theoretical orientation:

> Theory-specific models may also be especially difficult for new trainees, who sometimes are admonished to quickly identify a single therapeutic orientation that works for them and adhere to it unwaveringly. (Ridley & Jeffrey, 2017, p. 381)

One option for beginning counselors is to practice a non-theory-specific case conceptualization process, and then apply basic counseling skills with a client when addressing the treatment planning process. This eliminates the initial need for a theoretical perspective, which many beginning counselor trainees have not yet fully developed. In this chapter, we present the biopsychosocial assessment model of case conceptualization. This theory-free model examines three important domains to understanding the client and developing treatment plans. However, as counselors increasingly understand and embrace a theory, or an integrative theoretical approach, they can start to view the knowledge gained from the biopsychosocial assessment model through their theoretical prism.

THE BIOPSYCHOSOCIAL ASSESSMENT MODEL

Introduced during the 1970s by George Engel, to help the medical profession move to a more holistic way of understanding the person, the biopsychosocial assessment model is seen today as a comprehensive and integrative way of approaching case conceptualization and has been adopted by the mental health professions (Bolton & Gillett, 2019; Zubernis et al., 2017). The model looks at individual client issues but also examines broader systemic concerns as well as the interplay between the three domains it gathers information about. The biopsychosocial assessment model is like other contemporary models of case conceptualization that stress in-depth inquiry into the individual as well as an understanding of social environment issues.

As the name implies, the biopsychosocial assessment model calls for the collection of information from three domains in the client's life: biological, psychological, and sociocultural. Generally, this is completed through an assessment process that includes an intake interview, follow-up interviews, and the use of assessment instruments. Unfortunately, Meyer and Melchert (2011) found most therapists do not always collect information in a thorough and comprehensive way. Thus, using the biological, psychological, and sociocultural domains, they created several components of the three domains counselors could assess, which were based on standards put forth by researchers as well as the Joint Commission for the Accreditation of Health Care Organizations and the American Psychiatric Association. Table 9.1 identifies items that are often looked at within each domain.

TABLE 9.1 Components of the Biopsychosocial Assessment Domains

Biological Domain	Psychological Domain	Sociocultural Domain
General medical history	History of present illness	Employment
Medications	Individual psychiatric history	Legal issues
Childhood health history	Suicidal or homicidal ideation	Relationships
	Substance use history	Current living situation
	Childhood abuse history	Education history
	Mental status examination	Religion/spirituality
	Psychological traumas	Family history
	Personality styles/characteristics	Multicultural issues
	Behavioral observations	Military history
	Individual developmental history	Interests/hobbies

When using the biopsychosocial assessment model, one explores the components of each domain as well as how components in one domain may interact with other domains. Ultimately, themes, ideas about causation, and diagnoses will arise after such an in-depth look at the domains. Ideally, a treatment plan should emerge after examining the themes, causations, and diagnoses. After counselors have gained expertise in a theoretical orientation, they can apply that lens to their treatment plan (see Figure 9.2).

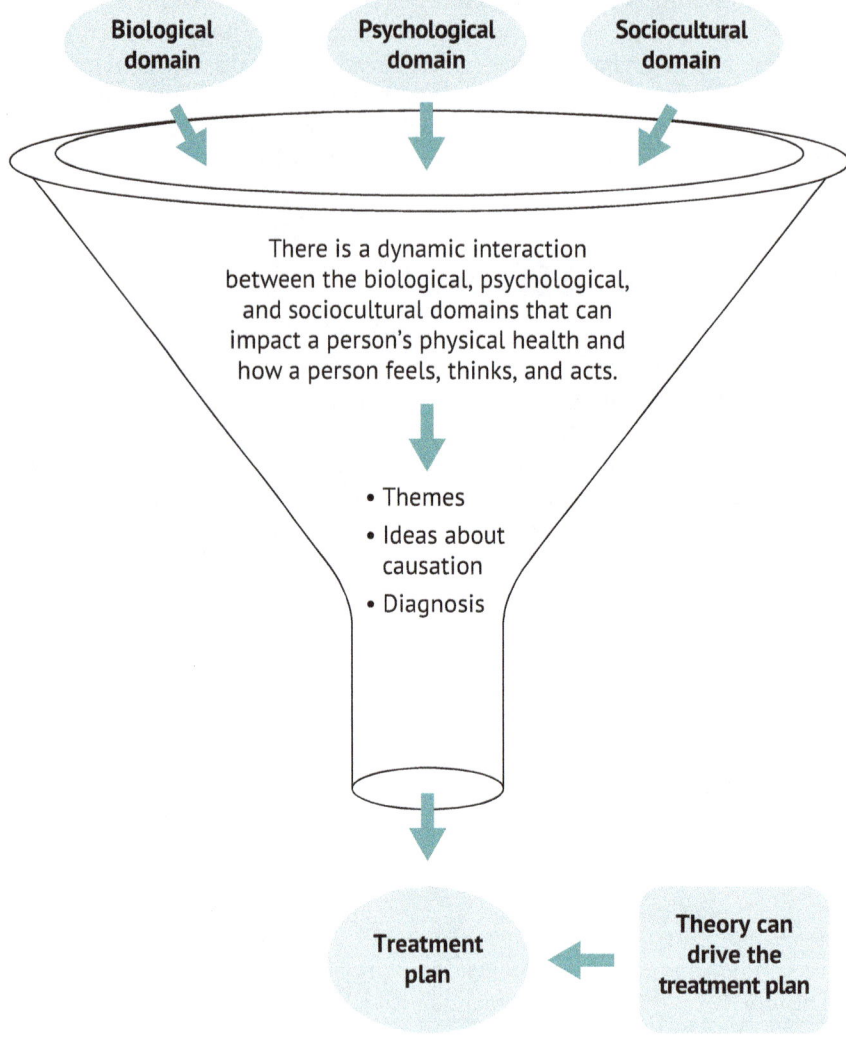

FIGURE 9.2 The Biopsychosocial Model

The Assessment Process

The key to conceptualizing your client is conducting a good assessment. Several assessment processes can be used, although all of them may not be used with all clients (Neukrug & Fawcett, 2020). In general, the more assessment techniques employed, the more information will be gained, and the better the outcome will be. However, counselors should consider the law of diminishing returns, in that one shouldn't overwhelm the client, make them feel frustrated, and/or go beyond saturation—that is, beyond the point

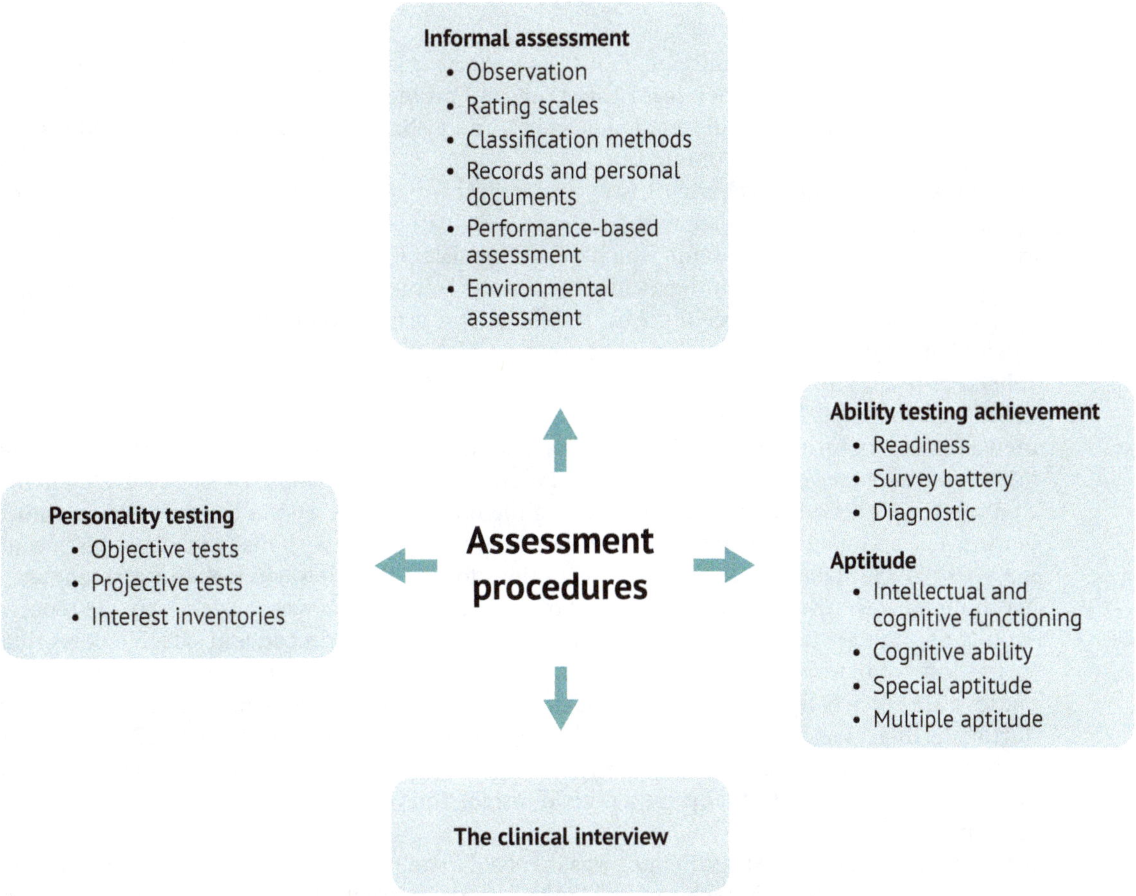

Informal assessment
- Observation
- Rating scales
- Classification methods
- Records and personal documents
- Performance-based assessment
- Environmental assessment

Assessment procedures

Personality testing
- Objective tests
- Projective tests
- Interest inventories

Ability testing achievement
- Readiness
- Survey battery
- Diagnostic

Aptitude
- Intellectual and cognitive functioning
- Cognitive ability
- Special aptitude
- Multiple aptitude

The clinical interview

FIGURE 9.3 Assessment Procedures

where information the counselor is gathering becomes redundant. Assessment can occur on many levels, such as conducting a clinical interview, applying informal techniques, and administering personality and ability tests (see Figure 9.3).

Using the Biopsychosocial Model With a Client

Jake Miller, a 34-year-old married male sought counseling due to extreme anxiety, concerns about his children's wellbeing, and problems in his marriage. Jake and his family are described in Appendix D, which offers an overview of the Miller family, and Appendix E, which is a psychological report about Jake which uses many of the assessment techniques delineated in Figure 9.3. After reading about Jake in the appendices, let's see how we might use the biopsychosocial model to understand him:

- Biological Domain
  - **general medical** history: No significant medical history. Currently, ongoing headaches, feeling tired much of the time, trouble sleeping, loss of weight.
  - **medications**: Currently on no medications. Took Luvox, 100 mg, at age 23 for anxiety and mild depression after meeting Angela, who was later to become his wife.
  - **childhood health history**: No significant medical history.

- ## Psychological Domain
  - **history of present illness**: Starting about 10 weeks ago, Jake began to have extreme anxiety, problems with sleep, headaches, loss of appetite, and problems with his marriage and children. Symptoms arose when his children, Luke, age 10, and Celia, age 7, accidentally knocked his car out of park and it rolled into the street.
  - **individual counseling/psychiatric history**: Jake saw counselors on two separate occasions, once when 13, 3 years after an incident with his twin sister, Justine, when they moved their father's car as a "joke," and it was hit by a semi, which caused his sister to have serious cognitive impairment. Jake felt guilt and anxiety over the incident and states counseling helped. Jake was in counseling again, at age 23, soon after meeting Angela, who later was to become his wife.
  - **suicidal or homicidal ideation**: None reported.
  - **substance use history:** None reported. States he is a social drinker.
  - **childhood abuse history**: None reported.
  - **mental status examination (MSE)**: Jake was casually and neatly dressed for the interview. He had appropriate eye contact and was oriented to time, place, and person. He often fidgeted in his chair, moving his body back and forth during the interview. He reports feeling "anxious most of the time" and notes he still feels guilty about the car accident with his twin sister, Justine, at the age of 10. He states he has been feeling anxious for the past 10 weeks since an incident with his children, when they knocked his car out of park, and it rolled down the driveway. He reports waking up multiple times at night, just to check that everyone is in bed and safe. He notes that he has lost some weight, which he believes is due to his disinterest in food as a result of his anxiety. He reports feeling tired much of the time and has ongoing headaches. At one point during the interview, when talking about the accident with Justine, he became tearful, saying, "I shouldn't have listened to her—it's all my fault." Jake's thoughts were clear, memory good, and he is above average intellectually. He has good insight and fair judgment. He reports no suicidal or homicidal ideation.
  - **psychological traumas**: At age 10, Jake was involved in an incident with his twin sister, Justine, when they moved their father's car as a "joke." The car was hit by a semi, which resulted in Justine having serious cognitive impairment. Jake seems to still carry evidence of this traumatic event, as noted by his current anxiety, sleep patterns, ongoing feelings of guilt about his sister's current level of functioning, and his controlling obsessive-compulsive behaviors, which involves trying to ensure safety in his home with his children and wife, often through demands and yelling.
  - **personality styles and characteristics**: Jake is currently showing some obsessive–compulsive behaviors related to worry regarding the safety of his children and his wife. This involves asking his wife to homeschool the children, yelling at his children whenever they are involved with what he describes as "rough play," waking up multiple times at night to ensure all the doors are locked, and ensuring the children are within visual distance of him, so they won't be harmed. Anxiety and periodic angry outbursts are associated with his obsessive-compulsive behaviors.
  - **behavioral observations**: Jake shows visual signs of anxiety through rapid speech, yelling at the children, constantly checking on the children, and getting up at night, sometimes multiple times, to ensure the doors are locked.
  - **individual developmental history**: Jake had a normal developmental history until the age of 10, when he and his twin sister Justine were involved in an incident in which they rolled their father's car into the street, and it was hit by a semi. His sister sustained severe cognitive impairment, and this traumatic moment in his life seemed to leave him with guilt, depression, and anxiety that periodically becomes worse at stressful times in his life.

- Sociocultural Domain
  - ○ **employment**: Employed as a mechanical engineer for 8 years.
  - ○ **legal issues**: None reported.
  - ○ **relationships**: Describes relationship with his wife and children as currently strained, since an incident in which his children accidentally rolled his car into the street. He states he is easily angered by his children, is vigilant about their safety, and has been controlling with his wife, insisting she homeschool the children to ensure their safety. He describes his relationship with his parents and wife's parents as "good," although he notes he and his parents continue to be "haunted" by the car accident (see "psychological trauma"). Jake notes his sexual relationship with his wife had been "normal" until his recent concerns regarding safety. He states they are "rarely intimate now."
  - ○ **current living situation**: Jake lives with wife, Angela, and children, Luke (10) and Celia (7).
  - ○ **education history**: Jake attended public school until college, where he obtained his bachelor's and master's degrees in mechanical engineering from the University of Kansas. He states he did well in school, particularly in math. However, he also noted that he always "wrote poorly" and thought he was "dyslexic." He was never tested for a learning disability.
  - ○ **religion/spirituality**: Jake states he is agnostic and that his wife, Angela, is Episcopalian, although he notes that "she is not very religious," and the family rarely, if ever, goes to church. He notes he'd rather "believe in science" than some "unknown God."
  - ○ **family history**: Jake has one sibling, a sister named Justine, who sustained serious cognitive impairment when the two of them were 10 years old and they were "playing" in their father's car and tried to move it, and it was hit by a semi. Jake continues to blame himself for the accident and states the accident continues to haunt him and his parents. Jake met his wife, Angela, in graduate school and has been married for 10 years. He describes his family as having been loving and healthy until a recent incident when his son, Luke, knocked the car out of park and it moved into the street. Jake's daughter, Celia, was also in the car. Jake states that since that time he has had a resurgence of anxiety and has wanted to control everyone in the family—mostly to ensure their safety. He notes that when the children are home, he constantly wants to make sure they are within visual distance. He also reports making sure that all the doors are locked at night, even waking up multiple times during the middle of the night to check. He states that whenever the children play "rough" games, he goes into a rage, yelling at them to stop it. He also notes that he has asked Angela to homeschool the children, as he is concerned that something "bad" will happen at school. This, he reports, has led to problems in his marriage. Meanwhile, Jakes states that Luke and Celia have been symptomatic since the incident with the car moving, with Luke "not listening to anyone" and Celia having ongoing stomachaches, which cause her, at times, to come home from school.

    Jake describes his parents as active, loving parents until the accident with Justine. He states that the accident led his mother to becoming despondent and reports she has "never been the same." It was also at that point that his father disengaged from the family. Jake feels like the family became "shattered" after the accident, with his father's distancing and mother's depression seeming to feed into his guilt about the accident.
  - ○ **multicultural issues**: Jake is White, and his wife, Angela, is biracial. Her father is Nigerian and moved to the United States. He is a college English professor. Angela's mother, a social worker, is White. Angela is her parent's biological daughter, and her parents also adopted two African American children, Marcus, who is 31, gay, and in a relationship, and Lillian, who is 29, heterosexual, and married. Jake describes his children as biracial. Until recently, he reports there were no major concerns regarding his children and seems accepting of his brother-in-law's sexual orientation. He notes that Angela has seen herself as White while visiting Nigeria and Black in the United States. He also states she had a "caretaking" personality growing up, especially relative

to her sister, who had a congenital hip deformity, who she was often asked to care for. He reports she struggles with her identity, which causes "issues" in their relationship from time to time, noting that sometimes she is "my caretaker" and other times she simply wants to be independent.
○ **financial resources**: Jake describes himself as "middle class" and reports no financial difficulties.
○ **military history**: None.
○ **interests/hobbies**: Jake has recently become involved with a national association that advocates for child-safe automobiles. Jake relates this involvement back to the traumatic event he had as a child, and he believes his skill as a mechanical engineer can be useful in the development of safer cars.

Themes and Ideas About Causation With Jake

After gathering information from the biopsychosocial model, we can begin to come up with themes, ideas about causation, and a diagnosis for Jake, all of which can be used in our treatment planning. For instance, when reviewing the biopsychosocial information, here are some of my thoughts about Jake:

- Jake is struggling with anxiety and obsessive-compulsive behaviors that seems to be related to an earlier incident in life.
- Jake's anxiety is negatively impacting his relationships with his children and his wife.
- Jake's early incident with his sister, Justine, was traumatic and has shaped his life in many ways.
- Jake may be struggling with PTSD from the original accident.
- Jake seems to continue to carry guilt from the original accident with his twin sister Justine.
- Jake's need to control his children and wife are related to his anxiety about their safety and negatively impacts his family.
- Jake's family of origin still seems to be struggling with the impact of the car accident and resulting cognitive impairment sustained by Justine. This impacts their relationship with Angela, Jake, Justine, and Luke.
- Jake has several current medical issues that seem to be related to his anxiety and worry, including headaches, trouble sleeping, and weight loss.
- Jake had some success with use of Luvox, when 23 years old, for similar symptoms.
- Jake's symptoms reverberate through the family and impact the children. The children are symptomatic, with Luke not listening and Celia having ongoing stomachaches and missing school.
- Jake seems to have good insight, but judgement may be interfering with his relationships.
- Jake's recent controlling attitudes and behaviors may be exasperating Angela's issues around her mixed feelings regarding being in a caretaking role.

All of the themes and ideas about causation are useful in determining a diagnosis and in developing a treatment plan. Let's turn to an understanding of how to make a diagnosis, eventually come back to a diagnosis for Jake, and then move on to understanding how to develop our treatment plan.

Using Case Conceptualization to Assist in Diagnosing Jake

In Chapter 8, we gave a quick overview of the *DSM-5-TR* and how to make a diagnosis (APA, 2022). Now that we understand how to use the *DSM-5-TR*, we can begin to look at one or more possible diagnoses with Jake. Referring to earlier in the chapter, where we used our case conceptualization process to come up with 12 themes and ideas about causation, we can begin to come up with some tentative diagnoses. For Jake, I come up with the following:

- Adjustment disorder, with anxiety (F43.21)
- Rule out generalized anxiety disorder (F41.1)

- Rule out posttraumatic stress disorder (F43.10)
- Rule out obsessive-compulsive disorder (F42.2)
- Possible spelling learning disability (F81.81)
- Relationship distress with spouse or intimate partner (Z63.0)
- Parent–child relational problem (Z62.820)
- High expressed emotion level within family (Z63.8)

Let's take a quick look at each of these:

- **adjustment disorder, with anxiety**: Since Jake's symptoms started about 10 weeks ago and appear to be a response to an "identifiable stressor" (the children knocking the car out of park), Jake's symptoms would fit the "adjustment disorder" category. Since he has classic signs of anxiety (e.g., feeling anxious, loss of weight, disinterest in food, trouble sleeping, obsessive thoughts), it seems apparent that the adjustment disorder is "with anxiety."
- **rule out generalized anxiety disorder**: In many ways, Jake meets all the symptoms necessary for a generalized anxiety disorder; however, to meet the criteria for this disorder, it must occur for at least 6 months. At this point, he does not meet that criterion. Should treatment not be successful, and he continues to have the same symptoms, he might later fit this category. Hopefully, treatment will be successful!
- **rule out posttraumatic stress disorder**: Jake has some of the symptoms of PTSD but probably does not fit all the criteria to have this disorder. For instance, he has been exposed to a traumatic situation (the original accident with his sister). He periodically does have flashbacks to the event and upsetting memories about it. He does blame himself, has difficulty sleeping, and is hypervigilant about ensuring safety. Also, his symptoms do create distress in his life. However, and importantly, he also has been able to go long periods of time with relatively little anxiety. In the end, he probably does not fit this diagnosis, although elements do exist.
- **rule out obsessive-compulsive disorder**: Although Jake technically meets the criteria for this disorder, since his current thoughts and behaviors are associated with a specific act, and because they have been occurring for a relatively short amount of time, it was decided to hold off on giving this disorder and see how it responds to treatment. However, it would be important to revisit this disorder if the behaviors and thoughts continue.
- **possible spelling disability**: Jake notes that he always has had trouble with spelling, and it impacted that aspect of his schooling. Relative to his other strengths in school, Jake could have a potential spelling disability. This can be explored further if Jake and his counselor think it will benefit his life.
- **relationship distress with spouse or intimate partner**: Clearly, Jake and Angela have not been getting along since the incident with his children. Their sexual relationship has diminished, and Angela is upset at Jake's controlling behavior and his need to have the children homeschooled.
- **parent–child relational problem**: Jake's response to his children has been to try and control their behavior. This often results in him yelling at them. They seem to have responded to his attempts at control through Celia's psychosomatic problems (stomachaches) and to Luke not listening. They also do not respond well to Jake's commands.
- **high expressed emotion level within family**: Jake, Angela, Luke, and Celia all seem on edge. Jake constantly tries to control everyone to ensure safety. The children act out at school and at home. Angela is upset as Jake attempts to control the children and push her toward homeschooling the children. The family's emotional level is high.

Now that we have come up with some themes, ideas about causation, and diagnoses for Jake, let's consider the treatment-planning process. This is the next step in helping Jake feel better about himself and assisting the family in feeling better about one another.

Treatment Planning for Jake

The treatment plan is the map of how you will work with your client. Based on the assessment process, the themes and ideas that were generated, and the diagnosis, the treatment plan often includes such things as identifying the client problems, suggesting treatment modalities, goals of counseling, and how change might be measured. The following represents a four-step treatment planning model. Keep the following quote in mind when creating a treatment plan:

> If a counselor has a poor understanding of the client's situation, applies an inaccurate diagnosis, or selects an inappropriate treatment approach, the client will suffer. (Kress & Paylo, 2019, p. 4)

A Four-Step Treatment Planning Model

Some have suggested counselors should consider four steps to treatment planning (Neukrug & Schwitzer, 2006; Schwitzer & Rubin, 2015). Using Jake as an example, let's see how we can (a) define the problems, (b) develop achievable goals, (c) decide on treatment modality, and (d) measure change.

Step 1: Defining the Problems

Remembering our case conceptualization, we might come up with the following 10 problems related to Jake's problems:

1. Jake struggles with anxiety.
2. Jake has feelings of guilt about the accident with Justine.
3. Jake tries to control the children and Angela to reduce his anxiety.
4. Angela's sense that she is feeling controlled by Jake negatively impacts Jake's relationship with her.
5. Jake lacks intimacy with Angela.
6. Jake has a lack of sleep, a loss of weight, and headaches.
7. As a result of Jake's yelling and controlling behaviors, Luke "is not listening to anyone."
8. As a result of Jake's yelling and controlling behaviors, Celia has stomachaches and misses school.
9. Jake's family of origin still seems "haunted" by the accident with Justine, which impacts Jake's ability to be close with his parents.
10. Jake's anxiety and attempts to control Angela feed into her negative feelings about always having to be the caretaker in her family.

Step 2: Developing Achievable Goals

After we have identified our problems, it is relatively easy to convert these into achievable goals. Let's look at the goals we might develop for Jake:

1. Reduce Jake's anxiety.

2. Find ways to help Jake deal with his guilt.

3. Reduce Jake's attempts at controlling the children and Angela.

4. Help Jake and Angela have a more equal and loving relationship.

5. Help Jake and Angela restore normalcy and intimacy to their relationship.

6. Increase Jake's ability to sleep, help him gain weight, and help him reduce his headaches.

7. Reduce Jake's yelling at Luke, and help Luke "listen" better.

8. Reduce Jake's yelling at Celia, and help her learn how to lessen her stomachaches.

9. Bring a sense of normalcy back to Jake's family of origin.

10. Reduce Jake's attempts to control Angela, and help Angela take a stand on what she wants in the relationship and the family.

Step 3: Deciding on Treatment Modalities

As achievable goals are determined for Jake, we can begin to consider what treatment modalities might be used to address those goals. In Jake's case, the following modalities come to mind, although all may not be implemented at once:

1. individual counseling focused on a reduction of Jake's anxiety and guilt

2. marital counseling to restore a sense of intimacy and health to Jake and Angela's relationship

3. family counseling with Jake and his family of origin to talk about the incident that resulted in Justine's cognitive impairment and to resolve family issues

4. psychiatric consultation for possible medication adjunct to assist Jake with his anxiety and obsessive-compulsive behaviors

5. possible referral to Celia and Luke's school counselor for support at school and to help them deal with the anxiety and shouting at home.

In addition, as one gains a sense of, and embraces, different theories and approaches, specific treatment modalities can be identified. For instance, to reduce Jake's anxiety, we might use a cognitive behavioral approach and medication (items 1 and 4). For his guilt (item 1), we might use an existential–humanistic approach, which carefully listens to his feelings. Couples counseling that focuses on communication skills and unsaid feelings with Jake and Angela seems important, as their relationship is central to their family doing well (item 2). Although short-term family counseling with Jake and his family of origin is important, it probably can occur after things calm down within Jake's immediate family (item 3).

Step 4: Measuring Change

Now that we know our goals and have decided our treatment modalities, measuring change is a naturally intuitive process. What follows are some of the different ways I came up with to measure change with Jake and his family:

1. reduction in anxiety, as measured verbally from Jake, using a scaling instrument that assesses anxiety from session to session (1 = no anxiety, 10 = extreme anxiety), and with an assessment instrument, such as the Beck Anxiety Inventory (BAI)

2. Reduction in yelling at the children and Jake's controlling behaviors (observations by Angela and children)

3. Increase in level of intimacy between Jake and Angela (self-report by Jake and Angela)

4. Self-report by Jake of reduction in guilt regarding the accident

5. Angela reporting increased satisfaction with Jake and decrease emotional volatility in family.

6. Jake's family of origin attending short-term family counseling

7. Over time, a reduction in the use of medication

8. Better sleep, increased weight, reduction in headaches (self-report and/or use of journal to document change).

9. Reduction of Celia's stomachaches by self-report of teachers, counselor, and parents.

10. Lessening of Luke's inattentiveness by self-report of parents. (see Reflection Exercise 9.1)

> **REFLECTION EXERCISE 9.1**
> **Measuring Change**
>
> Can you come up with additional ways to measure change? Reflect on Jake's situation and see if you can come up with two or three additional ways. Share your suggestions in class.

CASE CONCEPTUALIZATION PROCESS THROUGH A THEORETICAL LENS

As you increasingly become familiar with theories of counseling, you are likely to drift toward and embrace one theory, lean heavily on that theory, and integrate techniques from various other theories—or integrate two or more theories into your own theoretical approach (Corey, 2024). With well over 300 theories (Neukrug, 2015; Meichenbaum & Lilienfed, 2018), choosing a theoretical approach can be a difficult task. Today, there are generally four schools of psychotherapy within which most theories fall: psychodynamic, existential–humanistic, cognitive behavioral, and postmodern (Neukrug, 2015, 2023). Presented here is a brief description of each of these schools, followed by some thoughts on how a counselor who embraces that school of thought might view Jake's situation. If the case conceptualization process were to be used with Jake and then viewed through a theoretical lens, a more involved treatment plan could be developed. The following gives you a taste of this process.

Psychodynamic Approaches

Developed near the beginning of the 20th century but maintaining widespread popularity today, psychodynamic approaches vary considerably but contain some common elements. For instance, they all suggest that an unconscious and a conscious affect the functioning of the person in some deeply personal and "dynamic" ways. They all look at early child-rearing practices as being important in the development of personality. They all believe examining the past, and the dynamic interaction between the past and conscious and unconscious factors, are important in the therapeutic process. Although these have tended to be long-term approaches, in recent years, some have been adapted and used in relatively brief treatment modality formats. Some of the more popular psychodynamic approaches include psychoanalysis, Jungian therapy, Adlerian therapy, attachment therapy, and object-relations theory (see Box 9.1).

BOX 9.1 **Assisting Jake Using a Psychodynamic Perspective**

Those who embrace any of a number of psychodynamic approaches believe a strong ego can help a person withstand difficult times in life, as the ego knows how to find available resources to overcome life's obstacles. With Jake, something in his early childhood prevented him from developing an ego that could withstand such obstacles. This is why when his children had the incident with his car, Jake began to decompensate and develop serious anxiety with associated problems (e.g., lack of sleep, lack of eating, headaches, obsessive-compulsive thoughts and behaviors, and a need to control). The psychodynamic theorist would want to help Jake look at his early attachment to important caretakers, particularly his parents, so he can better understand what went awry. Ultimately, Jake would need to understand some of the reasons he did not develop a strong-enough ego, and through reparenting efforts with his counselor, can begin to learn new and healthier ways of functioning that can help him get through the most difficult times in life. This approach tends to be long term, as looking at the past and developing new and healthier ways of functioning through reparenting and ego building is an arduous process.

Existential-Humanistic Approaches

Loosely based on the philosophies of existentialism and phenomenology, existential–humanistic approaches were particularly prevalent during the latter part of the 20th century but continue to be widely used today. Existentialism examines the kinds of choices one makes to develop meaning and purpose in life and, from a psychotherapeutic perspective, suggests people can choose new ways of living at any point in their lives. Phenomenology is the belief that each person's reality is unique, and to understand the person, you must hear how that person has come to make sense of their world. These approaches tend to stress having a trusting and "real" relationship with the counselor, focusing on the here and now, and gently challenging clients to make new choices in their lives. Although generally shorter than the psychodynamic approaches, these therapies tend to be longer than the cognitive behavioral approaches. Some of the more well-known existential–humanistic approaches include existential therapy, Gestalt therapy, and person-centered counseling (see Box 9.2).

BOX 9.2 **Assisting Jake Using an Existential–Humanistic Perspective**

This approach views the counseling relationship as a joint journey that is based on the notion that Jake can only be understood and feel comfortable sharing his inner-most thoughts through a trusting, accepting, and empathic relationship. As this relationship is developed, Jake will feel increasingly safe within the counseling relationship and be open to talking about all aspects of himself. Therefore, it is likely that he will want to talk about his feelings about the car accident with Justine, the guilt he has felt, and how it has impacted his life with Justine, his parents, wife, and children. He will likely examine how his anxiety, and its associated behaviors, has negatively affected himself and others around him. His ability to change the present, by taking responsibility about the behaviors and relationship choices he has made, will increasingly take precedence within the counseling relationship. Slowly, Jake will examine how he can make new choices, so he can decrease his anxiety and have increasingly real and meaningful relationships with his wife and children, Justine, and his parents (see Reflection Exercise 9.2).

Cognitive Behavioral Approaches

Cognitive behavioral approaches look at how cognitions and/or behaviors impact one's current manner of living in the world and assume cognitions and/or behaviors have been learned and can be relearned. Although building a relationship is important in these approaches, it is seen as a way of building trust, so clients will be more likely to change specific behaviors and cognitions and not core to the theories, as in existential–humanistic approaches. These approaches tend to spend a limited amount of time examining the past, as they focus more on how present cognitions and behaviors affect the individual's feelings, thoughts, actions, and physiological responses. They all propose that after identifying problematic behaviors and/or cognitions, one can choose, replace, or reinforce new cognitions and behaviors that result in more effective functioning. These approaches tend to be shorter term than the psychodynamic or existential–humanistic approaches. Four of the most well-known approaches that constitute the cognitive behavioral school became popular during the latter part of the 20th century and continue to have widespread appeal today. They include behavior therapy, rational emotive behavior therapy (REBT), cognitive behavior therapy, and reality therapy. Two other more recent third-wave cognitive behavioral approaches that place a great emphasis on the context of the person include dialectical behavior therapy (DBT) and acceptance and commitment therapy (ACT); (see Box 9.3).

> **REFLECTION EXERCISE 9.2**
> **Jake Undergoing Existential–Humanistic Therapy**
>
> Now that you have a good sense of who Jake is and have conceptualized his life situation, consider how you might work with him from an existential–humanistic perspective. Then, review the video roleplay of Dr. Ed Neukrug with Jake. Is his work with Jake how you would have imagined it to be? Do you think the techniques he used fit the existential–humanistic perspective? Are there clear goals for Jake, and do you think he will eventually begin to reduce his anxiety and build more effective relationships with those he loves? Share your thoughts in class.

BOX 9.3   Assisting Jake Using a Cognitive Behavioral Perspective

After building a relationship, Jake will be asked to examine his cognitions and behaviors to see how cognitive distortions, irrational thinking, and negative core beliefs are impacting his feelings, physiological responses (e.g., high cortisol levels which cause stress), and behaviors. He will also examine how his behaviors are negatively impacting others around him. Through a psychoeducational process, he will be taught how he can change his thinking and his behaviors, so he can feel less anxious and act in healthier and more loving ways with Angela, his children, and his parents. He will be prescribed homework that will entail changing his irrational or faulty beliefs as well as practicing new behaviors that will help him feel better and act more loving to those around him. Through practice and reinforcement from his counselor and those around him, he will eliminate his irrational and faulty beliefs, develop new rational and healthy core beliefs, and develop new positive behaviors (see Reflection Exercise 9.3).

Postmodern Approaches

Narrative therapy, solution-focused brief therapy, and relational-cultural therapy are three recent approaches to the therapeutic milieu and are based on the philosophies of social constructivism and postmodernism. Postmodernism suggests that no one reality holds the truth, and we should question many of the past assumptions we took for fact. Those with this philosophy even doubt many of the basic assumptions of past popular therapies, which suggest certain structures cause mental health problems (e.g., id, ego, superego, a self-actualizing tendency, core beliefs, and an internal locus of control). Social constructivism suggests individuals construct meaning in their lives from the discourses they have with others and the language used in their culture and society. They suggest those in power, through language, behaviors, and laws, can create havoc for those whose identify as a minority (e.g., culturally diverse clients, women, individuals with disabilities, and sexual minorities). Thus, they encourage the counseling relationship to be highlighted by equality and nonpathology. Rather than harp on past problems that tend to be embedded in oppressive belief systems, postmodern approaches suggest clients can find exceptions to their problems and develop creative solutions and new ways of understanding their world. Postmodern approaches tend to be short-term therapies, with solution-focused brief therapy being considered a particularly short-term approach, sometimes lasting fewer than five sessions (see Box 9.4).

BOX 9.4   Applying a Postmodern Approach to Jake

Although postmodern approaches can be vastly different in how they work with the client, they all have the basic assumption that there is no inherent pathology "within" Jake, that Jake can develop new ways of living in the world, and that, through discourse, people can change. Thus, Jake's anxiety is not seen as embedded within his being, and counseling is seen as positive and forward moving. Since Jake's anxiety is clearly upsetting Jake and those around him, the postmodern counselor would want to understand Jake's story, or dominant, problem-saturated narrative, and begin to seek solutions that will help Jake and those around him feel better. The counselor will not act like an aloof expert or know-it-all. Instead, this counselor will show curiosity, be caring, and be humble about Jake's situation. Listening carefully to Jake's story, the postmodern counselor will help Jake explore past positive coping mechanisms, past exceptions to his current problem-dominated story (e.g., times when he did not have anxiety or use controlling behaviors), and identify new positive solutions to help Jake develop new narratives as he reauthors his life. Jake will begin to de-emphasize his current problem-saturated story and build new positive narratives and more helpful ways of living.

APPLYING CASE CONCEPTUALIZATION, DIAGNOSTIC FORMULATION, AND TREATMENT PLANNING

Hinkle and Dean (2017) have found roleplays can help beginning counselors increase cognitive complexity, sharpen reflection skills, and raise the affective awareness required to master the skills needed in case conceptualization. Of course, supervision can also be helpful in this process. In fact, some have found that supervisees have varying degrees of reflective practice skills (e.g., Ellis et al., 2013; Rausch & Gallo, 2017). At a basic level, the supervisee can describe therapeutic events using cause and effect. At the next level, the supervisee can examine patterns within cases. At the most advanced level, the supervisee can detect and reflect on patterns across cases in relation to self and challenge assumptions underlying conceptualizations. Wherever one is in the process, when counselor trainees learn more about the counseling process and increasingly engage in supervision, they will become better at case conceptualization, developing a diagnosis, and formulating a treatment plan (see Experiential Exercise 9.1).

EXPERIENTIAL EXERCISE 9.1 Practicing Case Conceptualization, Making a Diagnosis, and Treatment Planning

Part 1: Angela
Throughout this chapter you have examined how Jake's situation can be examined through the case conceptualization process. In addition, using Jake as an example, we demonstrated how to conduct an assessment, form a diagnosis, and develop a treatment plan. Finally, we briefly looked at how therapy might take place with Jake through the four major schools: psychodynamic, existential–humanistic, cognitive behavioral, and postmodern.

In getting to know Jake, you also obtained a glimpse into the world of Angela, Jake's wife. Using Appendices B and E, review Angela's situation one more time. In addition, you may want to view videos of Angela with Dr. Neukrug, undergoing a psychodynamic approach to therapy and a postmodern approach to counseling. This will give you additional information about Angela and allow you to reflect on these theoretical approaches.

After you have gained knowledge about Angela, as best as you can, use the biopsychosocial assessment model to conceptualize Angela's situation. Then, come up with a diagnosis using *DSM-5-TR*. Finally, develop a treatment plan for Angela. Share what you came up with in small groups.

Part 2: Roleplay
In addition to, or instead of, exploring Angela's situation, do a roleplay with a student, friend, or client, and use the biopsychosocial assessment model to develop your case conceptualization. Then, using *DSM-5-TR*, come up with a diagnosis of your client and develop a treatment plan based on your case conceptualization and diagnosis. Finally, consider what the process might look like if your client underwent a psychodynamic, existential–humanistic, cognitive behavioral, or postmodern approach to counseling. In small groups, share how the case conceptualization, diagnosis, and treatment-planning process went and how you envisioned counseling to unravel.

SUMMARY

The chapter started by defining case conceptualization, sometimes called case formulation, as the process the counselor uses to understand the client's situation, develop a diagnosis, and form treatment strategies that can lead to successful outcomes. We noted that this process can be theory or non-theory specific. Theory specific means the process of understanding your client is seen through the lens of your theoretical approach. We noted that most beginning counselors are not wed to any one theory, and we suggested for those individuals, it might be best to look at a non-theory-specific approach—in this case, applying the biopsychosocial approach from a non-theoretical perspective.

We next defined the biopsychosocial assessment model, introduced by George Engel during the 1970s. The model looks at several variables associated with biological, psychological, and sociocultural domains. We listed each of these variables. Offering a graphic, we pointed out that these domains interact with each other and that the model is holistic, as it looks at a broad range of variables that impact the person. We noted there is a dynamic interaction between these domains and that this interaction impacts how the person feels, thinks, and acts and that understanding this interaction can help us come up with ideas about causation, a diagnosis, and an eventual treatment plan.

To assess the three themes of the biopsychosocial model, we suggested that several assessment procedures could be used, including informal assessments, ability testing, personality testing, and the clinical interview. We noted that this often happens during the intake interview. Using Jake, we then went through each theme and gave an example of how each variable within each domain would be highlighted.

By assessing each variable within the three domains, we noted how the results could lead to themes and ideas about causation and offered 12 possible themes and ideas for Jake. We next noted how these 12 themes and ideas could be helpful in coming up with a diagnosis and, again using Jake as an example, offered a series of diagnoses for Jake.

The chapter then moved into a four-step treatment planning model based on the assessment process, the themes and ideas that were generated, and the diagnosis. This process includes (a) defining the problems, (b) developing achievable goals, (c) deciding on treatment modality, and (d) measuring change. Again, using Jake as an example, we gave some possible items to consider in each of these four areas.

As the chapter neared its conclusion, using Jake, we went on to give some examples of how the psychodynamic, existential–humanistic, cognitive behavioral, and postmodern schools of counseling might view Jake's situation. Using the same conceptualization model but viewing it through the lens of each of these four schools, we showed how four different treatment plans would be developed. We concluded the chapter by suggesting that you practice the case conceptualization process with Angela (Jake's wife) or a person of your choosing.

KEY WORDS AND TERMS

acceptance and commitment therapy (ACT)

Adlerian therapy

American Psychiatric Association (APA)

attachment therapy

behavior therapy

biological domain

biopsychosocial assessment model

by history

by self-report

case conceptualization

case formulation

cognitive behavior therapy

cognitive-behavioral approaches

criticisms of *DSM*

diagnosis

Diagnostic and Statistical Manual of Mental Disorders, Fifth Edition, Text Revision (*DSM-5-TR*)

dialectical behavior therapy (DBT)

existential therapy

existential–humanistic approaches

four-step model treatment planning model

Gestalt therapy

gnosis

ideas about causation

International Classification of Disease (*ICD*)

Jungian therapy

making and reporting diagnoses

medical conditions
mental disorders
narrative therapy
object-relations theory
ordering diagnoses
other specified disorders
person-centered counseling
postmodernism
principal diagnosis
psychoanalysis
psychodynamic
psychological domain
psychosocial and environmental
  stressors

rational emotive behavior therapy
  (REBT)
reality therapy
relational–cultural therapy
rule out
severity
specifiers
social constructivism
sociocultural domain
solution-focused brief
  therapy
step 1: define the problems
step 2: develop achievable
  goals

step 3: decide on treatment
  modalisties
step 4: measure change
subtypes
themes
third-party payments
third-wave cognitive behavioral
  approach
traits
treatment planning
unspecified disorder
Z codes

KEY NAME

Engel, George

CREDITS

Fig. 9.1: Edward Neukrug, Counseling and Helping Skills: Critical Techniques to Becoming a Counselor, p. 164. Copyright © 2019 by
  Cognella, Inc. Reprinted with permission.
Fig. 9.2: Ed Neukrug and Carolyn Cullen, Counseling and Helping Skills: Critical Techniques to Becoming a Counselor, ed. Edward
  Neukrug, p. 166. Copyright © 2019 by Cognella, Inc. Reprinted with permission.
Fig. 9.3: Edward Neukrug, The World of the Counselor: An Introduction to the Counseling Profession, p. 381. Copyright © 2022 by
  Cognella, Inc. Reprinted with permission.

CHAPTER 10

CASE MANAGEMENT

Learning Goals

- Learn about the broad range of case management activities used by CMHCs, including the following:
  - professional disclosure statements and informed consent
  - assessment
  - developing client goals
  - monitoring psychotropic medications
  - writing notes and reports
  - confidentiality of records
  - ensuring the security of records
  - documenting clients' contact hours
  - collaboration with other professionals
  - termination and making referrals
  - conducting follow-ups
  - practicing time management

INTRODUCTION

Once, when working at a mental health center as an outpatient therapist, I received a printout stating I had 140 clients. Some of them were monthly "med checks" or bimonthly clients, and some had already terminated counseling, but still, it was an enormous number of clients. Meeting once a week with 30 clients would be a bit much, especially with all the paperwork and other duties I had. Clearly, I had to somehow manage my cases, so I could see all of the clients as their treatment plan suggested.

Case management, which has been called the overall process involved in maintaining the optimal functioning of clients (Summers, 2016; Woodside & McClam, 2018), encompasses a broad range of activities, including providing informed consent and professional disclosure statements, assessment, developing client goals, monitoring psychotropic medications, writing notes and reports, confidentiality of records, ensuring security of client records, documenting client contact hours, collaboration with other

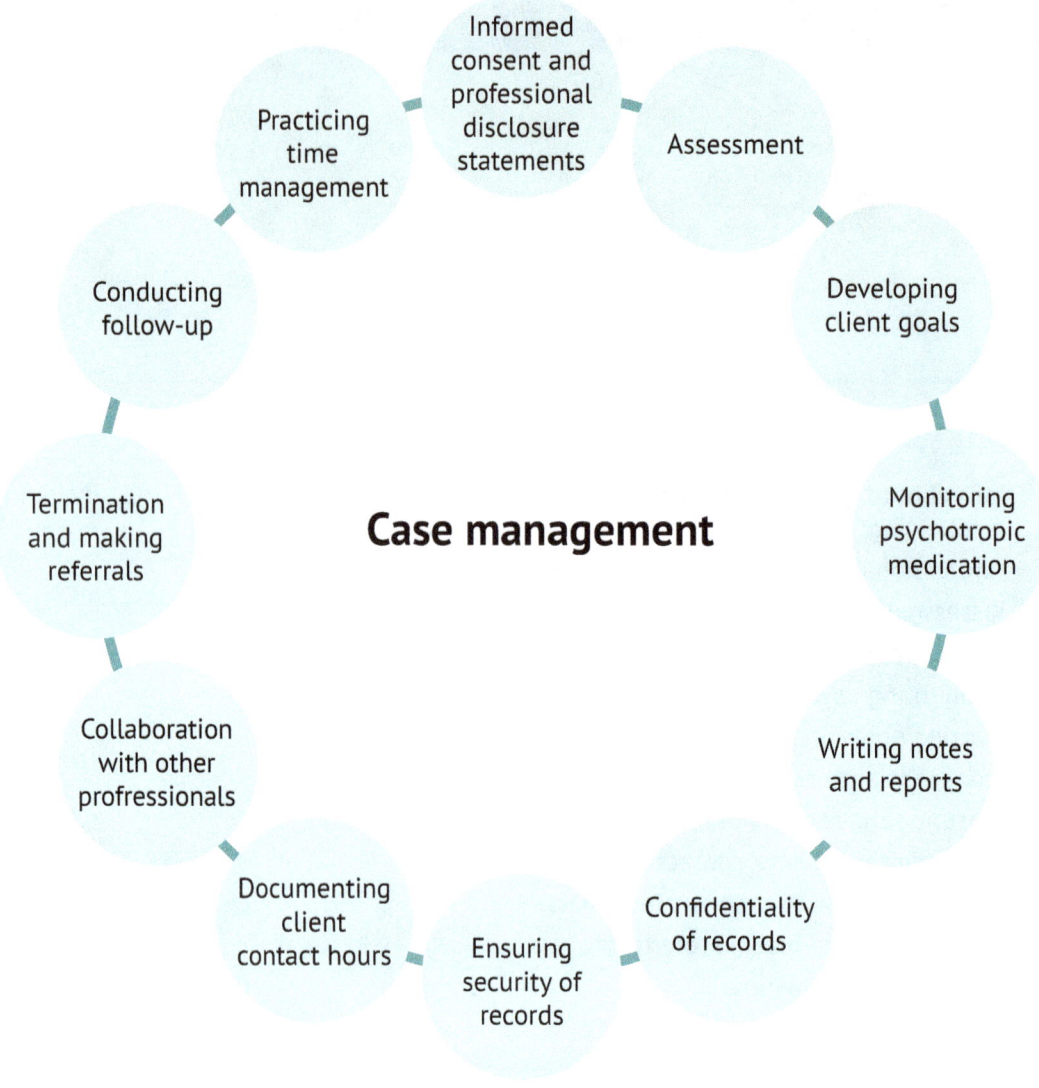

FIGURE 10.1   12 Aspects of Case Management

professionals, termination and making referrals, conducting follow-ups, and practicing time management. Although some of these tend to be done at specific times during the relationship, many need to be examined and reassessed throughout the relationship. Let's look at these 12 aspects of case management (see Figure 10.1).

PROFESSIONAL DISCLOSURE STATEMENTS AND INFORMED CONSENT

When clients begin counseling, they are usually handed a professional disclosure statement that summarizes the purposes, procedures, and nature of the counseling relationship and covers a wide net. For instance, the AMHCA and ACA Code of Ethics, as well as books on ethics, suggest the following areas be addressed in such a statement (ACA, 2014; AMHCA, 2020; Corey et al., 2024; Remley & Herlihy, 2020):

- the role of diagnosis
- supervision processes
- emergency procedures
- information about fees and billing
- the role of technology in counseling
- how assessment procedures will be used
- potential risks and benefits of counseling
- that clients can refuse services at any point
- the CMHC's theoretical approach to counseling
- the importance of each client's unique diversity
- information about clients' rights to confidentiality
- the CMHC's credentials, experience, and qualifications
- the limits to boundaries in the counseling relationship
- legal issues that might impact the counseling relationship
- how clients will participate in the ongoing counseling plan
- agency rules that might impact the counseling relationship
- how services will continue should the CMHC become incapacitated
- how records will be used and what rights clients have to their records
- the limits of confidentiality, especially relative to harm to self or others
- purposes, goals, techniques, and procedures of the counseling relationship

Near the beginning of each counseling relationship, clients can be given a written or electronic copy of the professional disclosure statement. After reviewing it, they can be asked if they have any other questions regarding treatment and if they feel comfortable signing an informed consent document, which involves them voluntarily agreeing to participate in counseling based on their understanding of its procedures, benefits, and risks, as noted in the professional disclosure statement (American Psychological Association [APA], 2023; see Experiential Exercise 10.1).

> **EXPERIENTIAL EXERCISE 10.1** **Writing Your Professional Disclosure Statement**
>
> Using the 20 professional disclosure items just noted, write your own professional disclosure statement. Keep it to two, single-spaced pages. Share your statement with others in class.

ASSESSMENT

One important function of the CMHC is to conduct a client assessment, which, at a minimum, involves a clinical interview but may also include administration of tests and informal assessment (Neukrug & Fawcett, 2020; Schwitzer & Rubin, 2015). Assessment helps the CMHC gain an in-depth understanding of the client, and the information gathered can be used in case conceptualization. Sometimes it also results in a psychological report of the client (see Chapter 9 and Appendix E).

The Clinical Interview

Probably the most important area of assessment, the clinical interview, allows the CMHC to gather information from a broad area of the client's life. Often, this interview takes place during the initial contact with the agency or setting and is called an intake interview.

A good clinical interview involves gathering information from several areas, including demographic information, the presenting problem or reason for referral, family background, significant medical/counseling history, substance use and abuse, educational and vocational history, other pertinent information, and the mental status exam. Gathering this information along with gathering and reporting test and informal assessment results can lead to a diagnosis, summary and conclusions, and recommendations. All of these elements are often written up in a psychological report (see Appendix E: Psychological Report and Appendix F: Categories Generally Assessed in a Psychological Report).

All areas of a clinical interview are important; however, the mental status exam needs special attention, as helpers often struggle with it. Although authors differ on what is included in a mental status exam, at the minimum, it generally contains information about the client's (a) appearance and behavior, or presentation of self; (b) affect, or emotional state; (c) thought components, or ability to think clearly; and (d) cognition, or memory state and orientation to the world (Akiskal, 2016; Washington State Department of Social and Health Services, 2018). The following provides short descriptions of these areas.

Appearance and Behavior

This includes observable appearance and behaviors during the clinical interview, such as manner of dress; hygiene; body posture; tics; significant nonverbal behaviors, such as eye contact or the lack thereof, wringing of hands, or swaying; and manner of speech, such as stuttering and tone.

Emotional State

Here, the examiner describes the client's affect and mood. Affect includes the client's current, prevailing feeling state (e.g., happy, sad, joyful, angry, or depressed) and may also be reported as constricted or full, appropriate or inappropriate to content, labile, flat, blunted, exaggerated, and so forth. The client's mood, on the other hand, represents the long-term, underlying emotional well-being of the client and is usually assessed through client self-report. Thus, a client may seem anxious and sad during the session (affect) and report that their mood has been depressed.

Thought Components

The manner in which the client thinks, or thought components, is generally broken down into the content and the process of thinking. Content includes such things as whether the client has delusions, distortions of body image, hallucinations, obsessions, suicidal or homicidal ideation, and so forth. A statement about a client's thought process often includes references to circumstantiality; coherence; flight of ideas; logical thinking; intact, as opposed to loose, associations; organization; and tangentiality.

Cognition

Whether a client is oriented to time, place, and person (knows what time it is, where they are, and who they are) is one important aspect of cognition and should generally be included in the mental status report. Other aspects include a write-up on the client's short- and long-term memory, an evaluation of the client's knowledge base and intellectual functioning, and a statement about the client's level of insight and ability to make judgments (see Appendix G for more information on writing a mental status, and then see Experiential Exercise 10.2).

> ## EXPERIENTIAL EXERCISE 10.2 **Writing a Mental Status Report**
>
> Find a partner and have one person roleplay a seriously impaired client, while the other, the counselor, assesses the client's mental status. Then, write a mental status report. After the first roleplay, switch roles, and have the second counselor assess the client and write the mental status report. Use the mental status report section of the psychological report found in Appendix E as a model. Appendix G can help you write your mental status report. When you have finished, discuss the following issues in class:
>
> 1. How difficult was it to assess a client's mental status?
> 2. What would have helped you in your assessment?
> 3. What questions might help you in assessing all four areas of the client's mental status?
> 4. What value do you see in conducting a mental status report?
> 5. Do you have other questions about the mental status report?

Administration of Tests

The administration of tests includes using instruments that have been shown to have test worthiness, which means they are valid (they measure what they are supposed to measure), reliable (they measure accurately), cross-culturally fair, and practical for the purpose for which they are being used (Neukrug & Fawcett, 2020). In many states, CMHCs can give a wide variety of educational and psychological tests, usually with the exception of projective testing and the more involved cognitive ability tests (e.g., intelligence testing). However, CMHCs should know their state laws to determine what tests they can give. Whatever testing they do conduct, CMHCs should be trained and competent in giving them, as outlined by AMHCA:

> CMHCs employ only those diagnostic tools and assessment instruments they are trained to use by education or supervised training and clinical experience.
>
> a. CMHCs seek appropriate workshops, supervision, and training to familiarize themselves with assessment techniques and the use of specific assessment instruments.
>
> b. CMHC supervisors ensure that their supervisees have adequate training in interpretation before allowing them to evaluate tests independently (AMHCA, 2020, Standard D3).

Informal Assessment

Informal assessment includes a wide variety of procedures that require little advanced training and are aimed at providing a quick and focused assessment of a client (Neukrug & Fawcett, 2020). Although generally not as valid or reliable as tests, they can be quickly administered and can be created to focus directly on a client's presenting concern. Some of the many types of informal assessment include observation; rating scales; classification methods, such as behavior or feeling word checklists (see Appendix H); environmental assessment, such as observing a person at their home or workplace; records and personal documents; and performance-based assessment, such as when a person is assessed on a task in a real-life situation. Informal assessments are often counselor made, and the number and types of instruments one can come up with is only limited by one's imagination. Reflection Exercise 10.1 shows one type of easily developed informal assessment. Can you come up with others?

REFLECTION EXERCISE 10.1 **Informal Assessment**

The following is an informal assessment of possible posttraumatic stress disorder (PTSD). This simple behavior checklist can be used as one measure to assess whether a person has PTSD.
   Check any items that you have experieced in the past month:*

- ☐ startled easily
- ☐ always on guard for hazards and peril
- ☐ engage in self-harmful behaviors (e.g., excessive drinking, cutting, head banging, punching self, and burning self)
- ☐ nightmares
- ☐ irritability
- ☐ angry and aggressive behaviors
- ☐ strong feelings of guilt or shame; suicidal feelings
- ☐ not able to manage your feelings

- ☐ excessive pain and sweating without apparent cause
- ☐ constant thoughts about past trauma
- ☐ avoiding people or things that would remind one of the trauma
- ☐ flashbacks
- ☐ problems concentrating
- ☐ sleeping difficulties
- ☐ distorted thoughts or forgetfullness about the original trauma
- ☐ feeling helpless

The time period can be changed.

After reviewing the checklist in Reflection Exercise 10.1, do you think it is valid (assesses what it's supposed to assess), reliable (consistently measures what it's supposed to measure), cross-culturally fair, and practical to use? This instrument, which was created by a quick internet search of the words "post-traumatic stress syndrome," could easily have issues with validity, reliability, and cross-cultural fairness but is practical, as it can be created quickly and focuses on the problem at hand. Of course, one must ask if it is worth creating such an instrument when your instrument may not be test worthy.

GOAL DEVELOPMENT

Goal development for clients is a critical aspect of most therapeutic approaches (Cooper & Law, 2018), and identifying specific goals should be a relatively easy process if the CMHC has completed a thorough assessment of the client. Some general rules of thumb include the following eight rules of goal attainment:

- **Goal development should follow the assessment process**.
- **Goal development should be collaborative**. Goals should not be "given" to the client but jointly developed.
- **Goals should be attainable**. If goals are too lofty, the client will feel like a failure if they are not met. If goals are too simple, they are less likely to help the client feel successful.
- **Progress toward goals should be monitored**. Not monitoring progress can lead clients to question their CMHC's ability or commitment. In addition, it can result in lack of follow-through on the part of clients. Lack of progress needs to be reviewed to determine whether goals need to be changed.
- **Goals can be changed**. If a client is not reaching their goals, discuss why. Were they too difficult or too easy? Were they the wrong goals? Were they not attempted due to lack of time or motivation? After determining why they were not reached, rework the goals and try again.
- **Develop new goals as former goals are reached**. As clients reach their goals, determine whether they are ready to work on new ones.

EXPERIENTIAL EXERCISE 10.3 Assessing Needs and Developing Goals

Part I
Spend 10 to 20 minutes interviewing another student who is roleplaying a client or discussing a real situation. While interviewing your client, assess the client's needs. When the interview is near completion, write down the client's needs as you view them. After you have finished, obtain feedback from your client regarding the accuracy of your assessment.

Part II
With your roleplay client in Part I, spend a minimum of 10 minutes developing your client goals. The goals should be an outgrowth of your client's needs formulated in Part I. Make sure the goal-setting process is collaborative and the client is comfortable with the goals developed.

- **Attainment of goals should be affirmed**. Clients work hard to reach their goals, and it is important that they are affirmed for their success.
- **Know when to stop**. Although it is important to keep clients moving forward, also know when to encourage a client to stop. Sometimes a client has simply finished!

With insurance companies and funding agencies increasingly wanting to know that client progress is being made, documenting progress toward goals has become even more important (Jensen-Doss, 2018; Woodside & McClam, 2018). In fact, some funding sources today will not renew funding if documentation of attainment toward goals is not demonstrated. The simplest way to document such progress is to make a note in the client's chart. Innovative CMHCs can create charts and graphs to visually document client progress (see Experiential Exercise 10.3).

MONITORING PSYCHOTROPIC MEDICATIONS

The use of psychopharmacology in the treatment of emotional problems has become widespread, and CMHCs are often in charge of monitoring psychotropic medications (see Chapter 7). With an increase in the types of medications available and the lessening of side effects, medications are now prescribed for almost any kind of psychological problem and, despite some challenges, should often be considered an adjunct to treatment (see Table 10.1 which is similar to Table 8.2).

TABLE 10.1 Advantages and Disadvantages of Psychotropic Medication

Advantages of Medication	Disadvantages of Medication
Medication can help motivate clients to work in the helping relationship.	Counseling can lead to autonomy; drugs can lead to dependence.
Medications can instill hope, as a person quickly begins to feel better.	Only counseling can address the complexity of the human condition.
Sometimes the quick response of medication can reduce the likelihood of a serious mental illness (e.g., schizophrenia) occurring again.	The positive effects of medications can lessen the desire for some clients to work on their problems.
Medication may help some people who are not helped by psychotherapy.	Targeted medications for some emotional problems increase beliefs that clients embody the illness and that they have little control over change.

(Continued)

TABLE 10.1 (*Continued*)

Advantages of Medication	Disadvantages of Medication
Sometimes, medications are more cost effective than psychotherapy.	Most psychotropic medications have side effects, and sometimes, these can be serious and long lasting.
The biological basis of some disorders means treatment by medication is crucial.	Psychotropic medications do not solve life's problems—only the client can.
The effectiveness of medication can be examined easily.	Outcome research on some psychotropic medication is mixed and confusing.

Although CMHCs cannot prescribe medication, they often consult with medical professionals who can prescribe. A working knowledge of medication can be helpful when consulting with these professionals. Therefore, CMHCs should know medication basics so they can (a) consult with physicians, particularly psychiatrists, psychiatric nurse practitioners, and, in some states and government agencies, psychologists; (b) be knowledgeable when assisting clients in adhering to their medication regime; (c) help identify potential side effects; and (d) have a sense of knowing whether the medication is working (see Chapter 7 for common psychotropic medications; see Experiential Exercise 10.4).

EXPERIENTIAL EXERCISE 10.4   Diagnosis and Medication: Helpful or Problematic?

In small groups, discuss whether medication would be helpful for these three vignettes. For Vignette 1, discuss whether the counselor should be suggesting what medication Joselin might want to take.

Vignette 1
Joselin is a 12-year-old middle school student, who has been assessed as having a panic disorder. She can do well in school, most of the time. However, a few times a week, she has severe panic attacks that end up with her leaving school and going home. They have become so intense and embarrassing that she now wants to be homeschooled. She has an older brother and twin younger sisters, all of whom seem to be doing well. Her father has a history of anxiety and her mother of depression, but their marriage is described as "solid." Joselin's mother and father fear Joselin's panic disorder is "genetic" and don't know what to do. She has just begun counseling, and her counselor is suggesting she gets a referral for possible antidepressant medication that also has antianxiety effects or whatever the prescribing health professional believes is best.

Vignette 2
John, a 35-year-old married male, has been having difficulties in his relationship with Steve (32), who he states is constantly thinking he is cheating on him, even though he is not. Steve also has delusional thoughts about the government having the ability to hear everyone's conversation through their phones. He has "secretly" told John about this but does not want others to know, as he's afraid they'll think he is crazy. Steve comes from a family in which schizophrenia is prevalent, and John is concerned that Steve is beginning to show some tendencies toward schizophrenia. John is hopeful he can help Steve receive treatment and medication quickly to ward of a "full-fledged schizophrenic episode."

(continued)

> **Vignette 3**
> Eduardo, a 27-year-old single male, has been dating Elicia for 3 years. He states Elicia has been pressuring him to get married and that he does not currently feel ready for marriage, although he says he loves her. He goes on to report that she is threatening to leave the relationship if he does not "take the next step." He describes himself as "severely depressed and anxious" and does not know what to do. He is considering going to counseling and hopes he can get some medication to help him through this difficult time in his life.

WRITING PROCESS NOTES, CASE NOTES, AND CASE REPORTS

Client records are a critical aspect of case management and are important for several reasons (Baird, 2019; Summers, 2016):

- They assist the CMHC in remembering what the client said.
- They help CMHCs conceptualize client problems and make diagnoses.
- They help determine whether clients have made progress.
- They are important when obtaining supervision.
- They may be used in court to show adequate client care took place.
- They are often mandated by insurance companies and government agencies to approve the treatment being given to clients.
- They are sometimes used in assessing agency effectiveness for funding sources.

The kinds of notes or reports you write will likely depend on the agency or institution in which you work. However, three types of notes and reports typically required at agencies and institutions include psychotherapy or process notes, case notes, and case reports.

Psychotherapy or Process Notes

Process notes, sometimes called psychotherapy notes, are relatively short notes written by CMHCs to highlight important points and summarize every meeting a client has with the CMHC. These notes are used to jog the memory of the CMHC for the next time they meet with the client. With some CMHCs having dozens of clients, process notes are useful and often essential.

Under the privacy rule of the Health Insurance Privacy and Portability Act (HIPAA), psychotherapy notes should not be viewed by an unauthorized person, and in the case of these kind of notes, clients have limited or no access to them (APA, 2013; U.S. Department of Health and Human Services, 2023a). The actual definition from HIPPA is as follows:

> [N]otes recorded (in any medium) by a health care provider who is a mental health professional documenting or analyzing the contents of conversation during a private counseling session or a group, joint, or family counseling session and that are separated from the rest of the individual's medical record. Psychotherapy notes excludes medication prescription and monitoring, counseling session start and stop times, the modalities and frequencies of treatment furnished, results of clinical tests, and any summary of the following items: Diagnosis, functional status, the treatment plan, symptoms, prognosis, and progress to date. (National Archives and Records Administration 2023, Psychotherapy Notes section)

Case Notes, Case Reports, Psychological Reports

Although the terms case notes and case reports are often used interchangeably, some view case reports as more involved and longer than case notes. Both case notes and case reports can include a wide variety of ways of summarizing client information. Some examples include the intake interview, highlights of a client's goals and objectives, periodic summaries of clients' progress, specialized reports for the courts or other agencies, transfer summaries, broad-based psychological reports, termination summaries, and more. In contrast to process (psychotherapy) notes, clients almost always have the right to access case notes and case reports.

Today, CMHCs often use sophisticated software to assist in their writing of case notes and case reports. Whether using such software or writing the report on your own, the minimum information found in such notes or reports usually includes the name of the client, the date, major facts noted during contact, progress made toward achieving client goals, and the CMHC's signature. More involved reports may include demographic information (e.g., date of birth, address, phone number, date of interview, and e-mail address); reason for report; family background; other pertinent background information (e.g., health information, vocational history, legal concerns, and history of adjustment issues/emotional problems/mental illness); mental status; assessment results; diagnosis; and a summary, conclusions, and recommendations section (see an example of a report in Appendix E).

Any written information about a client needs to be relatively objective and, based on observable behavior, not opinion. Based on the strength of the privileged communication law in the CMHC's state, what the CMHC writes could be subpoenaed by the courts, and the CMHC could be held liable for their statements. Therefore, writing from an objective, dispassionate point of view is essential when keeping case notes or case reports. Generally, the third person should be used in referring to the client. For example, it would be better to say, "Family information was gathered from Jim," rather than, "I collected family information from Jim." Any subjective information gathered from the client should be noted as such. To assist in this, begin subjective statements with phrases such as, "It seems that … ," "Jim noted that … ," "It appears that … ," "Jim reported that … ," "Claire related that … ," and "Claire recounted that. … "

When writing case notes, CMHCs should avoid biased statements and sexist attitudes, not use significant amounts of psychological jargon, and not make statements expressing their own values or opinions (unless the CMHC's opinions are called for, as when a court is asking for it or the CMHC is making a diagnosis). Also, CMHCs should write case notes or case reports, so other mental health professionals can readily understand them.

SOAP Notes

One approach to writing case notes that has gained popularity over the years is called SOAP notes (Woodside & McClam, 2018). These notes focus on the client's subjective understanding of what the client has experienced, the CMHC's objective description of what they understand the client's situation to be, the CMHC's assessment of the client's situation, and a description of the treatment plan. Using SOAP notes, Table 10.2 gives an example of how such a method is used with a depressed client. These notes are easy to keep, focused, and one can see progress over time.

TABLE 10.2 SOAP Notes/Reports

SOAP Element	Overview	Description
Subjective	Description by client of her experiences in the world	The client describes periodic depressive episodes and notes she feels sad much of the time and "mopes around" her house. Her sadness, she states, has been pervasive, and she reports having difficulty relating to others. She notes that she has difficulty starting and completing tasks and is concerned she is not properly parenting her children.

Objective	Description by counselor of client behaviors	The client looked disheveled when she came to the session. She had difficulty talking and sobbed periodically during the session. The client was given a Beck Depression Inventory, which she scored a 35 on, indicating severe depression. Behaviors described also indicate depression, including lack of sleep, loss of weight, and inability to get tasks done. On multiple occasions this has resulted in her children going to school without their lunch and without clean clothes. Depression started after the death of her mother, which occurred approximately 8 months ago.
Assessment	Summary of counselor's thinking with evidence of assessment of client	The client describes serious depression that seems congruent with a diagnosis of major depressive disorder of *DSM-5-TR*. This diagnosis is consistent with her symptoms of sadness, lack of motivation, difficulty sleeping and eating, not completing tasks, and difficulty relating to others. Behaviors, and test results, indicate ongoing depression.
Plan	Description of treatment plan by counselor	The treatment plan includes ongoing grief counseling regarding the death of her mother. This should start with rapport building and empathy but soon lead to defining goals, so she can attend to important issues in her life, such as ensuring adequate care of her children. Psychiatric consultation for possible antidepressant medication is planned within the next week. Monitoring of medication will occur during scheduled counseling sessions.

Whereas SOAP notes tend to be shorter summaries of what is going on in the client's life and in counseling, a psychological report, like the one in Appendix E, is a more involved assessment of the client's life. Try writing your own psychological report using the directions in Experiential Exercise 10.5.

EXPERIENTIAL EXERCISE 10.5 Writing a Psychological Report

Using the guidelines that follow, interview a student, and subsequently, write a psychological report. When complete, share it with others in small groups to gain feedback, or hand it in to your instructor, who will review it and give you feedback. Keep it to four single-spaced, 12-font pages. Use Appendix E as a model.

The following are some possible categories for a psychological report:

- demographic information (e.g., date of birth, address, phone number, and date of interview).
- reason for report
- family background
- other pertinent background information (e.g., health information, vocational history, or history of adjustment issues/emotional problems/mental illness)
- mental status
- assessment results, if any
- diagnosis
- summary and conclusions
- recommendations
- signature

CONFIDENTIALITY OF RECORDS

Today, confidentiality of records is protected by the HIPPA privacy rule, which sets limits and conditions on the release of information without the client's authorization (APA, 2013; U.S. Department of Health and Human Services, 2023a). However, there are some times when the CMHC is legally bound, or required, to release such information by law. This may occur

- when the CMHC is consulting with a professional or undergoing supervision for the benefit the client;
- in certain cases of mandatory reporting (e.g., child, spousal, older abuse);
- if the client is in danger of harming self or others;
- if the court subpoenas a client's records and the CMHC is not protected by privileged communication;
- if a client gives permission, in writing, to share information with others; and
- for certain information for health insurance companies or funding sources that are underwriting counseling services.

In addition to protecting the privacy of client records, HIPAA gives clients the rights to their health information, in most instances (Remley & Herlihy, 2020). Similarly, the Freedom of Information Act (FOIA) of 1974 allows individuals access to records maintained by a federal agency that contain personal information about the individual (U.S. Department of Justice, 2021), and states have followed suit with their own FOIA laws. Also, the Family Education Rights and Privacy Act (FERPA) assures individuals the right to access their own and their children's educational records (U.S. Department of Education, 2021).

On a more practical level, a client rarely asks to see their records. Nevertheless, if a client did make such a request, I would first attempt to talk with the client about what is in the records and try to understand why the client wants to know about the records. Sometimes, a client's request to see their records says more about progress (or lack of progress) in counseling than a real desire to see the records. If after talking with the client, they still want to see the records, I might suggest I would write a summary of the records. If this was still unsatisfactory, it is generally the client's legal right to have access to their records, and I would give them a copy. Finally, except in certain instances, parents generally have the right to view records of their children (C. Borstein, personal communication, January 5, 2023). AMHCA's (2020) Code of Ethics notes that clients have a right to "[o]btain information about their case record and to have this information explained clearly and directly" (Section 1.B.7.g). And ACA's (2104) Code of Ethics says the following:

> Counselors provide reasonable access to records and copies of records when requested by competent clients. Counselors limit the access of clients to their records, or portions of their records, only when there is compelling evidence that such access would cause harm to the client. Counselors document the request of clients and the rationale for withholding some or all of the records in the files of clients. (Section B.6.e., Client Access)

and

> When clients request access to their records, counselors provide assistance and consultation in interpreting counseling records. (Section B.6.f., Assistance with Records)

ENSURING SECURITY OF RECORDS

As outlined by ACA, client records need to be kept in secure places, such as locked file cabinets and password-secured computers: "Counselors ensure that records and documentation kept in any medium are secure and that only authorized persons have access to them" (ACA, 2014, Section B.6.b). Any records sent electronically need to be encrypted and HIPAA compliant. Under the

HIPPA security rule, ensuring security of records indicates that safeguards for administrative, physical, and technical matters are in place:

- **administrative safeguards:** Examples include having a process in place to identify risks, designating a security official, implementing a process to authorize access to information only when appropriate, providing training and supervision to workforce members, and performing periodic assessments of security policies and procedures.
- **physical safeguards:** Examples include implementing processes and procedures to limit unauthorized access to facilities, workstations, and devices.
- **technical safeguards:** Examples include technical policies and procedures to control access, ensure data integrity, and safeguard electronic transmission over a network. (Privacy Rights Clearinghouse, 2014, Section 3.c)

Clearly, CMHHCs need to be aware of the technological safeguards that need to be in place in the workplace, especially if the CMHC is an independent practitioner. In addition, clerical workers need to understand the importance of confidentiality when working with records. In fact, many agencies have clerical staff sign statements, often legally binding ones, acknowledging they understand the importance of the confidentiality of records and they will keep all correspondences and information confidential (see Reflection Exercise 10.2).

REFLECTION EXERCISE 10.2 How Secure Are Records?

Unfortunately, counselors, and others, sometimes forget how easily client records can be misplaced or information in the records can become available to the public. The following true stories highlight the ways information in records can be mishandled and stress the importance of keeping records secure and confidential:

- When working as an outpatient therapist at a mental health center, a client appropriated his paper records that had been left "lying around." Because the records were written in "psychologese," using diagnostic language, the client was understandably quite upset by what he found. He would periodically call emergency services and read his records over the phone to the emergency worker, while making fun of the language used in the records.
- While taking a class in my doctoral program, we were reviewing an intellectual test assessment of an adolescent that had been completed several years earlier. Suddenly, one of the students in class yelled out, "That's me!" Apparently, although there was no identifying name on the report, he recognized it as describing him.
- In 2014, 4.5 million medical records, including mental health records, were hacked from Community Health Systems (CHS; Pagliery, 2014). Although CHS thought they had a secure system, they found out otherwise, and due to HIPAA, individuals could now sue CHS for breach of information.
- The U.S. Department of Health and Human Services (2023b) lists hundreds of cases of "unsecured protected health information affecting 500 or more individuals" within the past 2 years.

Besides the obvious liability issues of these true scenarios, these examples show the importance of ensuring administrative, physical, and technical safeguards when securing client records.

DOCUMENTATION OF CONTACT HOURS

Documentation of contact hours and what occurred with clients during their counseling sessions has become increasingly important as CMHCs have had to respond to requirements set forth by insurance companies as well as local, state, and federal funding agencies (Summers, 2016). Every setting deals with documentation of client hours differently, and the resulting documentation is generally based on the following:

- the kinds of issues and goals clients tend to work on at the setting
- the expectation of the setting for the number and length of sessions
- the expectations of the setting for the kind of case notes or records that are needed
- client expectations about how often and how long they will be meeting
- the kind of case notes ethically and legally needed (e.g., process notes, case notes, and SOAP notes)
- the expectations of what will happen if a client meeting is cancelled or extended
- the expectations of funding agencies (e.g., insurance companies, state regulatory commissions, and state boards of education)
- laws regarding the amount of time the CMHC should meet with clients

Today, most clinical settings have a mechanism for recording client meeting times with CMHCs and how those meeting times are documented. As you consider the setting in which you want to work, think about the kinds of documentation that might be needed (see Experiential Exercise 10.6).

EXPERIENTIAL EXERCISE 10.6 **Ways of Documenting Hours**

Form groups of four or five students based on the setting in which you would like to work. After forming your groups, spend time consulting with an agency or search the internet for examples of the following (this assignment might take a few days):

1. What are the expectations regarding how often and how long clients will meet with their counselor?
2. How are client contact hours documented?
3. What kinds of case notes are expected? How are they documented?
4. What laws or regulations might dictate how documentation occurs?
5. How does payment occur as a result of documentation?
6. What happens regarding payment if a meeting is cancelled?

After your group has gathered this information, share what you found in class. Consider the different kinds of necessary documentation as you hear from students who are interested in working in different settings than your own.

COLLABORATING WITH OTHER PROFESSIONALS

These days, it is common for clients to be in other helping relationships in addition to a counseling relationship with a CMHC. With this in mind, most codes of ethics state that a CMHC should not enter into a counseling relationship with a client who is being served in a counseling capacity by another mental health professional (e.g., individual, couples and family, or group counseling), unless the other helper has been informed and agrees to the arrangement. In addition, when clients work with multiple helpers, they should secure permission to do so from the other helpers and work in a collaborative manner with all helpers involved (AMHCA, 2020, Section 1.B.4).

In addition to working closely with other mental health professionals, today's CMHCs are often found working side by side with professionals who are working with the same clients in a different capacity (e.g., MDs, lawyers, prison guards, occupational therapists, and physician assistants). In fact, working with mental health professionals and other professionals in integrated behavioral health care settings has become increasingly common, and CMHCs need to be proficient at collaborating with other professionals (Franklin, 2022). AMHCA's (2020) Code of Ethics notes that CMHCs should adhere to the following when collaborating and consulting with colleagues:

1. CMHCs treat colleagues and other professionals with respect.

2. CMHCs understand how related professions complement their work and make full use of other professional, technical, and administrative resources that best serve the interests of clients.

3. CMHCs treat professional colleagues with dignity and respect. Professional discourse should be free of personal attacks. CMHC recognize and respect professional cultural differences.

4. CMHCs respect the viability, reputation, and proprietary rights of organizations that they serve.

5. Credit is assigned to those who have contributed to a publication in proportion to their contribution.

6. CMHCs do not accept or offer referral fees from other professionals.

7. When CMHCs have knowledge of the impairment, incompetence, or unethical conduct of a mental health professional, they are expected to attempt to rectify the situation. Failing an informal resolution, CMHCs should bring such unethical activities to the attention of the appropriate state licensing board and/or the ethics committee of the professional association (Section II.A).

TERMINATION AND MAKING REFERRALS

Clients are terminated, or referred to other professionals, for numerous reasons, and this process should be as seamless as possible (Summers, 2016; Neukrug, 2019; Woodside & McClam, 2018). Some reasons for client termination or referral include being referred as a part of the treatment plan, the professional is leaving the agency, the death of the professional, the professional feeling incompetent to work with the client, and the client having reached their goals and being ready to move on to another form of treatment. However, it is not appropriate to refer a client due to value differences (see ACA, 2014). In these cases, the CMHC should find ways to work effectively with the client, despite such differences (e.g., undergo supervision).

When referring or terminating a client, the AMHCA (2020) Code of Ethics states that CMHCs should ensure clients have appropriate referrals or find other mechanisms to ensure their ongoing mental health. It notes the following:

CMHCs do not abandon or neglect their counseling clients.

a. Assistance is given in making appropriate arrangements for the continuation of treatment, when necessary, during interruptions such as vacation and following termination.

b. CMHCs may terminate a counseling relationship when it is reasonably clear that the client is no longer benefiting, when services are no longer required, when counseling no longer serves the needs and/or interests of the client, or when agency or institution limits do not allow provision of further counseling services.

c. CMHCs may terminate a counseling relationship when clients do not pay fees charged or when insurance denies treatment. In such cases, appropriate referrals are offered to the clients.

d. If CMHCs determine that services are not beneficial to the client, they avoid immediately terminating the counseling relationship. Instead, appropriate referrals are made. If clients decline the suggested referral, CMHCs may discontinue the relationship.

e. When CMHCs refer clients to other professionals, they will be collaborative.

f. CMHCs take steps to develop a safety plan if clients are at risk of being harmed or are suicidal. If necessary, they refer to appropriate resources and contact appropriate support. (Section 1.B.5)

Finally, when making a referral, a CMHC should gain client approval and gain permission from clients to talk with other professionals involved in the referral process. In addition, the client's referral process should be monitored to ensure confidentiality and ease of transition (see Experiential Exercise 10.7).

EXPERIENTIAL EXERCISE 10.7 Making Referrals

Find a fellow student; have one of you roleplay a CMHC, while the other roleplays a client. Choose one of the aforementioned reasons a counselor might refer or terminate a client, and then roleplay a situation in which such a referral or termination is to take place. Reflect on how it feels for you and the client to go through this process. Share your feelings in small groups or with the class.

CONDUCTING FOLLOW-UPS

Follow-up, another important function of case management, can be completed by a phone call, a letter, an elaborate survey of clients, or other ways. It can be done a few days to a few weeks after the relationship has ended and serves many purposes (Neukrug, 2019; Summers, 2016). A follow-up may be required by some funding agencies to ensure services have been adequate (how many times have you received a follow-up survey recently?). The following are a few reasons follow-ups are so important:

- They function as a check to see whether clients would like to return for counseling or be referred to a different counselor.
- They allow the CMHC to assess whether change has been maintained.
- They give the CMHC the opportunity to determine which counseling techniques have been most successful.
- They offer an opportunity to reinforce client change.
- They allow the CMHC to evaluate services provided to the client.

Follow-ups are one method for conducting program evaluation and ensuring excellence in services being rendered. These days, follow-ups are a necessary, and often critical, aspect of counseling services.

PRACTICING TIME MANAGEMENT

With ever-increasing caseloads and demands placed on CMHCs, time management has become crucial if the CMHC is to avoid burnout, compassion fatigue, and vicarious traumatization (Woodside & McClam, 2018). Time management strategies serve several purposes, including helping CMHCs ensure that all clients are seen within a reasonable period of time and helping CMHCs remember meetings, appointment times, and other obligations. Today, there are several helpful time management systems. Although this text will not delve into these different systems, suffice it to say that addressing time management concerns is paramount in today's world.

SUMMARY

This chapter reviewed 12 important areas of case management, or the overall process involved in maintaining the optimal level of functioning for clients, including providing informed consent and professional disclosure statements, assessment for treatment planning, developing client goals, monitoring psychotropic medications, writing notes and reports, confidentiality of records, ensuring security of client records, documenting client contact hours, collaboration with other professionals, termination and making referrals, conducting follow-ups, and practicing time management.

We started the chapter by highlighting the importance of 20 items critical to address in one's professional disclosure statement, which should be provided to the client in electronic or paper form. We noted that the items highlighted in this statement should be acknowledged in an informed consent document, which is signed by the client.

Relative to assessment for treatment planning, we noted that this process includes conducting a clinical interview, administering tests, and using informal assessment procedures and that these procedures are often part of the case conceptualization process and may result in a psychological report. We talked about the fact that the intake interview is often the first important clinical interview the client undergoes, and we identified several areas that are usually assessed during an interview, while spending a bit of time discussing the mental status report, which describes the client's appearance and behavior, affect, thought components, and cognition. Relative to testing, we talked about test worthiness, which means a test is valid, reliable, cross-culturally fair, and practical. We also noted that it was important to know state laws and one's own level of competence to give certain tests. Moving on to informal assessment, we pointed out that these procedures are usually less valid or reliable than tests, but are sometimes useful as a quick measure to use for focused areas of client concerns.

Next we examined goal development and identified eight rules of thumb in developing goals, including the idea that they should be an outgrowth of the assessment process, collaborative, attainable, monitored, changeable, developed anew when former ones are reached, affirming of clients when reached, and no longer needed when the client has reached an end point to counseling.

We next moved on to a discussion about monitoring client use of psychopharmacology. We pointed out advantages and disadvantages of such use and noted that psychotropic drugs are discussed in more detail in Chapter 7. We noted that it is important for CMHCs to have knowledge of psychotropic medications if they are to intelligibly consult with those who prescribe such drugs, be knowledgeable to assist clients in their medication regime, be helpful in identifying potential side effects, and have a sense of knowing whether the medication is working.

Knowing how to write process notes, case notes, and case reports was next discussed. We first identified several reasons case notes and case reports are important. We then defined psychotherapy notes, often called process notes, as notes that are used to jog the memory of the CMHC for the next time they see the client. We noted that the privacy rule of HIPPA underscores the notion that others should not see client records and that in the case of psychotherapy or process notes, clients have limited access to them. We then distinguished case notes from case reports and noted that case reports tend to be a bit more involved. We also noted that psychological reports are even more involved and referred to the example, in Appendix E. We also pointed out that written information about clients should be relatively objective and should not portray bias, sexism, psychological jargon, or an undue amount of counselor opinion. We described SOAP notes as a subjective understanding of what the client has experienced, an objective description of the client's situation, an assessment of the client's situation, and a description of the treatment plan. An example of SOAP notes was given.

A discussion of confidentiality of records highlighted when client records may be released, sometimes without client permission. These included (a) for consultation or supervision; (b) for mandatory reporting; (c) if the client is in danger of harming self or others; (d) court subpoenas when the CMHC is not protected by privileged communication; (e) if a client gives permission, in writing, to share information; and (f) certain information to health insurance companies or funding sources that are underwriting counseling services. We noted that clients generally have the right to their health records and educational records, as underscored by the HIPAA privacy rule, the Freedom of Information Act, and FERPA. We also noted that parents generally have rights to their children's records. When talking about the security of client records, we noted that the HIPPA security rule suggests administrative, physical, and technical safeguards be in place. We also noted that records should be encrypted, file cabinets locked, and computers password secured.

Relative to the documentation of contact hours, we identified eight items to consider when documenting client contact hours. These included client issues and goals, expectations of the setting, client expectations of length of counseling, ethical concerns, needed ethically and legal issues, if a client session is canceled or extended, expectations of funding agencies, and specific laws regarding amount of time CMHCs should meet with clients.

The chapter went on to note that when collaborating with other professionals, CMHCs should not conduct counseling with a client who is in an existing counseling relationship, unless the other helper has been informed and agrees to the arrangement. We also noted that when clients are in relationships with other non-mental health professionals, it may be important to collaborate with those individuals in the client's interest. We identified several ethical concerns from the AMHCA Code of Ethics relative to collaborating and consulting with colleagues.

When discussing termination and referral, we highlighted a number of situations in which plans for client referral or termination should be in place, including being referred as a part of the treatment plan, the professional leaving the agency, the death of the professional, the professional feeling incompetent to work with the client, and the client having reached their goals and being ready to move on to another form of treatment. We noted clients should not be referred due to value differences with the CMHC and that the CMHC should find ways to work with the client when this occurs (e.g., supervision). We also identified six reasons not to abandon or neglect clients that are addressed in the AMHCA code. Finally, we noted that when making referral, a CMHC should gain client approval, gain permission from clients to talk with other professionals, monitor the client's transition, and assure confidentiality.

As the chapter neared its conclusion, we talked about the importance of conducting follow-ups, as they are useful for checking to see if clients would like to come back, being able to assess whether change has been maintained, determining what techniques worked best, being able to reinforce change, and evaluating services that had been given to clients. We concluded the chapter with a brief discussion of practicing time management to avoid burnout, compassion fatigue, and vicarious traumatization.

KEY WORDS AND TERMS

administration of tests
affect
appearance and behavior
assessment

case notes
case reports
clinical interview
cognition

collaborating with other
 professionals
confidentiality of records
cross-cultural fairness

documentation of contact hours
eight rules of goal attainment
ensuring security of records
Family Education Rights and
  Privacy Act (FERPA)
follow-up
Freedom of Information Act
  (FOIA)
goal development
Health Insurance Privacy and
  Portability Act (HIPAA)
HIPPA privacy rule
HIPPA security rule

informal assessment
informed consent
intake interview
integrated behavioral health care
  settings
mental status exam
monitoring psychotropic
  medications
practical
privacy rule
privileged communication
process notes
professional disclosure statement

psychological report
psychopharmacology
psychotherapy notes
psychotropic medications
referral
reliable
SOAP notes
termination
test worthiness
thought components
time management
12 aspects of of case management
valid

CHAPTER 11

CONSULTATION AND SUPERVISION

Learning Goals

- Define consultation, the consultant, and the consultee.
- Understand the systemic nature of consultation and supervision.
- Review the history of consultation and its movement from a direct-service to process approach.
- Understand the different kinds of consultant-centered and consultee centered types of consultation.
- Review the stages of consultation.
- Define supervision, the supervisor, and the supervisee, and examine supervision's similarities and differences to consultation.
- Understand the importance of parallel process in supervision and how it can help to positively impact the counseling process.
- Review types of resistance that can occur in the supervisory relationship, and highlight the importance of understanding countertransference.
- Distinguish between individual, triadic, and group supervision.
- Review developmental, psychotherapy-based, and integrative models of supervision.
- Examine several ethical and legal issues in consultation and supervision.
- Understand professional issues related to supervision of graduate students and practicing counselors and become familiar with the Association for Counselor Education and Supervision.

INTRODUCTION

I've had a lot of experience with consultation and supervision over the years. Some has been good, and some not so good. I've supervised master's level counselors on their way to becoming LPCs—that was good. It's interesting and important work, as you assist a person in becoming better at what they do and watch them grow and mature. I've consulted with universities regarding their counseling programs. That was intense, as I talked with students, faculty, and administrators and reviewed curriculum and program needs. As a clinician, I've been supervised by several people at my work. Often, it was a designated supervisor, but when I was in private practice, I hired a "master therapist" to supervise my work. Being supervised for my work was usually a wonderful experience. However, one time I was supervised by a psychodynamic-oriented supervisor, and my style was clearly not in her toolbox—she fired me. That was devastating. I've consulted with school systems regarding the use of tests, and another time, I consulted with a school regrading a student who was quadriplegic and intellectually disabled and was mainstreamed into a third-grade classroom. That was heart-wrenching—and not in the way you might think. The third-grade students didn't mind him being mainstreamed, but when I talked with them individually, many, in fact most of them, were tearful, due to problems at home.

Within this chapter we're going to look at both consultation and supervision—there are similarities and differences in these two important counseling roles and functions. As a CMHC, you will consult with others, be consulted with, supervise others, and be supervised. We'll begin with consultation.

CONSULTATION

Consultation is an important part of the role of the CMHC. Here, we will first define consultation, noting its relationship to systemic change. Then, we will offer a brief history of consultation, and note the difference between outward and inward consultation. We will then discuss the difference between consultant-centered and consultee centered models of consultation and highlight six stages of consultation. Some examples of the consultation process will be provided.

CONSULTATION DEFINED

Although I personally like this simple definition—"me and you talking about [them] with the purpose of some change" (Fall, 1995, p. 151)—perhaps, a more professional one I might suggest is this: When a professional (the consultant), who has specialized expertise, meets with one or more other professionals to improve their work with current or potential clients. Whereas the consultant is the person who has been called in to do some type of consultation, the consultee is the point person, or the person identifying and inviting the consultant to consult (Falender & Shafranske, 2020). And in some cases, the consultee is not directly involved in the consultation process. For instance, the administrative head of an agency may hire a consultant to conduct a workshop on a new counseling technique for all the counselors at an agency. However, because the administrator is not a counselor, that person may not be included in the workshop.

Consultation is *not* a one-to-one, intense counseling experience. However, it does involve a person who has expertise in consultation skills meeting with others to increase their knowledge and skills (Corey et al., 2020). And in a different way than personal counseling, this too can be intense! For instance, consultation could include any of the following scenarios:

- A mental health agency director hiring a consultant to meet with agency personnel to help them better understand changes in the *Diagnostic and Statistical Manual-5-TR* (DMS-TR-5); (American Psychiatric Association, 2022).
- Counselors inviting a consultant to meet with them to discuss important issues on which the counselors may be focusing upon with their clients (e.g., values in counseling, LGBTQ+ issues, or trauma).
- An administrative director of an agency inviting a consultant to meet with agency personnel to lessen infighting, with the goal being a better-run, friendlier agency.
- A community mental health clinic director asking one of the counselors to develop a workshop for community members on how to identify and refer a depressed teenager.
- A clinical director asking a senior counselor to run a series of workshops for junior counselors on new government regulations concerning confidentiality.

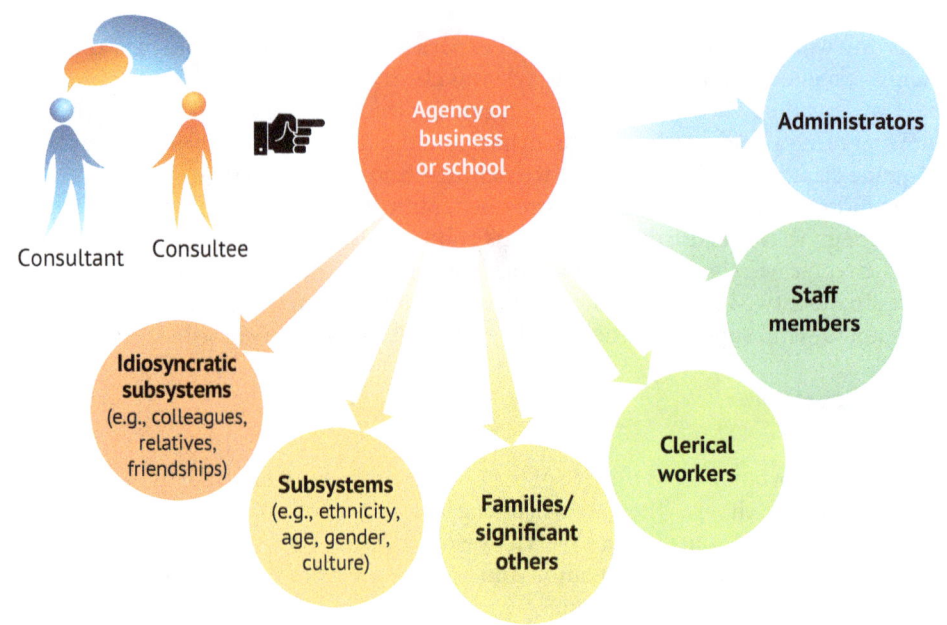

FIGURE 11.1 A Sample of the Many Subsystems in Consultation

Consultation is systemic, in that the effective consultant is able to see the multiple ways individuals within a system view a problem and realizes that any changes made in the system can affect the lives of many other people (Haslebo & Nielsen, 2000/2018; Moe & Perera-Diltz, 2009; see Figure 11.1).

A BRIEF HISTORY OF CONSULTATION

The Beginning of Clinical Mental Health Counseling Consultation

The 1940s and 1950s are considered the beginning of modern consultation methods (Kurpius & Robinson, 1978). At that time, a consultee, who was generally a supervisor or administrator of an organization, would invite a consultant to their setting with the expectation that the consultant, "the expert," would solve an existing problem. After coming to the setting, the consultant would have little contact with the consultee, and the consultant was pretty much left to their own devices to solve the problem. This became known as the direct-service approach to consultation.

> *Consider the following example:* An agency director finds that many of the clinicians do not understand how to appropriately make a diagnosis. The director then invites an expert on *DSM* to come into the agency and perform training for the clinicians.

By the end of the 1950s, the consultee would generally be included in the consultation process, along with the staff. This would help to ensure that if similar issues were to arise, the consultee would have the training to deal with the problem.

> *Consider the following example:* After finding several insurance forms have been returned for misdiagnosis and believing some clients may have been placed on the wrong medication due to similar errors, the clinical director of an agency asks a consultant to come in and teach the staff about the *DSM-5*. The clinical director sits in on the workshops to also gain knowledge and be able to handle the problem on their own, should the situation arise again.

As consultation models evolved, consultation was increasingly seen as a process-oriented approach in which the consultant would train others or "give away" their expertise to staff (Dougherty, 2014; Kurpius & Robinson, 1978).

> *Consider the following example:* The clinical director of an agency realizes the staff are not adequately trained in trauma-informed care. With the increase in mass shootings and other violent acts being epidemic, the director asks an expert on trauma-informed care to come to the agency and conduct a weeklong workshop on how to work with clients who have experienced trauma. At the end of the workshop, the staff now feels competent to do such work.

Consultation Becomes Legitimized

In 1963, Congress passed the Community Mental Health Centers Act, and a new era in the delivery of mental health services was upon us (Erickson, 2021). Providing federal funds for the creation of comprehensive mental health centers across the country, the act provided grants for short-term inpatient care, outpatient care, partial hospitalization, emergency services, and consultation and education services. For the first time, there was an acknowledgment that consultation was an important factor in the prevention of mental health problems. It was then that consultation in community agencies went in two directions: consulting outward and consulting inward.

Consulting Outward

The focus of outward consultation is assisting individuals who have mental health concerns but are not clients directly involved with the agency. For instance, a mental health counselor may consult with the parents and teachers of a child (e.g., helping them cope with a child who has behavioral problems) as well as with other mental health professionals the child might be seeing (e.g., setting up meetings to ensure future treatment strategies don't have cross purposes). A mental health counselor may also consult with schools, hospitals, businesses, and other social service agencies in any number of ways. For example, one consultant might assist teachers and counselors from a school system understand mood disorders in children. Another consultant might be asked by a local business to help reduce the general stress level of its employees, and a third consultant might help a social service agency understand some of its employees' internal conflicts.

Consulting Inward

In 1970, Gerald Caplan published a book called *Theory and Practice of Mental Health Consultation*, which became one of the best-known consultation delivery models. Similar to some of the models of consultation discussed earlier, Caplan's theory defined the role of the consultant in mental health agencies and made suggestions on ways to intervene in organizations (Caplan & Caplan-Moskovich, 2004). His theory, which is still very much in use today, looks inward at an agency, with the major focus ultimately being concern for the clients the agency serves (Erchul, 2009; Scott et al., 2015). He described four consultation roles a consultant might take on in an agency: (a) offering specific suggestions to a counselor who has asked for help in working with a client; (b) assisting a counselor in identifying problems the counselor has working with a client or a number of clients; (c) facilitating communication in the agency and educating agency staff and administrators about identified problems, so the agency runs more smoothly and clients get better service; and (d) working solely with administrators to facilitate communication and educate them about identified problems.

Current Models of Consultation

Today, we find an array of consultation models that speak to how consultants bring themselves into the consulting relationship and are reminiscent of the various models discussed, broken down into two orientations: consultant-centered consultation and consultee-centered consultation (Dougherty, 2014; Falender & Shafranske, 2020; Kampwirth & Powers, 2016; Schein, 2016).

Consultant-Centered Consultation

Three models of consultant-centered consultation, where the consultant imparts knowledge to the system, include the expert, prescriptive, and trainer/educator models:

- **expert consultation model**: In this model, the consultant is specifically brought into an organization because of their expertise in a specific area and asked to use this knowledge to provide solutions to specific problems.
- **prescriptive consultation model (doctor–patient model)**: In this model, the consultant collects information, diagnoses the problem, and makes recommendations to the consultee on how to solve the problem.
- **trainer/educator consultation model**: Often used in what has come to be known as "staff development," this model involves the consultant being hired to come into a system and teach or train staff members.

Consultee-Centered Consultation

Three models of consultee-centered consultation, where the consultant uses their helping skills to elicit knowledge from the system, include the collaborative, facilitative, and process-oriented models.

- **collaborative consultation model**: In this type of consultation, a partnership develops, in which the consultant offers expertise and also relies on the expertise of individuals in the system to offer input into the problems and solutions. This shared expertise model tends to focus on joint decision-making.
- **facilitative consultation model**: In this model, the consultant plays a facilitative role by helping individuals within the system communicate with one another, understand each other, and resolve conflicts among themselves.
- **process-oriented consultation model**: This consultant believes those involved in the consultation either do not have the answer or are withholding their expertise, with the confidence that the most effective resolution (resulting in the highest self-esteem and sense of ownership of the problem) would be for the system members to find their own solution. The consultant has faith that system members can change if the consultant is able to develop a trusting environment.

In choosing a model, the consultant needs to know their personality style, the people with whom they are working, and the problem to be addressed. For instance, one would likely not use an expert model if consulting with therapists who already have a fair amount of expertise in the situation being examined. Similarly, a consultant whose natural style is directive would have a more difficult time taking on a process-oriented style. And a consultant working with counselors who are providing less-than-adequate care on a suicide hotline might start with a consultant-centered style, as it would resolve some issues quickly, which is critical when people's lives are at stake.

Today, the Council on the Accreditation of Counseling and Related Educational Program (CACREP), (2016) requires consultation to be taught as part of the curriculum in a counselor education program, and models such as the ones just described are often taught in classes and may be practiced in practica and internships.

Stages of Consultation

Several authors have defined the process of consultation in similar ways, as they explain how a consultant enters a system, facilitates change, and leaves (Crothers et al., 2020; Dougherty, 2014; Scott et al., 2015). These processes tend to view the consultation process as consisting of the following stages: pre-entry, entry, goal setting, implementation, evaluation, and disengagement.

Stage 1: Pre-entry

In the initial stage, the consultant conceptualizes the problem, contacts the consulting system, and explains the purpose of consultation and their approach. Some ways to do this are through letters to employees, pre-entry meetings, or by having the consultee (e.g., an administrator who initially contacted the consultant) or a designated employee explain the purpose of the consultation.

Stage 2: Entry

The second stage of consultation is a three-pronged process that includes contacting the consulting system, exploring the problem, and defining the contract. First, the consultant contacts the consulting system, in such ways as having a series of meetings with all different work groups, meeting individually, or both. After contact, the consultant probes the system to obtain an initial understanding of the problem. This enables the consultant to discuss the contract with the organization, which can include confirming fees; setting up meetings; defining materials needed; deciding purpose, objectives, and ground rules; and setting an approximate termination date.

Stage 3: Goal Setting

The third stage, goal setting, involves three phases. The first, information gathering, is essentially a data-retrieval process. Based on the initial assessment of the problem and the contract decided in the second stage, the consultant is well situated to obtain reliable and valid data. This data-collection process ranges from obtaining specific, hard numerical data to sending out questionnaires to employees to generating data (information) from small group sharing and individual meetings with individuals in the consulting system. In the second phase, this data is analyzed, synthesized, and interpreted. This process allows the consultant to confirm, deny, or revise the initial identification of the problem obtained in the entry stage. Finally, the identification of the problem allows the consultant to set achievable goals for the organization and to begin to examine methods for change.

Stage 4: Implementation

During the fourth stage, the consultant collaboratively decides on strategies for change, and the implementation of those strategies begins with all those involved with the consultation. Although interventions can vary widely as a function of the consultant's model, the problems addressed should more or less be the same, and the results should focus on solving those problems. Generally, problems are defined contextually and push the system to make deep changes that will prevent future problems.

Stage 5: Evaluation

A good consultant wants to know what worked, what wasn't helpful, and perceived strengths and weaknesses of the consulting process. Evaluation includes asking participants for their judgments regarding the interventions that were made and whether the stated goals (change processes) were accomplished. Evaluation can be accomplished verbally or in writing throughout the consultation process (i.e., formative evaluation), through a statistical analysis of whether goals were reached near the end of the consulting process (i.e., summative evaluation), or through a combination of the two methods. At times, evaluation may result in the consultant discovering they are off track, and they may decide to recycle the process through the various stages.

Stage 6: Disengagement

Disengagement involves the consultant leaving the consulting relationship, hopefully because goals have been met. Usually, this happens at a preset time determined during the contract phase of Stage 2, although sometimes, this date will be revised based on new information gathered during the consulting process. During this stage, it is important that the consultant processes the results of the consulting relationship, including its successes and any interventions that may have been less successful, with all parties involved. The ending of any relationship involves loss, and the individuals involved should be given the opportunity to share their feelings about ending the consulting relationship (see Box 11.1, and then see Reflection Exercise 11.1).

BOX 11.1   An Example of Consultee-Centered Consultation at a Mental Health Center

A consultant is called in by the administrative director of a local mental health center. The director is concerned about morale at the center, saying they have heard people are unhappy and there is a depressed mood throughout. Not only is the director concerned about morale, but they are also worried because the number of billing hours has dropped in the past 6 months as a result of the mood in the agency. They ask the consultant to evaluate the situation and make recommendations.

The consultant first writes a letter to all staff and assistants explaining who they are, their consulting style, when they will be coming to the agency, what they will be doing, and approximately how long they will be there. In addition, the consultant discusses the limits of confidentiality, noting that after meeting with everyone at the agency, they will be sharing general feelings and discussing systemic dynamics and problems that seem to be occurring. The consultant notes that they will keep individual issues confidential but that their experience has shown that when people begin to discuss personal concerns, things sometimes leak out into the agency. The consultant encourages all agency personnel to avoid this if possible.

Before coming to the agency, the consultant develops a hierarchical plan to visit each work group. They start with the administration, meeting separately with the clinical, medical, and administrative directors. Next, they meet with the heads of each unit in the center (e.g., the outpatient director and day treatment director) and then with counselors and mental health assistants from each unit. This is followed by a meeting with the secretarial and clerical staff. They finish by meeting with the janitorial staff. Using empathy and basic listening skills, they meet first with each group and then individually with each member. While meeting with the staff, the consultant is also gathering data from the agency on changes in client flow, the economic status of the agency, salaries, types of degrees necessary for varying jobs, information flow (e.g., paper trails), and so forth.

(continued)

Following the consultant's initial contact with each unit and member of the agency, they gather all their information and spend 2 or 3 weeks determining what they consider to be the major problems in the agency. A report is written with the issues defined, and strategies for change are suggested. This report is sent to the agency director and distributed to agency personnel. Two weeks later, the consultant meets with the whole agency for a feedback session. Based on the feedback during that session, a revision to the report is written and distributed.

After approval from the agency, the consultant begins to implement the strategies for change. Throughout this process, they are receiving process feedback concerning what is working and what is not. The consultant adjusts their strategies based on this feedback. Finally, after the change process is initiated and directions for future change are determined, the consultant begins their termination from the agency. Closure is made through a series of agency group sessions, in which all who want to can come and give feedback in person. An anonymous written evaluation form is also made available to all personnel. A follow-up evaluation is completed 6 months later to see if change was indeed maintained.

Conclusion

Consultation comes in many different forms and is an important role of the CMHC. It is likely that as you continue in your career as a CMHC, you will be a consultant inward to those in an agency who work with clients, or outward to people outside of an agency. Usually, this occurs after a person has gained some amount of expertise. One special type of consultation is supervision, and through supervision, you will gain knowledge and skills that will assist you in becoming an expert CMHC and provide you with the confidence to become a consultant. But, let's take a look at this special kind of consultation—supervision.

> **REFLECTION EXERCISE 11.1**
> **Reviewing the Stages**
>
> After having read the example in Box 11.1, consider the stages of the consulting relationship, and determine whether this consultation process addressed each of the stages. Also consider what could have been done differently or better. Share in class.

SUPERVISION

Supervision of CMHCs is an important and expected part of the CMHC's role, as evidenced by (a) licensing boards requiring clinical supervision as part of the prerequisite to becoming licensed, (b) licensing boards setting more rigid standards for who can conduct clinical supervision and the activities that can count toward licensing, (c) agency administrators increasingly supporting the need for supervision, (d) the inclusion of supervisor standards in AMHCA's (2021) Standards for the Practice of Clinical Mental Health Counseling, (e) publication of the best practices in clinical supervision document (Borders et al., 2014), and (f) CACREP's (2016) focus on supervision in its standards. But what exactly is supervision, and how is it related to consultation?

Supervision Defined

Remember this simple quote from earlier in the chapter: "me and you talking about [them] with the purpose of some change" (Fall, 1995, p. 151)? Although it was previously used to define *consultation*, it also aptly speaks to supervision, which involves an ongoing consultative relationship between a supervisor and the counselor (the supervisee) that increases the counselor's skills and positively affects clients. A somewhat more involved definition of supervision can elucidate this further:

[Supervision is] a process in which one individual, usually a senior member of a given profession designated as the supervisor, engages in a collaborative relationship with another individual or group, usually a junior member(s) of a given profession designated as the supervisee(s) in order to (a) promote the growth and development of the supervisee(s), (b) protect the welfare of the clients seen by the supervisee(s), and (c) evaluate the performance of the supervisee(s). (ACA, 2014, Glossary)

Although it is a type of consultation, supervision differs from most other forms of consultation. For instance, whereas consultation is almost always time limited, supervision often involves an ongoing relationship between the supervisor and supervisee. Whereas most forms of consultation do not involve an intense interpersonal relationship that focuses on the consultee, supervision generally does, with the consultee being the supervisee. And whereas most forms of consultation do not have a direct evaluative responsibility for the consultee, in supervision, the supervisor is evaluating the supervisee in one fashion or another (Bernard & Goodyear, 2019; Corey et al., 2020; Kemer et al., 2019).

Because supervision is an intense, interpersonal relationship that sometimes delves into some very personal issues of the supervisee and how they may affect the client, it can sometimes be eye-opening, even therapeutic, for the supervisee. Although not therapy (Corey et al., 2020), supervision can sometimes cross over that imaginary line when supervisees' personal challenges impact their counseling practice. In these cases, the supervisor, in consultation with the supervisee, must decide if a referral to counseling for the supervisee would be appropriate.

Like consultation, supervision involves several systems, the most basic of which is that of supervisor–supervisee which impacts the counselor (supervisee) and the client. As in all homeostatic mechanisms, if you change one component, the whole system changes. That is the wonderful part of being a supervisor: If you impart knowledge to and facilitate growth in your supervisee, you will see your clients change. The system is responding. Take this one step further, and other systems will change. A rebound effect occurs, where the client now affects the systems in which they are involved—perhaps, their family and extended family: Throw a rock into a pond, and the ripples increasingly expand.

The manner in which systems are affected in supervision is complex. First and foremost, the simple act of supervision fine-tunes the counselor's skills and ultimately can positively affect the client and the systems in which they are involved. Sometimes, a parallel process occurs in the supervisory relationship, where the client–counselor relationship is mirrored in the supervisor–supervisee relationship (Bernard & Goodyear, 2019; Corey et al., 2020). This generally occurs when the counselor unconsciously takes on the traits of the client, which are repeated in the supervisory relationship (e.g., taking on the client's anxiety and expressing this anxiety in supervision). Parallel process is generally viewed as something that should be addressed in supervision and worked through, with the goal being to help the supervisee work effectively with the client (Koltz et al., 2012; Osherson, 2019; Zetzer et al., 2020). The scenario in Box 11.2 shows how a parallel process of Juan's work with his client Suzanne is being recreated in his supervisory relationship with Carla.

Good supervision will curtail the parallel process seen in Box 11.2, whereby the supervisor acts as an effective model for Juan and offers ideas Juan can use in his work with Suzanne. However, what would happen if Carla suddenly became anxious, believing she could not help Juan? You can see why being an effective supervisor is so important to both the supervisee and the client.

Sometimes it is argued that a reverse parallel process occurs (Borders & Brown, 2005/2022), such as when positive qualities in a supervisor (e.g., good empathic responding) are taken on by the counselor and subsequently passed on to the client. It is hoped that these qualities will ultimately be passed on by the client to others in their life. Whether it is a simple improvement in the knowledge base of the supervisee or the complexity of the parallel process, supervision involves a system that can have far-reaching effects.

BOX 11.2 Parallel Process

Juan is being supervised by Carla. One of his clients, Suzanne, is having panic attacks. Suzanne has two children, works full time, and is in graduate school. Her marriage is "rocky." Economically, she cannot cut back on work, and her dream is to finish her graduate degree. She comes to Juan pleading for help and noting that throughout the day, she is having panic attacks, and at night, she has difficulty sleeping. She is worried about being able to tend to her children and her studies because of her state of mind. A psychiatric consult and subsequent medication has resulted in little relief. She looks at Juan and says, "Please, you've got to help me—what should I do?" Juan is stymied and, at his first opportunity, discusses Suzanne's situation with Carla. Juan notes to Carla, "You know, since I've been working with Suzanne, I am filled with anxiety. I feel inadequate because I can't find a solution for her. I am thinking about her situation all the time, cannot stop obsessing about it, and am having trouble sleeping because I am worrying about her. It's even affecting my relationship with my partner."

Who Is the Supervisor?

Supervisors may be advanced students (e.g., doctoral students) or faculty supervising master's-level students in a counseling skills class, practicum, or internship. Or they may be individuals who are designated to supervise counselors at an agency. Or they could be individuals who are hired by counselors (the supervisees) to provide supervision as part of their requirement to become licensed. As ACA (2014) puts it, supervisors are "counselors who are trained to oversee the professional clinical work of counselors and counselors-in-training" (Glossary). Whoever the supervisor is, they should have obtained knowledge and competency in 206 aspirational standards representing the following 12 areas, as identified by the Best Practices in Clinical Supervision:

- initiating supervision
- goal setting
- giving feedback
- conducting supervision
- the supervisory relationship
- diversity and advocacy considerations
- ethical considerations
- documentation
- evaluation
- supervision format
- the supervisor
- supervisor preparation (i.e., supervision training and supervision of supervision; Borders et al., 2014)

The supervisor also has several roles and responsibilities, a few of which include ensuring the welfare of the client; informing the supervisees of policies and procedures relative to supervision; meeting regularly with the supervisee and ensuring proper termination; assuring that ethical, legal, and professional standards are being upheld; overseeing the clinical and professional development of the supervisee; and evaluating the supervisee (ACA, 2014, Section F). In addition, AMHCA's (2021) *Standards for the Practice of Clinical Mental Health Counseling*, provides 10 knowledge areas and 11 skills areas good supervisors should know (see Appendix I).

Like the effective counselor, the good supervisor is empathic, flexible, genuine, open, concerned, supportive, and able to build a strong supervisory alliance (Borders et al., 2014; Corey et al., 2020). In addition, the good supervisor is competent and able to evaluate the supervisee and knows the appropriate boundaries for supervision. Finally, good supervisors know counseling, have good client conceptualization skills, and are good at problem-solving.

Who Is the Supervisee?

One role of the supervisor is to evaluate the supervisee. According to ACA, the supervisee is "a professional counselor or counselor-in-training whose counseling work or clinical skill development is being overseen in a formal supervisory relationship by a qualified trained professional" (ACA, 2014, Glossary). The supervisee, in contrast, is learning from the evaluative process and building a professional identity (Bernard & Goodyear, 2019). Being subject to the evaluation of the supervisor, the supervisee is in a vulnerable position, and it is inevitable that, at some point in the supervisory relationship, supervisee resistance will occur. Of course, the amount and kind of resistance can be the result of several factors, including the following:

- **attachment and trust**: The ability to build trust and reduce resistance is likely related to the personality traits of both the supervisor and supervisee and their ability to form an effective relationship.
- **supervisor style**: Some supervisory styles allow supervisees to feel more in control, less threatened, and result in less supervisee resistance.
- **supervisee sensitivity to feedback**: Some supervisees are much more sensitive to evaluation and feedback, increasing resistance.
- **countertransference**: Some client issues will elicit defensiveness from the supervisee and result in inadequate responses by the counselor (supervisee). Similarly, supervisees can arouse defensiveness in supervisors, resulting in poor responses by the supervisor. As you can see, there certainly is enough defensiveness to go around. Unresolved issues on the part of a supervisee or supervisor can lead to countertransference and problems in supervision (see Figure 11.2).
- **developmental level**: As supervisees become more autonomous and independent from the supervisor, they naturally resist some of their supervisor's ideas as they increasingly believe in themselves.
- **supervisor characteristics**: Several supervisor characteristics can increase resistance, sometimes in unknown ways. They include age, race, cultural background, gender, power issues, and a wide variety of relationship dynamics (Bernard & Goodyear, 2019; Blacklund & Johnson, 2018).

Individual, Triadic, or Group Supervision?

Supervision can occur one on one (individual supervision), with one supervisor and two supervisees (triadic supervision), or in small groups (group supervision). Each type has its benefits. From a practical standpoint, group supervision allows several people to receive supervision at one time. Therefore, whether taking place in graduate school or at an agency, group supervision allows one supervisor to oversee several supervisees, usually four to eight. Group supervision has several advantages, including being exposed to multiple perspectives about an issue, viewing multiple ways counselors may respond to clients, hearing about different kinds of interventions, being able to learn how to do supervision by watching others undergo supervision, obtaining feedback from more than one individual, and normalizing experiences by seeing others who are dealing with similar issues (Bernard & Goodyear, 2019; Valentino et al., 2016). Another benefit is cost: For those who may be paying for supervision, group supervision is generally much less expensive than the $50 to $150 an hour that a supervisor might charge for individual supervision.

FIGURE 11.2 Countertransference Gone Awry

In recent years, triadic supervision has become more popular, probably because it appears to combine certain strengths of individual and group supervision and is recognized by CACREP (2016) as one method allowable when supervising students in practicum and internship. In this kind of supervision, two students meet with a supervisor (Borders et al., 2015). There are several potential advantages to this type of supervision, including the rapid building of trust in the supervisory relationship if students already know one another, vicarious learning from watching the other student get supervised, additional feedback from a third person (the other student), and the ability to practice supervision skills with the other student (Borders et al., 2012).

Although there are many benefits to group and triadic supervision, they may not offer the intimacy, intensity and depth found in individual supervision, and confidentiality is less assured when several individuals are involved, even when those individuals are counselors (Bernard & Goodyear, 2019; Borders et al., 2012). Also, individual supervision is more likely to result in a mentoring process in which a supervisee becomes the student of a master counselor. Furthermore, mismatches among supervisees, especially in terms of professional experience, personality characteristics, and expectations from supervision, may create challenges for supervisors in building rapport and cohesion in triadic and group supervision, whereas it's slightly less likely when matching a supervisee to an individual supervisor.

Models of Supervision

Corey et al. (2020) suggests three broad classes of supervision, which encompass several different models. These include developmental, psychotherapy-based, and integrative approaches to supervision.

Developmental Models

Developmental models view supervision as occurring in a series of stages, through which the supervisee will pass (Borders & Brown, 2005/2022). Therefore, the supervisor can rely on a certain amount of predictable growth as well as resistance, depending on the stage. Of course, individual supervisees may move faster or slower through these stages based on their personality style, their ability, and their fit with their supervisor. Awareness of developmental stages can assist the supervisor in developing strategies for growth based on the supervisee's particular stage (McNeil & Stoltenberg, 2016; Stoltenberg & McNeil, 2010). Although there have been several developmental models over the years, probably the best known is the integrated developmental model (IDM) of Stoltenberg and colleagues.

IDM proposes that during the course of supervision, supervisees will pass through the three main levels of development of IDM:

1. awareness of self and the client,
2. motivation to participate in the counseling process, and
3. increased autonomy (decreased dependency) in the counseling and supervision process.

Simultaneously, supervises increase their learning in eight domains of knowledge of IDM through the course of supervision and as they pass through the levels:

1. intervention skills competence,
2. assessment techniques,
3. interpersonal assessment,
4. client conceptualization,
5. individual differences,
6. theoretical orientation,
7. treatment plans and goals, and
8. professional ethics. (McNeil & Stoltenberg, 2016; Stoltenberg & McNeil, 2010)

In Level 1, counselors are anxious and have difficulty gaining insight into themselves and their clients. New to the field, they are highly motivated but are particularly dependent on their supervisor. As they enter Level 2, counselors are better able to focus on self and client and can show greater insight and empathy toward the client. However, realizing the complexity of the counseling relationship, their motivation sometimes decreases, as they wonder if they can be effective counselors. They struggle between dependency and autonomy—one moment feeling like they "get it," and the next moment believing they will never be truly accomplished in this field. Level 3 occurs when the counselor can easily understand self and develops deep understanding of the client. Here, counselors again become motivated as they realize their strengths and abilities. This leads to increased independence from their supervisor, as they become willing and ready to try new techniques and develop their own sense of professional identity (McNeil & Stoltenberg, 2016; Stoltenberg & McNeil, 2010; see Figure 11.3). Stoltenberg and McNeil (2010) also presented a final level, 3i, in which supervisees have increased awareness of their strengths and weaknesses across the eight domains and develop a unique understanding of their own integrative way of doing counseling.

Psychotherapy-Based Models

Many counselors who practice a particular type of therapy (e.g., Gestalt, person-centered, behavioral, etc.). believe it is best to receive supervision from a master therapist/supervisor who practices the same approach (Bernard & Goodyear, 2019; Watkins, 2012). This can occur in two ways:

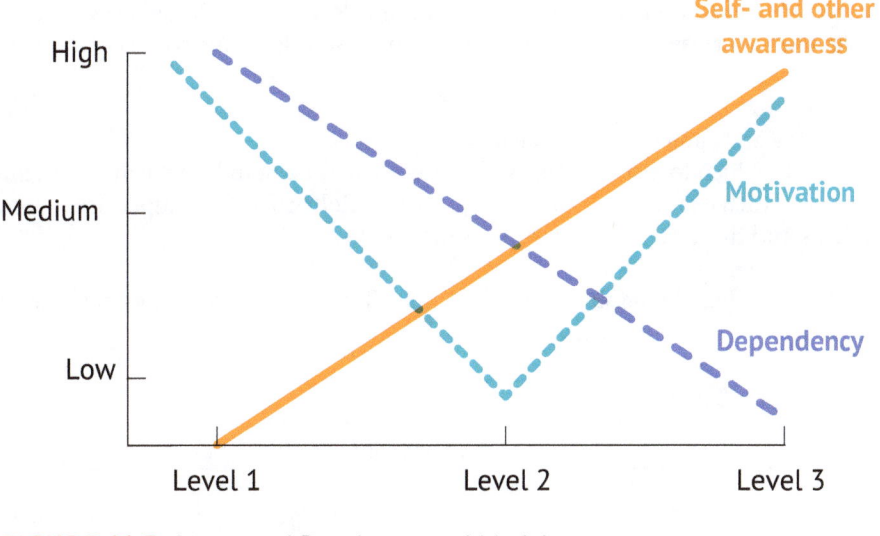

FIGURE 11.3 Integrated Developmental Model

- Supervision can be structured to model the supervisee's counseling approach.
  - **Example A**: A supervisor who is working with a behaviorally focused supervisee (counselor) models a behavioral supervision approach by identifying problems in supervision, collaboratively setting behavioral goals to work on, and then using specific behavioral techniques to reach those goals.
  - **Example B**: A supervisor working with a psychoanalytically oriented supervisee (counselor) does modified analysis with the supervisee.
  - **Example C**: A supervisor working with a person-centered supervisee (counselor) uses empathy, shows unconditional regard, and is genuine with their supervisee.

- During supervision knowledge can be imparted to the supervise to guide and teach the supervisee about new skills.
  - **Example A**: A supervisor offers advice on a new behavioral technique to a behaviorally oriented supervisee (counselor) who is not making progress with their client.
  - **Example B**: A supervisor suggests a specific psychoanalytic technique (e.g., dream analysis) to an analytically oriented supervisee (counselor) and describes the technique during a supervision session.
  - **Example C**: A supervisor describes advanced empathic responses to a person-centered supervisee (counselor).

Integrative Models

Perhaps more appropriately called meta-theory models, integrative models are not theory specific and can be used regardless of the theoretical approach of the supervisee. Two such models are Bernard's discrimination model (Bernard & Goodyear, 2019) and Kagan's interpersonal process recall approach (1980; Kagan & Kagan, 1997).

Bernard's discrimination model (Bernard, 2019) examines three supervisory roles, depending on the needs of the supervisee. These include a *didactic role*, in which the supervisor is a teacher; an *experiential role*, in which the supervisor is a time-limited counselor assisting the supervisee in working through issues affecting their ability as a therapist; and a *consultant role*, in which the supervisor is an objective colleague assisting the supervisee. As supervisors take on these roles, supervisees can focus on one of three domains of the discrimination model:

- *interventions* they are using or would like to use;
- *conceptualization*, which focuses on how supervisees are understanding client issues; and
- *personalization*, which examines what personal issues might affect how supervisees conceptualize client problems and the kinds of interventions they make.

Referring to Box 11.2 (with Juan being supervised by Carla), Table 11.1 demonstrates how the supervisor's roles can be applied to each focus of supervision.

TABLE 11.1 Roles of the Supervisor

	Roles of the Supervisor		
Focus of Supervision	Teacher	Counselor	Consultant
Intervention	Teach the supervisee how to implement techqniques.	Listen to the supervisee's concerns about their feelings of inadequacy relative to this client.	Offer a number of options when the supervisee requests specific techniques to use with the client.
Conceptualization	Note to the supervisee how the origin of panic attacks may be viewed in a number of ways (e.g., early childhood issues, temperament, or situational).	Connects the supervisee's own childhood issues related to anxiety, and consider whether these issues relate to the supervisee's fear of working with the client.	When the supervisee asks how temperament can affect anxiety, the supervisor responds with research concerning the genetics of temperament and its relationship to anxiety. The possibility of prescribing medication to dampen the effects of the temperament is discussed.
Personalization	Define *parallel process* to the supervisee and indicate how that concept might be at play in this case.	Listens to the supervisee discuss how their own issues raise anxiety and feelings of inadequacy.	When the supervisee asks how their parallel process can be halted, the supervisor makes a number of suggestions.

In Kagan's interpersonal process recall (IPR) approach (1980; Kagan & Kagan, 1997), there is a reliance on the ability of the supervisor and supervisee to build trust in the supervisory relationship, so the supervisee feels comfortable sharing their strengths and weaknesses as a counselor (similar to the personalization area from the discrimination model). In this type of supervision, the supervisor and supervisee review an audio or video recording of the supervisee with a client. The supervisee, supervisor, or both can control the recording, starting and stopping it when it is believed there is an important moment in the counseling relationship. The supervisor's role is to attend accurately to the feelings and thoughts of the supervisee and, when appropriate, ask leading questions to deepen the session. The following questions have been used in this inquiry session:

- What do you wish you had said to them?
- How do you think they would have reacted if you had said that?

- What would have been the risk in saying what you wanted to say?
- If you had the chance now, how might you tell them what you are thinking and feeling?
- Were there any other thoughts going through your mind?
- How did you want the other person to perceive you?
- Were those feelings located physically in some part of your body?
- Were you aware of any feelings? Does that feeling have any special meaning for you?
- What did you want them to tell you?
- What did you think they wanted from you?
- Did they remind you of anyone in your life? (Cashwell, 1994, p. 2)

In the tradition of some of the humanistic therapies, IPR is an approach that gives supervisees the ability to explore their feelings and thoughts about a therapeutic relationship within a trusting and safe environment. Supervisees, therefore, can get in touch with those aspects of themselves that prevent clients from moving forward and, thus, can be particularly useful when looking at cross-cultural bias (Ivers et al., 2017). In these cases, culturally relevant questions can be added, such as "What reaction did you have to your client's (culture/group affiliation/appearance [e.g., skin color, accent, disability, sexual orientation, or religious/spiritual beliefs])?" (Ivers et al., 2017, p. 292).

Conclusion

Each of the models discussed in this section offer a slightly different take on the supervisory process, and they are not necessarily exclusive of one another. For instance, one can adopt a developmental model and be orientation specific or use an integrative approach. If given a choice to choose a supervisor, a supervisee should pick the supervisor who offers the approach that best facilitates the supervisee's learning process as well as the therapeutic experience of the supervisee's clients. Whoever a supervisee chooses, there is evidence that the strength of the working alliance, or bond between the supervisor and supervisee, regardless of model, may be the most crucial factor for effective supervision (Enlow et al., 2019; Sterner, 2009).

ETHICAL AND LEGAL ISSUES IN CONSULTATION AND SUPERVISION

Ethical Issues in the Consulting Relationship

Several authors, as well as ethics codes, illuminate some key ethical issues specific to the consulting process (ACA, 2014; AMHCA, 2020; Dougherty, 2014; Gray, 2017; Kampwirth & Powers, 2016; Welfel, 2016). Some of these salient ethical issues in the consulting relationship include the following:

- **agreements**: Counselors should ensure agreements regarding consultation are obtained from all parties involved, especially with regard to confidentiality.
- **respect for privacy**: Client identities should be protected, and information should be discussed only for professional purposes.
- **growth toward self-direction**: The consultant should have as their primary goals the ability of those involved in consultation to become increasingly independent and able to use the skills the consultant imparts.
- **disclosure of confidential information**: Information should be kept confidential and discussed only for professional purposes.
- **multiple relationships**: Consultation often involves multiple relationships, and consultants should take steps to ensure all involved are clear about the purpose of the consulting relationships, the limits of the relationships, and the relationships' goals.

- **informed consent**: Counselors should give, in writing and verbally, to those involved in the consulting relationship information concerning the purpose of the consultation and should jointly decide how goals will be achieved. Those involved in consultation should give consent to the procedures.
- **consultant competency**: Counselors should ensure they have the competence and resources to conduct consultation and should refer when they do not.
- **clear understanding of goals and consequences**: Counselors should develop a "clear understanding" with those involved in the consulting relationship of the problem, goals, and consequences of an intervention.
- **cross-cultural issues**: Consultants should strive to understand and monitor their own biases, have knowledge of other cultures, and use interventions that will positively affect all in the system.

Ethical Issues in the Supervisory Relationship

Because supervision is technically a kind of consultation, one should be aware of the issues just discussed when supervising. However, some ethical issues in the supervisory relationship that have specifically stood out in supervision include the following:

- **supervisor preparation**: Supervisors should receive didactic and experiential training and develop competencies in supervisory methods.
- **client welfare**: Supervisors have a responsibility to monitor the welfare of the client and take appropriate action if the client is at risk of harming self or another person or if the supervisee cannot effectively work with a client.
- **informed consent**: Supervisors should obtain informed consent from their supervisees, and clients should be informed that the supervisee is in supervision with a supervisor and how that might affect confidentiality.
- **multicultural issues**: Supervisors should be aware of, and address how, issues of diversity affect the supervisory relationship.
- **relationship boundaries**: Supervisors should be aware of how power differentials play a role between themselves and their supervisees and respect appropriate professional and social boundaries.
- **sexual relationships**: Supervisors do not engage in sexual relationships with supervisees.
- **dual and multiple relationships**: Although dual relationships with some supervisees are inevitable (e.g., a supervisee taking a class from their supervisor or having a supervisor serve on a supervisee's dissertation committee), supervisors should be particularly sensitive to the potential for abuse of power in any dual relationship.
- **responsibility to clients**: Supervisors have a responsibility to ensure that adequate counseling is taking place between the supervisee (counselor) and client.
- **limitations of supervisees**: Supervisors have a responsibility to evaluate supervisees and find remedial assistance for them if they are not performing adequately. If supervisees are not able to function effectively, supervisors have the responsibility to recommend dismissal from their program or agency or not recommend them for a specific credential.
- **evaluation and accountability**: Supervisors have a responsibility to evaluate the supervisee's progress in supervision, ensure ongoing feedback to the supervisee, and document supervisory sessions.
- **endorsement**: Supervisors do not endorse unqualified supervisees for credentialing but, rather, take steps to help them become qualified. (ACA, 2014; AMHCA, 2020; Bernard & Goodyear, 2019; Corey, 2024)

LIABILITY IN CONSULTATION AND SUPERVISION

> A primary obligation of counseling supervisors is to monitor the services provided by supervisees. (ACA, 2014, F.1.a., Client Welfare section)

Because consultants and supervisors indirectly, but knowingly, effect change in clients, they can be held legally responsible for the potential negative results of their consultation or supervision (ACA, 2014; AMHCA, 2020, 2021; Welfel, 2016). This particularly came to light during the Tarasoff decision, when a counseling supervisor (and others) was held legally responsible for not taking action to ensure the safety of Tatiana Tarasoff, the former girlfriend of a client who eventually murdered Ms. Tarasoff (see Reflection Exercise 6.1 in Chapter 6). Thus, we see how consultants and supervisors can be held responsible for the work they perform.

PROFESSIONAL ISSUES IN SUPERVISION

Supervision of Graduate Students and Practicing Counselors

Graduate students will have several opportunities to receive supervision during clinical classes (e.g., a counseling skills class, a practicum, and an internship). Supervision is usually given by an advanced graduate student, a professor, a site supervisor, or a combination thereof. Often, students are required to record sessions or be supervised during live sessions (CACREP, 2016).

Although supervision is often conducted through the use of taped videos or written notes, increasingly, live supervision has become popular. Today, almost all counseling programs have rooms equipped with one-way windows, video streaming, or other technological advances that allow students to be viewed by supervisors during live counseling sessions or roleplays (Bernard & Goodyear, 2019; Corey et al., 2020). Students can receive immediate feedback through several methods, including having the supervisor walk in on the session, communicating through an earpiece, or calling on the supervisee's phone. Obviously, clients or those roleplaying need to be made aware of this in advance.

Recently, we have seen the use of cybersupervision, mostly for sessions that aren't live, although it can potentially be used for live sessions (Bender & Dykeman, 2016; Pennington et al., 2020; Woo et al., 2020). Some advantages include more flexibility around scheduling; easier access to supervisees when conducting group supervision; better use of the supervisee's time, as travel is not required; and more potential supervisors. Drawbacks include the access to, and expense of, technology; difficulty building a relationship compared to face-to-face supervision; problems with technology; confidentiality issues with technology; legal issues if supervision crosses state boundaries; and difficulty acting quickly if there is foreseeable harm.

After obtaining a degree in counseling, practicing counselors often receive supervision as part of their job or because it is a requirement for credentialing. Unfortunately, when counselors become licensed they often terminate supervision after obtaining their credential, which is not adhering to best practices. Finally, some practicing counselors receive mandated supervision as the result of an ethical violation or professional concern (Ahia & Boccone, 2017).

Professional Association for Counselor Supervision

The Association for Counselor Education and Supervision (ACES), a division of ACA, is specifically focused on issues of counselor training, including supervision. You might want to consider joining it if you are interested in counselor education and in supervision.

SUMMARY

This chapter examined two important types of helping relationships: consultation and supervision. We began by defining consultation, noting that it is a process whereby the consultant, who has specialized expertise, meets with one or more other professionals to improve their work with current or potential clients. We noted that the consultant is the person who has been called in to do some type of consultation, while the consultee is the point person, or the person identifying and inviting the consultant to consult.

The chapter then gave a brief history of consultation, noting that it first became popular during the 1940s and 1950s, when it was known as a direct-service approach, wherein the consultant would have little contact with the consultee and the consultant was left to their own devices to solve the problem. Over the years, however, it became increasingly more process oriented, as the consultee, and others participating in the consultation process, became increasingly involved with understanding the problem, so they would have the skills should a similar problem arise.

During the 1960s, with the passage of the Community Mental Health Centers Act, consultation became legitimized as an important function of what federally funded mental health centers did. Soon, consultation was seen as occurring in two directions: outward and inward. Consulting outward was when an agency would assist individuals who have mental health concerns but are not directly involved with the agency (e.g., community members and schools). Consulting inward, which Gerald Caplan is given credit for popularizing, was focused on how consultants can help counselors within agencies work more effectively with their clients. Today, we find two main models of consultation: consultant-centered consultation (expert, prescriptive, and trainer/educator models) and consultee centered consultation (collaborative, facilitative, and process-oriented models). As the chapter continued, we pointed out that, regardless of the approach a consultant uses, there are several predictable stages to the consulting process, including pre-entry, entry, goal setting, implementation, evaluation, and disengagement.

Turning to the next part of the chapter, we defined supervision as a special type of consultation that involves an intense interpersonally focused relationship that comprises a number of systems, with the most basic being that of the supervisor–supervisee or counselor–client. Although supervision and consultation have some similarities, we noted that in contrast to consultation, supervision is an ongoing relationship, involves an intense interpersonal relationship, and has a strong evaluative component to it. We noted that supervision can sometimes become very personal, and the supervisor should not "cross over" the imaginary line, where supervision becomes therapy. Instead, at this point, it may be appropriate for the supervisor to refer the supervisee to counseling. We noted that sometimes a parallel process occurs in the supervisory relationship, in which the client–counselor relationship is mirrored in the supervisor–supervisee relationship. Here, the supervisor can model how to deal with the supervisee in a similar fashion to how the supervisee should deal with the client.

Next, the chapter presented definitions of supervisor and supervisee. We then noted that Best Practices in Clinical Supervision includes 206 aspirational standards that can be found within 12 specific areas. We went on to identify some of the roles and responsibilities of a supervisor as well as some of the qualities embraced by good supervisors. The chapter then examined the role of the supervisor as evaluator and noted that this role can sometimes bring out supervisee resistance. We highlighted some reasons resistance occurs. In conducting supervision, we distinguished between individual, triadic, and group supervision and pointed out some of the advantages and disadvantages of each of these.

The chapter then examined three supervision models: developmental, psychotherapy-based, and integrative models. Developmental models, such as Stoltenberg's integrated developmental model (IDM), speak to predictable stages a supervisee will go through while in supervision, including three main levels of development related to awareness of self and client, motivation toward the counseling process, and developing increasing autonomy in the counseling and supervision process.

Psychotherapy-based models approach the supervisory process by using a specific counseling theory as their basis for the supervisory process. These approaches model, or teach, a specific psychotherapeutic approach. Integrative models are not theory specific and thus can be used with any supervisee. Specifically, the chapter highlighted two integrative models. Bernard's discrimination model looks at the supervisor in the role of teacher, counselor, and consultant and examines domains of supervision that include interventions, conceptualization, and personalization. Interpersonal process recall (IPR), views the supervisor's role as attending to the feelings and thoughts of the supervisee and, when appropriate, asks leading questions to deepen the session.

As the chapter continued, we looked at several ethical issues in the consulting relationship, and while most of those issues can be applied to supervision as well, we also noted some specific ethical issues related to the supervisory process. We also examined liability issues in consultation and supervision. Highlighting the Tarasoff case, we noted that supervisees (and consultants) may be held liable for what occurs to clients as a result of consultation and supervision.

The chapter went on to discuss different delivery systems of supervision, such as the use of taped videos, written notes about clients, and live supervision. We discussed ways students can receive immediate feedback during live supervision, such as walking in on a session, using an earpiece, or calling on a phone. We also noted that cybersupervision, mostly for supervisory sessions that aren't live, has become increasingly popular and discussed several advantages and disadvantages to this process. We noted that practicing counselors usually need to obtain supervision to become licensed but, unfortunately, do not always continue with supervision after obtaining their license. We concluded with a shout-out to ACES, a division of ACA that specifically focuses on counselor training, including supervision.

KEY WORDS AND TERMS

Bernard's discrimination model
Best Practices in Clinical Supervision
collaborative model
Community Mental Health Centers Act
consultant
consultant-centered consultation models
consultation
consultee
consultee-centered consultation models
consulting inward
consulting outward
countertransference
cybersupervision
developmental approach to supervision
Diagnostic and Statistical Manual, Fifth Edition, Text Revision (DSM-5-TR)
direct-service approach

eight domains of knowledge of IDM
ethical issues in the consulting relationship
ethical issues in the supervisory relationship
expert model
facilitative model
foreseeable harm
formative evaluation
four consultation roles
group supervision
homeostatic mechanisms
individual supervision
integrated developmental model (IDM)
integrative approach to supervision
Kagan's interpersonal process recall (IPR) model
liability in consultation and supervision
meta-theory models
parallel process

prescriptive model
process-oriented approach
process-oriented model
Stage 1: pre-entry
Stage 2: entry
Stage 3: goal setting
Stage 4: implementation
Stage 5: evaluation
Stage 6: disengagement
summative evaluation
supervisee
supervisee resistance
supervision
supervisors
systemic
Tarasoff decision
three domains of the discrimination model
three main levels of development of IDM
three supervisory roles of the discrimination model
trainer/educator model
triadic supervision

KEY NAME

Caplan, Gerald

PROFESSIONAL ASSOCIATIONS AND ORGANIZATIONS

Association for Counselor Education and Supervision (ACES)
Council on the Accreditation of Counseling and Related Educational Program (CACREP)

CREDITS

CHAPTER 12

DEVELOPING AND EVALUATING MENTAL HEALTH PROGRAMS

Ed Neukrug and Jeanel Franklin

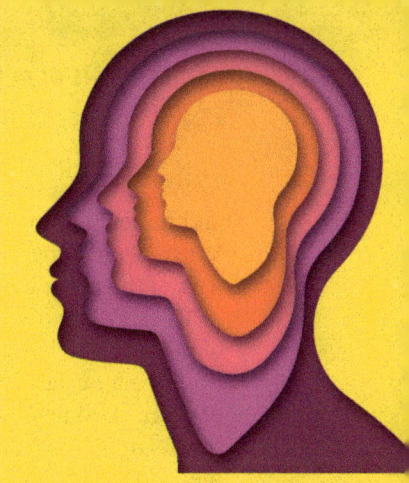

Learning Goals

- Learn the six steps in the development and evaluation of mental health programs.
- Using an example of individuals with borderline personality who have emotional dysregulation, examine how a counselor would develop and evaluate a program to work with these clients.
- Understand the difference between formative and summative program evaluation and how both can be used in the evaluation process.
- Learn how to develop a written evaluation report that addresses outcomes of program evaluation.
- Learn how to give an oral report that addresses outcomes of program evaluation.
- Understand important ethical and legal issues related to development and evaluation of programs, including adherence to underlying ethical principles; risks and benefits of a program; informed consent; confidentiality; and the role HIPAA and IRB boards play in protecting the privacy and security of information.

INTRODUCTION

Imagine you are a clinical mental health counselor (CMHC) employed at a mental health center. Due to your expertise in working with clients with borderline personality disorder (BPD), who, by definition, have trouble with emotional regulation, you are asked to conduct and evaluate a program to assist these clients in identification and management of their emotions. Where would you begin? What activities would you include in your program? How would you know if your program is effective?

What if you were asked to develop and evaluate a program for community members on understanding and reacting to individuals in the community who are potentially dangerous to themselves and others. Where would you begin, and what kinds of evaluation procedures would you use to assess the effectiveness of the program?

CMHCs can often be found designing, developing, implementing, managing, and evaluating a variety of programs to meet the social and mental health needs of their clients and consumers. This chapter will examine a number of factors in this process, including six steps in the development and evaluation of a program; two major types of program evaluation, formative and summative; ways of reporting evaluation results in writing and orally; and key ethical and legal considerations when developing and evaluating mental health programs.

SIX STEPS IN DEVELOPING AND EVALUATING A MENTAL HEALTH PROGRAM

Researchers and authors have suggested a series of steps in the development and evaluation of mental health programs (Calley, 2011; Kelley, 2022; U.S. Department of Health and Human Services, 2022). Six steps that are often identified include the following:

1. identifying your target population
2. operationalizing the problem
3. identifying goals and objectives of your program
4. designing specific strategies to reach your goals and objectives
5. developing evaluation techniques to evaluate whether you successfully implemented your strategies
6. analyzing the data from the evaluation techniques and making decisions on program change or curtailment

Keeping these steps in mind, those with expertise with the target population can develop, implement, and evaluate a mental health program. Let's take a brief look at each of these steps.

Step 1: Identifying Your Target Population

Target populations are often identified by the kinds of clients or consumers one is working with, the focus of the agency, and/or funding that has been obtained for research on specific clients or consumers. As one might expect, the target population will drive the goals and objectives and the strategies used in your program. In the example we use in this chapter, we identity adults with borderline personality disorder (BPD) as our target population.

Step 2: Operationalizing the Problem

Now that we have identified our target population, we need to decide what problem we want to focus upon. Those who are developing the program should have expertise with the target population, conduct research to understand the target population, and/or participate in continuing education about the target population. In researching adults with BPD, a short summary of some of the kinds of information we would find is highlighted in Box 12.1.

Clearly, the short summary of BPD in Box 12.1 shows that one of the major symptoms that individuals with BPD struggle with is emotional dysregulation. Individuals with emotional dysregulation often

BOX 12.1 Defining BPD

Adults diagnosed with BPD often have a difficult time functioning in relationships, engage in nonsuicidal self-injurious behavior (e.g., cutting), are at much higher risk of suicidal behaviors, and have a high amount of emotional dysregulation. In addition, they tend to have a difficult time in counseling and often leave practitioners feeling helpless, as they struggle to make progress with their clients. Kuo and Fitzpatrick (2015) summarize the symptoms needed for a diagnosis of BPD according to the *DSM-5*:

- frantic efforts to avoid imagined abandonment,
- instability in interpersonal relationships,
- identity disturbance,
- impulsivity,
- suicidal behaviors,
- emotional instability,
- chronic feelings of emptiness,
- inappropriate or intense anger, and
- stress-related paranoid ideation or dissociation (p. 294)

Although fewer than 2% of Americans are diagnosed with BPD, up to 20% of the inpatient psychiatric population have BPD, and 42.4% of those diagnosed with BPD seek treatment for the disorder (Chapman et al., 2022; Lenzenweger et al., 2007; National Institute of Mental Health, n.d.). In addition, ten Have et al. (2016) found that approximately 25% of people have one or two symptoms of BPD, and another nearly 4% have three or four symptoms of BPD. Thus, individuals with BPD or related disorders, as well as individuals who have some of the symptoms of BPD, make up a substantial percentage of those who seek counseling.

find themselves having suicidal ideation, angry outbursts, episodes of self-harm, extreme anxiety and depression, unstable relationships, low self-esteem, difficulty functioning and creating order in their lives, and other related symptoms (American Psychiatric Association, 2022; NIMH, n.d.). Although there are a variety of types of programs that could be developed for individuals with BPD, since emotional dysregulation is one aspect of BPD that can have a devastating impact on clients and their loved ones, creating a program to address this problem could be particularly useful for an individual's recovery. We could call the program "Understanding and Managing Emotions." In creating our program, additional research on this topic could be conducted, and programs that have been successfully used in the past can be examined as one develops their own unique program for this problem.

Step 3: Identifying Goals and Objectives of Your Program

Now that we have identified our target population and have operationalized our problem, we can focus on what goals and objectives we want. Oftentimes, this starts with individuals at the agency who have some amount of expertise with BPD examining the research that was conducted on emotional dysregulation and reviewing other programs that have been successfully used that focus on understanding and managing emotions. Hypothetically, this could result in the goals and objectives listed in Table 12.1.

TABLE 12.1 Goals and Objectives of Your Program

1. Help adults with BPD understand emotional dysregulation.
2. Help adults with BPD understand the genetic, learned, and environmental factors that lend themselves to emotional dysregulation.
3. Help adults with BPD examine the impact on self and others of emotional dysregulation.
4. Help adults with BPD learn techniques to lessen emotional dysregulation.
5. Help adults with BPD maintain emotional regulation over their lifetime.

Step 4: Designing Specific Strategies to Reach Your Goals and Objectives

Now that your goals and objectives have been identified, specific strategies to reach them can be designed. For example, Table 12.2 suggests a limited number of strategies for each goal or objective, although many more can be created to help participants understand emotional dysregulation (see Neukrug & Hays, 2023, Chapter 13). After reviewing Table 12.2, complete Exercise 12.1.

TABLE 12.2 Developing Strategies for Goals and Objectives

Goal and Objective 1: Help adults with BPD understand emotional dysregulation.

Strategy 1: Use the *DSM-5-TR*, journal articles, and books to develop a 90-minute didactic presentation on emotional dysregulation.

Goal and Objective 2: Help adults with BPD understand the genetic, learned, and environmental factors that lend themselves to emotional dysregulation.

Strategy 1: Provide a 2-hour workshop that provides examples, displays graphics, and solicits personal stories from clients to understand the genetic, learned, and environmental factors that might lend oneself to emotional dysregulation.

Goal and Objective 3: Help adults with BPD examine the impact on self and on others of emotional dysregulation.

Strategy 1: Provide a 2-hour group counseling experience, where clients can share how their experience with emotional dysregulation has impacted themselves and others.

Goal and Objective 4: Help adults with BPD learn techniques to decrease emotional dysregulation.

Strategy 1: Teach clients to identify typical characteristics of emotional dysregulation, as well as behaviors that are reflective of emotional dysregulation within themselves (e.g., high levels of anxiety, depression, self-harm behaviors, substance abuse, and angry outbursts).

Strategy 2: Teach and model mindfulness and meditation when experiencing emotional dysregulation.

Goal and Objective 5: Help adults with BPD maintain emotional regulation over their lifetime.

Strategy 1: Provide a variety of techniques for clients to be able to maintain emotional regulation over a long period of time, including mindfulness, meditation, medication, relaxation exercises, interpersonal skills, nutrition, exercise, and more.

EXPERIENTIAL EXERCISE 12.1 **Strategies for Reaching Your Goals and Objectives**

Using each of the five goals and objectives just discussed, come up with one additional strategy for each. Share them in class, refine them, and make a final list of additional strategies you might use to help individuals with BPD develop better regulation of their emotions. After you are finished, look at all the strategies that were developed, and reflect on the many ways that can be developed to assist individuals with BPD in regulating their emotions.

Step 5: Developing Evaluation Techniques to Assess Whether You Successfully Implemented Your Strategies

In your counseling program, you will take an assessment, research, and/or program evaluation course(s) and learn a wide variety of techniques that can be applied to evaluate programs. Table 12.3 offers just a few evaluation procedures that can be used with the five goals and objectives just discussed. After reviewing Table 12.3, complete Exercise 12.2.

TABLE 12.3 Evaluation Techniques

Goal and Objective 1: Help adults with BPD understand emotional dysregulation.

    Strategy 1: Use the *DSM-5-TR*, journal articles, and books to develop a 90-minute didactic presentation on emotional dysregulation.

        Evaluation Technique 1: Develop an evaluation instrument clients can use to assess how well the speaker was prepared, respectful, knowledgeable, interesting, and stimulating.

Goal and Objective 2: Help adults with BPD understand the genetic, learned, and environmental factors that lend themselves to emotional dysregulation.

    Strategy 1: Provide a 2-hour workshop that provides examples, displays graphics, and solicits personal stories from clients to understand the genetic, learned, and environmental factors that might lend oneself to emotional dysregulation.

        Evaluation Technique 1: Have clients anonymously write their reactions to the 2-hour workshop.

        Evaluation Technique 2: Give a quiz on the information learned during the workshop to assess the presenter's ability at helping clients learn.

Goal and Objective 3: Help adults with BPD examine the impact on self and on others of emotional dysregulation.

    Strategy 1: Provide a 2-hour group counseling experience, where clients can share how their experience with emotional dysregulation has impacted themselves and others.

        Evaluation Technique 1: As part of the group counseling experience, have clients share their feelings on the experience.

Goal and Objective 4: Help adults with BPD learn techniques to decrease emotional dysregulation.

    Strategy 1: Teach clients to identify typical characteristics of emotional dysregulation, as well as behaviors that are reflective of emotional dysregulation, within themselves (e.g., high levels of anxiety, depression, self-harm behaviors, substance abuse, and angry outbursts).

        Evaluation Technique 1: At the end of the seminar, have clients list each characteristic of emotional dysregulation they can remember from the seminar.

(Continued)

TABLE 12.3   (*Continued*)

Strategy 2: Teach and model mindfulness and meditation when experiencing emotional dysregulation.

Evaluation Technique 2: Create a 10-point rating scale that measures how well clients feel they have been able to practice mindfulness and meditation within 1 week of learning the techniques.

Goal and Objective 5: Help adults with BPD maintain emotional regulation over their lifetime.

Strategy 1: Provide a variety of techniques for clients to be able to maintain emotional regulation over a long period of time, including mindfulness, meditation, medication, relaxation exercises, interpersonal skills, nutrition, exercise, and more.

Evaluation Technique 1: Rank order the techniques to determine which have been most useful over the past week (or since you finished the program, 6 months ago).

Evaluation Technique 2: For each technique, use a rating scale that assesses how well the client believes they have mastered each of the techniques taught.

Evaluation Technique 3: Six months following treatment, clients will be given an assessment to evaluate their experience in treatment and their ability to maintain emotional regulation.

Evaluation Technique 4: Ask unbiased observers, or significant others, to provide written or verbal feedback regarding how they view the client is progressing after the program was completed (e.g., 1 month, 6 months, or a year).

EXPERIENTIAL EXERCISE 12.2   **Strategies for Reaching Your Goals and Objectives**

After examining each of the evaluation techniques identified in Table 12.3, come up with one additional technique or refine one or more of the techniques that are given. Share your new or refined evaluation techniques with the class, and after obtaining everyone's feedback, make a master list of additional evaluation techniques you might use to assess the effectiveness of your program.

Step 6: Analyzing the Data from the Evaluation Techniques and Making Decisions on Program Change or Curtailment

Depending on the types of evaluation techniques used, those with a background in data collection and interpretation can assess how successful the program has been. Success of the program can be an ongoing process that occurs while the program is progressing (formative evaluation) or an evaluation of the total program at its conclusion (summative evaluation). The next section of the chapter examines these two types of evaluation and offers a few examples of how the data might be collected. However, more involved courses in research, assessment, and program evaluation will offer expanded ideas on how to collect data.

FORMATIVE AND SUMMATIVE PROGRAM EVALUATION

Two common types of program evaluation used to obtain feedback are formative evaluation and summative evaluation (Formative and Summative Assessments, 2021). Whereas formative evaluation is typically completed during a program to improve and make modifications of the program while it is in process, summative evaluation is completed close to or after the conclusion of a program to determine whether a program should be continued, expanded, or eliminated. Often used to show accountability to funding agencies and agency administrators, summative evaluation is generally an involved and formal process that may have a strong research focus.

Conducting Formative Evaluation

There are innumerable ways to conduct formative evaluation, and a sampling of a few of them include asking for feedback, creating quizzes, using rating scales, and observation of your participants. The following highlights these methods, although there are many other forms of formative evaluation—often, just limited by your imagination.

Asking for Feedback

One method of asking for feedback is simply requesting that participants write down or verbally share their experience of an aspect of the program while it is occurring. For instance, we can develop this type of evaluation using Goal and Objective 2, Strategy 1 and Goal and Objectives 3, Strategy 1 from Table 12.3 (see Evaluation Techniques 1):

Goal and Objective 2: Help adults with BPD understand the genetic, learned, and environmental factors that lend themselves to emotional dysregulation.

> **Strategy 1:** Provide a 2-hour workshop that provides examples, displays graphics, and solicits personal stories from clients to understand the genetic, learned, and environmental factors that might lend oneself to emotional dysregulation.

>> **Evaluation Technique 1:** Have clients anonymously write their reactions to the 2-hour workshop.

Goal and Objective 3: Help adults with BPD examine the impact on self and on others of emotional dysregulation.

> **Strategy 1:** Provide a 2-hour group counseling experience, where clients can share how their experience with emotional dysregulation has impacted themselves and others.

>> **Evaluation Technique 1:** As part of the group counseling experience, have clients share their feelings on the experience.

Asking for feedback is a particularly easy evaluation method; however, some of the pitfalls include the following:

- When writing feedback, participants may or may not believe their feedback is truly anonymous.
- Participants may or may not be honest in their feedback.
- If feedback is done orally, in a group setting, participants may or may not be trusting while sharing their experiences.
- The feedback may or may not be taken seriously by the program leader in leading to changes to the program.

Creating Quizzes

When content knowledge is presented to participants, a program leader might want to obtain a sense of whether that knowledge has been assimilated. Creating a quiz is a simple and quick way of assessing knowledge assimilation. Since formative evaluation is examining whether the program, not the participants, has been successful (although one hopes that participants are successful), participants should not experience a sense of having to "pass the quiz" when it is administered. For instance, we can create a quiz using Goal and Objective 2, Strategy 1 from Table 12.3 (see Evaluation Technique 2):

Goal and Objective 2: Help adults with BPD understand the genetic, learned, and environmental factors that lend themselves to emotional dysregulation.

> **Strategy 1:** Provide a 2-hour workshop that provides examples, displays graphics, and solicits personal stories from clients to understand the genetic, learned, and environmental factors that might lend oneself to emotional dysregulation.

> > **Evaluation Technique 2:** Give a quiz on the information learned during the workshop to assess the presenter's ability at helping clients learn.

Development of a traditional quiz, such as the use of multiple choice and true–false items, would work in obtaining such knowledge. However, these days, there are multiple creative ways of creating quizzes online, where participants can respond anonymously on their phones or via other electronic means.

Using Rating Scales

There are a whole host of rating scales that can be used in evaluating a program. Three of the most common include Likert scales, numerical scales, and rank order scales (Neukrug & Fawcett, 2020). Let's take a quick look at each of these:

- **LIKERT SCALES**: Likert scales, sometimes called graphic scales, contain several items rated on the same theme and anchored by both numbers and a statement that correspond to the numbers. This type of scale is particularly good at assessing a program leader's ability to offer didactic presentations. For instance, for Goal and Objective 1, Strategy 1 from Table 12.3 we can create a Likert scale (See Evaluation Technique 1 and then view Box 12.2).

Goal and Objective 1: Help adults with BPD understand emotional dysregulation.

> **Strategy 1:** Use the *DSM-5-TR*, journal articles, and books to develop a 90-minute didactic presentation on emotional dysregulation.

> > **Evaluation Technique 1:** Develop an evaluation instrument clients can use to assess how well the speaker was prepared, respectful, knowledgeable, interesting, and stimulating.

- **NUMERICAL SCALES**: Numerical scales provide a written statement or question that can be rated from high to low on a number line. For instance, using Goal and Objective 4, Strategy 1 from Table 12.3 we can create a numerical scale (see Evaluation Technique 2, then Box 12.3):

Goal and Objective 4: Help adults with BPD learn techniques to decrease emotional dysregulation.

> **Strategy 1:** Teach clients to identify typical characteristics of emotional dysregulation and have them and acknowledge and accept their behaviors that are reflective of emotional dysregulation (e.g., high levels of anxiety, depression, self-harm behaviors, substance abuse, and angry outbursts).

BOX 12.2 Likert Scale Assessing Program Leader's Ability at Presenting Material

Relative to the program leader's ability at presenting the material today, indicate how strongly you agree or disagree with each of the following statements:

	Strongly disagree	Somewhat disagree	Neither agree nor disagree	Somewhat agree	Strongly agree
The leader seemed well-prepared.	1	2	3	4	5
The leader was respectful to the participants.	1	2	3	4	5
The leader seemed knowledgeable about the material being presented.	1	2	3	4	5
The leader was interesting.	1	2	3	4	5
The leader stimulated my interest in the material.	1	2	3	4	5
Overall, the leader was excellent in the workshop.	1	2	3	4	5

Evaluation Technique 2: Create a 10-point rating scale that measures how well clients feel they have been able to practice mindfulness and meditation within one week following learning the techniques.

BOX 12.3 Practicing Mindfulness

With "0" representing not having practiced mindfulness at all over the past week and "10" representing that you have practiced mindfulness thoroughly over the past week, circle the number on the scale below that best represents you.

0	1	2	3	4	5	6	7	8	9	10

- **RANK ORDER SCALES:** Rank order scales provide a series of words or statements the participant can place in hierarchical order based on their preferences. For instance, using Goal and Objective 5, Evaluation Technique 1, from Table 12.3 we can create a rank order scale (see Evaluation Technique 1, then Box 12.4):

Goal and Objective 5: Help adults with BPD maintain emotional regulation over their lifetime.

Strategy 1: Provide a variety of techniques for clients to be able to main emotional regulation over a long period of time, including mindfulness, meditation, medication, relaxation exercises, interpersonal skills, nutrition, exercise, and more.

Evaluation Technique 1: Rank order the techniques to determine which have been most useful over the past week (or since you finished the program, 6 months ago).

BOX 12.4 Rank Order Scale

Please rank order your preferred method of practicing emotional dysregulation. Place a "1" next to the item you most prefer, a "2" next to the item you second most prefer, and so on, down to an "8" next to the item you prefer least.

_____ Mindfulness
_____ Meditation
_____ Medication
_____ Relaxation exercises
_____ Interpersonal skills
_____ Nutrition
_____ Exercise
_____ Interpersonal skills

Observing Participants

Observation of your participants is an often overlooked, but important, aspect of formative evaluation. Consider whether your participants look bored, whether they are half asleep, whether they are participating in the program, and so forth. The best method of observation is to have non-biased colleague sit in on the program and be an objective observer of participants' behaviors. This person can help determine those aspects of the program participants like best and those aspects participants seem to be less interested or uninvolved in. Although generally not as powerful, family members and/or significant others can offer feedback about any changes they have observed in the client. Using Goal and Objective 5, Evaluation Technique 4, from Table 12.3 we can ask an observer to respond to their perceptions of how the individual is doing on any of a number of parameters (see Evaluation Technique 4, then Box 12.5).

BOX 12.5 Observation From a Spouse

Dear _____:

Thank you for agreeing to give us feedback regarding your observations of your spouse while she has been participating in learning some techniques to manage her emotions. We hope you can complete this form once a week during the time she is involved in the program.

On the form provided, can you tell us how frequently you believe your spouse is doing each of the following activities per week and how dedicated and thorough she seems to be doing each of the techniques. Also, can you tell us if she seems to have used each technique as a means of calming herself down when she has become highly emotional. Use as much space as you need. Your feedback is so important, and we thank you for your help!

Remember: frequency, dedication and thoroughness, and if used when highly emotional.

- Mindfulness
- Meditation
- Medication
- Relaxation exercises
- Interpersonal skills
- Nutrition
- Exercise

Goal and Objective 5: Help adults with BPD maintain emotional regulation over their lifetime.

> **Strategy 1:** Provide a variety of techniques for clients to be able to main emotional regulation over a long period of time, including mindfulness, meditation, medication, relaxation exercises, interpersonal skills, nutrition, exercise, and more.
>
> > **Evaluation Technique 4:** Ask unbiased observers, or significant others, to provide written or verbal feedback regarding how they view the client is progressing after the program was completed (e.g., 1 month, 6 months, or a year).

Conducting Summative Evaluation

Whereas formative evaluation examines the experience of participants while the program is running, summative evaluation assesses the experience of the whole program, either near the end of the program or sometime after the program has finished. Summative evaluation sometimes uses the same techniques as formative evaluation but focuses on the totality of the program. With this in mind, one can design a number of methods for conducting summative evaluation. Using our example of a program on managing emotions, one can (a) provide feedback on the leader's ability to offer didactic learning, (b) provide feedback about the whole program verbally or in writing, (c) complete rating scales that target many aspects of the program and compare the results to see which ones were most effective, (d) complete rating scales that target the whole program, and (e) develop and initiate research designs that compare the program to other similar programs. Here, we look at a limited number of the many summative evaluation techniques.

Provide Feedback on Didactic Learning

Box 12.2, which uses a Likert scale to determine the leaders' ability at presenting a piece of the program didactically, can be used as is or changed somewhat, but this time, the instrument has a focus on the totality of the program instead of one aspect of the program.

Asking for Feedback

As in formative evaluation, participants can be asked to give feedback about the program in writing or verbally. However, in this case, the focus is on the whole program. When feedback is given in writing, participants should be told whether their responses are anonymous.

Using Ratings Scales That Target Specific Aspects of Program

Numerical ratings scales, like the one in Box 12.3, can be used at the conclusion of a program to assess the effectiveness of a variety of learned skills. Or a series of numerical scales can be merged into one large scale that assesses the learning of several skills during the program (see Box 12.6).

Using Ratings Scales That Target the Whole Program

Varying forms of rating scales can be used to target all of what has been taught and learned in the program. Adapting a Likert scale is particularly amenable to this kind of rating (see Box 12.7).

BOX 12.6 Rating Techniques Learned in the Program

With "0" representing not being helpful and "10" representing being extremely helpful, circle the number that best matches how helpful the particular technique was to you in learning how to manage your emotions.

Mindfulness	0	1	2	3	4	5	6	7	8	9	10
Meditation	0	1	2	3	4	5	6	7	8	9	10
Medication	0	1	2	3	4	5	6	7	8	9	10
Relaxation exercises	0	1	2	3	4	5	6	7	8	9	10
Interpersonal skills	0	1	2	3	4	5	6	7	8	9	10
Nutrition	0	1	2	3	4	5	6	7	8	9	10
Exercise	0	1	2	3	4	5	6	7	8	9	10

Developing and Initiating Research Designs

Summative evaluation sometimes involves the use of specific research designs. For instance, in employing survey research, a university trying to decide if it should maintain its graduate counseling program might desire to survey all counseling students who have graduated within the past 5 years, as well as their employers, in an effort to assess how effective they believe the counseling program was in finding jobs and preparing them to become counselors.

Even true experimental designs can be employed in summative research. For example, if we wanted to determine whether an online program for teaching emotional dysregulation was as effective as

BOX 12.7 Likert Scale Assessing the Whole Program

Rate the whole program using the following scale:

	Strongly disagree	Somewhat disagree	Neither agree nor disagree	Somewhat agree	Strongly agree
I learned a lot from this program.	1	2	3	4	5
I am now much more adept at using a variety of skills in managing my emotions.	1	2	3	4	5
Overall, from the knowledge gained, I am much more adept at managing my emotions.	1	2	3	4	5
The program was interesting and worthwhile.	1	2	3	4	5
The leaders were knowledgeable and informative.	1	2	3	4	5
This program was critical to positive change in my life.	1	2	2	4	5

an in-person program for teaching emotional dysregulation, we might develop a true experimental design to compare the effectiveness of the two programs. Participants can be randomly assigned to online and in-person programs, and at the conclusion of the programs, participants can be assessed by an instrument to measure emotional dysregulation. A statistical comparison of the online and in-person programs can then be completed to determine if one program was more effective than the other in managing emotional dysregulation. Clearly, this would be a large undertaking and is generally only done when it is grant funded.

REPORTING EVALUATION RESULTS

Effective communication is an important part of well-designed evaluation procedures and requires careful consideration if evaluation results are to be understood and utilized. Although progress reports are provided to different stakeholders throughout an evaluation, a formal written evaluation report is often generated and provides an evaluation outline and summary, a description of the evaluation context, descriptions of program participants, a justification of evaluation criteria, data-gathering procedures, evaluation findings, and recommendations. In addition to a final report, oral presentations summarizing evaluation results are often given to communicate evaluation findings and recommendations. The purposes, content, and other considerations for each of these reporting methods are discussed in the following sections.

Writing an Evaluation Report

A formal written report of the evaluation serves the purposes of documentation, answering questions about the findings and methodology, and provides a reference for future decision-makers (Linfield & Posavac, 2019). The following are some of the key sections you may find in an evaluation report.

Evaluation Outline and Summary

Unlike abstracts for research articles, report summaries are longer (e.g., two pages) and can stand alone. It is helpful to think of the summary as a shortened version of the formal report that summarizes the sections of the entire report and includes a discussion of recommendations. When writing the summary, it is useful to include subheadings to assist readers in navigating the information contained in the summary. Keep in mind that the summary may be the only part of the report that administrators read; thus, it is important to include specific information.

Description of Evaluation Context

This section of the report contains details of the program setting, program staff, and purpose of the evaluation (Linfield & Posavac, 2019). Since it is impossible to know who will read the evaluation report, this section is written with the assumption that the reader has little knowledge of the program.

Descriptions of Program Participants

Not only do evaluation reports include a description of the context, but they also include a description of those who received the program's services. This section of the report contains information on participant demographics (e.g., age, education, and gender), how participants entered the program (e.g., were they self or other referred, or was their attendance court mandated?), as well as attrition rates and descriptions of those who did not complete the program. These descriptions help program administrators determine whether the target population for which the program was designed is being reached as well as strategies for improving the program (Linfield & Posavac, 2019).

Justification of Evaluation Criteria

Regardless of the type of evaluation (e.g., formative evaluation or summative evaluation), certain criteria are selected to measure participant needs and program outcomes and should be related to program goals and objectives. Describing why certain evaluation criteria were included and how they are related to program goals and objectives should be discussed here. This section might also be an appropriate place to discuss how issues related to statistical power and reliability as well as validity of measurement tools were considered and addressed (Linfield & Posavac, 2019).

Data-Gathering Procedures

Like the methodology or procedure section of a research article, this section of the report discusses how data in the evaluation was obtained, since the way information is gathered can impact the findings (Linfield & Posavac, 2019).

Evaluation Findings

This section contains the results and limitations of the analysis. Findings should be written in a manner that allows readers to gain a practical understanding of the results, and evaluators should anticipate potential misunderstandings to minimize the misuse of findings. One strategy to address reader misunderstanding is to include graphs and other visual depictions of data, which can be used to help readers interpret and understand findings. Evaluators should also discuss the limitations of the evaluation in this section of the report.

Recommendations

Recommendations for program improvement are best developed in consultation with stakeholders (Linfield & Posavac, 2019) and then written into the report. Adequate time should be set aside to ensure the meaning of the evaluation is understood and recommendations make sense for the program. Program managers likely know which recommendations are feasible for the program and should be involved when developing recommendations.

Oral Presentation of Evaluation Results

Oral presentations to program managers, administrators, and other stakeholders are used to supplement the formal written report. Oral presentations are beneficial because people are more likely to pay attention to an oral presentation than words in a report. In addition, oral presentation can be adjusted to fit the needs of the audience (Linfield & Posavac, 2019). Oral presentations are generally more interactive than written reports and provide stakeholders with an opportunity to ask questions about the evaluation.

Content of an Oral Presentation

Oral presentations of evaluation findings are designed to fit the needs of the audience and relay different information than the formal written report. These presentations typically begin with a short review of the reasons for the evaluation as well as the procedures used. Typically, oral presentations last 30 to 60 minutes, so most of the presentation time should focus on describing the findings, recommendations, and answering questions (Linfield & Posavac, 2019). In addition to the oral content of the presentation, presenters may include computer-projected visuals or handouts to assist in highlighting key points. These visuals can help increase the audience's understanding of the content and keep their attention focused on the message. The goal is to make the presentation memorable, so program managers will utilize the recommendations of the evaluation.

ETHICAL AND LEGAL ISSUES IN PROGRAM DEVELOPMENT AND EVALUATION

The ethical codes of the American Mental Health Counselors Association (AMHCA, 2020), American Counseling Association (ACA, 2014), and American Psychological Association (APA, 2016) have all set standards regarding conducting research and evaluation. In addition, federal regulations specify rules and procedures to follow when conducting programs and research with people. Based on these codes and legislative issues, Wilder (2007) summarizes some of the most salient ethical and legal issues when conducting and evaluating a program, including incorporating underlying ethical principles into your program and evaluation process, considering the risks and benefits of your program and evaluation procedures, providing informed consent, ensuring confidentiality, and the importance of following regulations according to HIPAA and IRB boards. Let's take a look at each of these.

Underlying Ethical Principles

Most ethical codes stress principles that should underpin all ethical behavior, including a focus on presenting programs and conducting program evaluation. As noted in Chapter 6, they include (a) autonomy, or protecting the independence, self-determination, and freedom of choice of clients and consumers; (b) nonmaleficence, or "doing no harm" when working with clients and consumers; (c) beneficence, or promoting the good of society, which can be fostered by focusing on the well-being of the client and the consumer; (d) justice, or providing equal and fair treatment to all clients and consumers; (e) fidelity, or maintaining trust in the relationship (e.g., keeping conversations confidential) and being committed to the client and consumer; and (f) veracity, or being truthful and genuine with the client and consumer within the context of the relationship (see Kitchener, 1984, 1986; Meara et al., 1996; Urofsky et al., 2008; Wilder, 2007).

Consider Risks and Benefits

When conducting and evaluating a program, evaluators should consider risks and benefits to the participants. For instance, some benefits to participating in our program to manage emotions include showing that our procedures worked and, ultimately, being able to use them again with other participants or refine them to make them even better in the future. One risk includes a client being triggered by one of the activities or items in the program or program evaluation questionnaires, resulting in negative feelings; experiences; and, perhaps, panic attacks. Relative to program evaluation, Wilder (2007) suggests the following to minimize the risks and maximize the benefits:

- Keep evaluation procedures as brief and convenient as possible to minimize disruptions in subjects' lives.
- Do not ask emotionally troubling questions, unless they are necessary to help you improve services.
- Provide incentives, such as food, money, or gift certificates. (p. 2)

Providing Informed Consent

As noted in Chapter 6, informed consent is a critical ethical issue in all aspects of mental health processes (Corey et al., 2024). When conducting and evaluating a program, individuals should be given information on what the program procedures are, understand risks and benefits, be told in advance about evaluation techniques, be able to choose whether they want to participate, know the qualifications of the individuals conducting the program and the evaluation techniques, know the limits of confidentiality, and be able to withdraw at any time.

Confidentiality

As best as possible, individuals who conduct and evaluate a program should ensure confidentiality (Corey et al., 2024). However, this is not always foolproof, as whenever you are working in group settings (e.g., our program on managing emotions), there is a possibility that some of the group members could talk about other members outside of the group, despite the fact that they were asked to keep information confidential. Thus, program leaders should encourage confidentiality of all participants but also identify the limits of such confidentiality and the penalties for breaking confidentiality (e.g., not continuing in the program). Relative to program evaluation, since the program leaders have control over how and what to evaluate, they can generally ensure confidentiality, although they may not be able to ensure anonymity. For instance, although all program evaluation responses can be kept confidential and held in secure places, sometimes a program evaluator can identify a person in the program by how they responded to items.

HIPAA and IRB Boards

All health care providers that collect information concerning the mental and physical health of individuals will need to protect the privacy and security of information obtained, according to the 1996 Health Insurance Portability and Accountability Act (HIPAA; American Psychiatric Association, 2013; U.S. Department of Health and Human Services, 2023). Thus, when conducting and evaluating a program, program leaders and evaluators should understand and abide by regulations relative to HIPAA. Disregarding HIPAA can result in large fines, a loss of license, and potential criminal implications.

In some cases, such as when programs are federally funded and designed using a research paradigm, they must be reviewed and approved by an institutional review board (IRB) that ensures the program complies with ethical codes and legal statutes in its protection of individuals (U.S. Food and Drug Administration, 2019). Those who conduct and evaluate programs should know when an IRB board has to approve a program as well as the process for having their program approved through the board.

SUMMARY

This chapter examined the development and evaluation of mental health programs. We began by identifying six steps in such development: Step 1: identifying your target population, step 2: operationalizing the problem, step 3: identifying goals and objectives of your program, step 4: designing specific strategies to reach your goals and objectives, step 5: developing evaluation techniques to examine whether you successfully implemented your strategies, and step 6: analyzing the data from the evaluation techniques and making decisions on program change or curtailment.

Focusing on one example—individuals with BPD who have emotional dysregulation—we next demonstrated how all the steps would be addressed. For instance, we suggested how to operationalize the problem (emotional dysregulation), how to identify goals and objectives for this problem, how to develop strategies for reaching the goals and objectives, and how to evaluate the efficacy of our strategies to make decisions on program change or curtailment. Using as a model a program to help individuals manage their emotions, we gave numerous examples of developing goals and objectives, strategies for change, and evaluation techniques of our program.

The next part of the chapter examined formative and summative program evaluation—two types of evaluation used to assess the efficacy of our program. We noted that formative evaluation is typically completed during a program to improve and make modifications of the program while it is in process and that summative evaluation is completed near to, or after, the conclusion of a program to determine whether a program should be continued, expanded, or eliminated.

In conducting formal evaluation, we highlighted a few of the many ways evaluation can be completed, including asking for feedback, creating quizzes, using rating scales, and observing your participants.

We then offered five ways summative evaluation could be conducted, including providing feedback on the leader's ability to offer didactic learning, providing feedback about the whole program verbally or in writing, completing rating scales that target many aspects of the program and comparing the results to see which ones were most effective, completing rating scales that target the whole program, and developing and initiating research designs that compare the program to other similar programs.

The next part of the chapter examined several aspects of written and oral evaluation reports. For written reports, we outlined the following key sections: the evaluation outline and summary, the description of evaluation context, descriptions of program participants, justification of evaluation criteria, data-gathering procedures, evaluation findings, and recommendations. We then discussed the importance of oral presentations and noted that they supplement the formal written report, are generally 30–60 minutes long, and are often paid more attention to than the written reports.

The chapter concluded with a review of ethical and legal issues in program development and evaluation. Here, we examined the underlying principles of autonomy, nonmaleficence, beneficence, justice, fidelity, and veracity when conducting program evaluation; the risks and benefits of conducting a program; the importance of providing informed consent when conducting a program; the importance and difficulty of ensuring confidentiality during a program; and the roles HIPAA and IRB boards play in protecting the privacy of individuals and the security of information obtained.

KEY WORDS AND TERMS

asking for feedback
autonomy
beneficence
borderline personality disorder (BPD)
confidentiality
creating quizzes
emotional dysregulation
fidelity
formal written evaluation report
formative evaluation
graphic scales
HIPAA
informed consent
IRB boards
justice
Likert scale
methods for conducting

summative evaluation
nonmaleficence
numerical scale
observation of your participants
oral presentations summarizing evaluation results
rank order scale
risks and benefits of your program and evaluation
six steps in developing and evaluating a mental health program
standards regarding conducting research and evaluation
Step 1: identifying your target population
Step 2: operationalizing the problem

Step 3: identifying goals and objectives of your program
Step 4: designing specific strategies to reach your goals and objectives
Step 5: developing evaluation techniques to evaluate whether you successfully implemented your strategies
Step 6: analyzing the data from the evaluation techniques and making decisions on program change or curtailment
summative evaluation
underlying ethical principles
using rating scales
veracity

APPENDIX A. ACA'S ETHICAL STANDARDS: A BRIEF OVERVIEW

ACA'S ETHICAL STANDARDS: A BRIEF OVERVIEW

ACA's ethical code has undergone several revisions since it was first adopted in 1961. However, because values of society and professional associations are always changing, and because codes change only periodically (e.g., every 10 years or so), the values reflected in a code sometimes lag behind the values of society and professional associations (Daniel-Burke, 2014; Kaplan et al., 2017; Ponton & Duba, 2009). Keeping this in mind, the nine sections of ACA's ethical code are briefly summarized next (ACA, 2014). The summary highlights aspects of the code; however, you are strongly encouraged to read the whole code in detail, which can be found visiting the knowledge center tab on the ACA website: www.counseling.org.

SECTION A: THE COUNSELING RELATIONSHIP

Highlighting important issues within the counseling relationship, this section stresses (a) the importance of respecting the client and looking out for the client's welfare and, to this end, keeping good records, having a plan for counseling, and supporting client networks (e.g., family, community, and religious) when appropriate; (b) obtaining informed consent prior to and during treatment; (c) consulting with others who are working with your client; (d) avoiding harm and not imposing one's own values; (e) not engaging in romantic or sexual relationships or personal virtual relationships with clients and those close to them; (f) maintaining appropriate boundaries and professional relationships with clients and documenting boundary extensions (e.g., attending a graduation ceremony); (g) knowing how to advocate for clients at various levels (e.g., individual, group, institutional, and societal); (h) understanding the importance of identifying roles when working with clients who may have a relationship with one another (e.g., clients who are simultaneously in individual, group, and family counseling); (i) knowing how to screen and protect clients participating in groups; (j) knowing how to establish fees, when bartering is justified, and whether to receive or give gifts; and (k) knowing how to effectively terminate and refer clients and not abandoning or neglecting clients in counseling (e.g., vacations, illnesses, and terminations).

SECTION B: CONFIDENTIALITY AND PRIVACY

Section B examines the importance of (a) respecting clients' rights to confidentiality and privacy, (b) knowing when to keep and break confidentiality (e.g., when there is "foreseeable harm"; during end-of-life decision-making; when a client has a contagious, life-threatening disease; or for court-ordered clients), (c) knowing when and how to share confidential information, (d) understanding the nature of confidentiality relative to group and family work, (e) understanding the nature of confidentiality when working with clients who lack the capacity to give informed consent (e.g., children and incapacitated adults), (f) preserving the confidentiality of records, and (g) making reasonable efforts at protecting a client's confidentiality when consulting with a colleague about that client.

SECTION C: PROFESSIONAL RESPONSIBILITY

This section discusses the importance of (a) knowing the ethical code; (b) practicing within one's professional competence and knowing what to do when one is professionally or psychologically impaired or incapacitated; (c) accurately advertising and promoting oneself; (d) accurately representing one's credentials and qualifications; (e) not discriminating against clients; (f) knowing one's public responsibilities, including not engaging in sexual harassment, accurately reporting information to third parties (e.g., insurance companies, courts), being accurate when using the media (e.g., radio talk shows), and not making unjustifiable treatment claims; (g) providing services that are empirically based or, if using a new procedure, explaining its potential risks and benefits to clients and minimizing risk and harm; and (h) ensuring the public can distinguish personal from professional statements.

SECTION D: RELATIONSHIPS WITH OTHER PROFESSIONALS

This section highlights the importance of (a) maintaining mutually respectful relationships with colleagues, employers, and employees despite differing counseling approaches; forming strong, interdisciplinary relationships with others; and addressing unethical situations and negative working conditions when they might arise and (b) when acting as a consultant, ensuring that one is competent, understands the needs of the consultee, and obtains informed consent from the consultee.

SECTION E: EVALUATION, ASSESSMENT, AND INTERPRETATION

This section highlights the importance of (a) using assessment tools to determine client welfare and ensuring the proper use and interpretation of such assessments; (b) being competent in the use of assessment instruments and appropriately using the information gained; (c) obtaining informed consent from clients; (d) releasing data only to those identified by clients; (e) making accurate diagnoses and taking into account cross-cultural issues; (f) choosing instruments based on good reliability, validity, and cross-cultural fairness; (g) ensuring proper testing conditions; (h) ensuring nondiscrimination; (i) knowing proper ways to score and interpret instruments; (j) ensuring test security; (k) ensuring test information is up to date and not obsolete; (l) ensuring that sound, scientific knowledge is used in the construction of assessment instruments; and (m) ensuring objective results when conducting forensic evaluations.

SECTION F: SUPERVISION, TRAINING, AND TEACHING

This section examines the importance of (a) supervisors being responsible for the welfare of their supervisees' clients; (b) supervisors obtaining ongoing training; (c) supervisors maintaining ethical relationships with supervisees, including respect for nonsexual boundaries; (d) supervisors obtaining informed consent from supervisees, ensuring access to consultation when they are not available, and ensuring that supervisees know standards and are familiar with proper procedures for termination; (e) students and supervisees knowing the ACA Code of Ethics, monitoring themselves to ensure that they are not impaired, and providing clients with a professional disclosure statement about their status as a counseling student or supervisee and how it affects confidentiality; (f) providing ongoing evaluation, assisting supervisees in securing remediation when necessary, and endorsing a supervisee only when they believe that the individual is qualified; (g) counselor educators being competent, infusing multicultural issues, integrating theory and practice, ensuring the rights of students, being careful when presenting "innovative" techniques, ensuring adequate field placements, and ensuring that students and supervisees present professional disclosure statements to clients; (h) counselor educators ensuring student welfare by offering orientations and providing self-help experiences; (i) counselor educators providing adequate program information and orientation, advising, providing self-growth experiences, and addressing personal concerns; (j) counselor educators identifying what is expected of students and working with students who may need referrals for remediation or counseling; (k) counselor educators knowing that they are prohibited from having a sexual relationship with current students or otherwise misusing the power they hold over students; and (l) counselor educators actively infusing multicultural competency into their training and working toward recruiting and retaining diverse faculty and students.

SECTION G: RESEARCH AND PUBLICATION

A wide range of ethical areas is discussed in this section, including (a) research responsibilities, such as the appropriate use of human research participants; (b) the rights of research participants, such as offering informed consent, ensuring confidentiality, and understanding the use of deception in research; (c) standards for maintaining appropriate boundaries and relationships with research participants; (d) methods for accurately reporting results; and (e) guidelines for accurately publishing results.

SECTION H: DISTANCE COUNSELING, TECHNOLOGY, AND SOCIAL MEDIA

Although issues related to distance counseling, technology, and social media are infused throughout the code, this new section highlights the importance of the following: (a) having knowledge of these areas and knowing the law; (b) conducting proper procedures for informed consent, confidentiality, and security of information; (c) making sure that the client you are corresponding with is actually the client; (d) in a distance counseling relationship, knowing the benefits and limitations, the boundaries, ensuring that clients are up to speed technologically, knowing how to identify other services if the distance counseling services are not effective, and educating clients on misunderstandings that might arise because of distance issues (e.g., mistaken nonverbals); (e) maintaining appropriate records in light of laws and informing clients about maintenance of records, maintaining links to information about credentials, providing accessibility for individuals with disabilities or those for whom English is not their first language; and (f) maintaining separate professional and personal social media websites, explaining to clients the benefits and drawbacks of the use of social media, respecting the privacy of clients' social media unless given consent, and avoiding the disclosure of clients' confidential information on social media.

SECTION I: RESOLVING ETHICAL ISSUES

This final section of the ethical code explains the proper steps to take in the reporting and resolution of suspected ethical violations. It addresses (a) possible conflicts between ethical codes and the law and using ethical decision-making models when dealing with ethical dilemmas; (b) how to deal with suspected violations, such as first addressing the individual informally and then, if no resolution is forthcoming or if the violation has caused harm to another, how to approach the appropriate ethics committee; and (c) the importance of working with ethics committees.

APPENDIX B. PRIVILEGE EXERCISE

1. If your ancestors were forced to come to the United States not by choice, take one step back.

2. If your primary ethnic identity is American, take one step forward.

3. If you were ever called names because of your race, class, ethnicity, gender, or sexual orientation, take one step back.

4. If there were people of color who worked in your childhood household as housekeepers, gardeners, and so on, take one step forward.

5. If you were ever ashamed or embarrassed of your clothes, house, car, and so on take one step back.

6. If your parents were professionals, doctors, lawyers, and so on take one step forward.

7. If you were raised in an area where there was a considerable amount of prostitution, drug activity, and so on take one stop back.

8. If you ever tried to change your appearance, mannerisms, or behavior to avoid being judged or ridiculed, take one step back.

9. If you studied the culture of your ancestors in elementary school, take one step forward.

10. If you went to school speaking a language other than English, take one step back.

11. If there were more than 50 books in your house when you grew up, take one step forward.

12. If you ever had to skip a meal or were hungry because there was not enough money to buy food when you were growing up, take one step back.

13. If you were taken to art galleries or plays by your parents during childhood, take one step forward.

14. If one of your parents was unemployed or laid off, not by choice, take one step back.

15. If you attended private school or summer camp, take one step forward.

16. If your family ever had to move because they could not afford the rent, take one step back.

17. If you were told that you were beautiful, smart, and capable by your parents, take one step forward.

18. If you were ever discouraged from academics or jobs because of race, class, ethnicity, gender or sexual orientation, take one step back.

19. If you were encouraged to attend college by your parents, take one step forward.

20. If you were raised in a single parent household, take one step back.

21. If your family owned the house where you grew up, take one step forward.

22. If you saw members of your race, ethnic group, gender or sexual orientation portrayed on television in degrading roles, take one step back.

23. If you were ever offered a good job because of your association with a friend or family member, take one step forward.

24. If you were ever denied employment because of your race, ethnicity, gender, or sexual orientation, take one step back.

25. If you were paid less, treated unfairly because of race, ethnicity, gender or sexual orientation, take one step back.

26. If you were ever accused of cheating or lying because of your race, ethnicity, gender, or sexual orientation, take one step back.

27. If you ever inherited money or property, take one step forward.

28. If you had to rely primarily on public transportation, take one step back.

29. If you were ever stopped or questioned by the police because of your race, ethnicity, gender or sexual orientation, take one step back.

30. If you were ever afraid of violence because of your race, ethnicity, gender, or sexual orientation, take one step back.

31. If you were generally able to avoid places that were dangerous, take one step forward.

32. If you were ever uncomfortable about a joke related to your race, ethnicity, gender, or sexual orientation but felt unsafe to confront the situation, take one step back.

33. If you were ever the victim of violence related to your race, ethnicity, gender, or sexual orientation, take one step back.

34. If your parents did not grow up in the United States, take one step back.

35. If your parents told you that you could be anything you wanted to be, take one step forward.

APPENDIX C. *DSM-5-TR* DIAGNOSTIC CATEGORIES

The *DSM-5-TR* offers an in-depth discussion of 22 broad diagnostic categories and their subtypes (APA, 2022). Depending on whether you include all possible combinations within the diagnostic categories (e.g., subtypes and specifiers), there are approximately 150 to 550 possible diagnoses in *DSM-5-TR*. The following offers very brief descriptions summaries of the categories. Please refer to the *DSM-5-TR* for an in-depth review of each disorder.

NEURODEVELOPMENTAL DISORDERS

This group of disorders typically refers to those that manifest during early development, although diagnoses are sometimes not assigned until adulthood. Examples of neurodevelopmental disorders include intellectual disabilities, communication disorders, autism spectrum disorders (incorporating the former categories of autistic disorder, Asperger's disorder, childhood disintegrative disorder, and pervasive developmental disorder), ADHD, specific learning disorders, motor disorders, and other neurodevelopmental disorders.

SCHIZOPHRENIA SPECTRUM AND OTHER PSYCHOTIC DISORDERS

The disorders that belong to this section all have one feature in common: psychotic symptoms—that is, delusions, hallucinations, grossly disorganized or abnormal motor behavior, and/or negative symptoms. The disorders include schizotypal personality disorder (which is listed again, and explained more comprehensively, in the personality disorders category in the *DSM-5-TR*), delusional disorder, brief psychotic disorder, schizophreniform disorder, schizophrenia, schizoaffective disorder, substance/medication-induced psychotic disorders, psychotic disorders due to another medical condition, and catatonic disorders.

BIPOLAR AND RELATED DISORDERS

The disorders in this category refer to disturbances in mood in which the client cycles through stages of mania or mania and depression. Both children and adults can be diagnosed with bipolar disorder, and the clinician can work to identify the pattern of mood presentation, such as rapid cycling, which is more often observed in children. These disorders include bipolar I, bipolar II, cyclothymic disorder, substance/medication-induced bipolar and related disorder, bipolar and related disorder due to another medical condition, and other specified or unspecified bipolar and related disorder.

DEPRESSIVE DISORDERS

Previously grouped into the broader category of "mood disorders" in *DSM-IV-TR*, these disorders describe conditions where depressed mood is the overarching concern. They include disruptive mood dysregulation disorder, major depressive disorder, persistent depressive disorder (also known as dysthymia), and premenstrual dysphoric disorder.

ANXIETY DISORDERS

There are a wide range of anxiety disorders, which can be diagnosed by identifying a general or specific cause of unease or fear. This anxiety or fear is considered clinically significant when it is excessive and persistent over time. Examples of anxiety disorders that typically manifest earlier in development include separation anxiety and selective mutism. Other examples of anxiety disorders are specific phobia, social anxiety disorder (also known as "social phobia"), panic disorder, and generalized anxiety disorder.

OBSESSIVE-COMPULSIVE AND RELATED DISORDERS

Disorders in this category all involve obsessive thoughts and compulsive behaviors, and the client feels compelled to perform them. Diagnoses in this category include obsessive–compulsive disorder, body dysmorphic disorder, hoarding disorder, trichotillomania (or hair-pulling disorder), and excoriation (or skin-picking) disorder.

TRAUMA- AND STRESSOR-RELATED DISORDERS

A new category introduced in the *DSM-5*, trauma and stress disorders emphasize the pervasive impact that life events can have on an individual's emotional and physical well-being. Diagnoses include reactive attachment disorder, disinhibited social engagement disorder, posttraumatic stress disorder (PTSD), prolonged grief disorder, acute stress disorder, and adjustment disorders.

DISSOCIATIVE DISORDERS

These disorders indicate a temporary or prolonged disruption to consciousness that can cause an individual to misinterpret identity, surroundings, and memories. Diagnoses include dissociative identity disorder (formerly known as multiple personality disorder), dissociative amnesia, depersonalization/derealization disorder, and other specified and unspecified dissociative disorders.

SOMATIC SYMPTOM AND RELATED DISORDERS

Somatic symptom disorders were previously referred to as "somatoform disorders" and are characterized by the experiencing of a physical symptom without evidence of a physical cause, suggesting a psychological cause. Somatic symptom disorders include somatic symptom disorder, illness anxiety disorder (formerly hypochondriasis), conversion (or functional neurological symptom) disorder, psychological factors affecting other medical conditions, and factitious disorder.

FEEDING AND EATING DISORDERS

This group of disorders describes clients who have severe concerns about the amount or type of food they eat to the point that serious health problems, or even death, can result from their eating behaviors. Examples include avoidant/restrictive food intake disorder, anorexia nervosa, bulimia nervosa, binge eating disorder, pica, and rumination disorder.

ELIMINATION DISORDERS

These disorders can manifest at any point in a person's life, although they are typically diagnosed in early childhood or adolescence. They include enuresis, which is the inappropriate elimination of urine, and encopresis, which is the inappropriate elimination of feces. These behaviors may or may not be intentional.

SLEEP-WAKE DISORDERS

This category refers to disorders in which one's sleep patterns are severely affected, and they often co-occur with other disorders (e.g., depression or anxiety). Some examples include insomnia disorder, hypersomnolence disorder, restless legs syndrome, narcolepsy, and nightmare disorder. A number of sleep–wake disorders involve variations in breathing, such as sleep-related hypoventilation, obstructive sleep apnea hypopnea, central sleep apnoea, and more.

SEXUAL DYSFUNCTIONS

These disorders are related to problems that disrupt sexual functioning or one's ability to experience sexual pleasure. They occur across sexes and include delayed ejaculation, erectile disorder, female orgasmic disorder, and premature (or early) ejaculation disorder, among others.

GENDER DYSPHORIA

Formerly termed "gender identity disorder," this category includes those individuals who experience significant distress with the sex they were assigned at birth and associated gender roles. This diagnosis has been separated from the category of sexual disorders, as it is now accepted that gender dysphoria does not relate to a person's sexual attractions.

DISRUPTIVE, IMPULSE CONTROL, AND CONDUCT DISORDERS

These disorders are characterized by socially unacceptable or otherwise disruptive and harmful behaviors that are outside the individual's control. Generally, more common in males than in females and often first seen in childhood, they include oppositional defiant disorder, conduct disorder, intermittent explosive disorder, antisocial personality disorder (which is also coded in the category of personality disorders), kleptomania, and pyromania.

SUBSTANCE-RELATED AND ADDICTIVE DISORDERS

Substance use disorders include disruptions in functioning as the result of a craving or strong urge. Often caused by prescribed and illicit drugs or the exposure to toxins, with these disorders, the brain's reward system pathways are activated when the substance is taken (or, in the case of gambling disorder, when the behavior is being performed). Some common substances include alcohol, caffeine, nicotine, cannabis, opioids, inhalants, amphetamine, phencyclidine (PCP), sedatives, hypnotics, and anxiolytics. Substance use disorders are further designated with the following terms: intoxication, withdrawal, induced, or unspecified.

NEUROCOGNITIVE DISORDERS

These disorders are diagnosed when one's decline in cognitive functioning significantly changes and is usually the result of a medical condition (e.g., Parkinson's or Alzheimer's disease), the use of a substance/medication, or a traumatic brain injury, among other phenomena. Examples of neurocognitive disorders (NCDs) include delirium and several types of major and mild NCDs, such as frontotemporal NCD, NCD due to Parkinson's disease, NCD due to HIV infection, NCD due to Alzheimer's disease, substance- or medication-induced NCD, and vascular NCD, among others.

PERSONALITY DISORDERS

The 10 personality disorders in the *DSM-5*; all involve a pattern of experiences and behaviors that are persistent, inflexible, and deviate from one's cultural expectations. Usually, this pattern emerges in adolescence or early adulthood and causes severe distress in one's interpersonal relationships. The personality disorders are grouped into the three following clusters, which are based on similar behaviors:

- **Cluster A:** paranoid, schizoid, and schizotypal. These individuals seem bizarre or unusual in their behaviors and interpersonal relations.
- **Cluster B:** antisocial, borderline, histrionic, and narcissistic. These individuals seem overly emotional and are melodramatic or unpredictable in their behaviors and interpersonal relations.
- **Cluster C:** avoidant, dependent, and obsessive compulsive (not to be confused with obsessive–compulsive disorder). These individuals tend to appear anxious, worried, or fretful in their behaviors.

PARAPHILIC DISORDERS

These disorders are diagnosed when the client is sexually aroused to circumstances that deviate from traditional sexual stimuli and when such behaviors result in harm or significant emotional distress. The disorders include exhibitionistic disorder, voyeuristic disorder, frotteuristic disorder, sexual sadism and sexual masochism disorders, fetishistic disorder, transvestic disorder, pedophilic disorder, and other specified and unspecified paraphilic disorders.

OTHER MENTAL DISORDERS

This diagnostic category includes mental disorders that did not fall within one of the previously mentioned groups and do not have unifying characteristics. Examples include other specified mental disorder due to another medical condition, unspecified mental disorders due to another medical condition, other specified mental disorder, and unspecified mental disorder.

MEDICATION-INDUCED MOVEMENT DISORDERS AND OTHER ADVERSE EFFECTS OF MEDICATIONS

These disorders are the result of adverse and severe side effects to medications, although a causal link cannot always be shown. Some of these disorders include neuroleptic-induced parkinsonism, neuroleptic malignant syndrome, medication-induced dystonia, medication-induced acute akathisia, tardive dyskinesia, tardive akathisia, medication-induced postural tremor, other medication-induced movement disorder, antidepressant discontinuation syndrome, and other adverse effect of medication.

OTHER CONDITIONS THAT MAY BE A FOCUS OF CLINICAL ASSESSMENT

Generally referred to as Z codes in *DSM-5-TR*, here we find a description of concerns that are not considered mental disorders but could be clinically significant, such as abuse/neglect; relational problems; psychosocial, personal, and environmental concerns; educational/occupational problems; housing and economic problems; and problems related to the legal system.

APPENDIX D.
THE MILLER FAMILY

Jake and Angela Miller recently celebrated their 10th anniversary with their friends, parents, and children. Jake's father and mother, Ted and Ann, were there, and they brought Jake's sister, Justine. Ted and Ann met in Atlanta and have been married for 42 years. Ted earned a law degree and has worked in corporate law ever since, while Ann worked as a piano teacher until her twins, Jake and Justine, were born. Jake is 34, and Angela is 33.

Angela's parents, Dexter and Evangeline, celebrated with the family. Dexter and Evangeline met at college in California in 41 years ago. Dexter, whose parents are from Nigeria, is an English professor at a midsize private university. Evangeline worked as a social worker facilitating adoptions. Due in part to her work, Evangeline and Dexter eventually adopted two children, who are African American, when Angela was five: Lillian, who was just an infant, and Markus, who was two. Angela is their only biological child. Lillian is a social worker, is married, and has two children. Markus is gay, lives with his partner, and just left his job as a high school English teacher to pursue his PhD in literature. Angela is biracial.

Jake and Angela met in graduate school, and today, Jake works as a structural engineer, and Angela is an art teacher at an elementary school. They have two children, Luke (10) and Cecile (7). Although the family and extended family have had few mental health concerns, recently, Jake has had some bouts with anxiety, which have begun to affect his relationship with his wife and children. The situation has become so difficult that it has placed a strain on Jake and Angela's relationship. In addition, their growing tensions might be contributing to problems their children recently started to experience at school.

JAKE

Until the age of 10, Jake remembers a happy childhood. From what he could tell, his parents, Ted and Ann, got along well. Ann seemed to have lots of friends she saw often and was active in the community, and Ted seemed content in his work. Jake describes his childhood like this: "I don't really remember anything *bad* happening when I was a kid. My parents seemed like they had a lot of fun together—they got along well, teased each other—they were affectionate and all that. What stands out for me is how much fun my twin sister, Justine, and I had when we were kids. We were into everything, climbing on the roof of the house or digging holes under the shed until the floor caved in—that kind of thing. There was nothing that Justine wouldn't try. She was funny, real quick, you know, and so brave. Nothing scared her. That was before the accident."

"One day Justine got it in her head that we would take Dad's car out of the garage and park it on the other side of the wooded area across the interstate. It was a joke for April Fool's Day. We were only 10, and of course, I was scared, but Justine was sure it would be a good trick, so before I knew it, we were in the car, and I was driving! Justine was laughing; I remember that she had her bare feet curled up under her and, as always, no seatbelt. I guess I didn't look or something 'cause right after I pulled the car out onto the interstate, a semi hit the car, and Justine went through the windshield. She was never the same. She was out for a long time, and when she finally came out of her coma, she had a serious brain injury. She had to learn to talk again and all that. When she did talk … well, she wasn't Justine anymore." Today, Justine is cared for by her parents and is able to maintain a job at a local fast-food restaurant. However, she continues to have serious cognitive impairment. Although Jake tends to get along with her, he periodically quips at her, telling her he thinks she can do better than she's been doing.

After the accident, Jake began to have problems with anxiety. He had a hard time sleeping through the night and had nightmares. "Things changed a lot at our house. It seemed like no one ever laughed anymore, and we didn't *do anything*. Before the accident, my parents would come up with something spontaneous and fun, and we would get up and go! But after Justine changed, well, things at the house got real quiet, and I always felt that something bad was going to happen. I was afraid to leave the house sometimes." Jake's parents took him to a psychiatrist briefly to address the nightmares and anxiety, but they did not talk about his feelings together as a family and rarely referred to the accident.

As the years passed, Jake's anxiety lessened, and he was only occasionally disturbed by anxiety or nightmares. He seemed to move on with his life and successfully finished high school, college, and graduate school. He met and married his wife while in graduate school. Soon after he married and had children, he became involved with a national association that advocates for child-safe automobiles, "just so nothing like what happened to Justine could happen to anyone else again."

Although Jake sounds proud when describing his wife and children, in recent months he has been struggling with a number of issues. Jake notes, "We've been having problems with Luke. He's fearless, like Justine was, and always into something! He's not bad, just mischievous, but lately he's been getting in trouble at school. A couple of months ago Luke and Cecile were playing in the car, and Luke knocked the car out of park. I was mowing the lawn and came around the corner just in time to see the car roll into the street. I felt my chest tighten; I couldn't breathe. I thought I was having a heart attack!" Since the incident with the car, I am anxious all the time. I can't sleep, and when I do, I have nightmares. I have been afraid for Angela to take the car and … I guess I've been difficult to deal with." He is constantly checking all the locks, making sure the care is in park, and always checking on the children. He has even asked Angela to homeschool the children to make sure that they are safe. He also is aware that his relationship with Angela is different: "Angela and I just seem kind of disconnected lately." Jake has also noted that his anxiety has caused him to miss work lately, and he is very concerned he will get a poor performance evaluation.

ANGELA

Angela is feeling at a loss. One afternoon she confided to the school counselor, "I really don't know what is happening to our family. Jake has just gotten so anxious that it is a full-time job keeping up with all his fears. He wants me to homeschool Celia and gets so angry with me for insisting Celia go to public school, and Luke just won't listen to him at all. I feel like I'm a character in one of those really bad movie-of-the-week-things. Sometimes I go into the bathroom, turn on the water in the tub, and cry. I don't want to live my life this way."

When Angela was growing up, she spent the fall and spring on a university campus and spent summers in Nigeria with her father's family. She notes, "I enjoyed spending time with my grandparents, but somehow, I always felt out of place. When I was in Nigeria my cousins treated me differently because, as far as they were concerned, I was 'White' and an American, but when I was back in America, I was 'Black.' But I really didn't feel 'Black' either. In fact, most of the time, I felt more like a Nigerian kid than an American. You'd never catch me talking to my parents or teachers the way the kids at school talked to adults!"

"No matter where we were, there was always one constant: my role as caretaker. Lillian, my adopted sister, was born with a congenital hip deformity that made walking difficult. It was my job to see to Lillian and make sure she had what she needed. I was never free to just go out and play with the other kids. I always had to stay near Lillian. I felt so trapped when I watched the other children on their bikes or playing chase. That's how I feel now, with Jake's demands, I feel trapped watching everyone else live their lives and still, after all these years, not really knowing who I am."

LUKE

Luke is 10, he's starting fifth grade this year. Luke has been a vibrant, active little boy since day one. He is curious and bright. His mother, Angela, has delighted in his willingness to try anything. He seems to live life fully and to feel things deeply. His laughter is contagious, but when Luke is angry, he can be difficult to reason with.

Luke's father spends a lot of time trying to rein Luke in: "He's like a wild horse sometimes. He can be so out of control." Luke doesn't always listen to warnings about safety—staying out of the car, for instance. If something breaks or someone is hurt, it is often Luke who is at the bottom of it. These incidents make Jake furious. Angela isn't comfortable with the way Jake yells at Luke, and lately, they have been fighting over it.

CECELIA

Cecelia is seven and is going to be in the second grade. Her mother explains, "Right away, we could see a difference between the two children. Celia is much more cautious—an observer. She tends to absorb whatever feeling is around her. She gets caught up in Luke's excitement, and she likes to join Luke in his adventures and pranks. Celia worries, though, and her hesitation sometimes makes Luke angry. A lot of the time Luke and Celia start out playing together but end up in an argument."

Recently, Celia has had problems with anxiety. What began as a mild resistance to going to school has become a real problem. More and more often, her mother gets a phone call from the school nurse saying that Celia has a stomachache and wants to come home. Angela became really worried when Celia got so anxious one morning about getting on the bus to go on a field trip that she wet her pants.

APPENDIX E. PSYCHOLOGICAL REPORT

Demographic Information

Name: Jake Miller	Ethnicity: Caucasian
Address: 5555 Anxiety Road, Apprehension, Kansas 66101	DOB: May 14, 1985
	Email: Jake.miller@gmail.com
Phone: 316.555.5555	Marital Status: Married

Presenting Problem/Reason for Referral

This 34-year-old married male sought out counseling due to extreme anxiety, concerns about his children's well-being, and problems in his marriage. He describes his anxiety and problems with his family as occurring about 10 weeks ago when his children, Luke (10) and Celia (7), were playing unsupervised in his car and knocked the car out of park. The car rolled, but no one was injured. He would like some help with his anxiety and hopes he can "return his family to normalcy."

Family Background

Jake notes that he met his wife, Angela, in graduate school and has been married for 10 years. They have two children, Luke (10) and Cecila (7). Jake reports that he has had bouts with anxiety over his lifetime, but it has become particularly difficult in recent months since the incident when Luke knocked his father's car out of park and the car rolled into the street. Celia was also in the car. Although no one was injured, Jake states that this incident set off a "surge of anxiety" and reminded him of a similar incident he had with his twin sister Justine when he was a child.

Jake's twin sister, Justine, is developmentally disabled. He states that when they were 10, Justine wanted to play a practical joke on his parents and urged Jake to move their parents' car. Jake states that he accidentally moved the car into the roadway, where a semi hit the car and caused serious cognitive impairment for Justine. Jake was not seriously injured. Jake reports feeling guilt since that time, blaming himself for the accident. Jake states that his parents, Ted and Ann, had a good relationship until the car accident. He notes that the family was always "having fun and laughing" up to that point. However, since then, he reports "a cloud over everyone in the family." Jake notes that he struggled with anxiety and depression after the accident for a few years but eventually overcame it after seeing a counselor at the age of 13.

Jake notes that since Luke knocked the car out of park, Jake has had a resurgence of anxiety and has wanted to control what everyone is doing in the family—mostly to ensure their safety. He notes that when the children are home, he constantly wants to make sure they are within visual distance. He also reports making sure all the doors are locked at night, even waking up sometimes during the middle of the night to check. He states whenever the children play "rough" games, he goes into a rage, yelling at them to stop it. He also notes that he has asked Angela to homeschool the children, as he is concerned that something "bad" will happen at school. This, he reports, has led to problems in his marriage. Meanwhile, Jakes states that Luke and Celia have been symptomatic since the accident, with Luke "not listening to anyone" and Celia have ongoing stomachaches, which cause her, at times, to come home from school.

Jake describes Angela as stubborn and not wanting to homeschool the children, which he would prefer to ensure his children's safety. He notes that Angela is biracial, and the oldest of three children, with a younger brother, Marcus, who is 31 and is gay, and Lillian, who is 29. Angela's siblings are both African American and adopted. Angela is her parents' only biological child. Jake states that Angela was often the "caretaker" in her family and struggled with her identity, as she felt "White" when spending the summers in Nigeria with her family and "Black" when back in the states, living at home. Jakes reports that Angela spent an inordinate amount of time caring for her sister, who had a congenital hip deformity.

Jake and Angela's parents are living, and they report that they have a "decent" relationship with them. However, Jake notes that issues from the past still haunt each of them, including the car accident with Jake and Angela's sense of not having a clear identity.

Significant Medical/Counseling History

Jake reports having been in counseling twice in his life. The first time was when he was 13, which he describes as beneficial and focused on his guilt over his accident. He saw the counselor for about 6 months. When he was 23, and met Angela, he states he felt mild depression and moderate anxiety and saw a counselor. After a psychiatric consult, he was prescribed 10 mg of Luvox. He states he saw the counselor for about 9 months, and between the Luvox and counseling, he began to feel better. He views his anxiety at that point in his life as feeling like he would be swallowed up in the relationship and not have any control in his life. He relays no significant medical history.

Substance Use and Abuse

Jake is a social drinker. He reports no illegal or prescribed abuse of substances.

Educational and Vocational History

From K–12, Jake attended public school. He reports that he always wanted to be a mechanical engineer and was always good at math. He states he did well in school but noted that he always "wrote poorly" and wondered if he was "dyslexic." He was never tested in school for a learning disability. He attended the University of Kansas, where he obtained his bachelor's and master's degrees in engineering. He has been at his current job, as a mechanical engineer, for 8 years. His father, Ted, was a lawyer, and his mother, Ann, a piano teacher. He states that they always pushed him to obtain a professional degree and were happy when he became an engineer.

Other Pertinent Information

Jake states he "loves Angela" and feels as if he is the cause of many of their problems. He hopes counseling will help "bring things back to the way they were." He notes that his sexual relationship with Angela was "normal" until recently, when they began to argue over the children and what Jake states Angela describes as "my controlling personality." He reports no legal problems. Jake states he is agnostic and his wife, Angela, is Episcopalian, although he notes that "she is not very religious" and the family rarely, if ever, goes to church. He says he'd rather "believe in science" than some "unknown God."

Mental Status

Jake was causally and neatly dressed for the interview. He had appropriate eye contact. He was oriented to time, place, and person. He often fidgeted in his chair, moving his body back and forth during the interview. He reports feeling "anxious most of the time" and notes that he still feels guilty about the situation with Justine. He states he has been feeling anxious for the past 3 months, since the incident with his children moving his car. He reports waking up multiple times at night, just to check that everyone is in bed and safe. He notes he has lost some weight, mostly, he believes, due to his disinterest in food as a result of his anxiety. He reports feeling tired much of the time and has ongoing headaches. At one point during the interview, when talking about the accident with Justine, he became tearful, saying, "I shouldn't have listened to her—it's all my fault." Jake's thoughts were clear, his memory was good, and he is above average intellectually. He has good insight and fair judgment. He reports no suicidal or homicidal ideation.

Assessment Results

The following assessment procedures were administered: the 16PF, the WRAT-IV, the kinetic family drawing, a sentence completion, the Beck Depression Inventory (BDI), the Beck Anxiety Inventory (BAI), and the Substance Abuse Subtle Screening Inventory (SASSI).

On the BDI, Jake's score of 14 shows mild to no depression. On the BAI, he scored a 36, which shows severe anxiety. Anxiety, and feelings of frustration, were also evidenced in his sentence completion, such as when he noted, "I see myself as <u>responsible for the accident</u>," "I get angry when I, <u>can't make things the way I want them to be</u>," and "The thing I'm most afraid to talk about is <u>the accident</u>." Sadness was noted when he stated, "I feel the saddest when I <u>think about the accident</u>." When asked to draw a picture of his family all doing something together, Jake drew them having a picnic. His family was all sitting at a table, Angela and Jake on opposite sides and the two kids sitting very close to one another and closer to Angela. Notably, a fence circumscribed the table, as if to keep everyone inside and safe. There were no smiles on anyone's faces, and the distance between Angela and Jake seemed significant.

On the 16PF, Jake had significantly high scores on the following: "rule consciousness," meaning he is conscientious, moralistic, staid, and rule bound; "perfectionism," meaning he has strong willpower and likes to exert control; and "tension," meaning he is tense, driven, and frustrated. He received low scores on "traditional," meaning he is conservative in his ideas and respects tradition, and on "practical," which means he is down-to-earth and conventional. On the global scores, which is a conglomeration of a number of the 16 factors, he scored high on "anxiety," "tough-mindedness," and "self-control." Jake's Holland code was an REI, which fits his current occupation of engineer. He showed no evidence of substance abuse on the SASSI.

On the WRAT-IV, Jake scored at the 92nd percentile in math, 75th percentile in reading, 70th percentile in sentence comprehension, and 35nd percentile in spelling. His reading composite score was at the 72nd percentile. These results indicate a possible learning disability in spelling.

Diagnosis

- adjustment disorder, with anxiety (F43.21)
- rule out generalized anxiety disorder (F41.1)
- rule out posttraumatic stress disorder (F43.10)
- possible spelling learning disability (F81.81)
- relationship distress with spouse or intimate partner (Z63.0)
- parent–child relational problem (Z62.820)
- high expressed emotion level within family (Z63.8)

Summary and Recommendations

This 34-year-old married male sought counseling due to increased anxiety, problems with sleep, ongoing headaches, loss of appetite, and problems in his marriage and with his children. He relates many of these issues to a history in his family of origin, when he was involved in a car accident at age 10 with his twin sister. At that time, at his sister's urging, he moved his parents' car and was accidentally struck by a semi, resulting in severe cognitive impairment for his sister. He was not injured. He reports feeling guilty and responsible for the accident. He attended counseling at age 13 for continued feelings of guilt and anxiety due to the accident. He was in counseling one other time, just prior to his marriage, for feelings of being overwhelmed and closed in.

Recently, his daughter and son were involved in an incident in which they pushed his car out of park and it moved down the driveway. Jake states that this incident caused a resurgence in his anxiety. He states that since that time, he has been trying to get a handle on his anxiety by keeping everyone safe in the home. He reports asking his wife to homeschool the children (which she has said no to), and he states he is constantly trying to control the family to ensure their safety.

Evidence of anxiety, a need to control, feelings of perfectionism, and tough-mindedness are evidenced throughout his clinical interview. He self-reports anxiety, which is confirmed by the BAI and the 16PF. Other tests, such as his KFD and the 16PF, reveal a need to control his family and ensure they are safe. The KFD also indicates distance from his wife and children. Some feelings of sadness and guilt, mostly related to the accident when he was a child, were noted in his clinical interview and the sentence completion.

Jake is a fairly insightful man, who is experiencing guilt, anxiety, and mild to no depression that appears to be related to the car accident he had with his twin sister when he was 10. His fears about something similar happening with his children are permeating his life, and he is having difficulty controlling the resulting anxiety. He attempts to control this anxiety by controlling others around him. This has resulted in symptoms in his children and problems in his marriage.

On a positive note, Jake has a good understanding of himself, is wanting to examine his life through counseling, and is wanting to heal his family problems. He is highly educated, bright, and hopeful about making changes in his life.

Recommendations

- Referral to a psychiatrist for possible medication to alleviate his anxiety.
- Counseling, 1 hour a week, to discuss past issues related to his car accident with his sister and current problems with his family.
- Possible marital counseling to relieve some of the stress in his marriage.
- Further testing for a possible learning disability in spelling, should Jake wish to pursue that.

_____

Signature

APPENDIX F. CATEGORIES GENERALLY ASSESSED IN A PSYCHOLOGICAL REPORT

Demographic Information

Name: D.O.B.:

Address: Age:

Phone: Sex:

Ethnicity: E-mail address:

Date of interview: Preferred Pronouns:

Name of interviewer:

Presenting Problem or Reason for Referral

- Who referred the client to the agency?
- What is the main reason the client contacted the agency?
- What is the reason for the assessment?

Family Background

- significant factors from the family of origin
- significant factors from the current family
- some specific issues that may be mentioned: where the individual grew up, sexes and ages of siblings, whether the client came from an intact family, who were the major caretakers, important stories from childhood, sexes and ages of current children, significant others, and marital concerns

Significant Medical/Counseling History

- significant medical history, particularly anything related to the client's assessment (e.g., psychiatric hospitalization or heart disease leading to depression)
- types and dates of previous counseling
- list of current and past medications along with dosage

Substance Use and Abuse

- use or abuse of food, cigarettes, alcohol, prescription medication, or illegal drugs
- counseling related to use and abuse

Educational and Vocational History

- educational history (e.g., level of education and, possibly, names of institutions)
- vocational history and career path (names and types of jobs)
- satisfaction with educational level and career path
- significant leisure activities

Other Pertinent Information

- legal concerns and history of problems with the law
- issues related to sexuality (e.g., sexual orientation, sexual dysfunction)
- trauma experienced
- financial problems
- other concerns

The Mental Status Exam

- appearance and behavior (e.g., dress, hygiene, posture, tics, nonverbals, manner of speech)
- emotional state (e.g., affect and mood)
- thought components (e.g., content and process: delusions, distortions of body image, hallucinations, obsessions, suicidal or homicidal ideation, circumstantiality, coherence, flight of ideas, logical thinking, intact as opposed to lo0se associations, organization, and tangentiality)
- cognitive functioning (e.g., orientation to time, place, and person; short- and long-term memory; knowledge base and intellectual functioning; insight and judgments)

Assessment Results

- List the assessment and test instruments used.
- Summarize the results.
- Avoid raw scores, and state results in unbiased manner.
- Consider using standardized test scores and percentiles.

Diagnosis

- *DSM-5* diagnoses
- Include other diagnoses, such as medical, rehabilitation, or other salient factors.

Summary and Conclusions

- integration of all previous information
- accurate, succinct, and relevant
- no new information
- inferences that are logical, sound, defendable, and based on facts in the report
- at least one paragraph that speaks to the client's strengths

Recommendations

- based on all the information gathered
- should make logical sense to the reader
- in paragraph form or as a listing
- usually followed by signature of an examiner

APPENDIX G. MENTAL STATUS EXAM GUIDELINES

The MSE must include detailed observations regarding the person's appearance, speech, attitude, behavior, mood, and affect. If not within normal limits, the MSE must also include detailed observations regarding the person's thought process and content, orientation, perception, memory, fund of knowledge, concentration, abstract thought, insight, and judgment.

TABLE G.1 Mental Status Exam Guidelines

Category	Examples of Observation Detail
Appearance	Is the person well groomed or unkempt?
	What is the person wearing?
	Are clothes appropriate for weather and situation?
Speech	Is the person's speech normal, pressured, tangential, or circumstantial?
Attitude and Behavior	Is the person calm, cooperative, uncooperative, or belligerent?
Mood	Is the person's mood euthymic, irritable, elevated, anxious, or depressed?
Affect	Is the person's affect within normal range, depressed, constricted, flat, labile, blunted, reactive and mood congruent, or tearful?
Thought Process and Content	Is the person goal directed and logical or disorganized?
	Are there any delusions, phobias, or obsessions/compulsions?
	Is the person suicidal and/or homicidal?
Orientation	Is the person oriented to time and place?
Perception	Did the person display signs of hallucinations or delusions during the interview?
Memory	Can the person remember past events (remote)?
	Can the person remember three of three objects after 5 minutes (recent)?
	How well can the person perform digit span (immediate)?
Fund of Knowledge	Is the person aware of current events? Give examples.
	Does the person know the names of the president and governor?
	Can the person answer simple geography questions, such as naming bordering states?

Category	Examples of Observation Detail
Concentration	Serial 7s or 3s.
	Spell the word "world" forward and backward.
	Is the person able to follow a three-step command?
Abstract Thought	Is the person able to interpret proverbs?
Insight and Judgment	Does the person have insight into their condition?
	Does the person show good judgment (e.g., when asked what they would do if they smelled smoke in crowded theater)?

APPENDIX H. FEELING WORD CHECKLIST

abandoned	disrespected	hurt	panicked	stupid
adored	distressed	impatient	paranoid	teased
aggravated	doubtful	impossible	passionate	tender
aggressive	drained	inadequate	peaceful	terrific
angry	dynamic	incapable	pitiful	terrified
anxious	eager	indecisive	playful	thoughtful
appreciated	elated	insecure	pleasant	thoughtless
apprehensive	embarrassed	inspired	pleased	thrilled
argumentative	empowered	interested	positive	tormented
ashamed	empty	intolerant	powerless	tranquil
assertive	energized	invigorated	precious	traumatized
assured	enlightened	invincible	pressured	troubled
awe	enthusiastic	irresistible	proud	trusting
awesome	envious	irresponsible	provoked	unaccepted
awful	exasperated	irritated	punished	unconcerned
betrayed	excited	jealous	quiet	understood
bitter	exhilarated	joyful	ready	undesirable
bliss	extraordinary	joyous	receptive	uneasy
bold	exuberant	jubilant	recognized	unfriendly
bored	failure	kind	rejected	unfulfilled
brilliant	fantastic	let down	relaxed	unhappy
broken-hearted	fearful	limitless	renewed	unhelpful
burdened	fearless	lonely	repulsive	unloved
calm	focused	lost	resentful	unsuccessful
capable	forced	lovable	resilient	unwanted
caring	free	loving	respected	unworthy
cheerful	frigid	lucky	restless	uplifted
comfortable	frustrated	lying	sad	upset
concerned	fulfilled	magical	satisfied	useless
confident	fun	mean	scared	valuable
confused	glad	mindful	selfish	valued
content	glowing	miraculous	serene	victimized
criticized	gracious	miserable	shameful	vindictive
decisive	grateful	misunderstood	shocked	warm
dejected	grieving	motivated	shy	wary
depressed	guilty	neglected	skeptical	weary
difficult	happy	nervous	sorrowful	whole
dirty	helpless	obligated	sour	wise
disappointed	honored	open	spectacular	worried
discontented	hopeful	oppressed	stifled	worthless
discouraged	hopeless	overwhelmed	strong	worthy
disgusted	humiliated	pained	stubborn	wrong

APPENDIX I. SUPERVISOR STANDARDS

AMHCA'S (2021) STANDARDS FOR THE PRACTICE OF CLINICAL MENTAL HEALTH COUNSELING

AMHCA recommends at least 24 continuing education hours or equivalent graduate credit hours of training in the theory and practice of clinical supervision for those clinical mental health counselors who provide pre- or post-degree clinical supervision to clinical mental health counseling students or trainees. AMHCA recommends that clinical supervisors obtain, on the average, at least 3 continuing education hours in supervision per year as part of their overall program of continuing education. Clinical supervisors should meet the following knowledge and skills criteria.

1. **Knowledge**

    a. Possess a strong working knowledge of evidence based and best practices orientation with clinical theory and interventions and application to the clinical process.

    b. Understand the client population and the practice setting of the supervisee.

    c. Understand and have a working knowledge of current supervision models and their application to the supervisory process. Maintain a working knowledge of the most current methods and techniques in clinical supervision knowledge of group supervision methodology including the appropriate use and limits of this modality.

    d. Identify and understand the roles, functions, and responsibilities of clinical supervisors including liability in the supervisory process. Communicates expectations and nature and extent of the supervision relationship.

    e. Maintain a working knowledge of appropriate professional development activities for supervisees. These activities should be focused on empirically based scientific knowledge.

    f. Show a strong understanding of the supervisory relationship and related issues, not limited to power differential, evaluation, parallel process, and isomorphic similarities and differences between supervision and counseling, and qualities that enhance the supervisor/supervisee working alliance for the benefit of clients served.

    g. Identify and define the cultural issues that arise in clinical supervision and be able to routinely incorporate cultural sensitivity into the supervisory process.

h. Understand and define the legal and ethical issues in clinical supervision including: *AMHCA Standards for the Practice of Clinical Mental Health Counseling* (Revised 2021)

  i. Applicable laws, licensure rules, and the AMHCA Code of Ethics, specifically as they relate to supervision

  ii. Supervisory liability, respondent superior, and fiduciary responsibility

  iii. Risk-management models and processes as they relate to the clinical process and to supervision

i. Possess a working understanding of the evaluation process in clinical supervision including evaluating supervisee competence and remediation of supervisee skill development. This includes initial, formative and summative assessment of supervisee knowledge, skills and self-awareness with provisions for clearly stated expectations, fair delivery of feedback, and due process. Supervision includes both formal and informal feedback mechanisms.

j. Maintain a working knowledge of industry recognized financial management processes and required recordkeeping practices including electronic records and transmission of records.

2. **Skills**

a. Possess a thorough understanding and experience in working with the supervisees' client populations. Be able to demonstrate and explain the counselor role and appropriate clinical interventions within the cultural and clinical context.

b. Develop, maintain and explain the supervision contract to manage supervisee relationships with clear expectations including:

  i. Frequency, location, length, and duration of supervision meetings

  ii. Supervision models and expectations of the supervisee and the supervisor

  iii. Liability and fiduciary responsibility of the supervisor

  iv. The evaluation process, instruments used, and frequency of evaluation

  v. Emergency and critical incident procedures

c. Demonstrate and model the ability to develop and maintain clear role boundaries and an appropriate balance between consultation and training within the supervisory r elationship.

d. Demonstrate the ability to analyze and evaluate skills and performance of supervisees including the ability to confront and correct unsuitable actions and interventions on the part of the supervisees. Provide timely substantive and formative feedback to supervisees, along with providing cumulative feedback and to train supervisees in techniques and methods in self-appraisal.

e. Present strong problem-solving and dilemma resolution skills and practice skills with supervisees.

f. Develop and demonstrate the ability to implement risk management strategies.

g. Practice and model self-assessment.

h. Seek consultation as needed.

i. Conceptualize cultural differences in therapy and in supervision. Incorporate and model this understanding into the supervisory process.

j. Possess an understanding of group supervision techniques and the role of group supervision in the supervision process.

k. Comply with applicable federal, state, and local law. Take responsibility for supervisees' actions, which include an understanding of recordkeeping and financial management rules and practice. (pp. 6–7)

REFERENCES

CHAPTER 1

Addiction-counselors.com. (2023). Addictions/substance abuse counselor requirements by state. https://www.addiction-counselors.com/

American Art Therapy Association. (2022). *About us.* https://arttherapy.org/about/

American Association of Marriage and Family Therapists. (2002–2023). *Home page.* https://www.aamft.org/

American Clinical Pastoral Education. (2020). *Home page.* https://acpe.edu/

American College Counseling Association. (n.d.). *Home page.* https://www.collegecounseling.org/

American Counseling Association (2023). *Knowledge center: Credential titles and levels.* https://www.counseling.org/knowledge-center/licensure-requirements/overview-of-state-licensing-of-professional-counselors

American Mental Health Counselors Association. (2020). *Code of ethics.* https://www.amhca.org/events/publications/ethics

American Mental Health Counselors Association. (2023a). *About us.* https://www.amhca.org/about/about-us

American Mental Health Counselors Association. (2023b). *Becoming essential.* https://www.amhca.org/about/mentalhealthcounselors

American Psychiatric Association. (2023). *About APA.* https://www.psychiatry.org/about-apa/vision-mission-values-goals

American Psychiatric Nurses Association. (2023). *About APNA.* https://www.apna.org/i4a/pages/index.cfm?pageid=3277

American Psychoanalytic Association. (2009–2023). *Home page.* https://apsa.org/

American Psychological Association. (2021). *APA guidelines on evidence-based psychological practice in health care.* https://www.apa.org/about/policy/psychological-practice-health-care.pdf

American Psychological Association. (2022). *About prescribing psychologists.* https://www.apaservices.org/practice/advocacy/authority/prescribing-psychologists

American Psychological Association. (2023a). *About APA.* https://www.apa.org/about

American Psychological Association. (2023b). *Careers in psychology.* https://www.apa.org/education-career/guide/careers

American Rehabilitation Counseling Association. (n.d.). *Home page.* http://www.arcaweb.org/

American School Counselor Association. (2023). *Home page.* https://www.schoolcounselor.org/

Association of Marital and Family Therapy Regulatory Boards. (n.d.). *Home page.* https://amftrb.org/

Art Therapy Credentials Board. (2021). *Home page.* http://www.atcb.org/

Association for Spiritual, Ethical, and Religious Values in Counseling. (2023). *Home page.* https://aservic.org/

Beierl, E. T., Murray, H., Wiedemann, M., Warnock-Parkes, E., Wild, J., Stott, R., Grey, N., Clark, D. M., & Ehlers, A. (2021). The relationship between working alliance and symptom improvement in cognitive therapy for posttraumatic stress disorder. *Psychiatry.* https://doi.org/10.3389/fpsyt.2021.602648

Castillo, J. H. (2018). Cognitive complexity in counseling and counselor education: A systematic and critical review. *The Journal of Counselor Preparation and Supervision, 11*(1). https://repository.wcsu.edu/jcps/vol11/iss1/3

Center for Credentialing and Education. (2023). *HS—BCP human services-board certified practitioner.* https://www.cce-global.org/hsbcp

College Student Educators International. (2004–2023). *Home page.* https://myacpa.org/

Commission on Accreditation for Marriage and Family Therapy Education. (n.d.). *Home page.* https://www.coamfte.org/

Council for the Accreditation of Counseling and Related Programs. (2016). *2016 CACREP standards.* https://www.cacrep.org/for-programs/2016-cacrep-standards/

Council for the Accreditation of Counseling and Related Programs. (2023a). *Find a program.* https://www.cacrep.org/directory/

Council for the Accreditation of Counseling and Related Programs. (2023b). *Why should I choose an accredited program?* https://www.cacrep.org/for-students/why-should-i-choose-an-accredited-program/

Council for the Accreditation of Counseling and Related Programs. (2023c). *2016 CACREP standards: Section 5.* https://www.cacrep.org/for-programs/2016-cacrep-standards/

Cuijpers, P., Reijnders, M., & Huibers, M. J. H. (2019). The role of common factors in psychotherapy outcome. *Annual Review of Clinical Psychology, 15,* 207–231. https://doi.org/10.1146/annurev-clinpsy-050718-095424

Deaver, S. (2015). Creative and expressive therapies: Overview. In E. Neukrug (Ed.), *The SAGE encyclopedia of theory in counseling and psychotherapy* (Vol. 1, pp. 253–256). SAGE Publications.

Egan, G. (2019). *The skilled helper: A problem management and opportunity-development approach to helping* (11th ed.). Cengage.

Elliott, R., Bohart, A. C., Watson, J. C., & Murphy, D. (2018). Therapist empathy and client outcome: An updated meta-analysis. *Psychotherapy, 55*, 399–410. http://dx.doi.org/10.1037/pst0000175

Escobar, J. I. (2012). Taking issue: Diagnostic bias: Racial and cultural issues. *Psychiatric Services, 63*(9), 847. http://ps.psychiatryonline.org/doi/pdf/10.1176/appi.ps.20120p847

Gelso, C. J., Kivlighan D. M., Jr., & Markin, R. D. (2018). The real relationship and its role in psychotherapy outcome: A meta-analysis. *Psychotherapy, 55*(4), 434–444. https://doi.org/10.1037/pst0000183434

Gompertz, K. (1960). The relation of empathy to effective communication. *Journalism Quarterly, 37*, 535–546.

Goodman, A. (2019, April 26). *AMHCA and ACA separate associations.* American Mental Health Counselors Association. https://www.amhca.org/blogs/howard-goodman/2019/04/26/amhca-and-aca-separate-associations.

Gutierrez, D., & Mullen, P. R. (2016). Emotional intelligence and the counselor: Examining the relationship of trait emotional intelligence to counselor burnout. *Journal of Mental Health Counseling, 38*(3), 187–200. http://dx.doi.org.proxy.lib.odu.edu/10.1774/mehc.38.3.01

Hilsenroth, M. (2018). Therapeutic alliance, empathy, and genuineness in individual adult psychotherapy: A meta-analytic review. *Psychotherapy Research, 28*(4), 593–605. https://doi.org/10.1080/10503307.2016.1204023

Hill, C. E., Spiegel, S. B., Hoffman, M. A., Kivlighan, D. M., & Gelso, C. J. (2017). Therapist expertise in psychotherapy revisited. *The Counseling Psychologist, 35*(1), 7–53, https://doi.org/10.1177/0011000016641192

Ivan, N., Gerber, R., Hughes, D., Battis, K., & Anderson, E. (2019). *Credentialing, licensing, and reimbursement of the SUD workforce: A review of policies and practices across the nation.* U.S. Department of Health and Human Services. https://aspe.hhs.gov/report/credentialing-licensing-and-reimbursement-sud-workforce-review-policies-and-practices-across-nation

International Association of Addictions and Offender Counselors. (n.d.). *Home page.* https://www.iaaocounselors.org/

International Association of Marriage and Family Counselors. (2018). *Home page.* https://www.iamfconline.org/

Kalkbrenner, M., & Neukrug, E. (2019). The utility of the revised fit, stigma, and value scale with counselor trainees: Implications for enhancing clinical supervision. *Clinical Supervisor, 38*, 262–280. https://doi.org/10.1080/07325223.2019.1634665

Kalkbrenner, M. T., Neukrug, E., & Griffith, S. A. (2019). Appraising counselor attendance in counseling: The validation and application of the revised Fit, Stigma, and Value Scale. *Journal of Mental Health Counseling, 41*(1), 21–35. https://doi.org/10.17744/mehc.41.1.03

Kaslow, N. J., Rubin, N. J., Forrest, L., Elman, N. S., Van Horne, B. A., Jacobs, S. C., Huprich, S. K., Benton, S. A., Pantesco, V. F., Dollinger, S. J., Grus, C. L., Behnke, S. H., Miller, D. S. S., Shealy, C. N., Mintz, L. B., Schwartz-Mette, R., Van Sickle, K., & Thorn, B. E. (2007). Recognizing, assessing, and intervening with problems of professional competence. *Professional Psychology: Research and Practice, 38*, 479–492. https://psycnet.apa.org/doi/10.1037/0735-7028.38.5.479

Koker, K. (2018, Spring). Chair's report. *CACREP connection.* https://www.cacrep.org/newsletter/spring-2018-cacrep-connection/

Laska, K. M., Gurman, A. S., & Wampold, B. E. (2014). Expanding the lens of evidence-based practice in psychotherapy: A common factors perspective. *Psychotherapy, 51*, 467–481. https://doi.org/10.1037/a0034332

Lawson, G., & Myers, J. E. (2011). Wellness, professional quality of life, and career-sustaining behaviors: What keeps us well? *Journal of Counseling and Development, 89*, 163–171. https://psycnet.apa.org/doi/10.1002/j.1556-6678.2011.tb00074.x

Lewis, J. A., Lewis, M. D., Daniels, J. A., & D'Andrea, M. J. (2011). *Community counseling: A multicultural-social justice perspective* (4th ed.). Cengage.

Lo, C., Cheng, T., & Howell, R. (2013). Access to and utilization of health services as pathway to racial disparities in serious mental illness. *Community Mental Health Journal, 50*(3), 251–257. https://doi.org/10.1007/s10597-013-9593-7

Martin, W. E., Easton, C., Wilson, S., Takemoto, M., & Sullivan, S. (2004). Salience of emotional intelligence as a core characteristic of being a counselor. *Counselor Education and Supervision, 44*(1), 17–30. https://doi.org/10.1002/j.1556-6978.2004.tb01857.x

Masters in Psychology and Counseling Accreditation Council. (2023a). *Home page.* http://mpcacaccreditation.org/

Masters in Psychology and Counseling Accreditation Council. (2023b). *Scope.* http://mpcacaccreditation.org/about-mpcac/scope/

McAuliffe, G. (Ed.). (2020). *Culturally alert counseling: A comprehensive introduction* (3rd ed.). SAGE Publications.

McAuliffe, G., & Eriksen, K. (Eds.). (2010). *Handbook of counselor preparation.* SAGE and the Association for Counselor Education and Supervision.

Minuchin, S. (1974). *Families and family therapy.* Harvard University Press.

National Alliance of Mental Illness. (2021). *African American mental health.* https://www.nami.org/Find-Support/Diverse-Communities/African-Americans

National Association of School Psychologists. (NASP). (2021). *About NASP.* https://www.nasponline.org/utility/about-nasp

National Board for Certified Counselors. (2023a). *NBCC specialty certifications.* https://www.nbcc.org/certification/specialtycertifications

National Board for Certified Counselors. (2023b). *State board directory.* https://www.nbcc.org/search/stateboarddirectory

National Board for Certified Pastoral Counselors. (2023). *Pastoral counselors.* http://nbcpc.org/

National Organization for Human Services. (n.d.). *About us.* https://www.nationalhumanservices.org/about-nohs

National Rehabilitation Counseling Association. (n.d.). *Home page.* https://nationalrehabcounselingassciation.wildapricot.org/

Neukrug, E., Bayne, H. Dean-Nganga, L., & Pusateri, C. (2013). Creative and novel approaches to empathy: A neo-Rogerian perpsective. *Journal of Mental Health Counseling, 35*(1), 29–42. https://doi.org/10.17744/mehc.35.1.5q375220327000t2

Neukrug, E., & Hays, D.G. (2023). *Counseling theory and practice* (3rd ed.). Cognella.

Neukrug, E. (2017, February 2). Creative and novel approaches to empathy. *Counseling Today.* https://ct.counseling.org/2017/02/creative-novel-approaches-empathy/

Neukrug, E. (2019). *Counseling and helping skills: Critical techniques to becoming a counselor.* Cognella.

Neukrug, E. (2021). *Skills and techniques for human service professionals: Counseling environment, helping skills, treatment issues* (2nd ed.). Cognella.

Nienhuis, J. B., Owen, J., Valentine, J. C., Black, S. W., Halford, T. C., Parazak, S. E., Budge, S., & Hilsenroth, M. (2018). Therapeutic alliance, empathy, and genuineness in individual adult psychotherapy: A meta-analytic review. *Psychotherapy Research, 28,* 593–605. http://dx.doi.org/10.1080/10503307.2016.1204023

Norcross, J. C., & Lambert, M. J. (2018). Psychotherapy relationships that work III. *Psychotherapy, 55*(4), 303–315. http://dx.doi.org.proxy.lib.odu.edu/10.1037/pst0000193

Norcross, J. C., & Wampold, B. E., & Lambert, M. J. (Eds.). (2019). *Psychotherapy relationships that work* (3rd ed., Vol. 2). Oxford University Press.

Norcross, J. C., & Wampold, B. E. (Eds.). (2019). *Psychotherapy relationships that work* (3rd ed., Vol. 2). Oxford University Press.

O*NET OnLine. (2023a). *Mental health counselors.* https://www.onetonline.org/link/summary/21-1014.00

O*NET Online. (2023b). *Substance abuse and behavioral disorder counselors.* https://www.onetonline.org/link/summary/21-1011.00

Person, M., Garner, C., Ghoston, M., & Petersen, C. (2020). Counselor professional identity development in CACREP and non-CACREP accredited programs. *The Journal of Counselor Preparation and Supervision, 13*(1). http://dx.doi.org/10.7729/131.1335

Peterson, S. (2020, February 6). *Celebrating the role of rehabilitation counseling. Counseling Today.* https://ct.counseling.org/2020/02/celebrating-the-role-of-rehabilitation-counseling/

Robiner, W. N., Tompkins, T. L., & Hathaway, K. M. (2019). Prescriptive authority: Psychologists' abridged training relative to other professions' training. *Clinical Psychology Science and Practice, 27*(1), 1–19. https://doi-org.proxy.lib.odu.edu/10.1111/cpsp.12309

Rogers, C. R. (1957). The necessary and sufficient conditions of therapeutic personality change. *Journal of Consulting Psychology, 21,* 95–103. https://psycnet.apa.org/doi/10.1037/h0045357

Rogers, C. R. (1989). A client-centered/ person-centered approach to therapy. In H. Kirschenbaum (Ed.), *The Carl Rogers reader* (pp. 135–152). Houghton Mifflin. (Original work published 1986)

Shaler, L. (2019, May 20). *Respecting the faith of clients and counselors. Counseling Today.* https://ct.counseling.org/2019/05/respecting-the-faith-of-clients-and-counselors/

Shaw, S. (2020, March 20). *Learning from highly effective counselors. Counseling Today.* https://ct.counseling.org/2020/03/learning-from-highly-effective-counselors/

Sommers-Flanagan, J. (2015). Evidence-based relationship practice: Enhancing counselor competence. *Journal of Mental Health Counseling, 37*(2), 95–108. https://doi.org/10.17744/mehc.37.2.g13472044600588r

Stokowski, L. A. (2018, January 4). *APRN prescribing law: A state-by-state summary. Medscape.* http://www.medscape.com/viewarticle/440315

Tschuschke, V., Koemeda-Lutz, M., von Wyl, A., Crameri, A., & Schulthess, P. (2022). The impact of clients' and therapists' characteristics on therapeutic alliance and outcome. *Journal of Contemporary Psychotherapy, 52,* 145–154 (2022). https://doi.org/10.1007/s10879-021-09527-2

Turkington, C. (1985). Analysts sued for barring non-MDs. *APA Monitor, 16*(5), 2.

Urofsky, R. (2013). The Council for Accreditation of Counseling and Related Educational Programs: Promoting quality in counselor education. *Journal of Counseling and Development, 91(1), 6–14.* https://doi.org/10.1002/j.1556-6676.2013.00065.x

U.S. Bureau of Labor Statistics. (2022). Substance abuse, behavioral disorder, and mental health counselors. *Occupational Outlook Handbook.* https://www.bls.gov/ooh/community-and-social-service/substance-abuse-behavioral-disorder-and-mental-health-counselors.htm

Wampold, B. E. (2010). The research evidence for common factors models: A historically situated perspective. In B. L. Duncan, S. D. Miller, B. E. Wampold, & M A. Hubble (Eds.), *The heart and soul of change* (2nd ed., pp. 49–82). American Psychological Association.

Wampold, B. E. (2015). How important are the common factors in psychotherapy? An update. *World Psychiatry, 14,* 270–277. https://doi.org/10.1002/wps.20238

Wampold, B. E. (2019). *The basics of psychotherapy: An introduction to theory and practice* (2nd ed.). American Psychological Association.

Wampold, B. E., & Budge, S. L. (2012). The relationship—and its relationship to the common and specific factors in psychotherapy. *The Counseling Psychologist, 40,* 601–623. https://doi.org/10.1177/0011000011432709

Wampold, B. E., & Imel, Z. E. (2015). *The great psychotherapy debate: The evidence for what makes psychotherapy work* (2nd ed.). Routledge.

U. S. Department of Health and Human Services. (2014). *Improving cultural competence: A treatment improvement protocol.* Substance Abuse and Mental Health Services Administration.

Zyromski, B., Hudson, T. D., Baker, E., & Granello, D. H. (2019). Guidance counselors or school counselors: How the name of the profession influences perceptions of competence. *Professional School Counseling, 22*(1), 1–10. https://doi.org/10.1177/2156759X19855654

CHAPTER 2

Addams, J. (2017). *Twenty years at Hull House.* Pantianos Classics. (Original work published 1910)

American Counseling Association. (2014). *Code of ethics.* http://www.counseling.org/resources/aca-code-of-ethics.pdf

American Counseling Association. (2015, May 12). *The latest news from ACA: More LPCs to be included under new TRICARE language*. https://www.counseling.org/news/updates/2015/05/12/more-lpcs-to-be-included-under-new-tricare-language

American Counseling Association. (2023a). *Government affairs: We did it! Medicare reimbursement now law*. https://www.counseling.org/government-affairs/federal-issues/medicare-mental-health-workforce-coalition

American Counseling Association. (2023b). *State licensing of professional counselors*. https://www.counseling.org/knowledge-center/licensure-requirements/overview-of-state-licensing-of-professional-counselors

American Counseling Association. (2023c). *Knowledge center: ACA licensure portability model FAQs*. https://www.counseling.org/knowledge-center/aca-licensure-portability-model-faqs

American Mental Health Counselors Association. (2023). *About us*. https://www.amhca.org/about/about-us

American Psychological Association. (2023). *APA history*. https://www.apa.org/about/apa/archives/apa-history

Arredondo, P., Toporek, R., Brown, S. P., Jones, J., Locke, D. C., Sanchez, J., & Stadler, H. (1996). Operationalization of the multicultural counseling competencies. *Journal of Multicultural Counseling and Development, 24*(1), 42–78. https://doi.org/10.1002/j.2161-1912.1996.tb00288.x

Aubrey, R. F. (1977). Historical development of guidance and counseling and implications for the future. *Personnel and Guidance Journal, 55*(6), 288–295. https://doi.org/10.1002/j.2164-4918.1977.tb04991.x

Aubrey, R. F. (1982). A house divided: Guidance and counseling in twentieth-century America. *Personnel and Guidance Journal, 61*, 198–204. https://doi.org/10.1002/j.2164-4918.1982.tb00312.x

Baxter, W. E. (1994). American psychiatry celebrates 150 years of caring. *Psychiatric Clinics of North America, 17*, 683–693.

Behnke, S. H. (1999). *O'Connor v. Donaldson*: Retelling a classic and finding some revisionist history. *American Academy of Psychiatric and the Law, 27*(1), 115–126.

Belgium, D. (1992). Guilt. In M. T. Burker & J. G. Miranti (Eds.), *Ethical and spiritual values in counseling* (pp. 53–66). American Association for Counseling and Development.

Bergman, D. (2020). President signs landmark bill opening the federal government to mental health counselors. *American Mental Health Counselors Association Blog*. https://www.amhca.org/blogs/david-bergman1/2020/10/20/president-signs-landmark-bill-opening-the-federal

Breasted, J. H. (1930). *The Edwin Smith surgical papyrus*. University of Chicago Press.

Breasted, J. H. (1934). *The dawn of conscience*. Scribner's.

Briddick, W. (2009a). Frank findings: Frank Parsons and the Parson family. *Career Development Quarterly, 57*(3), 207–214. https://doi.org/10.1002/j.2161-0045.2009.tb00106.x

Carkhuff, R. (1969). *Helping and human relations* (Vol. 2). Holt, Rinehart & Winston.

Chan, F., Chronister, J., Catalana, D., Chase, A., & Eun-Jeong, L. (2004). *Foundations of rehabilitation counseling. Directions of Rehabilitation Counseling, 15*, 1–11.

Charland, L. C. (2018). Lost in myth, lost in translation: Philippe Pinel's 1809 *Medico–Philosophical Treatise on Mental Alienation. International Journal of Mental Health, 47*(3), 245–249. https://doi.org/10.1080/00207411.2018.1483053

Claiborn, C. D. (Ed.). (1991). *Multiculturalism as a fourth force in counseling [Special issue]. Journal of Counseling and Development, 70*(1).

Colangelo, J. J. (2009). The American Mental Health Counselors Association: Reflection on 30 historic years. *Journal of Counseling & Development, 87*, 234–240. https://doi.org/10.1002/j.1556-6678.2009.tb00572.x

Council for the Accreditation of Counseling and Related Programs. (2023a). *About us: A brief history*. https://www.cacrep.org/about-cacrep/

Counseling Compact. (2022). *Inaugural meeting*. https://counselingcompact.org/wp-content/uploads/2022/09/Counseling-Compact-Inaugural-Meeting-Packet.pdf

Counseling Compact (2022b). *Home: What is the counseling compact*. https://counselingcompact.org/

Council for the Accreditation of Counseling and Related Programs. (2023b). *Find a program*. https://www.cacrep.org/directory/

Dilkes-Frayne, E., Savic, M., Carter, A., Kokanović, R., & Lubman, D. I. (2019). Going online: The affordances of online counseling for families affected by alcohol and other drug issues. *Qualitative Health Research, 29*(14), 2010–2022. https://doi.org/10.1177/1049732319838231

du Plock, S., & Tantum, D. (2019). History of existential–phenomenological therapy. In E. van Deurzen, E. Craig, A. Längle, K. J. Schneider, D. Tantum, & S. du Plock (Eds.), *The Wiley world handbook of existential therapy* (pp. 135–153). Wiley-Blackwell.

Egan, G. (1975). *The skilled helper: A model for systematic helping and interpersonal relating*. Brooks/Cole.

Ellwood, R. S., & McGraw, B. A. (2014). *Many peoples, many faiths: Women and men in the world religions* (10th ed.). Pearson.

Epstein, M. (2013). *The trauma of everyday life*. Penguin.

Erickson, B. (2021). Deinstitutionalization through optimism: The Community Mental Health Act of 1963. *The American Journal of Psychiatry, 16*(4), 6–7. https://psychiatryonline.org/doi/10.1176/appi.ajp-rj.2021.16040

Erikson, E. H. (1950). *Childhood and society*. Norton.

Evans, K. M., & Larrabee, M. J. (2002). Teaching the multicultural counseling competencies and revised career counseling competencies simultaneously. *Journal of Multicultural Counseling and Development, 30*(1), 21–39. https://doi.org/10.1002/j.2161-1912.2002.tb00475.x

Franklin, J. (2022). *Mental health counselors' perceptions of professional identity as correctional counselors in an integrated behavioral health care setting* [Doctoral dissertation, Old Dominion University]. ODU Digital Commons. https://digitalcommons.odu.edu/chs_etds/141

Ghassemi, A. E. (2017). Interprofessional collaboration between mental health counselors and nurses. *Creative Nursing, 23*(4), 242–247. http://dx.doi.org/10.1891/1078-4535.23.4.242

Gilbertson, J. (2020). *Telemental health: The essential guide to providing successful online therapy.* PESI Publishing and Media.

GovTrack. (n.d.). *H.R. 1795 — 94th Congress: Community Mental Health Centers amendments: Summary.* https://www.govtrack.us/congress/bills/94/hr1795/summary

Hanna, J. (2019, Fall). Outnumbered. *Harvard Ed. Magazine.* https://www.gse.harvard.edu/news/ed/19/08/outnumbered

Herr, E. L. (2013). Trends in the history of vocational guidance. *The Career Development Quarterly, 61*(3), 277–282. https://doi.org/10.1002/j.2161-0045.2013.00056.x

Hershenson, D. B. (2009). Historical perspectives in career development theory. In I. Marini & M. A. Stebnicki (Eds.), *The professional counselor's desk reference* (pp. 411–420). Springer.

Hoffman, L., Serlin, I. A., & Rubin, S. (2019). The history of existential–humanistic and existential integrative therapy. In E. van Deurzen, E. Craig, A. Langle, K. J. Schneider, D. Tantam, & S. du Plock (Eds.). *The Wiley Handbook of Existential Therapy* (pp. 235–246). John Wiley and Sons.

Hollis, J. W., & Dodson, T. A. (2000). *Counselor preparation 1999–2001: Programs, faculty, trends* (10th ed.). Taylor & Francis.

Ivey, A. E., & Gluckstein, N. (1974). *Basic attending skills: An introduction to micro counseling and helping.* Microtraining Associates.

Ivey, A., E., Ivey, M., & Zalaquett, C. P. (2018). *Intentional interviewing and counseling: Facilitating client development in a multicultural society* (9th ed.). Brooks/Cole.

Jones, L. K. (1994). Frank Parsons' contribution to career counseling. *Journal of Career Development, 20*(4), 287–294. https://doi.org/10.1177/089484539402000403

Kaplan, M., & Cuciti, P. L. (Eds.). (1986). *The Great Society and its legacy: Twenty years of U.S. social policy.* Duke University Press.

Kongstvedt, P. R. (2020). *Health insurance and managed care* (5th ed.). Jones and Bartlett.

Kottler, J. A., & Shepard, D. S. (2015). *Introduction to counseling: Voices from the field* (8th ed.). Cengage.

Kraft, D. P. (2011). One hundred years of college mental health. *Journal of American College Health, 59,* 477–482. https://doi.org/10.1080/07448481.2011.569964

Lambie, G., & Williamson, L. L. (2004). The challenge to change from guidance counseling to professional school counseling: A historical proposition. *Professional School Counseling, 8*(2), 124–131. https://www.jstor.org/stable/42732614

Liu, K., Miller, R., Dickmann, E., Monday, K. (2018). Virtual supervision of student teachers as a catalyst of change for educational equity in rural areas. *Journal of Formative Design in Learning, 2,* 8–19. https://doi.org/10.1007/s41686-018-0016-6

McDaniels, C., & Watts, G. A. (Eds.) (1994). Frank Parsons: Light, information, inspiration, cooperation [Special issue]. *Journal of Career Development, 20*(4).

National Board for Certified Counselors. (2023a). *About us.* https://www.nbcc.org/about

National Board for Certified Counselors. (2023b). *Specialty certifications.* https://www.nbcc.org/certification/specialtycertifications

National Certification Commission for Addiction Professionals. (2023). *Certification.* https://www.naadac.org/certification

National Security Archive. (1995–2017). *FOIA basics.* https://nsarchive2.gwu.edu/nsa/foia/guide.html

Neukrug, E. (1980). The effects of supervisory style and type of praise upon counselor trainees' level of empathy and perception of supervisor [Doctoral dissertation, University of Cincinnati]. *Dissertation Abstracts International, 41(04*A), 1496.

Neukrug, E. (2015). *The SAGE encyclopedia of counseling and psychotherapy.* SAGE Publications.

Neukrug, E. (2022). *The world of the counselor* (6th ed.). Cognella Academic Press.

Neukrug, E., & Hays, D. G. (2023). *Counseling theory and practice.* Cognella Academic Press.

New International Version Bible. (2022). *Bible Study Tools: Provers 12:18. https://www.biblestudytools.com/proverbs/12-18.html#:~:text=witness%20tells%20lies.-,18%20The%20words%20of%20the%20reckless%20pierce%20like%20swords%2C%20but,tongue%20lasts%20only%20a%20moment.*

O'Connor v. Donaldson, 422 U.S. 563 (1975). https://www.loc.gov/item/usrep422563/

O*NET OnLine. (2023). *Mental health counselors.* https://www.onetonline.org/link/summary/21-1014.00

Parsons, F. (1908). The Vocational Bureau. *The Arena, 40*(224), 3–16.

Peterson, S. (2020, February 6). *Celebrating the role of rehabilitation counseling.* https://ct.counseling.org/2020/02/celebrating-the-role-of-rehabilitation-counseling/

Piaget, J. (1954). *The construction of reality in the child.* Basic Books

Popple, P. R., Leighninger, L., & Leighninger, R. D. (2019). *Social work, social welfare, and American society* (9th ed.). Pearson.

Ratts, M. J., Singh, A. A., Nassar-McMillan, S., Butler, S. K., & McCullough, J. R. (2016). Multicultural and social justice counseling competencies: Guidelines for the counseling profession. *Journal of Multicultural Counseling and Development, 44*(1), 28–48. https://doi.org/10.1002/jmcd.12035

Remley, T. P., & Herlihy, B. (2020). *Ethical, legal, and professional issues in counseling* (6th ed.). Pearson.

Rochefort, D. A. (1984). Origins of the "third psychiatric revolution": The Community Mental Health Centers Act of 1963. *Journal of Health Politics, Policy, and Law, 9*(1), 1–30. https://doi.org/10.1215/03616878-9-1-1

Rogers, C. R. (1942). *Counseling and psychotherapy: New concepts in practice.* Houghton Mifflin.

Rogers, C. R. (1951). *Client-centered therapy: Its current practice, implications, and theory.* Houghton Mifflin.

Schneiderman, K. (2018, April 3). To stay or not to stay in managed care. *Psychology Today.* https://www.psychologytoday.com/us/blog/the-novel-perspective/201804/stay-or-not-stay-in-managed-care

Shallcross, L. (2009, December 5). Counseling profession reaches the big 50. *Counseling Today.* http://ct.counseling.org/2009/12/counseling-profession-reaches-the-big-5-0/

Simon, R. (2007). The most influential therapists of the past quarter-century. (2007). *Psychotherapy Networker.* https://www.psycho-therapynetworker.org/magazine/article/661/the-top-10

Smith, H. B., & Robinson, G. (1995). Mental health counseling: past, present, and future. *Journal of Counseling and Development, 74,* 158–162. https://doi.org/10.1002/j.1556-6676.1995

Solomon, M. (1918). The increasing importance of the biological viewpoint in psychopathology and psychiatry. *Journal of Abnormal Psychology, 13,* 168–171. https://doi.org/10.1037/h0070702

Super, D. E. (1953). A theory of vocational development. *American Psychologist, 8*(2), 185–190. https://doi.org/10.1037/h0056046

Sweeney, T. J. (1991). Counselor credentialing: Purpose and origin. In F. O. Bradley (Ed.), *Credentialing in counseling* (pp. 81–85). Association for Counselor Education and Supervision.

University of Cincinnati Online. (2023). *Substance abuse counselor – Licensure requirements by state.* https://online.uc.edu/substance-abuse-counselor-licensure-requirements-by-state/

U.S. Department of Education. (2017). *The Rehabilitation Act of 1973.* https://www2.ed.gov/policy/speced/reg/narrative.html

U.S. Department of Education. (2020). *U.S. Education Department commemorates 45 years of the IDEA.* https://sites.ed.gov/idea/department-commemorates-45-years-idea/

U.S. Department of Education. (2021). *Family Educational Rights and Privacy Act (FERPA).* https://www2.ed.gov/policy/gen/guid/fpco/ferpa/index.html

U.S. Department of Health and Human Services. (2017). *Understanding health information privacy.* https://www.hhs.gov/hipaa/for-professionals/faq/2088/does-hipaa-provide-extra-protections-mental-health-information-compared-other-health.html

U.S. Department of Health and Human Services. (2021). *Parity policy and implementation.* https://www.hhs.gov/about/agencies/advisory-committees/mental-health-parity/task-force/resources/index.html

Walsh, R., & Dasenbrook, N. (2010). Managed care update. *Counseling Today, 52*(9), 16–17.

Walsh, R., & Dasenbrook, N. (2016). Contracting strategies with managed care and other agencies. In I. Marini & M. A. Stebnicki (Eds.), *The professional counselor's desk reference* (2nd ed., pp. 49–54). Springer.

Weikel, W. J. (2010). *A brief history of the American Mental Health Counselors Association.* https://www.amhca.org/about/about-us/aboutamhca/history. (Original work published 1985)

Weissmann, G. (2008). Citizen Pinel and the madman at Bellevue. *Journal of the Federation of American Societies for Expermental Biology, 22,* 1289–1293. https://doi.org/10.1096/fj.08-0501ufm

Wheeler, A. M. N., & Bertram, B. (2019). *The counselor and the law: A guide to legal and ethical practice* (8th ed.). American Counseling Association.

Williamson, E. G., & Darley, J. G. (1937). *Student personnel work: An outline of clinical procedures.* McGraw-Hill.

Zuckerman, E. L. (2017). *The paper office: Forms, guidelines, and resources to make your practice work ethically, legally, and profitably* (5th ed.). Guilford.

Zwelling, S. S. (1990). *Quest for a cure: The public hospital in Williamsburg, Virginia, 1773–1885.* Colonial Williamsburg Foundation.

CHAPTER 3

American Art Therapy Association. (2022). *About the American Art Therapy Association.* https://arttherapy.org/about/

American Association for Marriage and Family Therapy. (2002–2023). *About AAMFT.* https://www.aamft.org/AAMFT/About

American Counseling Association. (2023a). *We did it! Medicare reimbursement now law.* https://www.counseling.org/government-affairs/federal-issues/medicare-reimbursement

American Counseling Association. (2023b). *About us: Our vision and mission: ACA's strategic plan.* https://www.counseling.org/about-us/about-aca/our-mission

American Mental Health Counselors Association. (2010). *A brief history of the American Mental Health Counselors Association.* *https://www.amhca.org/about/about-us/aboutamhca/history*

American Mental Health Counselors Association. (2020). *Code of ethics.* https://www.amhca.org/events/publications/ethics

American Mental Health Counselors Association. (2021). *AMHCA standards for the practice of clinical mental health counseling.* https://www.amhca.org/HigherLogic/System/DownloadDocumentFile.ashx?DocumentFileKey=cea86111-9bdb-984a-c14f-8528a3b3d83f&forceDialog=0

American Mental Health Counselors Association. (2023a). *Benefits of memberships.* https://www.amhca.org/members/benefits

American Mental Health Counselors Association. (2023b). *Medicare inclusion.* https://www.amhca.org/advocacy/medicare

American Mental Health Counselors Association. (2023c). *About: About us.* https://www.amhca.org/about/about-us

American Mental Health Counselors Association. (2023d). *AMHCA affiliated chapters.* https://www.amhca.org/about/chapters

American Mental Health Counselors Association. (2023e). *Credentialing certifications.* https://www.amhca.org/members/career/credential/apply

American Mental Health Counselors Association. (2023f). *About: Memberships. https://www.amhca.org/joinamhca*

American Mental Health Counselors Association. (2023g). *Membership: Student liability insurance.* https://www.amhca.org/members20/liabilityinsurance

American Mental Health Counselors Association. (2023h). *Advocacy: Policy agenda.* https://www.amhca.org/advocacy/policyagenda

American Psychiatric Association. (2023a). *About APA.* https://www.psychiatry.org/about-apa

American Psychiatric Association. (2023b). *APA's vision, mission, values, and goals.* https://www.psychiatry.org/about-apa/vision-mission-values-goals/vision-mission-values-goals

American Psychiatric Nurses Association. (2023). *About APNA.* https://www.apna.org/about-apna/

American Psychological Association. (2023). *About APA.* https://www.apa.org/about

Briddick, W. (2009a). Frank findings: Frank Parsons and the Parson family. *Career Development Quarterly, 57*(3), 207–214. https://doi.org/10.1002/j.2161-0045.2009.tb00106.x

Colangelo, J. J. (2009). the American Mental Health Counselors Association: Reflection on 30 historic years. *Journal of Counseling & Development, 87,* 234–240. https://doi.org/10.1002/j.1556-6678.2009.tb00572.x

Herr, E. L. (2013). Trends in the history of vocational guidance. *The Career Development Quarterly, 61*(3), 277–282. https://doi.org/10.1002/j.2161-0045.2013.00056.x

Huber, M. J., Walker, Q. D., Dunlap, P. N., Russell, V. E., & Richardson, T. V. (2019). A revisited inquiry: A survey of the members of the American Rehabilitation Counseling Association (ARCA). *Rehabilitation Counseling Bulletin, 62*(2), 121–127. https://doi.org/10.1177/0034355218755509

McDaniels, C., & Watts, G. A. (Eds.). (1994). Frank Parsons: Light, information, inspiration, cooperation [Special issue]. *Journal of Career Development, 20*(4).

National Association of School Psychologists. (2021). *Vision, core purpose, core values, and strategic goals.* https://www.nasponline.org/utility/about-nasp/vision-core-purpose-core-values-and-strategic-goals

National Association of Social Workers. (2023). *About NASW.* https://www.socialworkers.org/About

National Board for Certified Pastoral Counselors. (2023). *About NBCPC.* http://nbcpc.org/pastoral-counseling/article/about-the-national-board-for-certified-pastoral-counselors

National Organization of Human Services. (n.d.). *Our mission.* https://www.nationalhumanservices.org/our-mission

Pickren, W. E., & Fowler, F. D. (2003). Professional organizations. In D. K. Freedheim and I. B. Weiner (Eds), *Handbook of psychology (Vol. 1): History of psychology* (pp. 535–554). John Wiley & Sons, Inc.

Weikel, W. J. (2010). *A brief history of the American Mental Health Counselors Association.* American Mental Health Counselors Association. https://www.amhca.org/about/about-us/aboutamhca/history

CHAPTER 4

American Counseling Association. (2012). *The Affordable Care Act: What counselors should know.* https://www.counseling.org/PublicPolicy/PDF/What_counselors_should_know-the_Affordable_Care_Act_12-12.pdf

American Counseling Association. (2023). *Licensure and certification – State professional counselor licensure boards.* https://www.counseling.org/knowledge-center/licensure-requirements/state-professional-counselor-licensure-boards

Andrews, M. (2005–2023). *HMO, PPO, EPO: What health plan is best.* WebMD. https://www.webmd.com/health-insurance/news/20140815/hmo-ppo-epo-hows-a-consumer-to-know-what-health-plan-is-best

Armstrong, K. (2022, June 29). Tending the family tree: Intervening in intergenerational mental health. *Association for Psychological Science.* https://www.psychologicalscience.org/observer/tending-the-family-tree

Barker, P., & Chang, J. (2020). *Basic family therapy* (7th ed.). Wiley.

Bergman, D. (2020). President signs landmark bill opening the federal government to mental health counselors. *American Mental Health Counselors Association Blog.* https://www.amhca.org/blogs/david-bergman1/2020/10/20/president-signs-landmark-bill-opening-the-federal

Blau, G. M., Caldwell, B., & Lieberman, R. E. (2014). *Residential interventions for children, adolescents, and families.* Routledge.

Brennan, C. (2013). Ensuring ethical practice: Guidelines for mental health counselors in private practice. *Journal of Mental Health Counseling, 35,* 245–261. https://doi.org/10.17744/mehc.35.3.9706313j4t313397

Cashwell, C. S., Young, J. S., Fulton, C. L., Willis, B. T., Giordano, A., Daniel, L. W., Giordano, A., Daniel, L. W., Crocket, J., Tate. B. N., & Welch, M. L. (2013). Clinical behaviors for addressing religious/spiritual issues: Do we practice what we preach? *Counseling and values, 58*(1), 45–58. https:// doi.org/10.1002/j.2161-007X.2013.00024.x

Centers for Disease Control and Prevention. (2022). *U.S. Public Health Service syphilis study at Tuskegee.* https://www.cdc.gov/tuskegee/timeline.htm

Centers for Disease Control and Prevention. (2023). *Provisional drug overdose death counts.* https://www.cdc.gov/nchs/nvss/vsrr/drug-overdose-data.htm

Council for Accreditation of Counseling and Related Educational Programs (CACREP). (2016). *CACREP standards.* https://www.cacrep.org/for-programs/2016-cacrep-standards/

Dasenbrook, N. C. (2023). *The complete guide to private practice* (5th ed.). Crysand.

Erickson, B. (2021). Deinstitutionalization through optimism: The Community Mental Health Act of 1963. *The American Journal of Psychiatry Residents' Journal.* https://doi.org/10.1176/appi.ajp-rj.2021.160404

Ferguson's Careers in Focus. (2008). *Careers in focus: Therapists* (2nd ed.). Ferguson.

Fisher, G. L., & Harrison, T. C. (2020). *Substance abuse: Information for school counselors, social workers, therapists, and counselors* (6th ed.). Pearson.

Franklin, J. (2022). *Mental health counselors' perceptions of professional identity as correctional counselors in an integrated behavioral health care setting* [Doctoral dissertation, Old Dominion University]. ODU Digital Commons. https://digitalcommons.odu.edu/chs_etds/141

Fullen, M. C. (2018). Ageism and the counseling profession: Causes, consequences, and methods for counteraction. *The Professional Counselor, 8*(2). https://doi.org/10.15241/mcf.8.2.104

Garner, G. O. (2008). *Careers in social and rehabilitation services* (3rd ed.). Wiley.

Gladding, S., & Newsome. D. W. (2018). *Clinical mental health counseling in community and agency settings* (5th ed.). Pearson.

Hagerdorn, W. B., Culbreth, J. R., & Cashwell, C. S. (2012). Addiction counseling accreditation: CACREP's role in solidifying the counseling profession. *The Professional Counselor, 2*(2), 124–133. https://doi.org/10.15241/wbh.2.2.124

Henderson, D. A. & Thompson, C. L. (2015). *Counseling children* (9th ed.). Cengage.

Hodges, S. (2018). *101 careers in counseling.* Springer.

Hodges, S. J. (2019). *Careers in counseling* (2nd. ed.). Springer.

Hoff, K. A., Song, C. Wee, C. J. M., Phan, W. M. J., & Rounds, J. (2020). Interest fit and job satisfaction: A systematic review and meta-analysis. *Journal of Vocational Behavior, 123*(103503). https://doi.org/10.1016/j.jvb.2020.103503

Hull, C. E., Suarez, E. C., & Hartman, D. (2016). Developing spiritual competencies in counseling: A guide for supervisors. *Counseling and Values, 61*, 111–126. https://doi.org/10.1002/cvj.12029

Johnson, S. M. (2019). *Attachment theory in practice: Emotionally focused therapy with individuals, couples, and families.* Guilford.

Kampfe, C. M. (2015). *Counseling older people: Opportunities and challenges.* Wiley.

Link, A. (2013). *Group work with older adults: 85 therapeutic exercises for reminiscence, validation, and remotivation.* Professional Resource Press.

Maruschak, L. M., & Minton, T. D. (2020). *Correctional populations in the United States, 2017–2018.* U.S. Department of Justice. https://www.bjs.gov/content/pub/pdf/cpus1718.pdf

McWhirter, J. J., McWhirter, B. T., McWhirter, E. H., & McWhirter, R. J. (2016). *At-risk youth: A comprehensive response for counselors, teachers, psychologists, and human service professionals* (6th ed.). Cengage.

Military and Government Counseling Association. (n.d.). *Home page.* http://mgcaonline.org/

Military OneSource. (2020). *Counseling options for service members and their families.* https://www.militaryonesource.mil/confidential-help/non-medical-counseling/military-and-family-life-counseling/7-counseling-options-for-service-members-and-their-families/

National Board for Certified Counselors. (2023). *Tricare.* https://www.nbcc.org/govtaffairs/tricare

Nelson, J. A., & Wines, L. A. (2021). *Responding to critical cases in school counseling. Building on theory, standards, and experience for optimal interventions.* Routledge.

Niles, S. G., & Harris-Bowlsbey, J. H. (2021). *Career development interventions* (6th ed.). Merrill/Prentice Hall.

O*NET Occupational Information Network. (2015). *Residential counselors.* https://occupationalinfo.org/onet/27307.html#TASKS

Parker, R. M., & Patterson, J. B. (Eds.) (2012). *Rehabilitation counseling: Basics and beyond* (5th ed.). PRO-ED.

Ritter, J. A., Obermann, A., & Danhaoff, K. L. (2020). *101 careers in social work* (3rd ed.). Springer.

Sawyer, W., & Wagner, P. (2020, March 24). *Mass incarceration: The whole pie 2020.* Prison Policy Initiative. https://www.prisonpolicy.org/reports/pie2020.html

Schiffman, R. (2022, September 23). More psychotherapists are incorporating religion into their practices. *The Washington Post.* https://www.washingtonpost.com/religion/2022/09/23/psychotherapy-religion-spirituality/

Schweiger, W. K., Henderson, D. A., McCaskill, K., Clawson, T., & Collins, D. R. (2012). *Counselor preparation: Programs, faculty, trends* (13th ed.). Routledge.

Shaler, L. (2019, May 20). *Respecting the faith of clients and counselors.* Counseling Today. https://ct.counseling.org/2019/05/respecting-the-faith-of-clients-and-counselors/

Shaw, B. M., Bayne, H., & Lorelle, S. (2012). A constructivist perspective for integrating spirituality into counselor training. *Counselor Education and Supervision, 51*(4), 270–280. https://doi. org/10.1002/j.1556-6978.2012.00020.x

Substance Abuse and Mental Health Services Administration (n.d.). FindTreatment.gov: Find a treatment facility. http://findtreatment.samhsa.gov/

Substance Abuse and Mental Health Services Administration. (2020). *Key substance use and mental health indicators in the United States: Results from the 2019 National survey on drug use and health.* https://www.samhsa.gov/data/sites/default/$les/reports/rpt29393/2019NSDUHFFRPDFWHTM-L/ 2019NSDUHFFR1PDFW090120.pdf

Suitt, T. (2021). *High suicide rates among United States service members and veterans of the post-9/11 Wars.* Watson Institute, Brown University. https://watson.brown.edu/costsofwar/files/cow/imce/papers/2021/Suitt_Suicides_Costs%20of%20War_June%2021%202021.pdf

Sun, K. (2013). *Correctional counseling: A cognitive growth perspective.* Jones and Bartle Learning.

The Sentencing Project. (2022). *Research—Get the facts.* The Sentencing Project. https://www.sentencingproject.org/research/

Turner, L. H., & West, R. (2018). *Perspectives on family communication* (5th ed.). McGraw-Hill.

U. S. Bureau of Labor Statistics. (2022). *School and career counselors.* https://www.bls.gov/ooh/community-and-social-service/school-and-career-counselors.htm

U. S. Census Bureau. (2021). *U.S. marriage and divorce rates declined in last 10 years.* https://www.census.gov/library/stories/2020/12/united-states-marriage-and-divorce-rates-declined-last-10-years.html

U.S. Census Bureau. (2020). *65 and older population grows rapidly as baby boomers age.* https:// www.census.gov/newsroom/press-releases/2020/65-older-population-grows.html

U.S. Centers for Medicare and Medicaid Services. (n.d.). *How to pick a health insurance plan*. https://www.healthcare.gov/choose-a-plan/plan-types/

U.S. Department of Health and Human Services. (2022). *Mental health and substance use co-occurring disorders*. https://www.mentalhealth.gov/what-to-look-for/mental-health-substance-use-disorders

Woititz, J. G. (2002). *The complete ACOA sourcebook: Adult children of alcoholics at home, at work, and in love*. Health Communications.

CHAPTER 5

American Association of Christian Counselors. (2023). *IBCC Credential Types: Board of Christian Professional and Pastoral Counselors (BCPPC)*. https://www.aacc.net/ibcc-credential-types/

American Association of Marriage and Family Therapy. (2002–2023). *MFT licensing boards*. https://www.aamft.org/Directories/MFT_Licensing_Boards.aspx?WebsiteKey=8e8c9bd6-0b71-4cd1-a5ab-013b5f855b01

American Board of Professional Psychology. (2023). *Learn about specialty boards*. https://abpp.org/application-information/learn-about-specialty-boards/

American Board of Psychiatry and Neurology. (n.d.). *Become certified*. https://www.abpn.com/become-certified/

American Counseling Association. (2012). *A guide to state laws and regulations on professional school counseling*. https://www.counseling.org/publicpolicy/schoolcounselingregs2012.pdf

American Counseling Association. (2015, May 12). *The latest news from ACA: More LPCs to be included under new TRICARE language*. https://www.counseling.org/news/updates/2015/05/12/more-lpcs-to-be-included-under-new-tricare-language

American Counseling Association. (2023a). *Knowledge center: Licensure requirements for professional counselors, A state by state report*. https://www.counseling.org/knowledge-center/licensure-requirements

American Counseling Association. (2023b). *Licensure and certification—State professaionl counselor licensure boards*. https://www.counseling.org/knowledge-center/licensure-requirements/state-professional-counselor-licensure-boards

American Counseling Association. (2023c). *Accreditation, licensure and certification defined*. https://www.counseling.org/knowledge-center/licensure-requirements/accreditation-licensure-and-certification-defined

American Counseling Association. (2023d). *We did it! Medicare reimbursement now law*. https://www.counseling.org/government-affairs/federal-issues/medicare-reimbursement

American Mental Health Counselors Association. (2023a). *Applying for AMHCA credentialing certifications*. https://www.amhca.org/members/career/credential/apply

Advanced Nurses Credentialing Center. *Home page*. https://www.nursingworld.org/ancc/

American Psychiatric Nurses Association. (2023). *About APNA*. https://www.apna.org/i4a/pages/index.cfm?pageid=3277

American Psychological Association. (2023). *RxP: A chronology*. https://www.apaservices.org/practice/advocacy/authority/prescription-chronology

American School Counselor Association. (2023a). *About: State certification requirements*. https://www.schoolcounselor.org/About-School-Counseling/State-Requirements-Programs/State-Licensure-Requirements

American School Counselor Association. (2023b). *ASCA-certified school counselor*. https://www.schoolcounselor.org/Recognition/Certification

Association of Marital and Family Therapy Regulatory Boards. (n.d.). *Home page*. https://amftrb.org/

Association of Social Work Boards. (2023). *Home page*. https://www.aswb.org/

Bloom, J. (1996). *Credentialing professional counselors for the 21st century* (ED399498). ERIC. https://eric.ed.gov/?id=ED399498

Bradley, L. J. (1995). Certification and licensure. *Journal of Counseling and Development, 74*(2), 185–186. https://doi.org/10.1002/j.1556-6676.1995.tb01849.x

Britannica. (2023). Registration. In *The Britannica dictionary*. Retrieved April, 22, 2023 from https://www.britannica.com/dictionary/registration

Center for Credentialing and Education. (2023a). *About: Who we are*. https://www.cce-global.org/about

Center for Credentialing and Education. (2023b). *HS—BCP: Human Services—Board Certified Practitioner*. https://www.cce-global.org/credentialing/hsbcp

Commission on Rehabilitation Counselor Certification. (2021). *Home page*. https://www.crccertification.com/

Commission on the Accreditation of Marriage and Family Therapy Education. (n.d.). *Home*. https://www.coamfte.org/COAMFTE/Home/COAMFTE/Home.aspx?hkey=cea2ee4f-0499-4381-ab7d-d31b373f4ab6

Corey, G., Corey, M. S., & Corey, C. (2024). *Issues and ethics in the helping professions* (11th ed.). Cengage.

Council for the Accreditation of Counseling and Related Educational Programs. (2016). *CACREP standards*. https://www.cacrep.org/for-programs/2016-cacrep-standards/

Counseling Compact Commission. (2022). *Inaugural meeting*. https://counselingcompact.org/wp-content/uploads/2022/09/Counseling-Compact-Inaugural-Meeting-Packet.pdf

Counseling Compact Commission (2023). *Home: What is the counseling compact?* https://counselingcompact.org/

Cummings, N. A. (1990). The credentialing of professional psychologists and its implications for the other mental health disciplines. *Journal of Counseling and Development, 68*(5), 485–490. https:// doi.org/10.1002/j.1556-6676.1990.tb01395.x

Department of Veteran Affairs. (2018). *VA handbook transmittal sheet*. https://www.va.gov/vapubs/viewPublication.asp?Pub_ID=942&FType=2

Garcia, A. (1990). An examination of the social work profession's efforts to achieve legal regulation. Journal of Counseling and Development, 68, 491–497. https://doi.org/10.1002/j.1556-6676.1990.tb01396.x

Gilberston, J. (2020). Telemental health: The essential guide to providing successful online therapy. PESI.

Hosie, T. (1991). Historical antecedents and current status of counselor licensure. In F. O. Bradley (Ed.), Credentialing in counseling (pp. 23–52). Association for Counselor Education and Supervision.

Livingston, R. (1979). The history of rehabilitation counselor certification. Journal of Applied Rehabilitation Counseling, 10, 111–118. https://doi.org/10.1891/0047-2220.10.3.111

NAADAC. (2023a). About the NCC AP. https://www.naadac.org/about-the-ncc-ap

NAADAC. (2023b). States and boards using the NCC AP exams. https://www.naadac.org/states-using-ncc-ap-exams

National Association of Forensic Counselors (n.d.). Certifications offered, requirements, application download, and other important information. https://www.forensiccounselor.org/?Certifications_and_Memberships__NAFC_Certifications_Offered%2C_Requirements_and_Applications#Requirements

National Association of School Psychologists. (2021). Why become an NCSP? https://www.nasponline.org/standards-and-certification/national-certification/why-become-an-ncsp

National Association of School Psychologists. (2022). The nationally certified school psychologist (NCSP) credential: Number granted in the past year by institution and state and total active as of July 1, 2022. https://www.nasponline.org/Documents/Standards%20and%20Certification/Certification/NCSP_2021_to_2022%20.pdf

National Association of Social Workers. (2023). Apply for NASW social work credentials. https://www.socialworkers.org/Careers/Credentials/Apply-for-NASW-Social-Work-Credentials

National Board for Certified Counselors. (2023a). About us. https://www.nbcc.org/about

National Board for Certified Counselors. (2023b). Board certification. https://nbcc.org/certification

National Board for Certified Counselors. (2023c). TRICARE. https://www.nbcc.org/govtaffairs/tricare

National Board for Professional Teaching Standards. (2023). National board certification. https://www.nbpts.org/certification/

National Certified Pastoral Counselor. (2023). NBCPC certifications. http://nbcpc.org/pastoral-counselors/article/nbcpc-certifications

O'Connor, K. (2022). APA helps DBs protect safe prescribing. Psychiatric News. https://psychnews.psychiatryonline.org/doi/10.1176/appi.pn.2022.05.5.9

O*NET Online. (2022). Mental health counselors. https://www.onetonline.org/link/summary/21-1014.00

Olfson, M. (2016). Building the mental health workforce capacity needed to treat adults with serious mental illness. Health Affairs, 35(6), 983–990. https://doi.org/10.1377/hlthaff.2015.1619

Peterson, S. (2020, February 6). Celebrating the role of rehabilitation counseling. Counseling Today. https://ct.counseling.org/2020/02/celebrating-the-role-of-rehabilitation-counseling/

Remley, T. P., Herlihy, B., & Herlihy, S. B. (1997). The U.S. Supreme Court decision in Jaffe v. Redmond: Implications for counselors. Journal of Counseling and Development, 75, 213–218. https://psycnet.apa.org/doi/10.1002/j.1556-6676.1997.tb02335.x

Remley, T. P., & Herlihy, B. (2020). Ethical, legal, and professional issues in counseling (6th ed.). Pearson.

Robiner, W. N., Tompkins, T. L., & Hathaway, K. M. (2019). Prescriptive authority: Psychologists' abridged training relative to other professions' training. Clinical Psychology Science and Practice, 27(1), 1–19. https://doi.org.proxy.lib.odu.edu/10.1111/cpsp.12309

Scoville, E., & Newman, J. S. (2009, May). A very brief history of credentialing. ACP Hospitalist. http://www.acphospitalist.org/archives/2009/05/newman.htm

The Center for Addiction Studies and Research. (2022a). Virginia substance abuse certification. https://centerforaddictionstudies.com/certification-requirements/us-substance-abuse-certification/virginia

The Center for Addiction Studies and Research. (2022b). Credentialing information. https://centerforaddictionstudies.com/credentialing-information

U.S. Department of Health and Human Services. (2019). Credentialing, licensing, and reimbursement of the SUD workforce: A review of policies and practices across the nation. https://aspe.hhs.gov/reports/credentialing-licensing-reimbursement-sud-workforce-review-policies-practices-across-nation-0

Virginia Board of Counseling. (2022). Board of counseling: Laws and regulations. https://www.dhp.virginia.gov/counseling/counseling_laws_regs.htm

Virginia Department of Health Professions. (n.d.). Virginia board of counseling. https://www.dhp.virginia.gov/counseling/counseling_forms.htm

Walsh, R., & Dasenbrook, N. (2010). Managed care update. Counseling Today, 52(9), 16–17.

Walsh, R., & Dasenbrook, N. (2016). Contracting strategies with managed care and other agencies. In I. Marini & M. A. Stebnicki (Eds.), The professional counselor's desk reference (2nd ed., pp. 49–54). Springer.

CHAPTER 6

Ahia, C. E., & Boccone, P. J. (2017). Licensure board actions against professional counselors: Implications for counselor training and practice. VISTAS Online, 39, 1–13. https:// www.counseling.org/docs/default-source/vistas/article_396bce2bf16116603abcacti-0000bee5e7.pdf?sfvrsn=f5d84b2c_4

American Association of Marriage and Family Therapy. (2015). Code of ethics. https://www.aamft.org/Legal_Ethics/Code_of_Ethics.aspx

American Counseling Association. (2014). *Code of ethics*. https://www.counseling.org/resources/aca-code-of-ethics.pdf

American Counseling Association. (2023). *Liability insurance*. https://www.counseling.org/membership/liability-insurance

American Mental Health Counselors Association. (2020). *2020 AMHCA Code of Ethics*. https://www.amhca.org/events/publications/ethics

American Mental Health Counselors Association. (2023). *Membership: Student member benefits*. https://www.counseling.org/membership/aca-and-you/students

American Psychological Association. (2017). *Ethical principles of psychologists and code of conduct: Including 2010 and 2016 amendments*. http://www.apa.org/ethics/code/index.aspx

American Psychiatric Association. (2013). *The principles of medical ethics: With annotations especially applicable to psychiatry*. https://www.psychiatry.org/File%20Library/Psychiatrists/Practice/Ethics/principles-medical-ethics.pdf

American School Counselor Association. (2022). *ASCA ethical standards for school counselors*. https://www.schoolcounselor.org/getmedia/f041cbd0-7004-47a5-ba01-3a5d657c6743/Ethi-cal- Standards.pdf

Association for Specialists in Group Work. (2021). *Guiding principles for group work*. https://asgw.org/wp-content/uploads/2021/07/ASGW-Guiding-Principles-May-2021.pdf

Barsky, A. E. (2019). *Ethics and values in social work: An integrated approach for a comprehensive curriculum*. Oxford University Press.

Barsky, A. E. (2022). *Essential ethics for social work practice*. Oxford University Press.

Bray, B., (2019, November 21). *Multicultural encounters. Counseling Today*. https://ct.counseling.org/2019/11/multicultural-encounters/

Burkholder, J., Burkhold, D., & Gavin, M. (2020). The role of decision-making models and reflection in navigating ethical dilemmas. *Counseling and Values, 65*(1). https://doi.org/10.1002/cvj.12125

Carlisle, K., Levitt, D., Neukrug, E. (2022). Mental health counselors' perceptions of ethical behaviors. *Counseling and Values, 67*(1), 88–115. https://doi.org/10.1163/2161007X-67010005

Çerkez, Y., Manyeruke, G., Oduwaye, O., & Shimave, S. (2018). Ethical issues in counseling: A trend analysis. *Quality and Quantity, 52*, 223–233. https://doi.org/10.1007/s11135-017-0604-6

Commission on Rehabilitation Counselor Certification. (2023). *Code of professional ethics for rehabilitation counselors*. https://crccertification.com/wp-content/uploads/2022/10/2023-Code-of-Ethics.pdf

Corey, G., Corey, M. S., & Corey, C. (forthcoming). *Issues and ethics in the helping professions* (10th ed.). Cengage Learning.

Cottone, R. R., & Claus, R. E. (2011). Ethical decision-making models: A review of the literature. *Journal of Counseling and Development, 78*(3), 275–283. https://doi.org/10.1002/j.1556-6676.2000.tb01908.x

Freedman, J., & Combs, G. (1996). *Narrative therapy: The social construction of preferred realities*. Norton.

Gert, B. (2020). *The definition of morality*. Stanford encyclopedia of philosophy. https://plato.stanford.edu/entries/morality-definition/

Guterman, J. T., & Rudes, J. (2008). Social constructionism and ethics: Implications for counseling. *Journal of Counseling and Development, 52*, 136–144. https://doi.org/10.1002/j.2161-007X.2008. tb00097.x

Healthcare Provider Service Organization (HPSO). (2021). *Need a quote? Getting a quote is as easy as 1, 2, 3*. http://hpso.com/selection?refID=WW2GWi

Hendricks, C. B., Bradley, L. J., & Robertson, D. L. (2015). Implementing multicultural ethics: Issues for family counselors. *The Family Journal: Counseling and Therapy for Couples and Families, 23*(2), 190–193. https://doi.org/10.1177/1066480715573251

Hill, A. L. (2004). Ethical analysis in counseling: A case for narrative ethics, moral visions, and virtue ethics. *Counseling & Values, 48*(2), 131–148. htpps://doi:10.1002/j.2161-007X.2004. tb00240.x

International Association of Marriage and Family Counselors. (2016). *IAMFC code of ethics*. https://www.iamfconline.org/public/department3.cfm

Kaplan, D. M., Francis, P. C., Hermann, M. A., Baca J. V., Goodnough, G. E., Hodges, S., Spurgeon S. L., & Wade M. E. (2017). New concepts in the 2014 ACA code of ethics. *Journal of Counseling & Development, 95*, 110–120. https://doi.org/10.1002/jcad.12122

Kegan, R. (1982). *The evolving self: Problem and process in human development*. Harvard University Press.

Kegan, R. (1994). *In over our heads*. Harvard University Press.

Kitchener, K. S. (1984). Intuition, critical evaluation and ethical principles: The foundation for ethical decisions in counseling psychology. *Counseling Psychologist, 12*(3), 43–45. https://doi.org/10.1177/0011000084123005

Kitchener, K. S. (1986). Teaching applied ethics in counselor education: An integration of psychological processes and philosophical analysis. *Journal of Counseling and Development, 64*(5), 306–311. https://doi.org/10.1177/0011000084123005

Kleist, D., & Bitter, J. R. (2013). Virtue, ethics, and legality in family therapy. In J. Bitter (Ed.), *Theory and practice of family therapy and counseling* (pp. 43–65). Brooks/Cole.

Kohlberg, L. (1984). *The psychology of moral development: The nature and validity of moral stages*. Harper & Row.

Lambie, G. W., Hagedor, W. B., & Ieva, K. P. (2010). Social–cognitive development, ethical and legal knowledge, and ethical decision making of counselor education students. *Counselor Education and Supervision, 49*, 228–246. https://doi.org/10.1002/j.1556-6978.2010.tb00100.x

Lambie, G. W., Smith, H. L., & Ieva. K. P. (2009). Graduate counseling students' levels of ego development, wellness, and psychological disturbance: An exploratory investigation. *Adultspan Journal, 8*, 114–127. https://doi.org/10.1002/j.2161-0029.2009.tb00064.x

Landon, T. J., & Schultz, J. C. (2017). Exploring rehabilitation counseling supervisors' role in promoting counselor development of ethical fluency. *Rehabilitation Counseling Bulletin, 62*(1), 18–29. https://doi-org.proxy.lib.odu.edu/10.1177/0034355217728912

Letourneau, J. L. H. (2016). A decision-making model for addressing problematic behaviors in counseling students. *Counseling and Values, 61(2)*, 206–222. https://doi.org/10.1002/cvj.12038

Levitt, D. H., Tierney, Farry, T. J., & Mazzarella, J. R. (2015). Counselor ethical reasoning: Decision-making practice versus theory. *Counseling and Values, 61*(1), 84–99. https://doi.org/10.1002/j.2161-007X.2015.00062.x

Lloyd-Hazlet, J., & Foster, V. A. (2017). Student counselors' moral, intellectual, and professional identity development. *Counseling and Values, 62*(1), 90–105. https://doi.org/10.1002/cvj.12051

Luke, M. D., Goodrich, K. M., Gilbride, D. D. (2013). Testing the intercultural model of ethical decision making with counselor trainees. *Counselor Education & Supervision, 52*(3), 222–234. https://doi.org/10.1002/j.1556-6978.2013.00039.x

McAuliffe, G., & Eriksen, K. (Eds.). (2010). *Handbook of counselor preparation: Constructivist, develop-mental, and experiential approaches.* SAGE Publications.

Meara, N. M., Schmidt, L. D., & Day, J. D. (1996). Principles and virtues: A foundation for ethical decisions, policies, and character. The *Counseling Psychologist, 24*(9), 4–77. https://doi.org/10.1177/0011000096241002

Moyer, M., & Crews, C. (2017). *Applied ethics and decision making in mental health.* SAGE Publications.

National Association of Social Workers. (2021a). *Code of ethics.* https://www.socialworkers.org/About/Ethics/Code-of-Ethics/Code-of-Ethics-English

National Association of Social Workers. (2021b). *Highlighted revisions to the code of ethics.* https://www.socialworkers.org/About/Ethics/Code-of-Ethics/Highlighted-Revisions-to-the-Code-of-Ethics

National Association of Social Workers. (2023). *History of the NASW code of ethics.* https://www.socialworkers.org/About/Ethics/Code-of-Ethics/History

National Board for Certified Counselors (NBCC). (2016). *NBCC code of ethics.* https://www.nbcc.org/assets/Ethics/NBCCCodeofEthics.pdf

National Organization of Human Services (NOHS). (2015). *Ethical standards for human services professionals.* https://www.national-humanservices.org/ethical-standards-for-hs-professionals

Paul, R. E. (1977). Tarasoff and the duty to warn: Toward a standard of conduct that balances the rights of clients against the rights of third parties. *Professional Psychology, 8*(2), 125–128. https://doi.org/10.1037/h0078397

Perry, W. G. (1970). *Forms of intellectual and ethical development in the college years: A scheme.* Holt, Rinehart, & Winston.

Ponton, R., & Duba, J. (2009). The "ACA code of ethics": Articulating counseling's professional covenant. *Journal of Counseling & Development, 87*, 117–121. https://doi.org/10.1002/j.1556-6678.2009.tb00557.x

Purgason, L. L., Avent, J. R., Cashwell, C. S., Jordan, M. E., & Reese, R. F. (2016). Culturally relevant advising: Applying relational cultural theory in counselor education. *Journal of Counseling & Development, 94*, 429–436. https://doi.org/10.1002/jcad.12101

Raskin, J. D., & Debany, A. E. (2017). The inescapability of ethics and the impossibility of "anything goes": A constructivist model of ethical meaning making. *Journal of Constructivist Psychology, 31*(4), 343–360. https://doi.org/10.1080/10720537.2017.1383954

Remley, T. P., & Herlihy, B. (2020). *Ethical, legal, and professional issues in counseling* (6th ed.). Pearson.

Robinson, J., Moyer, M., Maghsoudi, M., & Martinez-Smith, C. (2020). Deconstructing ethical ambiguity: Ethical decision making when working with multiple ethical codes of conduct. *Journal of Professional Counseling: Practice, Theory & Research, 47*(2), 61–74. https://doi.org/10.1080/15566382.2020.1799675

Simon, S. B., Howe, L. W., & Kirschenbaum, H. (1995). *Values clarification: A practical, action-directed workbook.* Warner Books.

Urofsky, R., Engels, D., & Engebretson, K. (2008). Kitchener's principle ethics: Implications for counseling practice and research. *Counseling and Values, 53*(1), 67–78. https://doi.org/10.1002/j.2161-007X.2009.tb00114.x

Wagner, H. H., & Hill, N. R. (2015). Becoming counselors through growth and learning: The entry transition process. *Counselor Education & Supervision, 54*, 189–202. https://doi-org.proxy.lib.odu.edu/10.1002/ceas.12013

Welfel, E. R. (2016). *Ethics in counseling and psychotherapy: Standards, research, and emerging issues* (6th ed.). Cengage Learning.

Wilkinson, T., Smith, D., & Wimberly, R. (2019). Trends in ethical complaints leading to professional counseling licensing boards disciplinary actions. *Journal of Counseling & Development, 97*, 98–104. https://doi.org/10.1002/jcad.12239

CHAPTER 7

Ali, S., & Lee, C. C. (2019). Using creativity to explore intersectionality in counseling. *Journal of Creativity in Mental Health, 14*(4), 510–518. https://doi.org/10.1080/15401383.2019.1632767

Allen, J. R. (2020). *How we rise: Systemic racism and America today. Brookings Institute.* https://www.brookings.edu/blog/how-we-rise/2020/06/11/systemic-racism-and-america-today/

American Counseling Association. (2023). *Conversion therapy bans.* https://www.counseling.org/government-affairs/state-issues/conversion-therapy-bans

American Psychological Association. (2021). *Inclusive language guidelines.* https://www.apa.org/about/apa/equity-diversity-inclusion/language-guidelines.pdf

American Psychiatric Association. (2017). *Mental health disparities: LGBTQ.* https://www.psychiatry.org/File%20Library/Psychiatrists/Cultural-Competency/Mental-Health-Disparities/Mental-Health-Facts-for-LGBTQ.pdf

Arthur, M. M. L. (2007). Race. In G. Ritzer (Ed.), *The Blackwell encyclopedia of sociology.* https://doi.org/10.1002/9781405165518.wbeosr001

Blackless, M., Cjarivastra. A., Derryck, A., Fausto-Sterling, A., Lauzanne, K., & Lee, E. (2000). How sexually dimorphic are we? Review and synthesis. *American Journal of Human Biology, 12,* 151–166. https://doi.org/10.1002/(SICI)1520-6300(200003/04)12:2<151::AID-AJHB1>3.0.CO;2-F

Bray, B. (2019, November 21). *Multicultural encounters. Counseling Today.* https://ct.counseling.org/2019/11/multicultural-encounters/

Chou, V. (2017). *How science and genetics are reshaping the face debate of the 21st century.* Harvard University. https://sitn.hms.harvard.edu/flash/2017/science-genetics-reshaping-race-debate-21st-century/

Cipriani, R. (2016). Religion. In R. George (Ed.), *The Blackwell encyclopedia of sociology.* https://doi.org/10.1002/9781405165518.wbeosr048.pub2

Counselors for Social Justice. (2021). *About.* https://www.counseling-csj.org/about.html

Debunking the concept of race. (2005, July 30). *New York Times,* A28.

Duello, T. M., Rivedal, S., Wicland, C., & Weller, A. (2021). Race and genetics versus 'race' in genetics: A systematic review of the use of African ancestry in genetic studies. *Evolution, Medicine, and Public Health, 9*(1), 232-245. https://doi.org/10.1093/emph/eoab018

Ekstam, D. (2022). Change and continuity in attitudes toward homosexuality across the lifespan. *Journal of Homosexuality.* https://doi.org/10.1080/00918369.2021.2004795

Escobar, J. I. (2012). Taking issue: Diagnostic bias: Racial and cultural issues. *Psychiatric Services.* http://ps.psychiatryonline.org/doi/pdf/10.1176/appi.ps.20120p847

Fox, J., Eriksen, K., Jackson, S. A., & Weld, C. (2020). Religion and spirituality. In G. J. McAuliffe (Ed.), *Culturally alert counseling: A comprehensive introduction* (3rd ed., pp. 407–440). SAGE Publications.

Goodspeed-Grant, P., & Mackie, K. L., & Abraham, J. (2020). Social class. In G. McAuliffe (Ed.), *Culturally alert counseling: A comprehensive introduction* (3rd ed., pp. 315–346). SAGE Publications.

Grothaus, T., McAuliffe, G., & Danner, M. (2020). Social justice and advocacy. In G. McAuliffe (Ed.), *Culturally alert counseling: A comprehensive introduction* (3rd., pp. 41–62). SAGE Publications.

Hansen, N. D., Pepitone-Arreola-Rockwell, F., & Greene, A. F., (2000). Multicultural competence: Criteria and case examples. *Professional Psychology: Research and Practice, 31*(6), 652–660. https://doi.org/10.1037//0735-702831.6.652

Hays, D., & Erford, B. T. (2018). *Developing multicultural counseling competence: A systems approach* (3rd ed.). Pearson.

InterACT. (2021). *FAQ: What is intersex?* https://interactadvocates.org/faq/

Jenkins, R. (2007). Ethnicity. In G. Ritzer (Ed.), *The Blackwell encyclopedia of sociology.* https://doi.org/10.1002/9781405165518.wbeose068

Jennings, L. (2015). Prejudice. In G. Ritzer (Ed.), *The Blackwell encyclopedia of sociology.* https://doi.org/10.1002/9781405165518.wbeosp089.pub2

Johnson, A. G. (2006). *Privilege, power, and difference* (2nd ed.). McGraw-Hill.

Jones, J. M. (2022). LGBT identification in U.S. ticks up to 7.1%. Gallup. https://news.gallup.com/poll/389792/lgbt-identification-ticks-up.aspx

Kishimoto, K. (2018). Anti-racist pedagogy: From faculty's self-reflection to organizing within and beyond the classroom. *Race Ethnicity and Education, 21,* 540–554. https://doi.org/10.1080/13613324.2016.1248824

Kluckhohn, C., & Murray, H. A. (Eds.). (1948). *Personality in nature, society, and culture.* Knopf.

Lewis, J. A., Lewis, M. D., Daniels, J. A., & D'Andrea, M. J. (2011). *Community counseling: A multicultural–social justice perspective* (4th ed.). Cengage.

Lo, C., Cheng, T., & Howell, R. (2013). Access to and utilization of health services as pathway to racial disparities in serious mental illness. *Community Mental Health Journal, 50*(3), 251–257. https://doi.org/10.1007/s10597-013-9593-7

Macionis. J. J. (2019). *Sociology* (17th ed.). Pearson.

McAuliffe, G. (2020a). The practice of culturally alert counseling. In G. McAuliffe (Ed.), *Culturally alert counseling: A comprehensive introduction* (3rd ed., pp. 511–536). SAGE Publications.

McAuliffe, G. (2020b). *Culturally alert counseling: A comprehensive introduction* (3rd ed.). SAGE Publications.

McAuliffe, G. (2020c). Culture and diversity defined. In G. McAuliffe (Ed.), *Culturally alert counseling: A comprehensive introduction* (3rd ed., pp. 3–22). SAGE Publications.

McAuliffe, G. J., Kim, B. S. K., & Yong, S. P. (2020d). Ethnicity. In G. J. McAuliffe (Ed.), *Culturally alert counseling: A comprehensive introduction* (3rd ed., pp. 63–76). SAGE Publications.

McAuliffe, G. M., Grothaus, T., & Gomez, E. (2020e). Conceptualizing race and racism. In G. J. McAuliffe (Ed.), *Culturally alert counseling: A comprehensive introduction* (3rd ed., pp. 77–106). SAGE Publications.

Nadal, K. L. (2011). The racial and ethnic microaggressions scale (REMS): Construction, reliability, and validity. *Journal of Counseling Psychology, 58*(4), 470–480. https://doi.org/10.1037/a0025193

National Alliance of Mental Illness. (2023). *African American mental health.* https://www.nami.org/Find-Support/Diverse-Communities/African-Americans

National Human Genome Research Project. (2018). *Human genomic variation.* https://www.genome.gov/dna-day/15-ways/human-genomic-variation

Notestine, L. E., & Leeth, C. (2020). Gender. In G. McAuliffe (Ed*.), Culturally alert counseling: A comprehensive introduction* (3rd ed., pp. 347–368). SAGE Publications.

O'Dowd, M. F. (2020, February 3). Explainer: What is systemic racism and institutional racism? *The Conversation.* https://theconversation.com/explainer-what-is-systemic-racism-and-institutional-racism-131152

Parker, K., Horowitz, J. M., & Brown, A. (2022). *Americans' complex views on gender identity and transgender issues.* Pew Research Center. https://www.pewresearch.org/social-trends/2022/06/28/americans-complex-views-on-gender-identity-and-transgender-issues/

PBS News Hour. (2023, January 12). *Wisconsin Republicans block ban on 'conversion therapy."* https://www.pbs.org/newshour/politics/wisconsin-republicans-block-ban-on-conversion-therapy

Pew Research Center. (2013). *LGBT in changing times.* http://www.pewresearch.org/packages/lgbt-in-changing-times/

Pew Research Center. (2019). *Attitudes on same-sex marriage.* https://www.pewresearch.org/religion/fact-sheet/changing-attitudes-on-gay-marriage/

Pickering, M. (2017). Stereotypic and stereotypes. In G. Ritzer (Ed.), *The Blackwell encyclopedia of sociology.* https://doi.org/10.1002/9781405165518.wbeoss263.pub2

Public Religion Research Institute. (2021). *The 2020 census of American religion.* https://www.prri.org/research/2020-census-of-american-religion/

Ratts, M. J. (2009). Social justice counseling: Toward the development of a fifth force among counseling paradigms. *Journal of Humanistic Counseling, Education, and Development, 48*(2), 160–172. https://doi.org/10.1002/j.2161-1939.2009.tb00076.x

Ratts, M. J. (2011). Multiculturalism and social justice: Two sides of the same coin. *Journal of Multicultural Counseling and Development, 39*(1), 24–37. https://doi.org/10.1002/j.2161-1912.2011.tb00137.x

Ratts, M. J., Singh, A. A., Nassar-McMillan, S., Butler, S. K., & McCullough, J. R. (2015). *Multicultural and social justice counseling competencies: Guidelines for the counseling profession.* American Counseling Association. https://www.counseling.org/docs/default-source/competencies/multicultural-and-social-justice-counseling-competencies.pdf?sfvrsn=20

Ratts, M. J., Singh, A. A., Nassar-McMillan, S., Butler, S. K., & McCullough, J. R. (2016). Multicultural and social justice counseling competencies: Guidelines for the counseling profession. *Journal of Multicultural Counseling and Development, 44*(1), 28–48. https://doi.org/10.1002/jmcd.12035

Sewell, H. (2009). *Working with ethnicity, race, and culture in mental health.* Jessica Kingsley.

Shin, R. Q., Welch, j. C., Kaya, A. E., Yeung, J. G., Obana, C., Sharma, R., VErnay, C. N., & Yee, S. (2017). The intersectionality framework and identity intersections in the *Journal of Counseling Psychology* and the *Counseling Psychologist*: A content analysis. *Journal of Counseling Psychology, 64*(5), 458–474. http://dx.doi.org/10.1037/cou0000204

Smith, T. B., & Trimble, J. E. (2016). Participation of clients of color in mental health services: A meta-analysis of treatment attendance and treatment completion/attrition. In T. B. Smith & J. E. Trimble (Eds.), *Foundations of multicultural psychology: Research to inform effective practice* (pp. 95–114). American Psychological Association. https://doi.org/10.1037/14733-005

Spillman, L. (2016). Culture. In G. Ritzer (Ed.) *The Blackwell encyclopedia of sociology.* https://doi.org/10.1002/9781405165518.wbeosc182.pub2

Sue, D. W., Alsaidi, S., Awad, M. N., Glaeser, E., Calle, C. Z., & Mendez, N. (2019). Disarming racial microaggressions: Microintervention strategies for targets, White allies, and bystanders. *American Psychologist, 74*, 128–142. http://dx.doi.org/10.1037/amp0000296

Sue, D. W., Sue, D., Neville, H. A., & Smith, L. (2022). *Counseling the culturally diverse: Theory and practice* (9th ed.). Wiley.

Sue, D. W., & Torino, G. C. (2005). Racial–cultural competences: Awareness, knowledge, and skills. In R. T. Carter (Ed.), *Handbook of racial–cultural psychology and counseling: Theory and research* (pp. 3–18). Wiley.

Szymanski, D. & Carretta, R. F. (2020). Counseling lesbian, gay, bisexual, and transgendered clients. In G. J. McAuliffe (Ed.), *Culturally alert counseling: A comprehensive introduction* (3rd ed., pp. 369–406). SAGE Publications.

Tarver, S. Z., & Herring, M. H., (2019). Training culturally competent practitioners: Student reflections on the process. *Journal of Human Services, 39*, 7–18.

U. S. Census Bureau. (2020*). Demographic turning points for the United States: Population projections for 2020 to 2060.* https://www.census.gov/content/dam/Census/library/publications/2020/demo/p25-1144.pdf

U.S. Census Bureau. (2021). *Quick facts: Population estimates 2021.* https://www.census.gov/quickfacts/fact/table/US/PST045221

U.S. Census Bureau (2022). *Quick facts: United States.* https://www.census.gov/quickfacts/fact/table/US/PST045216

U. S. Department of Health and Human Services. (2014). *Improving cultural competence: A treatment improvement protocol.* Substance Abuse and Mental Health Services Administration.

U.S. Department of Homeland Security. (2022). *Legal immigration and adjustment of status report fiscal year 2022, quarter 2.* https://www.dhs.gov/immigration-statistics/special-reports/legal-immigration#File_end

Tarver, S. Z., & Herring, M. H., (2019). Training culturally competent practitioners: Student reflections on the process. *Journal of Human Services, 39*, 7–18.

Vitt, L. A. (2020). Class. In G. Ritzer (Ed.), *The Blackwell encyclopedia of sociology.* https://doi.org/10.1002/9781405165518.wbeosc048.pub2

CHAPTER 8

Allsopp, K., Read, J., Corcoran, R., & Kinderman, P. (2019). Heterogeneity in psychiatric diagnostic classification. *Psychiatric Research, 279*, 15–22. https://doi.org/10.1016/j.psychres.2019.07.005

American Counseling Association. (2014). *Code of ethics.* https://www.counseling.org/resources/aca-code-of-ethics.pdf

American Mental Health Counselors Association. (2020). *Code of ethics.* https://www.amhca.org/events/publications/ethics

American Psychiatric Association. (2013). *Cultural concepts in DSM-5*. https://www.psychiatry.org/File%20Library/Psychiatrists/Practice/DSM/APA_DSM_Cultural-Concepts-in-DSM-5.pdf

American Psychiatric Association. (1994). *Diagnostic and statistical manual of mental disorders* (4th ed.).

American Psychiatric Association. (2000). *Diagnostic and statistical manual of mental disorders* (4th ed., text revision).

American Psychiatric Association. (2022a). *Diagnostic and statistical manual of mental disorders* (5th ed., text revision).

American Psychiatric Association. (2022b). Attention to culture, racism, and discrimination in DSM-5-TR. https://www.psychiatry.org/File%20Library/Psychiatrists/Practice/DSM/DSM-5-TR/APA-DSM5TR-AttentiontoCultureRacismandDiscrimination.pdf

American Psychological Association. (2023). *Abnormal*. In *APA Dictionary of Psychology*. Retrieved April 23, 2023 from https://dictionary.apa.org/abnormal

Bandura, A. T., Ross, D., & Ross, S. A. (1963). Imitation of film-mediated aggressive models. *Journal of Abnormal and Social Psychology*, *67*, 3–11. https://doi.org/10.1037/h0048687

Beck, J. (2020). *Cognitive therapy: Basics and beyond* (3rd ed.). Guilford Press.

Bishop, A. (2015). Freudian psychoanalysis. In E. Neukrug (Ed.*), The SAGE encyclopedia of theory in counseling and psychotherapy* (Vol. 1, pp. 437–441). SAGE Publications.

Bonino, J. L., & Hanna, F. J. (2018). Who owns psychopathology? The DSM: Its flaws, its future, and the professional counselor. *Journal of Humanistic Counseling*, *57*, 118–137. https://doi.org/10.1002/johc.12071

Bridge, J. A., Iyengar, S., Salary, C. B., Barbe, R. P., Birmaher, B., Pincus, H. A., & Brent, D. A. (2007). Clinical response and risk for reported suicidal ideation and suicide attempts in pediatric antidepressant treatment: A meta-analysis of randomized controlled trials. *JAMA*, *297*, 1683–1696. https://doi.org/10.1001/jama.297.15.1683

Cabaniss, D. L., Cherry, S., Douglas, C. J., & Schwartz, A. (2017). *Psychodynamic psychotherapy: A clinical manual* (2nd ed.). John Wiley & Sons.

Carlisle, K., Levitt, D., & Neukrug, E. (2022). Mental health counselors' perceptions of ethical behaviors. *Counseling and Values*, *67*(1), 88–115. https://doi.org/10.1163/2161007X-67010005

Clark, L. A., & Watson, D. (2008). Temperament: An organizing paradigm for trait psychology. In O. P. John, R. W., Robins, & L. A. Pervin (Eds.), *Handbook of personality: Theory and research* (3rd ed., pp. 265–287). Guilford Press.

Courtet, P., & Lopez-Castroman, J. (2017). Antidepressants and suicide risk in depression. *World Psychiatry*, *16*(3), 317–318. https://doi.org/10.1002/wps.20460

Crocker, S. F., & Philippson, P. (2005). Phenomenology, existentialism, and Eastern thought in Gestalt therapy. In A. L. Woldt & S. M. Tolman (Eds.), Gestalt therapy: History, theory, and practice (pp. 65–80). SAGE Publications.

DeBattista, C. (2017). Psychostimulants and wakefulness-promoting agents. In A. F. Schatzberg & C. B. Nemeroff (Eds.), *Textbook of psychopharmacology* (5th ed., pp. 1083–1104). American Psychiatric Press.

DeSilva, R., Aggarwal, N. K., & Lewis-Fernández, R. (2018). The *DSM-5* cultural formulation interview: Bridging barriers toward a clinically integrated cultural assessment in psychiatry. *Psychiatric Annals*, *48*(3), 154–159. https://doi.org/10.3928/00485713-20180214-01

Douglas Harper. (2019). *Diagnosis*. In *Online Etymology Dictionary*. Retrieved April 22, 2023, from https://www.etymonline.com/word/diagnosis

Ellis, A., & Harper, R. A. (1997). *A guide to rational living* (3rd ed.). Wilshire Book Company.

Eriksen, K., & Kress, V. (2005). *Beyond the DSM story: Ethical quandaries, challenges, and best practices*. SAGE Publications.

Eriksen, K., & Kress, V. (2006). The *DSM* and the professional identity: Bridging the gap. *Journal of Mental Health Counseling*, *28*, 202–217. https://doi.org/10.17744/mehc.28.3.4f39a6wr1n3fceh2

Eriksen, K., & Kress, V. (2008). Gender and diagnosis: Struggles and suggestions for counselors. *Journal of Counseling and Development*, *86*, 152–162. https://doi.org/10.1002/j.1556-6678.2008.tb00492.x

Fawcett, J., & Busch, K. A. (1998). Stimulants in psychiatry. In A. F. Schatzberg & C. B. Nemeroff (Eds.), *Textbook of psychopharmacology* (2nd ed., pp. 503–522). American Psychiatric Press.

Foster, V., & McAdams, C. (2009). A framework for creating a climate of transparency for professional performance assessment: Fostering student investment in gatekeeping. *Counselor Education and Supervision*, *48*, 271–284. https://doi.org/10.1002/j.1556-6978.2009.tb00080.x

Freedman, J., & Combs, G. (1996). *Narrative therapy: The social construction of preferred realities*. W. W. Norton and Company.

Gaete, J., Sutherland, O., Couture, S., & Strong, T. (2017). DSM diagnosis and social justice: Inviting counselor reflexivity. In D. Pare & C. Audet (Eds.), *Social justice in counseling* (pp. 197–212). Routledge.

Gergen, K. J. (1985). The social constructionist movement in modern psychology. *American Psychologist*, *40*, 266–275. https://doi.org/10.1037/0003-066X.40.3.266

Gergen, K. J. (2015). *An invitation to social construction* (3rd ed.). SAGE Publications.

Ghaemi, S. N. (2018). After the failure of the DSM: Clinical research of psychiatric diagnosis. *World Psychiatry*, *17*(3), 301–302. https://doi.org/10.1002/wps.20563

Goldberg, J. F., & Ernst, C. L. (2019). *Managing the side effects of psychotropic medications* (2nd ed.). American Psychiatric Publishing.

Halstead, R. W. (2015). *Assessment of client core issues* (2nd ed.). American Counseling Association.

Henein, F., Prabhakar, D., Peterson, E. L., Williams, L. K., & Ahmedani, B. K. (2016). A prospective study of antidepressant adherence and suicidal ideation among adults. *The Primary Care Companion for CNS Disorders*, *18*(6), 1–4. https://www.doi.org/10.4088/PCC.16l01935

Horowitz, A. V. (2021). *DSM: History of psychiatry's bible*. Johns Hopkins University Press.

Ivey, A., E. & Ivey, M. (1998). Reframing *DSM-IV*: Positive strategies from developmental counseling and therapy. *Journal of Counseling and Development, 76*(3), 334–350. https://doi.org/10.1002/j.1556-6676.1998.tb02550.x

Jackson, C. (2012). Diagnostic disarray. *Therapy Today, 23*(3), 4–8.

Jacobs, M. (2017). *Psychodynamic counselling in action.* SAGE Publications.

Jozefowiez, J., & Staddon, J. E. R. (2015). Operant conditioning. In E. Neukrug (Ed.). *The SAGE encyclopedia of theory in counseling and psychotherapy* (Vol. 2, pp. 738–742). SAGE Publications.

Kamali, M., Krishnamurthy, V. B., Baweja, R., Saunders, E. F. H., & Gelenberg, A. J. (2017). Lithium. In A. F. Schatzberg and C. B. Nemeroff (Eds.), *Textbook of psychopharmacology* (5th ed., pp. 889–922). American Psychiatric Press.

Kinderman, P., Allsopp, K., & Cooke, A. (2017). Responses to the publication of the American Psychiatric Association's *DSM-5. Journal of Humanistic Psychology, 57*(6), 625–649. https://doi-org.proxy.lib.odu.edu/10.1177%2F0022167817698262

Kress, V., Eriksen, K., Rayle, A., & Ford, S. (2005). The *DSM-IV-TR* and culture: Considerations for counselors. *Journal of Counseling and Development, 83*, 97–104. https://doi.org/10.1002/j.1556-6678.2005.tb00584.x

Krishnan, K. R. R. (2017). Monoamine oxidase inhibitors. In A. F. Schatzberg and C. B. Nemeroff (Eds.), *Textbook of psychopharmacology* (5th ed., pp. 283–304). American Psychiatric Press.

Letourneau, L. H. (2016). A decision-making model for addressing problematic behaviors in counseling students. *Counseling and Values, 61*, 206–222. https://doi.org/10.1002/cvj.12038

Maia, S., & Jozefowiez, J. (2015). Classical conditioning. In E. Neukrug (Ed.), *The SAGE encyclopedia of theory in counseling and psychotherapy* (Vol. 1, pp. 163–167). SAGE Publications.

McElroy, S. L., & Keck, P. E., Jr. (2017). Topirmate. In A. F. Schatzberg & C. B. Nemeroff (Eds.), *Textbook of psychopharmacology* (5th ed., pp. 1017–1038). American Psychiatric Press.

Miller, G. (2012). Criticism continues to dog psychiatric manual as deadline approaches. *Science, 336*, 1088–1089. https://www.doi.org/10.1126/science.336.6085.1088

Moreira, V. (2012). From person-centered to humanistic–phenomenological psychotherapy: The contribution of Merleau-Ponty to Carl Rogers's thought. *Person-Centered & Experiential Psychotherapies,11*(1), 48–63. https://doi.org/10.1080/14779757.2012.656410

Mukherjee, S. (2016). *The gene: An intimate history.* Scribner.

Nasrallah, H. A., & Tandon, F. (2017). Classic antipsychotic medications. In A. F. Schatzberg and C. B. Nemeroff (Eds.), *Textbook of psychopharmacology* (5th ed., pp. 603–622). American Psychiatric Press.

National Institute of Mental Health. (2022). *Mental health medications.* https://www.nimh.nih.gov/health/topics/mental-health-medications/index.shtml

Nelson, J. C. (2017). Tricyclic and tetracyclic drugs. In A. F. Schatzberg & C. B. Nemeroff (Eds.), *Textbook of psychopharmacology* (5th ed., pp. 305–334). American Psychiatric Press.

Neukrug, E., & Hays, D. G. (2023). *Counseling theory and practice* (3rd ed.). Cognella Academic Press.

Nishino, S., Sakai, N., Mishima, K., Mignot, E., Dement, W. C. (2017). Sedative–hypnotics. In A. F. Schatzberg and C. B. Nemeroff (Eds.), *Textbook of psychopharmacology* (5th ed., pp. 1051–1082). American Psychiatric Press.

Nye, R. D. (2000). *Three psychologies: Perspectives from Freud, Skinner, and Rogers* (6th ed.). Brooks/Cole.

Patron, J., Serra-Cayuela, A., Han, B., Li, C., & Wishart D. S. (2019). Assessing the performance of genome-wide association studies for predicting disease risk. *PLoS One, 14*(12). https://doi.org/10.1371/journal.pone.0220215

Perkins, A., Ridler, J., Browes, D., Peryer, G., Notley, C., & Hackmann, C. (2018). Experiencing mental health diagnosis: A systemic review of service user, clinician, and career perspectives across clinical settings. *The Lancet Psychiatry, 5*(9), 747–764. https://doi.org/10.1016/S2215-0366(18)30095-6

Pirodsky, D. M., & Cohn, J. S. (1992). *Clinical primer of psychopharmacology* (2nd ed.). McGraw-Hill.

Preston, J. D., O'Neal, J. H., Talaga, M. C., & Moore, B. A. (2021). *Handbook of clinical psychopharmacology for therapists* (9th ed.). New Harbinger Publications.

Procyshyn, R. M., Bezchlibnyk-Butler, K. Z., & Jeffries J. J. (Eds.). (2019). *Clinical handbook of psychotropic drugs.* Hogrefe Publishing.

Rice, R. (2015). Narrative therapy. In E. Neukrug (Ed.), *The SAGE encyclopedia of theory in counseling and psychotherapy* (Vol. 2, pp. 695–700). SAGE Publications.

Robinson, D. S., & Rickels, K. (2017). Buspirone. In A. F. Schatzberg and C. B. Nemeroff (Eds.), *Textbook of psychopharmacology* (5th ed., pp. 585–602). American Psychiatric Press.

Rogers, C. R. (1951). *Client-centered therapy: Its current practice, implications, and theory.* Houghton Mifflin.

Rogers, C. R. (1957). The necessary and sufficient conditions of therapeutic personality change. *Journal of Consulting Psychology, 21*, 95–103. *https://doi.org/10.1037/h0045357*

Rogers, C. R. (1959). A theory of therapy, personality and interpersonal relationships as developed in the client- centered framework. In S. Koch (Ed.), *Psychology: A study of science, Vol. 3: Formulations of the person and the social context* (pp. 184–256). McGraw-Hill.

Rogers, C. R. (1980). *A way of being.* Houghton Mifflin.

Rogers, C. R. (1989). A therapist's view of the good life: The fully functioning person. In H. Kirschenbaum & V. Henderson (Eds.), *The Carl Rogers reader* (pp. 409–419). Houghton Mifflin. (Original work published 1961)

Rudes, J., & Guterman, J. T. (2007). The value of social constructionism for the counseling profession: A reply to Hansen. *Journal of Counseling and Development, 85*, 387–392. https://doi.org/10.1002/j.1556-6678.2007.tb00606.x

Schatzberg, A. F., & DeBattista, C. (2019). *Schatzberg's manual of clinical psychopharmacology* (9th ed.). American Psychiatric Publication.

Sheehan, D. V. (2017). Benzodiazepines. In A. F. Schatzberg & C. B. Nemeroff (Eds.), *Textbook of psychopharmacology* (5th ed., pp. 563–584). American Psychiatric Press.

Sherman, N., & Field, T. A. (2017). Psychopharmacology basics. In T. A. Field, L. K. Jones, & L. A. Russell-Chapin (Eds.), *Neurocounseling: Brain-based clinical approaches* (pp. 168–178). American Counseling Association.

Sinacola, R. S., Peters-Strickland, T., & Wyner, J. D. (2020). *Basic psychopharmacology for mental health professionals* (3rd ed.). Pearson.

Skinner, B. F. (1971). *Beyond freedom and dignity*. Knopf.

Stein, D. J., Szatmari, P., Gaebel, W., Berk, M., Vieta, E., Maj, M., de Vries, Y. A., Roest, A. M., de Jonge, P., Maercker, A., Brewin, C. R., Pike, K. M., Grilo, C. M., Fineberg, N. A., Briken, P., Cohen-Kettenis, P. T., & Reed, G. M. (2020). Mental, behavioral and neurodevelopmental disorders in the ICD-11: An international perspective on key changes and controversies. *BMC Medicine, 18*(21), 1–24. https://doi.org/10.1186/s12916-020-1495-2

Stübner, S., Grohmann, R., Greil, W., Zhang, X., Müller-Oerlinghausen, B., Bleich, S., Rüther, E., Möller, H. -J., Engel, R., Falkai, P., Toto, S., Kasper, S., Neyazi, A. (2018). Suicidal ideation and suicidal behavior as rare adverse events of antidepressant medication: Current report from the AMSP Multicenter Drug Safety Surveillance Project. *International Journal of Neuropsychopharmacology, 21*(9), 814–821. https://doi.org/10.1093/ijnp/pyy048

Substance Abuse and Mental Health Services Administration. (2020). *Key substance use and mental health indicators in the United States: Results from the 2019 National survey on drug use and health*. https://www.samhsa.gov/data/sites/default/files/reports/rpt29393/2019NSDUHFFRPDFWHTML/2019NSDUHFFR1PDFW090120.pdf

Swenson, L. C. (1997). *Psychology and the law for the helping professions* (2nd ed.). Brooks Cole.

Videbeck, S. L. (2019). *Psychiatric mental health nursing* (8th ed.). Lippincott, Williams, & Wilkins.

Wilkinson, T., Smith, D., Wimberly, R. (2019). Trends in ethical complaints leading to professional counseling licensing boards disciplinary actions. *Journal of Counseling & Development, 97*, 98–104. https://doi.org/10.1002/jcad.12239

Wilson, N. (2015). Contemporary psychodynamic-based therapies: Overview. In E. S. Neukrug (Ed.), *The SAGE encyclopedia of theory in counseling and psychotherapy* (Vol. 1, pp. 229–234). SAGE Publications.

Wolpe, J. (1969). *The practice of behavior therapy*. Pergamon Press.

CHAPTER 9

American Psychiatric Association. (2022). *Diagnostic and statistical manual of mental disorders* (5th ed., text revision).

Berman, P. S. (2019). *Case conceptualization and treatment planning: Integrating theory with clinical practice* (3rd ed.). SAGE Publications.

Bolton, D., & Gillett, G. (2019). *The biopsychosocial model of health and disease: New philosophical and scientific developments*. Palgrave MacMillan

Bucci, S., French, L. & Berry, K. (2016). Measures assessing the quality of case conceptualization: A systematic review. *Journal of Clinical Psychology, 72*, 517–533. https://doi.org/10.1002/jclp.22280

Corey, G. (2019). *The art of integrative counseling* (4th ed.). American Counseling Association.

Ellis, M. V., Hutman, H., & Deihl, L. M. (2013). Chalkboard case conceptualization: A method for integrating clinical data. *Training and Education in Professional Psychology, 7*(4), 246–256. https://psycnet.apa.org/doi/10.1037/a0034132

Hinkle, M. S., & Dean, L. M. (2017). Creativity in teaching case conceptualization skills: Role-play to show the interconnectedness of domains. *Journal of Creativity in Mental Health, 12*(3), 388–401. https://psycnet.apa.org/doi/10.1080/15401383.2016.1249813

Kress, V. E., & Paylo, M. J. (2019). *Treating those with mental disorders: A comprehensive approach to case conceptualization and treatment* (2nd ed.). Pearson.

Meichenbaum, D., & Lilienfeld, S. O. (2018). How to spot hype in the field of psychotherapy: A 19-Item Checklist. *Professional Psychology: Research and Practice, 49*(1), 22–30. https://doi.org/10.1037/pro0000172

Meyer, L., & Melchert, T. P. (2011). Examining the content of mental health intake assessments from a biopsychosocial perspective. *Journal of Psychotherapy Integration, 21*(1), 70–89. https://www.doi.org/10.1037/a0022907

Neukrug, E. (Ed.). (2015). *The SAGE encyclopedia of theory in counseling and psychotherapy* (Vols. 1–2). SAGE Publication.

Neukrug, E. (2023). *Theory, practice, and trends in human services: An introduction* (6th ed.). Cognella.

Neukrug, E., & Fawcett, R. (2020). *Essentials of testing and assessment: A practical guide for counselors, social workers, and psychologists* (3rd ed., enhanced ed.). Cengage Learning.

Neukrug, E. S. & Schwitzer, A. M. (2006). *Skills and tools for today's counselor and psychotherapists from natural helping to professional counseling*. Brooks/Cole.

Rausch, M. A., & Gallo, L. L. (2017). Counselor in training 360 degree case conceptualization process for group supervision. *The Journal of Counselor Preparation and Supervision, 10*(1), 1–26. https://digitalcommons.sacredheart.edu/jcps/vol10/iss1/1

Ridley, C. R., & Jeffrey, C. E. (2017). The conceptual framework of thematic mapping in case conceptualization. *Journal of Clinical Psychology, 73*(4), 376–392. https://doi.org/10.1002/jclp.22355

Schwitzer, A. M., & Rubin, L. C. (2015). *Diagnosis and treatment planning skills: A popular culture casebook approach* (2nd ed.). SAGE Publications.

Sperry, L., & Sperry, J., (2020). *Case conceptualization: Mastering this competency with ease and confidence* (2nd ed.). Routledge.

Zubernis, L., & Snyder, M. (2016). *Case conceptualization and effective interventions: Assessing and treating mental, emotional, and behavioral disorders.* SAGE Publications.

Zubernis, L., Snyder, M., & Neale-McFall, C. (2017). Case conceptualization: Improving understanding and treatment with the temporal/contextual model. *Journal of Mental Health Counseling, 39*, 181–194. https://www.doi.org/10.17744/mehc.39.3.01

CHAPTER 10

Akiskal, H. S. (2016). The mental status examination. In S. H. Fatemi, & P. J. Clayton (Eds.), *The medical basis of psychiatry* (pp. 3–16). Springer.

American Counseling Association. (2014). *Code of ethics.* https://www.counseling.org/resources/aca-code-of-ethics.pdf

American Mental Health Counselors Association. (2020). *Code of ethics.* https://www.amhca.org/events/publications/ethics

American Psychological Association. (2013). *HIPAA: What you need to know: The privacy rule—A primer for psychologists.* https://www.apaservices.org/practice/business/hipaa/hippa-privacy-primer.pdf

American Psychological Association. (2023). *Informed consent.* In *American Psychological Association Dictionary of Psychology.* Retrieved April 24, 2023 from https://dictionary.apa.org/informed-consent

Baird, B. N. & Mollen, D. (2019). *The internship, practicum, and field placement handbook: A guide for the helping professions* (8th ed.). Routledge.

Cooper, M., & Law, D. (Eds.). (2018). *Working with goals in psychotherapy and counseling.* Oxford University Press.

Corey, G., Corey, M. S., Corey, C., & Callanan, P. (2024). *Issues and ethics in the helping professions* (11th ed.). Cengage Learning.

Franklin, J. (2022). *Mental health counselors' perceptions of professional identity as correctional counselors in an integrated behavioral health care setting* [Doctoral dissertation, Old Dominion University]. ODU Digital Commons. https://digitalcommons.odu.edu/chs_etds/141

Jensen-Doss, A., Haimes, E. M. B., Smith, A. M., Lyon, AR, Lewis, CC, Stanick, C. F., Hawley, K. M. (2018). Monitoring treatment progress and providing feedback is viewed favorably but rarely used in practice. *Administration and Policy in Mental Health and Mental Health Services Research, 45*(1), 48–61. https://doi.org/10.1007/s10488-016-0763-0

National Archives and Records Administration. (2023). *164.501 Definitions: Psychotherapy notes.* Code of Federal Regulations. https://www.ecfr.gov/current/title-45/subtitle-A/subchapter-C/part-164/subpart-E/section-164.501

Neukrug, E. (2019). *Counseling and helping skills: Critical techniques to becoming a counselor.* Cognella.

Neukrug, E., & Fawcett, R. (2020). *Essentials of testing and assessment: A practical guide for counselors, social workers, and psychologists* (3rd ed., enhanced version). Cengage Learning.

Pagliery, J. (2014, August 18). *Hospital network hacked, 4.5 million records stolen.* CNN Business. http://money.cnn.com/2014/08/18/technology/security/hospital-chs-hack/index.html

Privacy Rights Clearinghouse. (2014). *Protecting health information: The HIPAA security and breach notification rules.* https://www.privacyrights.org/consumer-guides/protecting-health-information-hipaa-security-and-breach-notification-rules

Remley, T. P., & Herlihy, B. (2020). *Ethical, legal, and professional issues in counseling* (6th ed.). Pearson.

Schwitzer, A. M., & Rubin, L. C. (2015). *Diagnosis and treatment planning skills: A popular culture casebook approach* (2nd ed.). SAGE Publications.

Summers, N. (2016). *Fundamentals of case management: Skills for the human services.* Cengage Learning.

U.S. Department of Education. (2021). *Family Educational Rights and Privacy Act (FERPA).* https://www2.ed.gov/policy/gen/guid/fpco/ferpa/index.html?

U.S. Department of Health and Human Services. (2023a). *HIPPA for professionals* https://www.hhs.gov/hipaa/for-professionals/index.html

U.S. Department of Health and Human Services. (2023b). *Breach portal: Notice to the secretary of HHS breach of unsecured protected health information.* https://ocrportal.hhs.gov/ocr/breach/breach_report.jsf

U.S. Department of Justice. (2021). *Freedom of information act guide: 2004 Edition.* http://www.usdoj.gov/oip/introduc.htm

Washington State Department of Social and Health Services. (2018). *Mental status exam guidelines.* https://www.dshs.wa.gov/sites/default/files/forms/pdf/13-865add.pdf

Woodside, M. R., & McClam, T. (2018). *Generalist case management: A method of human service delivery* (5th ed.). Cengage Learning.

CHAPTER 11

Ahia, C. E., & Boccone, P. J. (2017). Licensure board actions against professional counselors: Implications for counselor training and practice. *VISTAS Online, 39.* https://www.counseling.org/docs/default-source/vistas/article_396bce2bf16116603abcacff-0000bee5e7.pdf?sfvrsn%A0=%A0f5d84b2c_4

American Counseling Association. (2014). *Code of ethics.* http://www.counseling.org/resources/aca-code-of-ethics.pdf

American Mental Health Counselors Association. (2020). *Code of ethics.* https://www.amhca.org/events/publications/ethics

American Mental Health Counselors Association. (2021). *AMHCA standards for the practice of clinical mental health counseling.* https://www.amhca.org/viewdocument/2021-amhca-standards-for-the-practi

American Mental Health Counselors Association. (2020). *Code of ethics.*

American Psychiatric Association. (2000). *Diagnostic and statistical manual of mental disorders* (4th ed., text revision).

Bender, S., & Dykeman, C. (2016). Supervisees' perceptions of effective supervision: A comparison of fully synchronous cybersupervision to traditional methods. *Journal of Technology in Human Services, 34*(2), 326–337. https://doi.org/10.1080/15228835.2016.1250026

Bernard, J. M., & Goodyear, R. K. (2019). *Fundamentals of clinical supervision* (6th ed.). Pearson.

Blacklund, M., & Johnson, V. (2018, August 8). *The beauty of client and supervisee resistance. Counseling Today.* https://ct.counseling.org/2018/08/the-beauty-of-client-and-supervisee-resistance/

Borders, L. D., & Brown, L. L. (2022). *The new handbook of counseling supervision.* Routledge. (Original work published 2005)

Borders, L. D., Brown, J. B., & Purgason, L. L. (2015). Triadic supervision with practicum and internship counseling students: A peer supervision approach. *The Clinical Supervisor, 34*(2), 232–248. https://doi.org/10.1080/07325223.2015.1027024

Borders, L. D., Glosoff, H. L., Welfare, L. E., Hays, D. G., DeKruyf, L., Fernando, D. M., & Page, B. (2014). Best practices in clinical supervision: Evolution of a counseling specialty. *The Clinical Supervisor, 33*(1), 26–44. https://doi.org/10.1080/07325223.2014.905225

Borders, L. D., Welfare, E., Greason, P. B., Paladino, D. A., Mobley, A. K., Villalba, J. A., & Wester, K. L. (2012). Individual and triadic and group: Supervisee and supervisor perceptions of each modality. *Counselor Education & Supervision, 51*(4), 281–295. https://doi.org/10.1002/j.1556-6978.2012.00021.x

Caplan, G. (1970). *The theory and practice of mental health consultation.* Basic Books.

Caplan, G., & Caplan-Moskovich, R. B. (2004). Recent advances in mental health consultation and mental health collaboration. In N. M. Lambert, I. Hylander, & J. H. Sandoval (Eds.), *Consultee-centered consultation: Improving the quality of professional services in schools and community organizations* (pp. 21–35). Lawrence Erlbaum.

Cashwell, C. S. (1994). *Interpersonal process recall (ED37232). ERIC.* https://eric.ed.gov/?id=ED372342

Council for Accreditation of Counseling and Related Educational Programs. (2016). *2016 standards.* https://www.cacrep.org/for-programs/2016-cacrep-standards/

Corey, G., Haynes, R. H., Moulton, P., & Muratori, M. (2020). *Clinical supervision in the helping professions: A practical guide.* Wiley.

Corey, G., Corey, M. S., & Corey, C. (2024). *Issues and ethics in the helping professions* (11th ed.). Cengage.

Crothers, L. M., Hughes, T. L., Kolbert, J. B., & Schmidt, A. J. (2020). *Theory and cases in school-based consultation: A resource for school psychologists, school counselors, special educators, and other mental health professionals.* Routledge.

Dougherty, A. M. (2014). *Psychological consultation and collaboration in school and community settings* (6th ed.). Cengage.

Enlow, P., Mcwhorter, L., & Genuario, K. (2019) Supervisor–supervisee interactions: The importance of the supervisory working alliance. *Training and Education in Professional Psychology, 13*(3), 206–211. https://doi.org/10.1037/tep0000243

Erchul, W. (2009). Gerald Caplan: A tribute to the originator of mental health consultation. *Journal of Educational and Psychological Consultation, 19*(2), 95–105. https://doi.org/10.1080/104744109028884186

Erickson, B. (2021). Deinstitutionalization through optimism: The Community Mental Health Act of 1963. *The American Journal of Psychiatry Residents' Journal.* https://doi.org/10.1176/appi.ajp-rj.2021.160404

Falender, C. A., & Shafranske, E. P. (2020). *Consultation in psychology: A distinct professional practice.* In C. A. Falender & E. P. Shafranske (Eds.), *Consultation in psychology: A competency-based approach.* American Psychological Association.

Fall, M. (1995). Planning for consultation: An aid for the elementary school counselor. *The School Counselor, 43,* 151–157.

Gray, B. (2017). Culture, cultural competence and the cross-cultural consultation. *Journal of Pediatrics and Child Health, 54,* 343–345. https://doi.org/10.1111/jpc.1379

Haslebo, G., & Nielsen, K. S. (2018). *Systems and meaning: Consulting in organizations.* Routledge. (Original work published 2000)

Ivers, N. N., Rogers, J. L., Borders, L. D., & Turner, A. (2017). Using interpersonal process recall in clinical supervision to enhance supervisees' multicultural awareness. *The Clinical Supervisor, 36,* 282–303. https://doi.org/10.1080/07325223.2017.1320253

Kagan, N. (1980). Influencing human interaction Eighteen years with IPR. In A. I. Hess (Ed.), *Psychotherapy supervision: Theory, research, and practice* (pp. 262–283). Wiley

Kagan, N., & Kagan, N. I. (1997). Interpersonal process recall: Influencing human interaction. In C. E. Watkins, (Ed.). *Handbook of Psychotherapy Supervision* (pp. 296–309). New York: John Wiley

Kampwirth, T. J., & Powers, K. M. (2016). *Collaborative consultation in the schools: Effective practices for students with learning and behavior problems* (6th ed.). Pearson.

Kemer, G., Sunal, Z., Li, C., & Burgess, M. (2019). Beginning and expert supervisors' descriptions of effective and less effective supervision. *The Clinical Supervisor, 38,* 116–134. https://doi.org/10.1080/07325223.2018.1514676

Koltz, R. L. (2014). Parallel process and isomorphism: A model for decision making in the supervisory triad. *The Family Journal: Counseling and Therapy for Couples and Families, 20*(3), 233–238. https://doi.org/10.1177/1066480712448788

Kurpius, D. J., & Robinson, S. E. (1978). An overview of consultation. *Personnel and Guidance Journal, 56,* 321–323. https://doi.org/10.1002/j.2164-4918.1978.tb04637.x

McNeill, B. W., & Stoltenberg, C. D. (2016). *Supervision essentials for the integrative developmental model.* American Psychological Association.

Moe, J. L., & Perera-Diltz, D. M. (2009). An overview of systemic-organizational consultation for professional counselors. *Journal of Professional Counseling: Practice, Theory & Research, 37,* 27–37.

Osherson, S. (2019, May 25). Why good supervision in psychotherapy matters: What happens early on in training can shape the rest of your career. *Psychology Today.* https://www.psychologytoday.com/us/blog/listen/201905/why-good-supervision-in-psychotherapy-matters

Pennington, M., Patton, R., & Kataflasz, H. (2020). Cybersupervision in psychotherapy. In H. Weinberg & A. Rolnick (Eds.), *Theory and practice of online therapy: Internet-delivered interventions for individuals, groups, families, and organizations* (pp. 79–96). Routledge.

Schein, E. H. (2016). *Humble consulting: How to provide real help faster.* Berrett-Koehler.

Scott, D. A., Royal, C. W., & Kissinger, D. B. (2015). *Counselor as consultant.* SAGE Publisher.

Sterner, W. (2009). Influence of the supervisory working alliance on supervisee work satisfaction and work-related stress. *Journal of Mental Health Counseling, 31*(3), 249–263. https://psycnet.apa.org/doi/10.17744/mehc.31.3.f35441502401831g

Stoltenberg, C. D., & McNeil, B. W. (2010). *IDM supervision: An integrative developmental model of supervising counselors and therapists* (3rd ed.). Routledge.

Valentino, A. L., LeBlanc, L. A., & Sellers, T. P. (2016). The benefits of group supervision and a recommended structure for implementation. *Behavior Analysis Practice, 9*(32), 320–328. https://doi.org/10.1007/s40617-016-0138-8

Watkins, C. E., Jr. (2012). Psychotherapy supervision in the new millennium: Competency-based, evidence-based, particularized, and energized. *Journal of Contemporary Psychotherapy, 42,* 193–203. https://doi.org/10.1007/s10879-011-9202-4

Welfel, E. R. (2016). *Ethics in counseling and psychotherapy: Standards, research, and emerging issues* (6th ed.). Cengage.

Woo, H., Dondanville, A., Jang, H., Na, G., Jang, Y. (2020). A content analysis of the counseling literature on technology integration: American Counseling Association (ACA) counseling journals between 2000 and 2018. *International Journal for the Advancement of Counselling, 42,* 319–333, https://doi.org/10.1007/s10447-020-09406-w

Zetzer, H. A., Hill, C. E., Hopsicker, R. J., Krasno, A. M., Montojo, P. C., Plumb, E. I. W., Hoffman, M. A., & Donahue, M. T. (2020). Parallel process in psychodynamic supervision: The supervisor's perspective. *Psychotherapy, 57*(2), 252–262. https://doi.org/10.1037/pst0000274

CHAPTER 12

American Counseling Association. (2014). *Code of ethics.* http://www.counseling.org/resources/aca-code-of-ethics.pdf

American Mental Health Counselors Association. (2020). *2020 AMHCA Code of Ethics.* https://www.amhca.org/events/publications/ethics

American Psychiatric Association. (2000). *Diagnostic and statistical manual of mental disorders* (4th ed., text revision).

American Psychological Association. (2013). *HIPAA: What you need to know: The privacy rule—A primer for psychologists.* https://www.apaservices.org/practice/business/hipaa/hippa-privacy-primer.pdf

American Psychological Association. (2016). *Ethical principles of psychologists and code of conduct: Including 2010 and 2016 amendments.* http://www.apa.org/ethics/code/

Calley, N. G. (2011). *Program development in the 21st century: An evidence-based approach to design, implementation, and evaluation.* SAGE Publications.

Chapman, J., Jamil, R. T., & Fleisher, C. (2022). *Borderline personality disorder.* National Center for Biotechnology Information. https://www.ncbi.nlm.nih.gov/books/NBK430883/

Corey, G., Corey, M. S., & Corey, C. (forthcoming). *Issues and ethics in the helping professions* (10th ed.). Cengage Learning.

Formative and Summative Assessments. (2021). *Poorvu Center for Teaching and Learning.* Yale University. https://poorvucenter.yale.edu/Formative-Summative-Assessments

Kelley, A. (2022). *Treatment program evaluation: Public health perspectives on mental health and substance use disorders.* Routledge.

Kitchener, K. S. (1984). Intuition, critical evaluation and ethical principles: The foundation for ethical decisions in counseling psychology. *Counseling Psychologist, 12*(3), 43–45. https://doi.org/10.1177/0011000084123005

Kitchener, K. S. (1986). Teaching applied ethics in counselor education: An integration of psychological processes and philosophical analysis. *Journal of Counseling and Development, 64*(5), 306–311. https://doi.org/10.1177/0011000084123005

Kuo, J. R., & Fitzpatrick, S. (2015). Dialectical behavior therapy. In E. Neukrug (Ed.), *The SAGE encyclopedia of theories in counseling and psychotherapy* (Vol. 1, pp. 292–297). SAGE Publications.

Lenzenweger, M. F., Lane, M., Lorganger, A. W., & Kessler, R. C. (2007). *DSM–IV* personality disorders in the national comorbidity survey replication. *Biological Psychiatry, 62,* 553–564. https://doi.org/10.1016/j.biopsych.2006.09.019

Linfield, K. J. & Posavac, E. J. (2019). *Program evaluation: Methods and case studies* (9th ed.). Routledge.

Meara, N. M., Schmidt, L. D., & Day, J. D. (1996). Principles and virtues: A foundation for ethical decisions, policies, and character. *The Counseling Psychologist, 24*(9), 4–77. https://doi. org/10.1177/0011000096241002

National Institute of Mental Health. (n.d.). *Personality disorders.* https://www.nimh.nih.gov/health/statistics/personality-disorders.shtml

Neukrug, E. S., & Fawcett, R. C. (2020). *Essentials of testing and assessment: A practical guide for counselors, social workers, and psychologists* (3rd ed., enhanced version). Cengage.

Neukrug, E. S., & Hays, D. (2023). *Counseling theory and practice* (3rd ed.). Cognella.

ten Have, M., Verheul, R., Kaasenbrood, A., van Dorsselaer, S., Tuithof, M., Kleinjan, M., & de Graaf, R. (2016). Prevalence rates of borderline personality disorder symptoms: A study based on the Netherlands Mental Health Survey Incidence Study. *BMC Psychiatry, 16,* 1–10. https://doi.org/10.1186/s12888-016-0939-x

Urofsky, R., Engels, D., & Engebretson, K. (2008). Kitchener's principle ethics: Implications for counseling practice and research. *Counseling and Values, 53*(1), 67–78. https://doi.org/10.1002/j.2161-007X.2009.tb00114.x

U.S. Department of Health and Human Services. (2022). *Evaluate your program.* https://www.samhsa.gov/workplace/employer-resources/evaluate-program

U.S. Department of Health and Human Services. (2023). *HIPPA for professionals.* https://www.hhs.gov/hipaa/for-professionals/index.html

U.S. Food and Drug Administration. (2019). *Institutional review boards (IRBs) and protection of human subjects in clinical trials.* https://www.fda.gov/about-fda/center-drug-evaluation-and-research-cder/institutional-review-boards-irbs-and-protection-human-subjects-clinical-trials

Wilder, C. H. (2007). *Ethical issues: Tips for conducting program evaluation.* Amber H. Wilder Foundation. https://www.wilder.org/sites/default/files/imports/crimevictimservices12_10-07Web.pdf

INDEX

www.ingramcontent.com/pod-product-compliance
Lightning Source LLC
Chambersburg PA
CBHW081428210125
20639CB00019B/1588